SOFTWARE SYSTEMS ARCHITECTURE

SOFTWARE SYSTEMS ARCHITECTURE

Working with Stakeholders Using Viewpoints and Perspectives

NICK ROZANSKI
EOIN WOODS

✦ Addison-Wesley

Upper Saddle River, NJ ▪ Boston ▪ Indianapolis ▪ San Francisco
New York ▪ Toronto ▪ Montreal ▪ London ▪ Munich ▪ Paris ▪ Madrid
Capetown ▪ Sydney ▪ Tokyo ▪ Singapore ▪ Mexico City

Many of the designations used by manufacturers and sellers to distinguish their products are claimed as trademarks. Where those designations appear in this book, and the publisher was aware of a trademark claim, the designations have been printed with initial capital letters or in all capitals.

The authors and publisher have taken care in the preparation of this book, but make no expressed or implied warranty of any kind and assume no responsibility for errors or omissions. No liability is assumed for incidental or consequential damages in connection with or arising out of the use of the information or programs contained herein.

The publisher offers excellent discounts on this book when ordered in quantity for bulk purchases or special sales, which may include electronic versions and/or custom covers and content particular to your business, training goals, marketing focus, and branding interests. For more information, please contact:

U. S. Corporate and Government Sales
(800) 382-3419
corpsales@pearsontechgroup.com

For sales outside the U. S., please contact:

International Sales
international@pearsoned.com

Visit us on the Web: www.awprofessional.com

Library of Congress Cataloging-in-Publication Data

Rozanski, Nick.
    Software systems architecture : working with stakeholders using viewpoints and perspectives / Nick Rozanski, Eoin Woods.
        p.   cm.
    Includes bibliographical references and index.
    ISBN 0-321-11229-6 (hardcover : alk. paper)
    1. Computer software—Development.   2. Computer architecture.   I. Woods, Eoin.   II. Title.

QA76.76.D47R696 2005
005.3—dc22   2005004600

ISBN 0-321-11229-6
Text printed in the United States on recycled paper at R.R. Donnelley in Crawfordsville, Indiana.
7th   Printing   August 2010

CONTENTS

The Accessibility Perspective   474
The Development Resource Perspective   479
The Internationalization Perspective   485
The Location Perspective   489
The Regulation Perspective   495
The Usability Perspective   499

PART V   **PUTTING IT ALL TOGETHER   505**

CHAPTER 29   **WORKING AS A SOFTWARE ARCHITECT   507**
The Architect in the Project Lifecycle   507
The Architect in Different Types of Projects   513

APPENDIX   **OTHER VIEWPOINT SETS   517**
Kruchten "4+1"   517
RM-ODP   518
Siemens (Hofmeister, Nord, and Soni)   519
SEI Viewtypes   520
Garland and Anthony   520

                   BIBLIOGRAPHY   523

                   INDEX   531

PREFACE

The authors of this book are both practicing software architects who have worked in this role, together and separately, on information system development projects for quite a few years. During that time, we have seen a significant increase in the visibility of software architects and in the importance with which our role has been viewed by colleagues, management, and customers. No large software development project nowadays would expect to go ahead without an architect—or a small architectural group—in the vanguard of the development team.

While there may be an emerging consensus that the software architect's role is an important one, there seems to be little agreement on what the job actually involves. Who are our clients? To whom are we accountable? What are we expected to deliver? What is our involvement once the architectural design has been completed? And, perhaps most fundamentally, where are the boundaries between requirements, architecture, and design?

The absence of a clear definition of the role is all the more problematic because of the seriousness of the problems that today's software projects (and specifically, their architects) have to resolve.

- The expectations of users and other stakeholders in terms of functionality, capability, time to market, and flexibility have become much more demanding.
- Long system development times result in continual scope changes and consequent changes to the system's architecture and design.
- Today's systems are more functionally and structurally complex than ever and are usually constructed from a mix of off-the-shelf and custom-built components.
- Few systems exist in isolation; most are expected to interoperate and exchange information with many other systems.

- Getting the functional structure—the design—of the system right is only part of the problem. How the system behaves (i.e., its quality properties) is just as critical to its effectiveness as what it does.

- Technology continues to change at a pace that makes it very hard for architects to keep their technical expertise up-to-date.

When we first started to take on the role of software architects, we looked for some sort of software architecture handbook that would walk us through the process of developing an architectural design. After all, other architectural disciplines have behind them centuries of theory and established best practice.

For example, in the first century A.D., the Roman Marcus Vitruvius Pollio wrote the first ever architectural handbook, *De architectura libri decem* ("Ten Books on Architecture"), describing the building architect's role and required skills and providing a wealth of material on standard architectural structures. In 1670, Anthony Deane, a friend of diarist Samuel Pepys, a former mayor of the English town of Harwich and later a member of Parliament, published a ground-breaking textbook, *A Doctrine of Naval Architecture*, which described in detail some of the leading methods of the time for large ship design. Deane's ideas and principles helped systematize the practice of naval architecture for many years. And in 1901, George E. Davis, a consulting engineer in the British chemical industry, created a new field of engineering when he published his text *A Handbook of Chemical Engineering*. This text was the first book to define the practical principles underpinning industrial chemical processes and guided the field for many years afterward.

The existence of such best practices has a very important consequence in terms of uniformity of approach. If you were to give several architects and engineers a commission to design a building, a cruise liner, or a chemical plant, the designs they produced would probably differ. However, the processes they used, the ways they represented their designs on paper (or a computer screen), and the techniques they used to ensure the soundness of their designs would be very similar.

Sadly, our profession has yet to build any significant legacy of mainstream industrial best practices. When we looked, we found a dearth of introductory books to guide practicing information systems architects in the details of doing their jobs.

Admittedly, we have an abundance of books on specific technologies, whether it's J2EE, CORBA, or .NET, and some on broader topics such as Web services or object orientation (although, because of the speed at which software technology changes, many of these become out-of-date within a few years). There are also a number of good general software architecture books, several of which we refer to in later chapters. But many of these books aim to lay down principles that apply across all sorts of systems and so are written in quite general terms, while most of the more specific texts are aimed at our colleagues in the real-time and embedded-systems communities.

We feel that if you are a new software architect for an information system, the books that actually tell you how to do your job, learn the important things you need to know, and make your architectural designs successful are few and far between. While we don't presume to replace the existing texts on software architecture or place ourselves alongside the likes of Vitruvius, Deane, and Davis, addressing these needs was the driving force behind our decision to write this book.

Specifically, the book shows you

- What software architecture is about and why your role is vitally important to successful project delivery
- How to determine who is interested in your architecture (your *stakeholders*), understand what is important to them (their *concerns*), and design an *architecture* that reflects and balances their different needs
- How to communicate your architecture to your stakeholders in an understandable way that demonstrates that you have met their concerns (the *architectural description*)
- How to focus on what is *architecturally significant*, safely leaving other aspects of the design to your designers, without neglecting issues like performance, resilience, and location
- What important activities you most need to undertake as an architect, such as identifying and engaging stakeholders, using scenarios, creating models, and documenting and validating your architecture

Throughout the book we primarily focus on the development of large-scale information systems (by which we mean the computer systems used to automate the business operations of large organizations). However, we have tried to present our material in a way that is independent of the type of information system you are designing, the technologies the developers will be using, and the software development lifecycle your project is following. We have standardized on a few things, such as the use of Unified Modeling Language (UML) in most of our diagrams, but we've done that only because UML is the most widely understood modeling language around. You don't have to be a UML expert to understand this book.

We didn't set out to be the definitive guide to developing the architecture of your information system—such a book would probably never be finished and would require the collaboration of a huge number of experts across a wide range of technical specializations. Also, we did not write a book of prescriptive methods. Although we present some activity diagrams that explain how to produce your deliverables, these are designed to be compatible with the wide range of software development approaches in use today.

What we hope we have achieved is the creation of a practical, practitioner-oriented guide that explains how to design successful architectures for information systems and how to see these through to their successful implementation. This is the sort of book that we wish had been available when we started out as software architects, and one that we expect to refer to even now.

You can find further useful software architecture resources, and contact us to provide feedback on the book's content, via our Web page: www.viewpoints-and-perspectives.info. We look forward to hearing from you.

ACKNOWLEDGMENTS

This book would never have appeared without the advice, assistance, and support of a lot of people.

We are very grateful to the many reviewers who commented on the text at various stages of its creation, including Gary Birch, Chris Britton, Kelley Butler, Sholom Cohen, Dan Haywood, Sallie Henry, Andy Longshaw, Robert Nord, Dan Paulish, Martyn Thomas, and Hans van Vliet.

We'd also like to thank the team members at Addison-Wesley for all of their work to make the book a reality, including Kim Boedigheimer, John Fuller, Peter Gordon, Chrysta Meadowbrooke, Simon Plumtree, and Elizabeth Ryan.

Other people who provided us with advice, encouragement, and inspiration at various times include Felix Bachmann, Dave Borthwick, David Emery, Wolfgang Emmerich, Rich Hilliard, Philippe Kruchten, Roland Leibundgut, Mike Mackay, Dave Maher, Mark Maier, Lucia Rapanotti, and Gaynor Redvers-Mutton.

We would also like to thank our families for their constant love, encouragement, and support throughout the project.

ABOUT THE AUTHORS

NICK ROZANSKI

Nick Rozanski is an Enterprise Technical Architect for Marks and Spencer, the United Kingdom's largest clothing and food retailer. His current architectural portfolio is focused on integration and workflow, but he also has a strong interest in information architecture and in the role and practice of the software architect.

Nick has worked in IT since 1980 for several large and small systems integrators, including Logica, Capgemini, and Sybase. He has taken senior roles on a wide range of programs for clients in finance, retail, manufacturing, and government. His technology background includes enterprise application integration, package implementation, relational database, data replication, and object-oriented software development. He is also an experienced technical instructor and certified internal project auditor.

Nick was educated at the Universities of Cambridge and Manchester, United Kingdom.

EOIN WOODS

Eoin Woods has been working in the software engineering field since 1990 for companies including Ford, Groupe Bull, Sybase, and currently Zühlke Engineering, where he works as a principal consultant, based in the firm's London office.

Eoin works primarily as a consultant software architect and has led applied research, server product development, and large-scale information systems implementation work. He specializes in the financial markets domain, working with a range of investment and trading organizations. Eoin's main technical professional interests are software architecture, distributed systems, computer security, and data management.

Eoin holds B.Sc. and M.Sc. degrees in Software Engineering from Brunel and Manchester universities. He is a professional member of the British Computer Society and the Institution of Electrical Engineers and is a chartered engineer.

1

INTRODUCTION

oday's large-scale software systems are among the most complex structures ever built by humans, containing millions of lines of code, thousands of database tables, and hundreds of components, all running on dozens of computers. This presents some formidable challenges to software development teams—and if these challenges aren't addressed early, systems are delivered late, over budget, or with an unacceptably poor level of quality.

Most projects nowadays recognize the importance of appointing a software architect, or in some cases a group of software architects, to provide technology guidance and leadership to the rest of the team. However, as an industry, there is no generally accepted definition of what software architects do, how they do it, and what they are expected to deliver.

STAKEHOLDERS, VIEWPOINTS, AND PERSPECTIVES

This book is intended as a practical guide for software architects, whether you are experienced or just starting your career. It focuses on three fundamental concepts: stakeholders, viewpoints, and perspectives. To understand why these concepts are important to you, let's look at an example of how the practice of software architecture often unfolds.

EXAMPLE Sally is a software architect who works for a large commercial organization. As one of the most senior members of the IT staff, Sally gets involved in a lot of different activities, but her key role is leading the definition and design of the organization's information systems. One of these systems is taking most of her time and attention at present.

It all starts simply enough: Sally is asked to start looking at options for replacing the current stock management system (which is batch-based and fairly elderly) with a more modern system that would better support the changing needs of the business. In particular, the business wants the system to be more interactive and to allow employees to process stock movements in real time rather than entering data and seeing the results the next day. The time lag imposed by the current system is a real competitive disadvantage and also leads to mistakes because of the lack of immediate feedback.

At first glance, the problem doesn't seem too complicated. Sally talks to a few people around the organization about the new system's requirements, and soon she has some idea of how to get started. Interviewing the business analysts and some of the main users at the head office suggests some key requirements, which seem fairly straightforward. Sally starts to sketch possible solutions.

However, as she discusses her ideas around the company, Sally meets some people with very different ideas about the key requirements for the system. The users at the distribution depots claim to need totally different information than the staff members at the head office need. Back at the head office, the commercial managers say it is crucial that they have real-time summary reporting throughout the day. However, this would slow the main transaction flow significantly, which isn't acceptable to the people in the logistics group that is actually paying for the system.

Sally also interviews people outside the immediate business area, and they all have opinions too. The IT operations group members are worried about adopting new technology and don't think they can administer the application server that Sally is planning to use. The IT auditors inform her that they need a two-year archive of all stock release authorizations in case of possible fraud. Leaving aside the difficulty of collecting it, that's a lot of stock movement data to keep in the system.

Sally is struggling to reconcile the conflicting requirements of many of the people she has interviewed. She is also worried that she may have left out someone important or failed to address a key requirement.

The architect in our example is working with a number of different people, each with different interests in and concerns about the new system. Traditionally, software developers have concentrated on the needs of end users and sometimes developers, but as our example illustrates, this is far too narrow a view if you want to create a system that satisfies everyone affected by it.

We call the people affected by our system its stakeholders. Because stakeholder needs are why the system is being created in the first place, meeting these needs is your chief goal as an architect. To do this, you need to clearly identify your stakeholders, work with them to understand their concerns, balance their inevitably conflicting priorities, and design an architecture that addresses their requirements as effectively as possible.

We talk about stakeholders throughout the book. We explore the concept in Part I, explain how to work effectively with them in Part II, and show you how to create architectures that meet their needs in Parts III and IV. For now, let us continue with our example.

Sally has done some work to understand and involve her stakeholders, and although she may not feel she can meet all of their concerns, at least she now feels that she has a good understanding of what those concerns are.

Based on her understanding of the important stakeholder needs, Sally starts her architectural design in earnest. She sketches the functional structure of the system, identifying the key components and planning how they will work together to provide the required functionality. While she's thinking about this, she starts grouping components into processes and working out where these processes will run in the data center. In order to meet the concerns of the operations group, Sally adds some system management components to her design that should make it more manageable. She realizes she needs to think about the data in the system, so she adds the main data stores and annotates the data flows between the key components. This sidetracks her for a while, as it's quite involved, but within a couple of weeks Sally has a detailed architecture model to show people.

She's pretty unhappy about the responses she gets from the people who received her document. Most of them don't reply at all, and those who do seem to be concerned about minor details of the system or even the way she formatted the document. Sally heads off to talk to some of the end users, developers, and IT operations staff who reviewed the architecture in order to find out why they didn't provide better feedback.

The result of her stakeholder chats is a bit demoralizing—no one seems to have grasped the most important features of her model. The developers are distracted by the operational components such as servers and disk arrays, and they worry about the way the application will be deployed to the data center, which isn't their primary responsibility. The IT operations people are pleased to see their system management software in the model, but they keep asking questions about data stores and data flows, when it seems quite obvious to Sally that this is not their concern. The end users don't really understand anything and keep asking, "But what will it do?" Sally feels this is pretty unfair because she has taken great pains to make sure that everything the system could do was documented somewhere.

In spite of producing a detailed architectural design, Sally doesn't seem to have helped anyone understand her system. It isn't clear to her how she can reorganize it in order to get her messages across more clearly.

Sally is facing a problem familiar to many architects: How can you describe something as multifaceted as the architecture of a complex system to the different people who need to understand it? Indeed, this has been a problem for software engineers since the early days of computing.

If you read the more recent literature on software architecture, one of the first useful discoveries you will make is the concept of an architectural view. An *architectural view* is a description of *one aspect* of a system's architecture and is an application of the timeless problem-solving principle of "divide and conquer." By considering a system's architecture through a number of distinct views, you can understand, define, and communicate a complex architecture in a partitioned fashion and thus avoid overwhelming your readers with its overall complexity. Examples of architectural views include the system's functional structure, information organization, and the deployment environment.

Although describing an architecture using views helps partition the architectural description and make it easier to understand, it still leaves you with the problem of deciding which views to use and how to create each one. Again, many of us have faced this problem in the past. A proven solution is to use template views, called *architectural viewpoints*, to guide the process of developing the views that describe your architecture.

Using viewpoints and views to guide the architecture definition process is a core theme of this book. We introduce, explain, and contextualize them in Part I, while Part III contains a complete set of viewpoint definitions you can use directly on your own architecture projects. For now, let's see how Sally uses viewpoints in our example.

Sally decides to use a set of viewpoints to create a view-based architectural description. This results in an effective representation of an architecture that seems to meet the majority of the needs that her discussions with stakeholders have revealed. Her ideas are approved, and development of the first version of the system begins. The software development goes fairly well, but some new complications emerge.

Having looked at the integration test logs and talked to some of the system testers, Sally starts to worry about system performance. She didn't think much about performance earlier because no one seemed to be concerned about it, but the performance she is seeing, even with test data volumes, seems pretty poor to her.

At the same time, some of the security and audit group members are raising concerns about system security. Again, they didn't mention this when Sally was gathering requirements, but now that the system is starting to take shape, they're talking about protecting parts of the system from different users and asking how they can be sure that the system databases aren't updated by support staff without authorization. This is even more troublesome because, although Sally feels pretty confident about sorting out performance problems, she's far less sure about security.

Finally, the corporate business continuity group recently sent out a stern e-mail reminding everyone of the need for all systems to be recoverable to a physically remote disaster recovery site within eight hours of a major failure. Sally wasn't aware that this group worked with IT at all; the mainframe applications that she normally deals with inherit their disaster recovery facilities automatically from the mainframe environment, and she hasn't needed to worry about this before.

Although it looks as if the system will provide the functionality that people requested, Sally is concerned that they will still be unhappy with it because it won't be quick enough, won't address their security concerns, or won't be available after any major systems failure.

Having recognized these problems, Sally isn't sure what to do about them. She knows about performance and availability, but she's not clear about how to increase the system's level of security. Leaving aside her technical knowledge, Sally doesn't know how to redesign her system in a way that balances these different concerns—concerns that no one mentioned when she was capturing requirements.

The architect in our example has realized that *what* a system does is only part of the story and that *how* the system provides its services often has a huge impact on the perceptions that stakeholders have of it. The architecture you choose for your system dictates how quickly it runs, how secure it is, how available it is, how easy it is to modify, and many other nonfunctional factors, which we collectively term *quality properties*. Designing a system that exhibits acceptable quality properties is a crucial part of your role as an architect.

Achieving your quality goals is a cross-structural aspect of the architecture definition process (in fact, quality properties are also often known as *cross-cutting concerns*) and is likely to impact all of the different structures that make up your architecture. This means that achieving your quality goals is likely to affect all of the views in your architectural description.

We have found that the conventional view and viewpoint approach works very well for the definition of architectural structures but is less helpful when considering quality properties. We need a better way to ensure that our architecture exhibits the quality properties required of it and to organize our architectural knowledge about quality properties. In order to do this, we have defined a new concept. The *architectural perspective* is analogous to a viewpoint, but rather than addressing a type of architectural structure, a perspective addresses a particular quality property (such as performance, security, or availability).

Applying perspectives to views to ensure they exhibit the required quality properties is another important theme of this book. We provide an overview of perspectives in Part I, while Part IV contains a complete set of perspective definitions you can use directly on your own architecture projects in order to avoid the kinds of problems that troubled the architect in our example.

Recapping, the core themes of this book are stakeholders, viewpoints, and perspectives.

- *Stakeholders* are the people for whom we build systems. A key part of your role as an architect is knowing how to work with stakeholders in order to create an architecture that meets their complex, overlapping, and often conflicting needs.
- *Viewpoints* (and views) are an approach to structuring the architecture definition process and the architectural description, based on the principle of separation of concerns. Viewpoints contain proven architectural knowledge to guide the creation of an architecture, described in a particular set of views (each view being the result of applying the guidance in a particular viewpoint).
- *Perspectives* are a complementary concept to viewpoints that we introduce in this book. Perspectives contain proven architectural knowledge and help structure the architecture definition process by separating concerns but focusing on cross-structural quality properties rather than architectural structures.

In this book we introduce, explain, and explore these three concepts and define an approach for creating effective architectures for your information systems. Of course, the approach we present is a simplification; architecture definition isn't a linear flow that can be easily written down but is in reality an incremental process involving an iterative cycle of information capture, model development, review, and refinement. What we present here is a practical, proven framework for tackling the architecture definition process and handling the challenges that make software architecture such a fascinating job.

THE STRUCTURE OF THIS BOOK

The book is divided into five parts.

- Part I provides an introduction to and review of the basic concepts we use throughout the book (e.g., stakeholder, architectural description, viewpoint, view, and perspective) and describes the role of the software architect.

- Part II describes the most important activities you need to undertake as an architect, such as agreeing on a project's scope, identifying and engaging stakeholders, using scenarios and patterns, creating models, and documenting and validating your architecture.

- Part III is a catalog of the six most important viewpoints you will need when creating your architectural description: the Functional, Information, Concurrency, Development, Deployment, and Operational viewpoints.

- Part IV is a catalog of the most important perspectives for information systems, including Security, Performance and Scalability, Availability and Resilience, Evolution, Location, Development Resource, Internationalization, and a number of others.

- Part V pulls these concepts together and explains how you can start to put our ideas into practice.

WHO SHOULD READ THIS BOOK

This book will clearly be of interest to you if you are a software architect or would like to become one. It presents a number of concepts with which you will be familiar and others that may be new to you. We hope it will help explain and clarify your role, establish your boundaries, and improve the way you do your job. For experienced architects, the reference material in Parts III and IV is likely to be particularly helpful for day-to-day use.

Parts of the book may interest some architectural stakeholders too. Sponsors and senior management on system development projects who work with architects on the demand side of the relationship will want to read Part I, the introductory chapters of Parts III and IV (about viewpoints and perspectives, respectively), and Part V. The same applies to users.

Software developers (particularly designers) and support and maintenance staff may also find much helpful material in this book and will probably want to focus on Parts III and IV in more detail, in order to better understand the aspects of the architecture definition process that interest them.

CONVENTIONS USED

To help make the text easy to read and refer back to, you will find some standard features throughout the book.

- We provide formal *definitions* of all of the important terms we use—either a reiteration of the accepted definition where its use is widespread or our own definition where the term (or our use of it) is new.
- We define a number of *principles* that underpin the theoretical aspects of the book. A principle is a fundamental statement of belief, approach, or intent that forms a basis for developing our ideas.
- We present *strategies* and *checklists* that will help you successfully apply our principles in your day-to-day work as an architect.
- We include a number of *examples* to illustrate the text. These are, for the most part, based on real projects with which one or the other of us has been involved in the past (with names changed to protect the innocent).

PART I

ARCHITECTURE FUNDAMENTALS

2

SOFTWARE ARCHITECTURE CONCEPTS

One of the problems encountered when we talk about architecture for software systems is that the terminology has been loosely borrowed from other disciplines (such as building architecture or naval architecture) and is widely used, inconsistently, in a variety of situations. For example, the term *architecture* is used to refer to the internal structure of microprocessors, the internal structure of machines, the organization of networks, the structure of software programs, and many other things.

This chapter defines and reviews some of the core concepts that underpin the discussion in the remainder of the book: *software architecture*, *architectural elements*, *stakeholders*, and *architectural descriptions*.

SOFTWARE ARCHITECTURE

Computers can be found everywhere in modern society—not just in data centers or on desks but also in cars, washing machines, and credit cards. Whether they are big or small, simple or complex, all computer systems are made up of the same three fundamental parts: hardware (e.g., processors, memory, disks, network cards); software (e.g., programs or libraries); and data, which may be either transient (in memory) or persistent (on disk or ROM).

When you try to understand a computer system, you are interested in what its individual parts actually do, how they work together, and how they interact with the world around them—in other words, its *architecture*. The best definition of architecture that we have read, and the one widely accepted in the architectural community, comes from work done in the Software Architecture group of the Software Engineering Institute (SEI) at Carnegie-Mellon University in Pittsburgh.

DEFINITION The **architecture** of a software-intensive system is the structure or structures of the system, which comprise software elements, the externally visible properties of those elements, and the relationships among them.

Let's look at two key parts of this definition in a bit more detail, namely, a system's *structures* and its *externally visible properties*.

System Structures

There are two types of system structure of interest to the software architect: *static* (design-time organization) and *dynamic* (runtime organization).

1. The *static structures* of a system tell you what the design-time form of a system is—that is, what its elements are and how they fit together.

DEFINITION The **static structures** of a software system define its internal design-time elements and their arrangement.

Internal design-time software elements might be modules, object-oriented classes or packages, database stored procedures, services, or any other self-contained code unit. Internal data elements include classes, relational database entities/tables, and data files. Internal hardware elements include computers or their constituent parts such as disk or CPU and networking elements such as cables, routers, or hubs.

The static arrangement of these elements defines—depending on the context—the associations, relationships, or connectivity between these elements. For software modules, for example, there may be static relationships such as a hierarchy of elements (module *A* is built from modules *B* and *C*) or dependencies between elements (module *A* relies on the services of module *B*). For classes, relational entities, or other data elements, relationships define how one data item is linked to another one. For hardware, the relationships define the required physical interconnections between the various hardware elements of the system.

2. The system's *dynamic structures* show how the system actually works—that is, what happens at runtime and what the system does in response to external (or internal) stimulus.

DEFINITION The **dynamic structures** of a software system define its runtime elements and their interactions.

These internal interactions may be flows of information between elements (element A sends messages to element B) or the parallel or sequential execution of internal tasks (element X invokes a routine on element Y), or they may be expressed in terms of the effect they have on data (data item D is created, updated many times, and finally destroyed).

Externally Visible System Properties

External properties manifest themselves in two different ways: *externally visible behavior* (what the system does) and *quality properties* (how the system does it).

1. *Externally visible behavior* tells you what a system does from the viewpoint of an external observer.

DEFINITION The **externally visible behavior** of a software system defines the functional interactions between the system and its environment.

These external interactions form a set similar to the ones we considered for dynamic structure. This includes flows of information in and out of the system, the way that the system responds to external stimuli, and the published "contract" or API that the architecture has with the outside world.

External behavior may be modeled by treating the system as a black box so that you don't know anything about its internals (if you make request P to a system built in compliance with the architecture, you are returned response Q). Alternatively, it may consider changes to internal system state in response to external stimuli (submitting a request R causes the creation of an internal data item D).

2. *Quality properties* tell you how a system behaves from the viewpoint of an external observer (often referred to as its nonfunctional characteristics).

DEFINITION A **quality property** is an externally visible, nonfunctional property of a system such as performance, security, or scalability.

There is a whole range of external architectural characteristics that may be of interest: How does the system perform under load? What is the peak throughput given certain hardware? How is the information in the system protected from malicious use? How often is it likely to break? How easy is it to manage, maintain, and enhance? How easily can it be used by people who are disabled? Which of these characteristics are relevant depends on your circumstances and on the concerns and priorities of your stakeholders.

External Properties and Internal Organization

Let's explore these concepts in more detail by means of a simple example.

EXAMPLE An airline reservation system supports a number of different transactions to book airline seats, update or cancel them, transfer them, upgrade them, and so forth. Figure 2–1 shows the context for this system.

The *externally visible behavior* of the system (what it does) is its response to the transactions that can be submitted by customers, such as booking a seat, updating a reservation, or canceling a booking. The *quality properties* of the system (how it does it) include the average response time for a transaction under a specified load, the maximum throughput the system can support, system availability, and the time required to repair defects.

Faced with these requirements, there are a number of ways that an architect could design a system for it. Over the next few pages we outline two possible architectural approaches for this system.

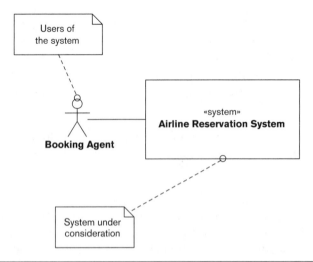

FIGURE 2–1 CONTEXT DIAGRAM FOR AN AIRLINE BOOKING SYSTEM

The architect could design a solution for the airline reservation system based around a **client/server** or **two-tier** deployment approach. (In fact, client/server is an example of an *architectural style*, as we will see in Part II.) In this approach, shown in Figure 2–2, a number of clients (which present information to customers and accept their input) communicate with a central server (which stores the data in a relational database) via a wide-area network (WAN).

The *static structure* (design-time organization) for this client/server deployment architecture consists of the client programs (which in this example are further broken down into presentation, business logic, database, and network layers), the server, and the connections between them. The *dynamic structure* (runtime organization) is based on a request/response model: Requests are submitted by a client to the server over the WAN, and responses are returned by the server to the client.

Alternatively, the architect could take a **three-tier** or **thin-client** deployment approach, where only the presentation processing is performed on the clients, with the business logic and database access performed in an application server, as shown in Figure 2–3.

The *static structure* for this deployment architecture consists of the client programs (which in this example are further broken down into presentation and network layers), the application server (here, business logic, database, and network layers), the database server, and the connections between

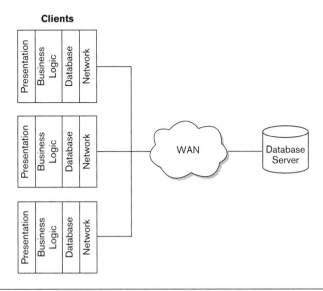

FIGURE 2–2 CLIENT/SERVER ARCHITECTURE FOR AN AIRLINE BOOKING SYSTEM

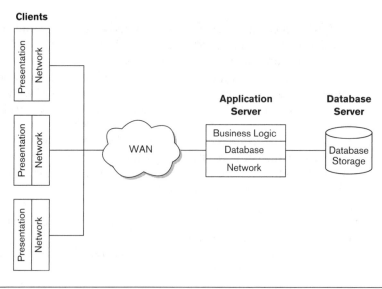

Clients

FIGURE 2–3 THIN-CLIENT ARCHITECTURE FOR AN AIRLINE BOOKING SYSTEM

them. The *dynamic structure* is based on a three-tier request/response model: Requests are submitted by a client to the application server over the WAN, the application server submits requests to the database server if necessary, and responses are returned by the application server to the client.

The architect might identify the two-tier approach as appropriate for the architecture because of its relative operational simplicity, because it can be developed quickly by the organization's software developers, because it can be delivered at lower cost than other options, or for a range of other reasons.

Alternatively, the architect may consider the three-tier approach to be right for the architecture because it provides better options for scalability as workload increases, because less powerful client hardware is needed, because it may offer better security, or for other reasons.

Whichever approach the architect considers to be most appropriate, she chooses it because it provides the best match between the system properties promised by the approach and the requirements of the system.

In this example, there are two possible solutions to the problem, based around a client/server approach and a three-tier approach, respectively. We call these *candidate architectures*.

DEFINITION A **candidate architecture** for a system is a particular arrangement of static and dynamic structures that has the potential to exhibit the system's required externally visible behaviors and quality properties.

Although the candidate architectures have different static and dynamic structures, each must be able to meet the system's overall requirements to process airline bookings in a timely and efficient manner. However, although all candidate architectures are believed to share the same important externally visible behaviors (in this case, responses to booking transactions) and general quality properties (such as acceptable response time, throughput, availability, and time to repair), they are likely to differ in the specific set of quality properties that each exhibits (such as one being easier to maintain but more expensive to build than another).

In each case, the extent to which the candidate actually exhibits these behaviors and properties must be determined by further analysis of its static and dynamic structures. For example, the client/server model might meet the functional requirements better because it supports functionally richer clients; the three-tier model might deliver better throughput and response time because it is more loosely coupled.

It is part of the architect's role to derive the static and dynamic structures for each of the candidate architectures, understand the extent to which they exhibit the required behaviors and quality properties, and select the best one. Of course, what is meant by "best" may not always be clear; we will return to this issue in Part II.

We can capture the relationship between the externally visible properties of a system and its internal structure and organization as follows.

- The externally visible behavior of a system (what it does) is determined by the combined functional behavior of its internal elements.
- The quality properties of a system such as performance, scalability, and resilience (how it does it) arise from the quality properties of its internal elements. (Typically, a system's overall quality property is only as good as the property of its worst-behaving or weakest internal element.)

The Importance of Software Architecture

Every computer system, large or small, is made up of pieces that are linked together. There may be a small number of these pieces, or perhaps only one, or there may be dozens or hundreds; and this linkage may be trivial, or very complicated, or somewhere in between.

Furthermore, every system is made up of pieces that interact with each other and the outside world in a deterministic (predictable) way. Again, the behavior may be simple and easily understood, or it may be so convoluted that no one person can understand every aspect of it. However, this behavior is still there and still (in theory at least) describable.

In other words, every system has an architecture, in the same way that every building, bridge, and battleship has an architecture—and every human body has a physiology.

This is such an important concept that we will state it formally as a principle here.

PRINCIPLE Every computer system has an architecture, whether or not it is documented and understood.

The architecture of a system is an intrinsic, fundamental property that is present whether or not it has been documented and is understood. It follows that every system has precisely one architecture—although, as we will see, it can be represented in a number of ways.

ARCHITECTURAL ELEMENTS

Throughout this book, we standardize the term *architectural element* to refer to the pieces from which systems are built.

DEFINITION An **architectural element** (or just element) is a fundamental piece from which a system can be considered to be constructed.

The nature of an architectural element depends very much on the type of system you are considering and the context within which you are considering its elements. Programming libraries, subsystems, deployable software units (e.g., Enterprise Java Beans and Active X controls), reusable software products (e.g., database management systems), or entire applications may form architectural elements in an information system, depending on the system being built.

An architectural element should possess the following key attributes:

- A clearly defined set of *responsibilities*
- A clearly defined *boundary*
- A set of clearly defined *interfaces*, which define the *services* that the element provides to the other architectural elements

Architectural elements are often known informally as *components* or *modules*, but these terms are already widely used with established specific meaning. In particular, the term *component* tends to suggest the use of a programming-level component model (such as J2EE or .NET), while *module* tends to suggest a programming language construct. Although these are valid architectural elements in some contexts, they won't be the type of fundamental system element used in others.

For this reason, we deliberately don't use these terms from now on. Instead, we use the term *element* throughout the book to avoid confusion (following the lead of others, including Perry and Wolf [PERR92] and Bass, Clements, and Kazman [BASS03]—see the Further Reading section at the end of this chapter for more details).

STAKEHOLDERS

Traditional software development has been driven by the need of the delivered software to meet the requirements of users. Although the definition of the term *user* varies, all software development methods are based around this principle in one way or another.

However, the people affected by a software system are not limited to those who use it. Software systems are not just used: They have to be *built* and *tested*, they have to be *operated*, they may have to be *repaired*, they are usually *enhanced*, and of course they have to be *paid for*. Each of these activities involves a number—possibly a significant number—of people in addition to the users. Each of these groups of people has its own requirements, interests, and needs to be met by the software system.

We refer collectively to these people as *stakeholders*. Understanding the role of the stakeholder is fundamental to understanding the role of the architect in the development of a software product or system. We define a stakeholder as follows.

DEFINITION A **stakeholder** in a software architecture is a person, group, or entity with an interest in or concerns about the realization of the architecture.

The definition comes from IEEE Standard 1471 [IEEE00] on architectural description, which we discuss in more depth in Part II. For now, let's look at a couple of key concepts from this definition.

People, Groups, and Entities

First of all, consider the phrase "person, group or entity." As we shall see in this book, those with an interest in an architecture stretch far more widely than just its developers, or even its developers and users. A much broader community than this is affected by the realization of the architecture, such as those who have to support it, deploy it, or pay for it.

Specifying the architecture is a key opportunity for the stakeholders to direct its shape and direction. You will find, however, that some stakeholders are more interested in their roles than others, for a variety of reasons that have little to do with architecture. Part of your role, therefore, is to engage and galvanize, to persuade people of the importance of their involvement, and to obtain their commitment to the task.

A stakeholder often represents a class of person, such as user or developer, rather than an individual. This presents some problems because it may not be possible to capture and reconcile the needs of all members of the class (all users, all developers) in the time available. Furthermore, you may not have the stakeholders at hand (e.g., when developing a new product). In either case, you need to select some representative stakeholders who will speak for the group. We'll come back to this in Part II.

Interests and Concerns

Now consider the phrase "interest in or concerns about." This criterion is—deliberately—a broad one, and its interpretation is entirely specific to individual projects.

We use the term *concern* here, incidentally, not just because the IEEE standard uses it but also because it is particularly appropriate to the process of architecture. As you will see when you start to develop your architecture, you are engaged in a process of discovery as much as one of capture—in other words, this early in the system development lifecycle, your stakeholders may not yet know precisely what their requirements are.

DEFINITION A **concern** about an architecture is a requirement, an objective, an intention, or an aspiration a stakeholder has for that architecture.

Many concerns will be common among stakeholders, but some concerns will be distinct and may even conflict. Resolving such conflicts in a way that leaves stakeholders satisfied can be a significant challenge.

EXAMPLE Some of the important attributes of a software development project are often shown as a triangle whose corners represent cost, quality, and time to market. Ideally we would like a project to have high quality, zero cost, and immediate delivery, but we know this isn't possible. The *quality triangle* in Figure 2–4 shows that it is necessary to make

FIGURE 2–4 THE QUALITY TRIANGLE

compromises between these three attributes, and the best you are likely to achieve is two out of three.

For example, a high-quality system tends to take longer to build and to cost more. Conversely, it is often possible to reduce the initial development time but, assuming costs are kept roughly constant, this comes at the expense of reducing the quality of the delivered software.

One or more of these attributes is likely to be important to different stakeholders, and it is the architect's job to understand which of these attributes is important to whom and to reach an acceptable compromise when necessary. We'll talk more about how to do this in Part II.

The Importance of Stakeholders

Stakeholders (explicitly or implicitly) drive the whole shape and direction of the architecture, which is developed solely for their benefit and to serve their needs. Stakeholders ultimately make or direct the fundamental decisions about scope, functionality, operational characteristics, and structure of the eventual product or system—under the guidance of the architect, of course. Without stakeholders, there would be no point in developing the architecture because there would be no need for the system it will turn into, nor would there be anyone to build it, deploy it, run it, or pay for it.

PRINCIPLE Architectures are created solely to meet stakeholder needs.

It follows that if a system does not meet the needs of its stakeholders, it cannot be considered a success—no matter how well it conforms to good architectural practice. In other words, architectures must be evaluated with respect to stakeholder needs as well as abstract architectural and software engineering principles.

PRINCIPLE A good architecture is one that successfully meets the objectives, goals, and needs of its stakeholders.

Part II explores the concept of stakeholders in more detail and explains how they can be classified, identified, selected, and engaged in the development of the architecture.

ARCHITECTURAL DESCRIPTIONS

An architecture for a software system can be an incredibly complex thing. Part of the architect's role is to describe this complexity to the people who need to understand it. The architect does this by means of an *architectural description*.

DEFINITION An **architectural description (AD)** is a set of products that documents an architecture in a way its stakeholders can understand and demonstrates that the architecture has met their concerns.

"Products" in this context consists of a range of things—particularly *architectural models*, but also *scope definition*, *constraints*, and *principles*. We discuss each of these in more detail in Part II.

A description of an architecture has to present the essence of the architecture and its detail at the same time—in other words, it must provide an overall picture that summarizes the whole system, but it also must decompose into enough detail that it can be validated and the described system can be built.

Although it is true that every system has an architecture, it is unfortunately not true that every system has an AD. Even if an architecture is documented, it may be documented only in part, or the documentation may be out of date or unused.

Strictly speaking, therefore, our definition describes a *good* AD. However, an AD that its stakeholders cannot understand or that doesn't demonstrate to them that their concerns have been met is really not worth having—in fact, it can be more of a liability than an asset. The AD needs to contain all of (and ideally only) the information needed to communicate the architecture effectively to those stakeholders who need to understand it.

PRINCIPLE Although every system has an architecture, not every system has an architecture that is effectively communicated via an architectural description.

Of course, the chances of project success are far less if the AD is inadequate.

EXAMPLE The AD for the airline reservation system referred to earlier focused strongly on the static deployment structure (the key hardware and software elements) and to a lesser extent on its external behavior (the requests that users could make). Because most users would have a customer at a sales desk or on the end of a telephone, quick response time and system reliability are paramount.

If the AD for such a system does not consider the quality properties of the system in any detail—in particular, if there is no clear definition of response-time requirements nor any performance models—it is quite likely that when the system is deployed, it will deliver poor performance, particularly under peak load.

The solution to this is to identify a group of users who can agree on what the performance requirements are, and then the architect can balance these against what analysis and testing reveal is practically possible. This helps avoid the significant amount of enhancement and tuning inevitably required when performance problems emerge later in the lifecycle.

The architect writes the AD and is also one of its major users. You use the AD as a memory aid, a basis for analysis, a record of decisions, and so on. However, you are only one of the users of the AD. To a lesser or greater extent, all of the other stakeholders need to understand the architecture (or at least parts of it) as it relates to them. If the AD does not help with this, it has failed.

PRINCIPLE A good architectural description is one that effectively and consistently communicates the key aspects of the architecture to the appropriate stakeholders.

Nowadays there is a plethora of techniques, models, architecture description languages, and other ways to document architectures. Choosing the right ones for a particular system development is a significant challenge in its own right; you need to take into account the characteristics of the system and the skills and capabilities of its stakeholders.

Part II explores the concept of ADs in more detail, and Parts III and IV explain the different elements of an AD and how to create them.

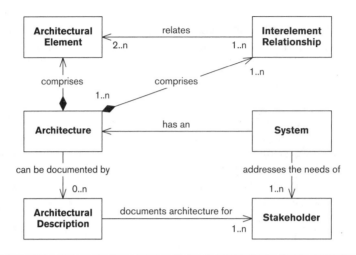

FIGURE 2-5 CORE CONCEPT RELATIONSHIPS

INTERRELATIONSHIPS BETWEEN THE CORE CONCEPTS

The important relationships between our core concepts are illustrated in the UML class diagram in Figure 2–5. The diagram brings out the following relationships between the concepts we have discussed so far.

- A system is built to address the needs, concerns, goals, and objectives of its stakeholders.
- The architecture of a system is comprised of a number of architectural elements and their interelement relationships.
- The architecture of a system can potentially be documented by an AD (fully, partly, or not at all). In fact, there are many potential ADs for a given architecture, some good, some bad.
- An AD documents an architecture for its stakeholders and demonstrates to them that it has met their needs.

SUMMARY

In this chapter we laid our foundations by defining and discussing some concepts and terms we will be using throughout the rest of the book.

- The *architecture* of a system defines four different aspects: its *static structure*, its *dynamic structure*, its *externally visible behavior*, and its *quality properties*. Each of these aspects is important, although not always addressed. Every computer system has an architecture, even if we don't understand it.

- A *candidate architecture* for a system is one that has the potential to exhibit the system's required externally visible behaviors and quality properties. Most problems have several candidate architectures, and it is the job of the architect to select the best one.

- An *architectural element* is a clearly identifiable, architecturally meaningful piece of a system.

- A *stakeholder* is a person, group, or entity with an interest in or concerns about the realization of the architecture. Stakeholders include users but also many people, such as developers, operators, and acquirers. Architectures are created solely to meet stakeholder needs.

- An *architectural description* is a set of products that documents an architecture in a way its stakeholders can understand and demonstrates that the architecture has met their concerns. Although every system has an architecture, not every system has an effective AD.

FURTHER READING

We have aligned our language and concepts in this chapter with the only formal general standard we are aware of in the field of software architecture—IEEE Standard 1471 [IEEE00]. According to its own introduction, this standard "addresses the activities of creation, analysis, and sustainment of architectures of software-intensive systems, and the recording of such architectures in terms of architectural descriptions." Our conceptual model is based on the one presented in the standard.

Much of our thinking on software architecture concepts is based on the work done by the Software Architecture group of the Software Engineering Institute. The book by Bass, Clements, and Kazman [BASS03] is a thorough introduction to the main ideas in the field of software architecture and provides a lot more depth and background on the fundamental concepts than we provide here.

One of the original books on software architecture is by Shaw and Garlan [SHAW96]. This book provides a minimalist and elegant introduction to the fundamental ideas in software architecture, including overviews of an AD, architectural styles, and possible tool support. Even earlier than this, one of the original papers in the software architecture field, by Perry and Wolf [PERR92], is well worth reading for its clear focus on the important elements of the discipline.

Another clear and thought-provoking overview of software architecture appears in a book that is actually the report from a research project funded by the European Commission [JAZA00] (which is unfortunately out of print at present). The first chapter provides an interesting introduction to the field.

If you want to take a wider view of software architecture, a useful book may be the cross-disciplinary *Art of Systems Architecting* [MAIE00]. This book is novel in that it introduces and discusses the idea of architecture (and "architecting") being a set of principles and techniques valid across all complex systems domains. A particular emphasis is placed on architecture heuristics, and a set of interesting heuristics is provided. Examples are taken from buildings, manufacturing, social systems, IT, and collaborative systems.

3

VIEWPOINTS AND VIEWS

When you start the daunting task of designing the architecture of your system, you will find that you have some difficult architectural questions to answer.

- What are the main functional elements of your architecture?
- How will these elements interact with one another and with the outside world?
- What information will be managed, stored, and presented?
- What physical hardware and software elements will be required to support these functional and information elements?
- What operational features and capabilities will be provided?
- What development, test, support, and training environments will be provided?

A common temptation—one you should strongly avoid—is to try to answer all of these questions by means of a single, heavily overloaded, all-encompassing model. This sort of model (and we've all seen them) will probably use a mixture of formal and informal notations to describe a number of aspects of the system on one huge sheet of paper: the functional structure, software layering, concurrency, intercomponent communication, physical deployment environment, and so on. Let's see what happens when we try to use an all-encompassing model in our AD, by means of an example (see page 28).

As the example shows, this sort of AD is really the worst of all worlds. Many writers on software architecture have pointed out that it simply isn't possible to describe a software architecture by using a single model. Such a model is hard to understand and is unlikely to clearly identify the architecture's most

EXAMPLE Although the airline reservation system we introduced in Chapter 2 is conceptually fairly simple, in practice some aspects of this system make it very complicated indeed.

- The system's data is distributed across a number of systems in different physical locations.
- A number of different types of data entry devices must be supported.
- The system must be able to present some information in different languages.
- The system must be able to print tickets and other documents on a wide range of printers.
- The plethora of international regulation complicates the picture even further.

After some discussion, the architect draws up a first-cut architecture for the system, which attempts to represent all of its important aspects in a single diagram. This model includes the full range of data entry devices (including various dumb terminals, desktop PCs, and wireless devices), the multiple physical systems on which data is stored or replicated data is maintained, and some of the printing devices that must be supported (the model does not cover remote printing because it is done at a separate facility). The model is heavily annotated with text to indicate, for example, where multilanguage support is required and where data must be audited, archived, or analyzed to support regulatory requirements.

However, no details of the network interfaces between the different components are included—these are abstracted out into a network icon because these are so complex. (In fact, the network design is probably the most complicated aspect of the architecture, requiring support for a number of different and largely incompatible network protocols, routing over public and private networks, synchronous and asynchronous interactions, and varying levels of service reliability and availability.) Furthermore, the model does not address any of the implications of having the same data distributed around multiple systems.

Because it is so complex and tries to address a wide mix of concerns in the same diagram, the model fails to engage any of the stakeholders. The users find it too complex and difficult to understand (particularly because of the large number of physical hardware components represented). The technology stakeholders, on the other hand, tend to disregard it because of the detail that is left out, such as the network topology. The legal

> team members can't use it to satisfy themselves that the regulatory aspects will be adequately handled, and the sponsor finds it completely incomprehensible.
>
> Furthermore, the architect spends an inordinate amount of time keeping it up-to-date—every time a new type of data entry device or printer is discussed, for example, the diagram needs to be updated and reprinted on a very large sheet of paper.
>
> Because of these problems, the diagram soon becomes obsolete and is eventually forgotten. Unfortunately, the issues that the model fails to address do not disappear and thus cause many problems and delays during the implementation and the early stages of live operation.

important features. It tends to poorly serve individual stakeholders because they struggle to understand the aspects that interest them. Worst of all, because of its complexity, a monolithic AD is often incomplete, incorrect, or out-of-date.

PRINCIPLE It is not possible to capture the functional features and quality properties of a complex system in a single comprehensible model that is understandable by and of value to all stakeholders.

We need to represent complex systems in a way that is manageable and comprehensible by a range of business and technical stakeholders. A widely used approach—the only successful one we have found—is to attack the problem from different directions simultaneously. In this approach, the AD is partitioned into a number of separate but interrelated **views**, each of which describes a separate aspect of the architecture. Collectively, the views describe the whole system.

To help you understand what we mean by a view, let's consider the example of an architectural drawing for one of the elevations of an office block. This portrays the building from a particular aspect, typically a compass bearing such as northeast. The drawing shows features of the building that are visible from that vantage point but not from other directions. It doesn't show any details of the interior of the building (as seen by its occupants) or of its internal systems (such as plumbing or air conditioning) that influence the environment its occupants will inhabit. Thus the blueprint is only a partial representation of the building; you have to look at—and understand—the whole set of blueprints to grasp the facilities and experience that the whole building will provide.

Another way that a building architect might represent a new building is to construct a scale model of it and its environs. This shows how the building will look from all sides but again reveals nothing about its interior form or its likely internal environment.

STRATEGY A complex system is much more effectively described by using a set of interrelated views, which collectively illustrate its functional features and quality properties and demonstrate that it meets its goals.

Let's take a look at what this approach means for software architecture.

ARCHITECTURAL VIEWS

An architectural view is a way to portray those aspects or elements of the architecture that are relevant to the concerns the view intends to address—and, by implication, the stakeholders for whom those concerns are important.

This idea is not new, going back at least as far as the work of David Parnas in the 1970s and more recently Dewayne Perry and Alexander Wolf in the early 1990s. However, it wasn't until 1995 that Phillipe Kruchten of the Rational Corporation published his widely accepted written description of viewpoints, *Architectural Blueprints—The 4+1 View Model of Software Architecture*. This suggested four different views of a system and the use of a set of scenarios (use cases) to check their correctness. Kruchten's approach has since evolved to form an important part of the Rational Unified Process (RUP).

More recently, IEEE Standard 1471 has formalized these concepts and brought some welcome standardization of terminology. In fact, our definition of a view is based on and extends the one from the IEEE standard.

DEFINITION A **view** is a representation of one or more structural aspects of an architecture that illustrates how the architecture addresses one or more concerns held by one or more of its stakeholders.

When deciding what to include in a view, ask yourself the following questions.

- What class(es) of stakeholder is the view aimed at? A view may be narrowly focused on one class of stakeholder or even a specific individual, or it may be aimed at a larger group whose members have varying interests and levels of expertise.
- How much technical understanding do these stakeholders have? Acquirers and users, for example, will be experts in their subject areas but are unlikely to know much about hardware or software, while the converse may apply to developers or support staff.

- What stakeholder concerns is the view intended to address? How much do the stakeholders know about the architectural context and background to these concerns?

- How much do these stakeholders need to know about this aspect of the architecture? For nontechnical stakeholders such as users, how competent are they in understanding its technical details?

As with the AD itself, one of your main challenges is to get the right level of detail into your views. Provide too much detail, and your audience will be overwhelmed; too little, and you risk your audience making assumptions that may not be valid.

STRATEGY Include in a view only the details that further the objectives of your AD—that is, those details that help explain the architecture to stakeholders or demonstrate that stakeholder concerns are being met.

VIEWPOINTS

It would be hard work if every time you were creating a view of your architecture you had to go back to first principles to define what should go into it. Fortunately, you don't have to do that.

In his introductory paper, Kruchten defined four standard views, namely, Logical, Process, Physical, and Development. The IEEE standard makes this idea generic (and does not specify one set of views or another) by proposing the concept of a *viewpoint*.

The objective of the viewpoint concept is an ambitious one—no less than making available a library of templates and patterns that can be used off the shelf to guide the creation of an architectural view that can be inserted into an AD. We define a viewpoint (again after IEEE Standard 1471) as follows.

DEFINITION A **viewpoint** is a collection of patterns, templates, and conventions for constructing one type of view. It defines the stakeholders whose concerns are reflected in the viewpoint and the guidelines, principles, and template models for constructing its views.

Architectural viewpoints provide a framework for capturing reusable architectural knowledge that can be used to guide the creation of a particular type of (partial) AD.

In a relatively unstructured activity like architecture definition, the idea of the viewpoint is very appealing. If we can define a standard approach, a standard language, and even a standard metamodel for describing different aspects of a system, stakeholders can understand any AD that conforms to these standards once familiar with them.

In practice, of course, we haven't achieved this goal yet. There are no universally accepted ways to model software architectures, and every AD uses its own conventions. However, the widespread acceptance of techniques such as entity-relationship models and of modeling languages such as UML takes us some way toward this goal.

In any case, it is extremely useful to be able to categorize views according to the types of concerns and architectural elements they present.

STRATEGY When developing a view, whether or not you use a formally defined viewpoint, be clear in your own mind what sorts of concerns the view is addressing, what types of architectural elements it presents, and who the viewpoint is aimed at. Make sure that your stakeholders understand these as well.

INTERRELATIONSHIPS BETWEEN THE CORE CONCEPTS

To put views and viewpoints in context, we can now extend the conceptual model we introduced in Chapter 2 to illustrate how views and viewpoints contribute to the overall picture (see Figure 3–1).

We have added the following relationships to the diagram we originally presented as Figure 2–5.

- A viewpoint defines the aims, intended audience, and content of a class of views and defines the concerns that views of this class will address.
- A view conforms to a viewpoint and so communicates the resolution of a number of concerns (and a resolution of a concern may be communicated in a number of views).
- An AD comprises a number of views.

THE BENEFITS OF USING VIEWPOINTS AND VIEWS

Using views and viewpoints to describe the architecture of a system benefits the architecture definition process in a number of ways.

- *Separation of concerns*: Describing many aspects of the system via a single representation can cloud communication and, more seriously, can result in independent aspects of the system becoming intertwined in the

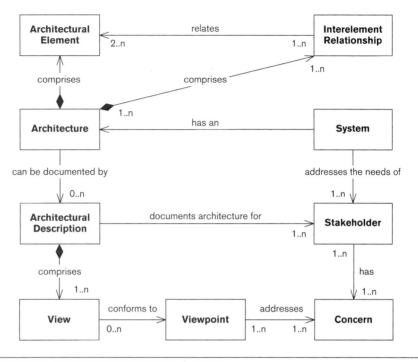

FIGURE 3-1 VIEWS AND VIEWPOINTS IN CONTEXT

model. Separating different models of a system into distinct (but related) descriptions helps the design, analysis, and communication processes by allowing you to focus on each aspect separately.

- *Communication with stakeholder groups*: The concerns of each stakeholder group are typically quite different (e.g., contrast the primary concerns of end users, security auditors, and help-desk staff), and communicating effectively with the various stakeholder groups is quite a challenge. The viewpoint-oriented approach can help considerably with this problem. Different stakeholder groups can be guided quickly to different parts of the AD based on their particular concerns, and each view can be presented using language and notation appropriate to the knowledge, expertise, and concerns of the intended readership.

- *Management of complexity*: Dealing simultaneously with all of the aspects of a large system can result in overwhelming complexity that no one person can possibly handle. By treating each significant aspect of a system separately, the architect can focus on each in turn and so help conquer the complexity resulting from their combination.

- *Improved developer focus*: The AD is of course particularly important for the developers because they use it as the foundation of the system design. By separating out into different views those aspects of the system that are particularly important to the development team, you help ensure that the right system gets built.

VIEWPOINT PITFALLS

Of course, the use of views and viewpoints won't solve all of your software architecture problems automatically. Although we have found that using views is really the only way to make the problem manageable, you need to be aware of some possible pitfalls when using the view-based approach.

- *Inconsistency*: Using a number of views to describe a system inevitably brings consistency problems. It is theoretically possible to use architecture description languages to create the models in your views and then cross-check these automatically (much as graphical modeling tools attempt to check structured or object-oriented methods models), but there are no such machine-checkable architecture description languages in widespread use today. This means that achieving cross-view consistency within an AD is an inherently manual process and so, to assist with this, Chapter 22 includes a checklist to help you ensure consistency between the standard viewpoints presented in our catalog in Part III.

- *Selection of the wrong set of views*: It is not always obvious which set of views is suitable for describing a particular system. This is influenced by a number of factors, such as the nature and complexity of the architecture, the skills and experience of the stakeholders (and of the architect), and the time available to produce the AD. There really isn't an easy answer to this problem, other than your own experience and skill and an analysis of the most important concerns that affect your architecture.

- *Fragmentation*: When you start to describe your architecture, one temptation is to create a large number of views. This can lead to your architecture being described by many independent models, each in a separate view, making the AD difficult to follow. Each separate view also involves a significant amount of effort to create and maintain. To avoid fragmentation and minimize the overhead of maintaining unnecessary descriptions, you should eliminate views that do not address significant concerns for the system you are building. In some cases, you may also consider creating hybrid views that combine models from a number of views in the viewpoint set (e.g., creating a combined deployment and concurrency view). Beware, however, of the combined views becoming difficult to understand and maintain because they address a combination of concerns.

OUR VIEWPOINT CATALOG

Part III of this book presents our catalog of six core viewpoints for information systems architecture: the Functional, Information, Concurrency, Development, Deployment, and Operational viewpoints. Although the viewpoints are (largely) disjoint, we find it convenient to group them as shown in Figure 3–2.

- The Functional, Information, and Concurrency viewpoints characterize the fundamental organization of the system.
- The Development viewpoint exists to support the system's construction.
- The Deployment and Operational viewpoints characterize the system once in its live environment.

Table 3–1 briefly describes our viewpoints.

Of course, not all of these viewpoints may apply to your architecture, and some will be more important than others. You may not need views of all of these types in your AD, and in some cases there may even be other more specialized viewpoints that you need to identify and add yourself. This means that your first job is to understand the nature of your architecture, the skills and experience of the stakeholders, and the time available and other constraints, and then to come up with an appropriate selection of views.

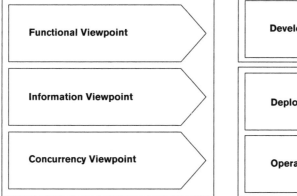
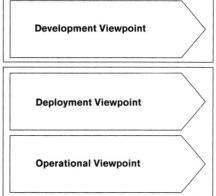

FIGURE 3–2 VIEWPOINT GROUPINGS

TABLE 3-1 VIEWPOINT CATALOG

Viewpoint	Definition
Functional	Describes the system's functional elements, their responsibilities, interfaces, and primary interactions. A Functional view is the cornerstone of most ADs and is often the first part of the description that stakeholders try to read. It drives the shape of other system structures such as the information structure, concurrency structure, deployment structure, and so on. It also has a significant impact on the system's quality properties such as its ability to change, its ability to be secured, and its runtime performance.
Information	Describes the way that the architecture stores, manipulates, manages, and distributes information. The ultimate purpose of virtually any computer system is to manipulate information in some form, and this viewpoint develops a complete but high-level view of static data structure and information flow. The objective of this analysis is to answer the big questions around content, structure, ownership, latency, references, and data migration.
Concurrency	Describes the concurrency structure of the system and maps functional elements to concurrency units to clearly identify the parts of the system that can execute concurrently and how this is coordinated and controlled. This entails the creation of models that show the process and thread structures that the system will use and the interprocess communication mechanisms used to coordinate their operation.
Development	Describes the architecture that supports the software development process. Development views communicate the aspects of the architecture of interest to those stakeholders involved in building, testing, maintaining, and enhancing the system.
Deployment	Describes the environment into which the system will be deployed, including capturing the dependencies the system has on its runtime environment. This view captures the hardware environment that your system needs (primarily the processing nodes, network interconnections, and disk storage facilities required), the technical environment requirements for each element, and the mapping of the software elements to the runtime environment that will execute them.
Operational	Describes how the system will be operated, administered, and supported when it is running in its production environment. For all but the simplest systems, installing, managing, and operating the system is a significant task that must be considered and planned at design time. The aim of the Operational viewpoint is to identify system-wide strategies for addressing the operational concerns of the system's stakeholders and to identify solutions that address these.

SUMMARY

Capturing the essence and the detail of the whole architecture in a single model is just not possible for anything other than simple systems. If you try to do this, you will end up with a model that is unmanageable and does not adequately represent the system to you or any of the stakeholders.

By far the best way of managing this complexity is to produce a number of different representations of all or part of the architecture, each of which focuses on certain aspects of the system, showing how it addresses some of the stakeholder concerns. We call these *views*.

To help you decide what views to produce and what should go into any particular view, you use *viewpoints*, which are standardized definitions of view concepts, content, and activities.

The use of views and viewpoints brings many benefits, such as separation of concerns, improved communication with stakeholders, and management of complexity. However, it is not without its pitfalls, such as inconsistency and fragmentation, and you must be careful to manage these.

In this chapter, we introduced our viewpoint catalog, comprising the Functional, Information, Concurrency, Development, Deployment, and Operational viewpoints, which we describe in detail in Part III.

FURTHER READING

A lot of useful guidance on creating ADs using views (including a discussion of when and how to combine views) and thorough guidance for creating the documentation for a wide variety of types of view can be found in Clements et al. [CLEM03]. Other references that help to make sense of viewpoints and views are IEEE Standard 1471 [IEEE00] and Kruchten's "4+1" approach [KRUC95]. One of the earliest explicit references to the need for architectural views appears in Perry and Wolf [PERR92].

Some of the other viewpoint taxonomies that have been developed over the last decade or so—including Kruchten's "4+1"; RM-ODP; the viewpoint set by Hofmeister et al. [HOFM00]; and the set by Garland and Anthony [GARL03]—are described in the Appendix, together with recommendations for further reading in this area.

Part III, where we describe our viewpoint catalog in detail, contains references for specific view-related reading.

4

ARCHITECTURAL PERSPECTIVES

In Chapter 3, we explained how we use viewpoints (such as the Functional, Information, and Deployment viewpoints) to guide the process of capturing and representing the architecture as a set of views, with the development of each view being guided by the use of a specific viewpoint. When creating a view, your focus is on the issues, concerns, and solutions pertinent to that view. So, for an Information view, for example, you focus on things such as information structure, ownership, transactional integrity, data quality, and timeliness.

Many of the important concerns that are pertinent to one view are much less important when considering the others: Data ownership, for example, is not key to formulating the Concurrency view, nor is the development environment a major concern when considering the Functional view. (Of course, the *decisions* taken in one view can have a considerable impact on the others, and it is a big part of the architect's job to make sure that these implications are understood. However, the *concerns* addressed in different views are largely different.)

Although the views, when combined, form a representation of the whole architecture, we can consider them largely independent of one another—a disjoint partition of the whole architectural analysis. In fact, for any significant system, you usually *must* partition your analysis this way because trying to address the entire problem is too much to understand or describe in a single piece.

QUALITY PROPERTIES

Many architectural decisions address concerns that are common to many or all views. These concerns are normally driven by the need for the system to exhibit a certain quality property rather than to provide a particular function.

In our experience, trying to address these aspects of an architecture by using viewpoints doesn't work well. Let's look at an example to understand why.

EXAMPLE Security is clearly a vital aspect of most architectures. It has always been important to be able to restrict access to data or functionality to appropriate classes of users, and in the age of the Internet, good external and internal security is even more important. If some of your systems are exposed to the wider world, they are vulnerable to attack, and the consequences of a breach can be disastrous for finances or public relations. (The large number of high-profile Internet security failures in Europe and North America during the early part of the millennium illustrates this clearly.)

In our experience, security is often not thought through properly early in the project lifecycle. Part of the reason for this is that security is hard—the means for achieving an appropriate level of security are complex and require sophisticated analysis. Also, it may be considered to be "someone else's problem"—the responsibility of a specialist security group rather than of the organization as a whole. You may be surprised, therefore, that we have not included a Security viewpoint in our catalog to go along with the others (Functional, Information, Deployment, and so forth).

We used to approach concerns like security just like that ourselves. We used a Security viewpoint and started to consider which classes of stakeholders have concerns in this area, what this viewpoint should consist of, and how a typical Security view might actually look.

However, experience taught us that security is an important factor that affects aspects of the architecture addressed by most if not all of the other viewpoints we presented in Chapter 3. Furthermore, which of the system's security qualities are significant depends on which viewpoint we are considering. Here are some examples.

- From the Functional viewpoint, the system needs the ability to identify and authenticate its users (internal and external, human and mechanical). Security processes should be effective but unobtrusive, and any external processes exposed to the outside world need to be resilient to attack.
- From the Information viewpoint, the system must be able to control different classes of access to information (read, insert, update, delete). The system may need to apply these controls at varying levels of granularity (e.g., defining object-level security within a database).
- From the Operational viewpoint, the system must be able to maintain and distribute secret information (e.g., keys and passwords) and must be up-to-date with the latest security updates and patches.

> When we consider the system from the Development, Concurrency, and Deployment viewpoints, we'll probably also find aspects of the architecture that will be affected by security needs.
>
> So our overall criterion of "the system must be secure" actually breaks down *across* the viewpoints into a number of more specific criteria.

As the example shows, there is an inherent need to consider quality properties such as security in each architectural view. Considering them in isolation just doesn't make sense, so using a viewpoint to guide the creation of another view for each quality property doesn't make sense either.

ARCHITECTURAL PERSPECTIVES

Going back to our example, although security is clearly important, representing it in our conceptual model of software architecture as another viewpoint doesn't really work. A comprehensive security viewpoint would have to consider process security, information security, operational security, deployment security, and so on: In other words, it would affect exactly the aspects of the system that we have considered so far using our viewpoints.

Rather than defining another viewpoint and creating another view, we need some way to modify and enhance our *existing* views to ensure that our architecture exhibits the desired quality properties. We therefore need something in our conceptual model that can be considered "orthogonal" to viewpoints, and we have coined the term *architectural perspective* (which we shorten to *perspective*) to refer to it.

DEFINITION An **architectural perspective** is a collection of activities, tactics, and guidelines that are used to ensure that a system exhibits a particular set of related quality properties that require consideration across a number of the system's architectural views.

Although our use of the term *perspective* is new, many of the ideas behind it clearly aren't. The issues addressed by perspectives are often referred to as *nonfunctional requirements* of the architecture, although we prefer not to use this term.[1]

---

1. Although it is true that the perspectives tend to address concerns that are distinct from what the system actually does, the division of concerns as *functional* or *nonfunctional* is often quite artificial, and we try to avoid the use of these terms. Perspectives can have an impact on how a system works, sometimes significantly, and using these terms can imply that these areas are somehow less important than functionality.

With perspectives, we are trying to *systematize* what a good architect does anyway—understand the quality properties that are required; assess and review the architectural models to ensure that the architecture exhibits the required properties; identify, prototype, test, and select architectural tactics to address cases when the architecture is lacking; and so on. A perspective provides a framework to guide and formalize this process. This means that you never work with perspectives in isolation but instead use them with each view to analyze and validate the qualities of your architecture and to drive further architectural decision making. We describe this as *applying* the perspective to the view.

Different quality properties, such as security, performance, availability, or usability, vary in their applicability to different types of systems. Usability, for example, is unlikely to be particularly important to an infrastructure project with little or no functionality exposed to users. However, broad categories of systems are likely to have similar overall quality property requirements and common ways of meeting them, so we intend perspectives to be defined in sets, with each set aimed at a particular category of system. In this book we focus on large-scale information systems and have therefore defined a set of perspectives for systems in that domain.

In our experience, the most important perspectives for large information systems include *Security* (ensuring controlled access to sensitive system resources), *Performance and Scalability* (meeting the system's required performance profile and handling increasing workloads satisfactorily), *Availability and Resilience* (ensuring system availability when required and coping with failures that could affect this), and *Evolution* (ensuring that the system can cope with likely changes). We define these perspectives in detail in Part IV, along with a number of less widely applicable perspectives such as *Regulation* (the ability of the system to conform to local and international laws, quasi-legal regulations, company policies, and other rules and standards).

You will find these perspective definitions useful whether you are just starting out as an architect or already have significant experience in the role. You can use the definitions in a number of different ways.

- A perspective is a useful *store of knowledge*, helping you quickly review your architectural models for a particular quality property without having to absorb a large quantity of more detailed material.

- A perspective acts as an effective *guide* when you are working in an area that is new to you and you are not familiar with its typical concerns, problems, and solutions.

- A perspective is a useful *memory aid* when you are working in an area that you are more familiar with, to make sure that you don't forget anything important.

In general, you should try to apply your perspectives, even if only informally, as early as possible in the design of your architecture. This will help prevent you from going down architectural blind alleys in which you develop a model that is functionally correct but offers, for example, poor performance or availability.

Like viewpoints, it is important to define perspectives by using a standard structure, to make them easy to use and to ensure that they all approach a subject area in the same general way. The perspective definitions in Part IV are all structured in the following manner.

- *Applicability*: This section explains which of your views are most likely to be affected by applying the perspective. For example, applying the Evolution perspective might affect your Functional view more than your Operational view.

- *Concerns*: This information defines the quality properties that the perspective addresses.

- *Activities*: In this section, we explain the steps for applying the perspective to your views—identifying the important quality properties, analyzing the views against these properties, and then making architectural design decisions that modify and improve the views.

- *Architectural tactics*: An **architectural tactic** is an established and proven approach you can use to help achieve a particular quality property (e.g., defining different processing priorities for different parts of the system's workload and managing this by using a priority-based process scheduler to achieve satisfactory overall system performance). Each perspective identifies and describes the most important tactics for achieving its quality properties.[2]

- *Problems and pitfalls*: This section explains the most common things that can go wrong and gives guidance on how to recognize and avoid them.

- *Checklists*: The checklists provide a list of questions to help you make sure you have addressed the most important concerns, considered the most appropriate tactics, and avoided the most common pitfalls.

- *Further reading*: Our perspective descriptions are necessarily brief, helping you understand the most important issues, problems, and proven practices. The Further Reading section provides a number of pointers to further information.

---

2. Don't confuse tactics with design patterns (which we discuss in Part II). Although tactics and patterns are both valuable sources of design knowledge, a tactic is much more general and less constraining than a classical design pattern because it does not mandate a particular software structure but provides general guidance on how to design a particular aspect of your system. See the Further Reading section at the end of this chapter for some references on tactics.

APPLYING PERSPECTIVES TO VIEWS

The informal diagram in Figure 4–1 shows how you apply perspectives to your views. The key point is that you apply each relevant perspective to some or all of the views in order to address that perspective's system-wide quality property concerns. The architectural views contain the description of the architecture, while the perspectives guide you through the process of analyzing and modifying your architecture to make sure it exhibits a particular quality property.

Although every perspective can be applied to every view (in other words, the relationship between perspectives and views is many-to-many), in practice, because of time constraints, you usually apply only *some* of the perspectives to *some* of the views. An easy way to understand this process is to think of a two-dimensional grid, with views along one axis and perspectives along another, as shown in Figure 4–2.

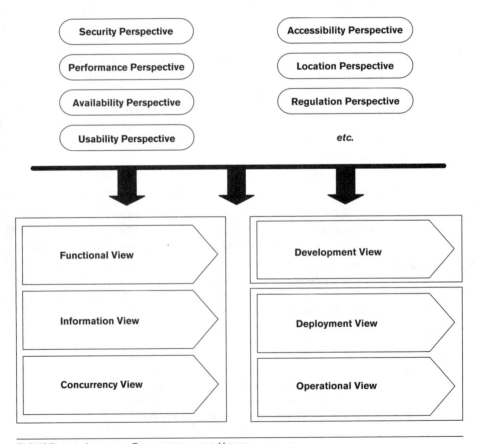

FIGURE 4-1 APPLYING PERSPECTIVES TO VIEWS

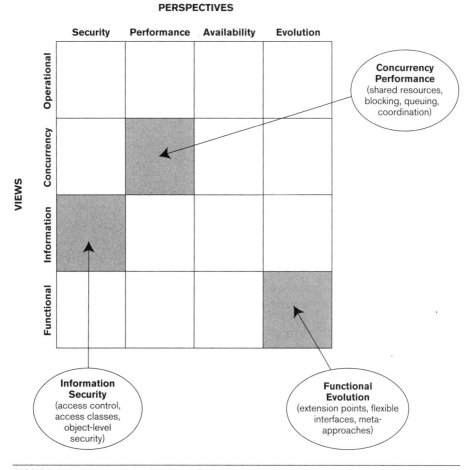

FIGURE 4-2 EXAMPLES OF APPLYING PERSPECTIVES TO VIEWS

Each rectangle in the grid represents the application of a perspective to a view, and the contents of the rectangle define the important qualities and concerns at that intersection. Here are some examples.

- When you apply the Security perspective to the Information view, it guides the design of your architecture so that, for example, it includes appropriate data access control and data ownership.
- When you apply the Performance perspective to the Concurrency view, it guides the design of your architecture so that, for example, a suitable process structure is used, and shared resources will not lead to contention.

▪ When you apply the Evolution perspective to the Functional view, it guides the design of your architecture so that, for example, you consider the types of changes that will be required and build in the right level of flexibility.

When you are working on a particular view, look along the rows of the grid to remind yourself of the important non-view-specific qualities and how they manifest themselves in that view. You may even want to draw up a grid like the one shown in Figure 4–2 to record which perspectives you intend to apply to which views. A good way to do this is to consider how important each perspective is to each view for your system, as illustrated in Table 4–1.

EXAMPLE Going back to our example of security, having decided on a candidate architecture for your system and captured it as a set of views, you would then apply the Security perspective in order to ensure that the system meets its security requirements.

To apply this perspective, you would perform a number of activities, as listed in the perspective's definition, such as identifying the sensitive resources in the system, identifying the threats that the system faces, and deciding how to mitigate each threat by using suitable security processes and technology. The result would typically be some changes to your candidate architecture such as those listed here.

▪ You might decide to partition the system differently in order to easily restrict access to parts of it. This would affect your Functional view.

▪ Your security design might introduce new hardware and software elements to the system to limit access or to add additional guarantees

TABLE 4–1 TYPICAL VIEW AND PERSPECTIVE APPLICABILITY

		Perspectives		
Views	Security	Performance and Scalability	Availability and Resilience	Evolution
Functional	Medium	Medium	Low	High
Information	Medium	Medium	Low	High
Concurrency	Low	High	Medium	Medium
Development	Medium	Low	Low	High
Deployment	High	High	High	Low
Operational	Medium	Low	Medium	Low

(such as encryption to ensure privacy). You would need to add these new elements to your Deployment view to define where they fit, and you might need to update the Development view to define how these new elements should be used.

■ You might identify new operational procedures to support secure operation (e.g., certificate management) or modify existing procedures to ensure security (e.g., handling backups of sensitive data). These procedural changes will modify the Operational view.

Applying the Security perspective has not resulted in a new security view but has identified a number of modifications to your existing views that help address your stakeholder's security concerns.

CONSEQUENCES OF APPLYING A PERSPECTIVE

Applying a perspective to a view can lead to *insights*, *improvements*, and *artifacts*.

Insights

Applying a perspective almost always leads to the creation of something—usually some sort of a model—that provides an insight into the system's ability to meet a required quality property. Such a model demonstrates either that the architecture meets its required quality properties or (more likely in the early stages of architecture definition) that it is deficient in some way.

EXAMPLE Applying the Security perspective might reveal the existence of a number of significant security threats that are not countered by the system in its current form. You would then need to understand these threats, understand what the risks are, and understand the impact these risks have on your architecture.

These insights normally drive further architectural design activity and are usefully recorded in their own right as rationales for significant design decisions.

Improvements

If applying the perspective tells you that the architecture will not meet one of its quality properties, the architecture needs to be improved. In this case, you may need to change an existing model in the view, create additional models to further develop the content of the view, or perhaps do both of these.

> **EXAMPLE** Applying the Performance and Scalability perspective to your Deployment view might demonstrate that you need to replicate the application servers in order to be capable of scaling to meet expected demand. This could lead to a change to the Deployment model to show several servers instead of one and possible changes to the Functional or Information views to support this load balancing.

These improvements are, of course, integral to the AD and should be given as much prominence as your original models.

Artifacts

Some of the models and other deliverables created as a result of applying a perspective will be of only passing interest and will probably be discarded once the insight or improvement they reveal is understood. However, other outputs of applying a perspective are of significant lasting value and are important supporting architectural information. These outputs, which we term **artifacts**, are a valuable outcome of applying a perspective and should be preserved.

> **EXAMPLE** Applying the Location perspective to your Deployment view might result in a spreadsheet that models the physical network to show that there is sufficient bandwidth and capacity for the expected traffic. This spreadsheet is a useful artifact that is likely to be needed in the future to investigate the probable impact of changes to the system or the network. You should retain and reference this artifact from the AD.

Artifacts are typically captured as documents, models, or implementations, which are referenced from the AD as supporting information. Small documents can be integrated into the AD as appendices, but take care to avoid creating a huge document because this can become unwieldy and difficult to read and maintain.

INTERRELATIONSHIPS BETWEEN THE CORE CONCEPTS

To put perspectives in context, we can now add a further piece to our conceptual model, as shown in Figure 4–3.

We have added the following relationships to update the similar diagram we showed previously as Figure 3–1.

- The content of a view can be shaped by a number of perspectives, in order to ensure the system's ability to exhibit the quality properties considered by that perspective.
- A perspective addresses a number of concerns of the system's stakeholders.

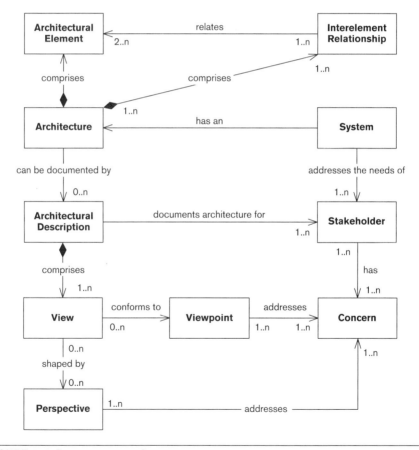

FIGURE 4–3 PERSPECTIVES IN CONTEXT

THE BENEFITS OF USING PERSPECTIVES

Applying perspectives to a view benefits your AD in several ways.

- The perspective provides common conventions, measurements, or even a notation or language you can use to *describe* the system's qualities. For example, the Performance perspective defines standardized measures such as response time, throughput, latency, and so forth, as well as how they are specified and captured.

- The perspective defines *concerns* that guide architectural decision making to help ensure that the resulting architecture will exhibit the quality properties considered by the perspective. For example, the Performance perspective defines standard concerns such as response time, throughput, and predictability. Understanding and prioritizing the concerns that a perspective addresses helps you bring a firm set of priorities to later decision making.

- The perspective describes how you can *validate* the architecture to demonstrate that it meets its requirements across each of the views. For example, the Performance perspective describes how to construct mathematical models or simulations to predict expected performance under a given load and techniques for prototyping and benchmarking.

- The perspective may offer recognized *solutions* to common problems, thus helping to share knowledge between architects. For example, the Performance perspective describes how hardware devices may be multiplexed to improve throughput.

- The perspective helps you work in a *systematic* way to ensure that its concerns are addressed by the system. This helps you organize the work and make sure that nothing is forgotten.

PERSPECTIVE PITFALLS

As with any technique, you should take some care when applying perspectives as there are some potential pitfalls.

- Each perspective addresses a single, closely related set of quality property concerns. There will often be conflicts between the solutions suggested by different perspectives (e.g., a highly evolvable system may be less efficient, and thus less performant, than a less flexible one). An important part of your role as a software architect is to balance such competing needs.

- The stakeholder concerns and priorities are different for every system, so the degree to which you should consider each perspective varies considerably.
- Perspectives contain established, general advice for ensuring a system exhibits certain quality properties. However, every situation is different, and it is important that you think about the advice and its relevance to your situation and then apply it appropriately.

OUR PERSPECTIVE CATALOG

Part IV of this book defines several perspectives (see Table 4–2), which form a set intended for application to the architectures of large-scale information systems.

TABLE 4–2 PERSPECTIVE CATALOG

Perspective	Desired Quality
Accessibility	The ability of the system to be used by people with disabilities
Availability and Resilience	The ability of the system to be fully or partly operational as and when required and to effectively handle failures that could affect system availability
Development Resource	The ability of the system to be designed, built, deployed, and operated within known constraints around people, budget, time, and materials
Evolution	The ability of the system to be flexible in the face of the inevitable change that all systems experience after deployment, balanced against the costs of providing such flexibility
Internationalization	The ability of the system to be independent from any particular language, country, or cultural group
Location	The ability of the system to overcome problems brought about by the absolute location of its elements and the distances between them
Performance and Scalability	The ability of the system to predictably execute within its mandated performance profile and to handle increased processing volumes
Regulation	The ability of the system to conform to local and international laws, quasi-legal regulations, company policies, and other rules and standards
Security	The ability of the system to reliably control, monitor, and audit who can perform what actions on what resources and to detect and recover from failures in security mechanisms
Usability	The ease with which people who interact with the system can work effectively

As we have said, there are many perspectives, and it is not usually feasible to consider all perspectives in the context of all of the views. Not every perspective is relevant to every system and view, and there may be instances where you don't need to consider some of the perspectives at all.

STRATEGY Apply only the most relevant perspectives to your views. Base your selection on the needs of the stakeholders, the relevant importance of the different quality properties to them, and your own experience and judgment.

SUMMARY

Viewpoints and views are an excellent way to partition your architecture into a set of interrelated models. However, these are often assessed for completeness and correctness against only functional requirements, rather than against other system qualities such as performance and scalability. This can result in a system that is functionally correct but exhibits poor response time or is insecure or unreliable. A mechanism is required to make sure this doesn't happen.

We define a *perspective* as a collection of activities, tactics, and guidelines you use to ensure that the system will exhibit a particular set of related qualities, properties, or behaviors. Using perspectives gives you a framework for the analysis and improvement of your architectural models against the qualities the perspective addresses.

Applying a perspective to a view allows you to ensure that the architecture, as represented in that view, is fit for its purpose as far as that perspective is concerned. This is an iterative process: You create models in your views, assess these models against criteria defined in the perspective, revise your view models according to the outcome of this analysis, and iterate again.

We can compare and contrast our notions of view, viewpoint, and perspective—probably the three most important concepts in this book—as follows.

- A *view* is a representation of all (or part of) an architecture—that is, a way to document its architecturally significant features according to a related set of concerns. A view captures a description of one or more of the architectural structures of the system. Architects use views to explain the architectural structure of the system to stakeholders and to demonstrate that the architecture will meet their concerns. A view comprises a set of tangible architectural products, such as principles and models; the complete set of views of an architecture forms the AD.
- A *viewpoint* guides the process of creating a particular type of view. A viewpoint defines the concerns addressed by the view and the approach for creating and describing that aspect of the architecture.

- A *perspective* guides the process of designing the architecture so that it exhibits one or more important *qualities*. As such, a perspective can be considered analogous to a viewpoint, but for a related set of quality properties rather than a type of architectural structure. We also use perspectives as a means of capturing common problems and pitfalls and identifying solutions to them.

There are many perspectives, and it is not usually feasible or useful to apply all perspectives to all views.

FURTHER READING

The idea of considering quality properties explicitly as part of architecture definition certainly isn't new (although the perspective approach and framework we have introduced here is new). Standard books such as *Software Architecture in Practice* [BASS03], *Evaluating Software Architectures* [CLEM02], and *Design and Use of Software Architectures* [BOSC00] all discuss quality properties and are well worth reading for more background in this area.

One particularly relevant area of academic work is the study of tactics being undertaken at the SEI as part of its software architecture research. Sets of generic tactics for various quality properties are outlined in Chapter 5 of Bass et al. [BASS03], while the SEI Web site (www.sei.cmu.edu) contains links to a number of technical reports that discuss tactics further.

5

THE ROLE OF THE SOFTWARE ARCHITECT

I f you gathered a group of software architects in a room and asked them to describe the jobs they do, you would probably end up with at least a dozen different definitions. More tellingly, if you asked the people with whom the architects work how their colleagues fill their working hours, you would probably get still more definitions.

Our own practical experience supports this. On some projects, the person with the title of architect has a very hands-on, directional involvement in the nuts and bolts of designing, coding, and testing. Alternatively, architecture may be viewed as an ivory tower from which pronouncements are handed down at intervals to the build and implementation teams. Architect is also often used as a generic title to denote a senior technical member of staff (such as the Java architect that a number of organizations now have).

Architects may specialize in one area, such as networking, middleware, or database design, to the exclusion of others; occasionally, the architect may not even have a system development background at all, having entered through another route such as business analysis. The title may also be further qualified in various ways such as application architect, data architect, or even enterprise architect, without being clear what these roles involve.

So before we consider how you perform your job as an architect, we need to understand exactly what that job *is*—what your responsibilities are, where your boundaries are, what areas you should delegate to others, and how you work alongside the other members of the team to ensure a successful software delivery.

In this chapter, we establish a definition of the software architect's role, including what you are and are not expected to do to fulfill this role and what qualities you need to possess in order to be a successful architect. We will also explore how this role relates to others involved in the product or system development process.

THE ARCHITECTURE DEFINITION PROCESS

The last concept in our model of software architecture captures the process used to design an architecture and create an AD for it. We call such a process *architecture definition*.

 DEFINITION Architecture definition is a process by which stakeholder needs and concerns are captured, an architecture to meet these needs is designed, and the architecture is clearly and unambiguously described via an architectural description.

This process is often called *architectural design*, and we say this informally ourselves. However, in the book we tend to avoid this term because of the potential confusion between its usage as a process and as an artifact.

The goal of an architecture definition process is to design an architecture that meets the needs of its stakeholders. There are three aspects to this, as shown in Figure 5–1.

- *Capturing stakeholder needs*, that is, understanding what is important to stakeholders (possibly helping them reconcile conflicts such as functionality versus cost) and recording and agreeing on these needs

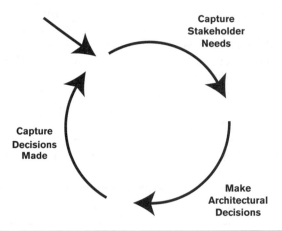

FIGURE 5–1 ARCHITECTURE DEFINITION

- *Making a series of architectural design decisions* that result in a solution that meets these needs, assessing it against the stakeholder needs, and refining this solution until it is adequate
- *Capturing the architectural design decisions* made, in an AD

These activities form the core of the architecture definition process and are normally performed iteratively. We talk more about this in Part II, in particular how stakeholder needs and concerns relate to functional and architectural requirements. For now, we'll leave you with another principle.

PRINCIPLE A good architecture definition process is one that leads to a good architecture, documented by an effective architectural description, which can be realized in a time-efficient and cost-effective manner.

Architecture Definition Isn't Just Design

A common question that arises is whether architecture definition is "just" part of design or whether there is something more to it. It's true that architecture definition incorporates elements of design and also of requirements analysis, but as we shall see in this book, it is a separate activity from each of these.

- Design is an activity focused on the solution space and targeted primarily at one group of people—the developers. It works within a clearly defined set of constraints (the system's requirements) and is essentially a process of translating these into the specifications for a conformant system. Historically, design has tended not to focus as much on the needs of other groups such as operations or support, assuming that their needs have been captured in the requirements specification.
- Requirements analysis, on the other hand, is an activity focused on the problem space that (in its purest forms) ignores the needs and constraints of groups like developers and systems administrators because it focuses on what is desired rather than what is possible. It also works within a clearly defined set of constraints (the system's required scope), although within these it tends to have much more freedom than the design process does.

Architecture definition resolves this tension by bridging the gap between the problem and solution spaces, as shown in Figure 5–2. Its focus is to understand the needs of everyone who has an interest in the architecture, to balance these needs, and to identify an acceptable set of tradeoffs between these where necessary. The tradeoffs take into account the constraints that exist

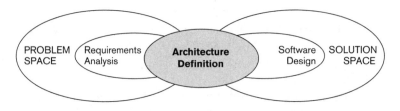

FIGURE 5-2 ARCHITECTURE DEFINITION, REQUIREMENTS ANALYSIS, AND SOFTWARE DESIGN

(e.g., technical feasibility, timescales, resources, deployment environment, costs, and so on).

Although your role as a software architect incorporates elements of design and of requirements capture, there are some key differences between it and the other two roles, the most significant of which revolve around its *scope*.

- You have to take input from a much wider range of people than just the user community (as we have seen in our discussion of stakeholders).
- You have to consider a much wider range of concerns than just functionality (as we have seen in our discussion of views and perspectives).
- You have to consider the big picture as well as the details.

Architecture definition is often more a process of *discovery* rather than just capture. At the early stages when—with luck—you start to be involved, the stakeholders may have only hazy ideas of their expectations of the system. Furthermore, there may be a number of conflicting ideas about how the system should be built, and there are likely to be big gaps in technical knowledge and developer experience in the proposed solution elements.

Although theory says that you should not start to think about the solution until you understand the problem—and we like this approach, as a theory—in practice, stakeholders start to think about technology solutions from day one. You can't avoid this; you just have to manage it.

The Boundary between Requirements Analysis and Architecture Definition

Part of your role as an architect is to be involved in the process of analyzing, understanding, and prioritizing the system's requirements. This also allows you to start assessing the difficulty involved in implementing each requirement.

Your role does not include requirements gathering, and ideally you will be presented with a complete, consistent, prioritized list of the requirements for the system. However, requirements analysts often struggle to trade off requirements against each other; while part of this process involves understanding the relative business value of requirements, it must also take into account the associated costs and risks.

Many of the requirements specified initially are likely to be difficult to implement because the requirements analysts have little or no insight into the implementation options. As an architect, you are ideally placed to provide this insight so that the importance of each requirement can be considered in the context of the likely cost of providing it.

STRATEGY Work with the requirements analysts to understand the system's requirements and their relative importance. For each important requirement, consider the likely difficulty of implementing it and feed this back to the requirements analysts to help them understand what can and cannot be achieved.

The Boundary between Architecture Definition and Design

One of the most important decisions you will have to make as an architect is whether something is important enough for you to worry about or whether it can safely and more appropriately be left until the detailed design phase—in other words, whether it is *architecturally significant*. Phillipe Kruchten neatly captured the essence of architectural significance in his definition, which we paraphrase here.

PRINCIPLE A concern, problem, or system element is **architecturally significant** if it has a wide impact on the structure of the system or on its important quality properties such as performance, scalability, security, reliability, or evolvability.

Of course, whether something is architecturally significant or not is a largely subjective decision driven by your judgment, skill, and expertise (and that of your stakeholders) and by the circumstances of individual projects. For example, where a new technology is involved, questions around reliability and performance may be very significant, whereas they may be far less so in a system where the technologies are established and well understood by the developers.

Your job as an architect is to get the right balance between maintaining a high-level view and exploring the detail—something that will become easier with practice. Beware, however, of assuming that all architectural concerns are found at the abstract level; often, the devil is in the details. You need to consider aspects of your architecture at all levels, from the strategy to the code. It is also important to keep considering whether your judgment is correct and to make sure that as your AD develops, you continue to review whether your scope is appropriate.

STRATEGY As you are designing the architecture, review the areas you have determined as being architecturally significant or not, and revise these as necessary in the light of your deeper understanding of your stakeholders' concerns and of the architecture itself.

THE ROLE OF THE ARCHITECT

We can now define the role of the architect in the following principle.

PRINCIPLE The architect is responsible for designing, documenting, and leading the construction of a system that meets the needs of all its stakeholders.

We see four aspects to this role:

1. To identify and engage the stakeholders
2. To understand and capture the stakeholders' concerns
3. To create and take ownership of the definition of an architecture that addresses these concerns
4. To take a leading role in the realization of the architecture into a physical product or system

A common theme in most descriptions of what the architect does is something along the lines of "the architect owns the big picture." We certainly support this view. One of your responsibilities as an architect is to develop and maintain a high-level view of the main elements in the product or system, which is subsequently translated into a detailed design, coded, tested, and deployed.

But this isn't all. You need to ensure that the big picture you develop is right for your situation. As we have seen, every problem has a number of possible architectural solutions, and every architecture has a number of possible representations. You must select an architecture that is fit for purpose and then document that architecture in an appropriate way.

Traditionally, the architect is viewed as making primarily an up-front contribution to system development—in other words, being heavily involved in the inception stages of the project. However, your responsibility does not end there. In fact, we find in general that the architect's involvement during the software development lifecycle conforms to the pattern illustrated in Figure 5–3.

This figure shows the architect's depth of involvement during each major development iteration of the system's delivery. During the initial phases, your involvement is intense. You are fully occupied in defining and agreeing on scope, agreeing on and validating requirements, and providing the technical leadership to make the decisions that will shape the architecture.

Your involvement typically lessens during the detailed design and code phases, while the product or system is being built, tested, and integrated. In practice, you may take a different role during this period, such as design authority or designer. If so, you are likely to be involved in mentoring, reviews, problem resolution, and technical leadership. In any case, if the architecture needs any changes, you must lead the change process.

Your involvement peaks again prior to and during acceptance, as you provide support and guidance to help resolve the last-minute problems that inevitably occur and to ensure a smooth deployment.

 STRATEGY Stay involved with the development process beyond the creation of the AD and through construction, acceptance, and handover (possibly at a reduced level of involvement).

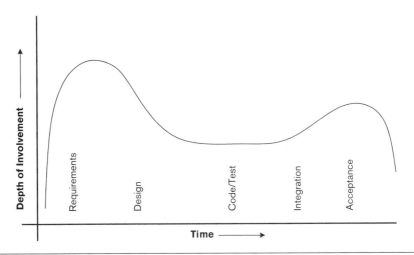

FIGURE 5–3 THE ARCHITECT'S INVOLVEMENT

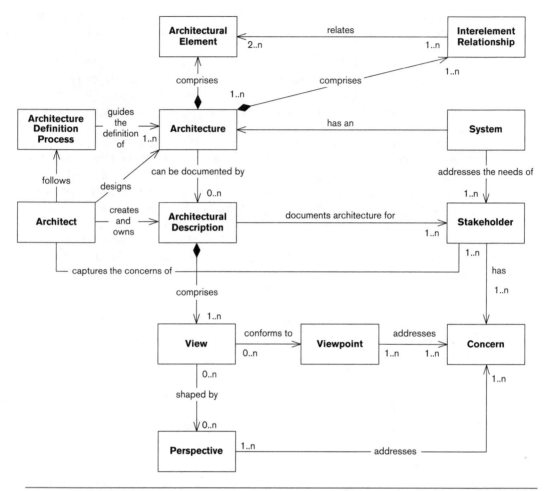

FIGURE 5-4 Architecture Definition and the Architect in Context

Interrelationships between the Core Concepts

We can now add two final pieces to our relationship diagram, namely, the process of architecture definition and the architect, as shown in Figure 5–4.

We have added the following relationships to augment the earlier versions of the model shown in previous chapters (e.g., Figure 4–3).

- The architect captures and consolidates the concerns of the stakeholders.
- The architect designs an architecture that meets these concerns.

- The architect creates and owns the AD.
- An architecture definition process guides the definition of the architecture.
- The architect follows the architecture definition process to carry out all of these tasks.

Architectural Specializations

So far, we have viewed the architect as a generalist who deals with all aspects of the system under development. This isn't always the case, especially on large projects where a team of architects may be working together. Everything we talk about in this book—stakeholders, views, principles, models—applies equally to such specialists, within their scope.

You are likely to see architects take on some of the following specializations.

- *Product architect*: The product architect is responsible for the delivery of one or more releases of a software product to external customers (and typically would stay associated with the product over a number of release cycles). The product architect is a key member of a product development team and oversees the technical integrity of the product. One specific challenge faced by the product architect is identifying user stakeholders, especially before the first release.

- *Domain architect*: Domain architecture is a specialization of the general architectural function, focusing on a particular domain of interest, such as the business architecture, data architecture, network architecture, and so on. Domain architects are particularly valuable for working on large, complex, or groundbreaking systems or for filling gaps in the knowledge of the software architect.

- *Solution architect*: In contrast with the domain architect, the solution architect specifically takes a broad, high-level view of the entire solution.

- *Enterprise architect*: Really good enterprise architects are among the most sought-after personnel in IT. Where the software architect concerns herself with a single (albeit probably complex and important) system, the enterprise architect has responsibility for the cross-system information systems architecture of the whole enterprise, including sales and marketing, client-facing systems, products and services, purchasing and accounts, the supply chain, human resources, and so forth.

THE ORGANIZATIONAL CONTEXT

Let's look at how your role as a software architect compares with those of the other key personnel on software development projects.

Business Analysts

A business analyst is responsible for capturing and documenting detailed business requirements, typically focusing on stakeholders from the user community, and ensuring that these are correct, complete, and consistent. You will often draw on the specialized knowledge of the business analyst, especially when dealing with views of interest to acquirers, users, and assessors.

Project Managers

A project manager is responsible for ensuring delivery of the product or system and meeting commercial priorities for resources, costs, and timescales. You will often help the project manager develop plans or assess them for reasonableness. You will also provide the project manager with technical information, feedback, advice, risk assessment, and so on throughout the project lifecycle.

Design Authorities

A design authority (sometimes referred to as a technical design authority) takes overall responsibility for the quality of the internal element designs for the system. In our experience, the architect often fills this role as the project moves into the design phase. The design authority takes the architectural views as her input and acts as guide and leader to the software developers who design, build, test, and integrate the product or system.

We have found that design authority is often the role actually performed by people who have the job title of technical architect. These key people are often the primary technical points of contact for how the system is implemented and how the underlying technology platform works. This role on the project is crucial and must be filled by an extremely strong staff member. However, making tradeoffs between requirements and possibilities for the system's stakeholders is not an inherent part of being a technical design authority, although it is a key part of the architect's role. Therefore we argue that the technical design authority plays a design role rather than an architectural one.

The boundary between the design authority and the architect is probably the hardest one to define formally. One guideline we find useful when deciding whether an issue is architecturally significant is to consider its impact on stakeholders. If the outcome of a decision is likely to have a significant impact on important stakeholders or requires tradeoffs between stakeholder needs, the architect should probably be responsible for the decision. If the decision is visible only within the development team, it is probably a design authority issue.

Of course, it is not always possible to make this assessment up front, and it is essential that the two roles cooperate fully. Let's consider a couple of examples to see how this might work in practice.

EXAMPLE Architecture definition for a new system has identified the need for a relational database, from the industry-leading supplier, for persistent storage of transaction data. The imminent new release of the database server will provide some significant new technology features and potential improvements in performance.

Functionally, the system would look identical whether it were built on the current or new version of the relational database management system. However, taking on the new version presents some commercial risk related to availability of skills, confidence in the new platform, and the potential problems associated with any point-zero release.

Because of the possible commercial impact, we would tend to involve the architect in this decision.

EXAMPLE In integration tests, some end-user queries have been falling far short of their performance requirements, taking a minute or more to complete under peak load. Monitoring and analysis have suggested that some database tables need to be internally restructured, indexes modified, and objects spread more evenly across physical disks. Access to data, which occurs via stored procedures, will not be affected (other than being much faster).

Because these changes have no visible stakeholder impact (other than to make the system compliant), it seems reasonable not to involve the architect in what are essentially internal systems decisions and to instead make this the responsibility of the design authority.

Technology Specialists

A technology specialist provides detailed expertise in one specific area. Where the architect provides breadth, the technology specialist provides depth, and the combination of the two can be extremely powerful.

Broadly speaking, it is the technology specialist's responsibility to provide detailed facts, to assess the architecture for technical feasibility, and to spot pitfalls early. You should be able to take the information provided by the technology specialist and apply it to addressing the problems you need to solve.

You should always make the best use of the skills and knowledge of your colleagues in the organization. It's not possible to know everything about everything, and as an architect you aren't expected to.

PRINCIPLE The architect provides and oversees the architectural breadth and works closely with both business-focused and technology-focused specialists who provide the specialist depth.

Developers

The architect's involvement doesn't end with handing over the completed and accepted AD. Although your level of participation may decrease during the build and test phases, you will still maintain a technology leadership role to ensure that the team adheres to the spirit and the letter of the AD.

This may involve mentoring staff through the detailed design process, reviewing designs as they are completed to ensure conformance to the system's architectural principles, arbitrating technology disputes, or even developing pieces of the implementation if required. You are likely to get involved in integration and system testing to ensure that the tests exercise an appropriate selection of functional and operational characteristics.

You will also need to lead the change process if (as is likely) the AD requires any modifications during the development.

THE ARCHITECT'S SKILLS

Although the job of the architect traditionally has a technology focus, and in nearly all cases the architect herself has a strong technology background, we have seen that the role is much broader than merely drawing up technical plans and designs.

You must have an across-the-board understanding of technology at a high level and of the real-world issues and problems the system is required to solve. You should have real experience with designing and building systems, although it may not always be possible to have direct, practical knowledge of the specific technologies you plan to use. (This is an example of when you must draw on the experience of technology specialists.)

Typically you will also have one or more areas of deeper technical expertise; this may not apply to your current project but will give you the ability to recognize a good design when you see one.

People skills are also very important, such as the ability to build consensus, facilitate change, and rapidly learn about unfamiliar business areas and technologies. Above all, you must earn and maintain the confidence of all of your stakeholders, from senior management and users to developers, third parties, and operational staff.

THE ARCHITECT'S RESPONSIBILITIES

A *pro forma* list of responsibilities for an architect would include the following items.

- Ensure that the scope, context, and constraints are documented and accepted.
- Identify, engage, and enfranchise your stakeholders.
- Facilitate the making of system-level decisions, ensuring that they are made on the basis of the best information and are aligned with stakeholder needs.
- Capture and interpret input from technical and domain specialists (and represent this accurately to stakeholders as needed).
- Define and document the system structure and form.
- Define and document strategies, standards, and guidelines to direct the build and deployment of the system.
- Ensure that the architecture meets the system quality attributes.
- Develop and own the AD (i.e., manage all changes to it).
- Help ensure that agreed-upon architectural principles and standards are applied to the finished system or product.
- Provide technical leadership.

SUMMARY

We have discussed two distinct concepts in this chapter, the final chapter of Part I.

- *Architecture definition* is a process whereby stakeholder needs and concerns are captured, an architecture to meet these needs is designed, and the architecture is fully and unambiguously described via an AD.
- The *architect* is the person (or group) responsible for designing, documenting, and leading the construction of an architecture that meets the needs of all its stakeholders.

There is no single commonly accepted definition of the software architect's role. The role of the architect includes elements of requirements capture and high-level design but is more than either of these. In this chapter, we defined the four main responsibilities of the architect: to identify and engage the stakeholders, to understand and capture their concerns, to create and take ownership of the AD, and to take a leading role in the realization of the architecture.

We presented some architectural specializations that you may encounter (or even choose to take on) such as product architects, domain architects, solution architects, and enterprise architects. We also compared and contrasted the role of the architect with other key project roles such as business analysts, project managers, design authorities, technology specialists, and developers. We considered when the architect is important: primarily during the early stages of system development and during acceptance, with a lesser role during the build and test phases.

Finally, we itemized the skills that a good architect should possess and presented the architect's responsibilities.

FURTHER READING

Most of the architecture books we mentioned earlier in Part I contain some discussion of the architect's role. In addition, McGovern et al. [MCGO04] contains a good discussion of roles related to software and enterprise architecture.

The definition of *architecturally significant* that we paraphrased earlier in this chapter can be found in Kruchten [KRUC00].

PART II

THE PROCESS OF SOFTWARE ARCHITECTURE

6

INTRODUCTION TO THE SOFTWARE ARCHITECTURE PROCESS

It is not our aim in this book to define another software development method nor to radically change existing models of the software development lifecycle. However, many software development methods fail to clearly define the role of software architecture in the development lifecycle. If they discuss it at all, they usually view architecture definition as merely the first part of software design—and we hope this book will show you that this view is far too simplistic.

As we have seen, architecture definition is a broad, creative, dynamic activity that is much more about discovering stakeholder concerns, evaluating options, and making tradeoffs than simply capturing information. At the outset, your stakeholders may have some fundamental disagreements about scope, objectives, and priorities. It may be necessary to change direction, possibly even significantly, partway through the exercise as a result of information you have uncovered through your work.

Although every situation is different, there is a core set of activities you will usually need to perform as part of architecture definition for any project. We describe these activities in the following chapters. You may need to do other things during architecture definition too, but you will probably need to perform most of the activities we describe in Part II to avoid creating future problems.

Part II begins by presenting a generic and straightforward process for architecture definition, which you can use to help plan your own architecture definition work and to align your plans with those for the other parts of the development. The subsequent chapters look at each of the key activities of the process, namely:

- Agreeing on scope and context, constraints, and baseline architectural principles
- Identifying and engaging stakeholders
- Identifying and using architectural scenarios
- Using architectural styles and patterns
- Producing architectural models
- Documenting the architecture
- Validating the architecture

For each of these activities, we provide practical advice and guidance, including checklists to help make sure you haven't forgotten anything, and pointers to further reading.

7

THE ARCHITECTURE DEFINITION PROCESS

Architecture definition starts early in the project lifecycle, when scope and requirements are often still unclear and the current view of the system may differ substantially from what is eventually built. For this reason, architecture definition tends to be a more fluid activity than later tasks such as designing, building, and testing, when the problem you are solving is better understood. When you start, you don't fully know the size and extent of your system, where the complexity is, what the most significant risks are, or where you will encounter conflict among your stakeholders.

In this chapter, we outline a simple process of architecture definition that applies (in some way) to most software development projects, irrespective of the development approaches used. You can use the process we describe with most forms of the software development lifecycle—from the very structured and formal to those founded on iterative or agile principles.

The material in this chapter will help you plan your own architecture definition work and align your plans with those for the other parts of the development. Of course, the way you do this will vary according to the needs of your project, the method you are following, the time available, and the skills of you and your team. You will be most successful if you use this chapter as a framework or starting point for developing your own personalized architecture definition process.

GUIDING PRINCIPLES

For an architecture definition process to be successful, it must adhere to the following principles.

- It must be driven by *stakeholder concerns*, as we discussed in Part I. As we will see, stakeholder concerns are the core—but by no means the only—inputs to the process. Furthermore, the process must *balance* these concerns effectively where they conflict or have incompatible implications.

- It must encourage the effective *communication* of architectural decisions, principles, and the solution itself to stakeholders.

- It must ensure, on an ongoing basis, that the architectural decisions and principles are *adhered to* throughout the lifecycle up to the final deployment.

- It must (as much as possible, given the fluid nature of architecture definition) be *structured*. In other words, it must comprise a series of one or more steps or tasks, with a clear definition of the objectives, inputs, and outputs of each step. Typically, the outputs from one step are the inputs to subsequent steps.

- It must be *pragmatic*—that is, it must consider real-world issues such as lack of time or money, shortage of specific technical skills, unclear or changing requirements, the existing context, and political considerations.

- It must be *flexible* so that it can be tailored to particular circumstances. (This is sometimes referred to as a *toolkit* or *framework* approach, with the idea that you use those elements of the toolkit you need and ignore the rest.)

- It must be *technology-neutral*. That is, it must not mandate that the solution is based around any specific technology, architectural pattern, or development style, nor should it dictate any particular modeling, diagramming, or documentation style.

- It must *integrate* with the chosen software development lifecycle.

- It must align with good *software engineering practices* and *quality management standards* (such as ISO 9001) so that it can integrate easily with existing approaches.

Having set out our ground rules, let's consider the context in which architecture definition operates, starting with where we want to end—its outcomes.

PROCESS OUTCOMES

Clearly, the main goal of architecture definition is to develop a sound architecture and to manage the production and maintenance of all of the elements of an AD that captures it. However, there are some desirable secondary outcomes or consequences of architecture definition, such as the following.

- *Clarification of requirements and of other inputs to the process*: Your stakeholders may not be absolutely clear what they want, and it may take some time to pin them down.

- *Management of stakeholders' expectations*: Your architecture will inevitably need to make compromises around your stakeholder concerns. It is far better to make these compromises visible and clearly understood early in the life of the project than to let them emerge later.

- *Identification and evaluation of architectural options*: There is rarely just one solution to a problem. When there are several potential solutions, your analysis will reveal the strengths and weaknesses of each and justify the chosen solution.

- *Description of architectural acceptance criteria* (indirectly): Architecture definition should lead to a clear understanding of the conditions that must be met before the stakeholders will accept the architecture as conforming to their requirements (e.g., it must provide a particular function, achieve certain response times, or restart in less than a given time period).

- *Creation of a set of design inputs* (ideally): Such information as guidance for and constraints on the software design process will help ensure the integrity of your architecture.

Having defined the goals that our architecture definition process must meet, let us continue by considering the context that the process must work within.

THE PROCESS CONTEXT

Architecture forms the bridge between requirements and design, performing the tradeoffs necessary to satisfy the demands of both. In process terms, this means that architecture definition sits between requirements analysis and software construction (design, code, and test). A good model for the interaction between requirements, architecture, and construction is the Three Peaks model (see Figure 7–1), an extension of Bashar Nuseibeh's Twin Peaks model.

The three triangles (the peaks) in the diagram represent the major software development activities of requirements analysis, architecture definition, and construction; the widening of the shapes at their bases represent an increasing level of detail as time goes on while the system is developed. The curling arrows show how requirements and architecture as well as architecture and construction are intertwined at a progressively increasing level of detail during system development. Although the specification, architecture, and implementation of the system are quite distinct, as the Three Peaks model illustrates, they have profound effects on each other and so cannot be considered in isolation.

The following key relationships exist between software architecture and the requirements and construction activities of the software lifecycle.

- Requirements analysis provides the context for architecture definition by defining the scope and the system's desired functionality and quality properties.

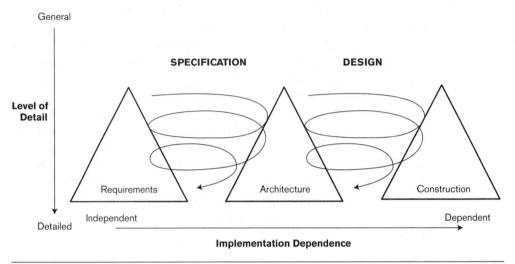

FIGURE 7-1 ARCHITECTURE DEFINITION CONTEXT—THE THREE PEAKS MODEL (BASED ON NUSEIBEH [NUSE01])

- Architecture definition often reveals inconsistent and missing requirements and also helps stakeholders understand the relative costs and complexities of meeting their concerns. This feeds back into requirements analysis to clarify and add requirements and to prioritize these when tradeoffs are made between stakeholders' aspirations and what can be achieved given time and budget constraints.

- When architecture definition has resulted in an architecture that appears to meet an acceptable set of user requirements, the construction of the system can be planned.

- Construction is often organized as a set of incremental deliveries, each of which aims to provide a useful set of functions and to leave the system in a stable, usable state (albeit an incomplete one). The construction of each increment provides further feedback to architecture definition, validating or indicating problems with the architecture as currently specified; hence, there is architecture definition activity throughout the lifecycle.

Requirements analysis, architecture definition, and software construction have a strong, interconnected set of relationships. Requirements analysis provides an initial context for architecture definition but is then itself affected by architecture definition as requirements are understood more fully. In turn, architecture definition drives the implementation process, but each piece of construction performed provides feedback about the effectiveness and utility of the architecture in use.

SUPPORTING ACTIVITIES

Our architecture definition process assumes that the following will be available to you and accepted by the sponsor and other stakeholders before you start:

- A definition of the system's baseline scope and context
- A definition of key stakeholder concerns

Our process also assumes that a broad range of stakeholders have been identified and engaged.

In reality, it is rare for the baseline scope and concerns to be captured to an appropriate level of detail at this early stage, and it is unlikely that any stakeholders (other than perhaps developers and occasionally users) will have been brought on board and engaged in the process. It can be a big challenge to discover and consolidate these inputs and then to gain agreement on them from an engaged stakeholder community before you can even think about a solution. We present a number of techniques for doing this in Chapters 8 and 9.

At the other end of the process, once you have an AD, you will often want to deliver a skeleton system implementation as the first development increment. Such an implementation can be very valuable because it offers a practical validation of the architecture, acts as a credibility test for the system's stakeholders, and provides a framework in which the development team can work.

The slightly extended UML activity diagram in Figure 7–2 shows how architecture definition relates to the following supporting activities. The square boxes with underlined names represent key inputs to and outputs from the process.

- Define the initial scope and context.
- Engage the stakeholders.
- Capture first-cut concerns.
- Define the architecture.
- Create a skeleton system.

Having defined the initial scope and context for your system with the acquiring stakeholders, you can then identify and engage all of the other stakeholders who have an interest in the system. Capturing their concerns provides a primary input, along with the scope and context, to architecture definition. (As we will see, both the scope and the concerns as defined at this point may change, subject to stakeholder agreement, during architecture definition.)

Architecture definition results in an AD and normally a set of guidelines and constraints to guide the system construction. Once you have an AD, you can (if you have the time and resources) create a skeleton system that will act as an evolvable prototype of the system you want to build.

We describe each of these supporting activities in Tables 7–1 through 7–5.

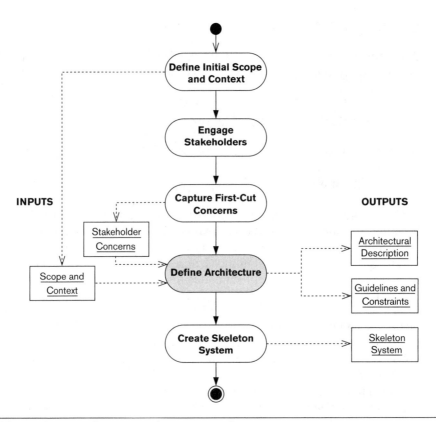

FIGURE 7–2 Activities Supporting Architecture Definition

TABLE 7–1 Define the Initial Scope and Context

Aims	To clearly define the boundaries of the system's behavior and responsibilities and the operational and organizational context within which the system exists.
Inputs	Acquirer needs and vision; organizational strategy; enterprise IT architecture.
Outputs	Initial statements of the goals of the system and what is included and excluded from its responsibilities; initial system context definition.
Comments	This step is primarily a process of understanding strategic and organizational objectives and how the system helps meet them, along with some analysis to understand which other systems need to interact with this one. We talk about this activity in Chapter 8. Note that the scope as defined here may change (subject to stakeholder agreement) during architecture definition.

TABLE 7-2 ENGAGE THE STAKEHOLDERS

Aims	To identify the system's important stakeholders and to create a working relationship with them.
Inputs	Scope and context; organizational structure.
Outputs	Definition of each of the stakeholder groups, with one or more named, engaged people who will represent the group.
Comments	This step involves understanding the organizational context you are working in and identifying the key people who will be affected by the system. You can then start to get to know their representatives and begin building a working relationship with them. We talk more about this activity in Chapter 9.

TABLE 7-3 CAPTURE FIRST-CUT CONCERNS

Aims	To clearly understand the concerns that each stakeholder group has about the system and the priorities they place on each concern.
Inputs	Stakeholder list; scope and context.
Outputs	Initial definition of a set of prioritized concerns for each stakeholder group.
Comments	This step often starts with your initial stakeholder meetings. It normally involves a series of presentations and meetings with representatives of each stakeholder group that allow you to explain what you aim to achieve and allow the stakeholders to explain their interests in the system. We talk more about this activity in Chapter 9. Note that the concerns as defined here may change (subject to stakeholder agreement) during architecture definition.

TABLE 7-4 DEFINE THE ARCHITECTURE

Aims	To create the AD for the system.
Inputs	Stakeholder list; scope and context.
Outputs	AD; guidelines and constraints.
Comments	We describe this step in detail in the Architecture Definition Activities section of this chapter.

TABLE 7-5 CREATE A SKELETON SYSTEM

Aims	Optional step to create a working (albeit limited) implementation of your architecture that can evolve into a delivered system during the system construction phase of the lifecycle.
Inputs	AD; associated guidelines and constraints.
Outputs	A limited working system that illustrates that the system can address at least one of your scenarios.
Comments	If you have the time and resources available to allow the creation of a skeleton system, it forms an effective bridge between architecture definition and software construction. This step allows the architect and the developers to build a working system that can execute at least a simple functional scenario the system is meant to address. The skeleton system acts as a validation of your architecture (and an important proof point for many stakeholders) as well as a framework for the software construction phase.

ARCHITECTURE DEFINITION ACTIVITIES

Your biggest difficulty as an architect is the amount of uncertainty and change you face as you bring your stakeholders together. Although you will be working from an agreed-upon scope—or if not, you will produce one as a matter of urgency—this is likely to change as the implications of including or excluding certain features emerge and as the stakeholders better understand the significance of what they are requesting. Functional and quality property requirements are also likely to evolve, perhaps significantly.

For this reason, our architecture definition process is an iterative one. In other words, you need to repeat the main steps several times before you produce a finished AD. Of course, for a small or simple architecture, you may produce the completed AD after the first iteration, but for anything complex, unfamiliar, or contentious, a single iteration is unlikely to suffice. Also, the architecture will keep evolving as the system is developed, so you will return to this cycle of activities throughout the project.

The UML activity diagram in Figure 7–3 illustrates our process, which involves the following steps.

1. Consolidate the inputs.
2. Identify scenarios.
3. Identify the relevant architectural styles.
4. Produce a candidate architecture.
5. Explore the architectural options.
6. Evaluate the architecture with the stakeholders.
7A. Rework the architecture.
7B. Revisit the requirements.

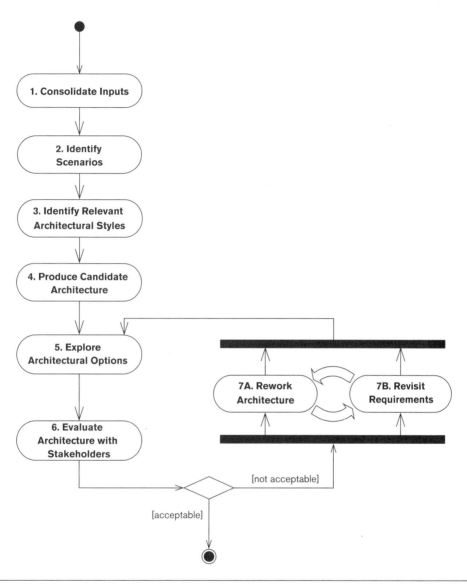

FIGURE 7-3 DETAILS OF ARCHITECTURE DEFINITION

Although it is obviously a simplification of the reality of architecture definition, you may find our model useful in discussions with management, colleagues, and stakeholders.

The curved arrows between steps 7A and 7B in the figure indicate that
these steps are not done in isolation: There is often a heavy interaction between

them as reworking the architecture may suggest changes to requirements and vice versa. For example, simplifying the concurrency model may necessitate changes to the order in which the system performs some tasks. Of course, all such changes should be reviewed and ratified with stakeholders.

The individual steps in this process are described in Tables 7–6 through 7–13.

TABLE 7-6 STEP 1: CONSOLIDATE THE INPUTS

Aims	To understand, validate, and refine the initial inputs.
Inputs	Raw process inputs (scope and context definition, stakeholder concerns).
Outputs	Consolidated inputs, with major inconsistencies removed, open questions answered, and (at a minimum) areas requiring further exploration identified.
Activities	Take the raw process inputs, resolve inconsistencies between them, answer open questions, and delve deeper where necessary, to produce a solid baseline.
Comments	It is rare for you to be provided with a consistent, accurate, and agreed-upon set of process inputs. During this step you take the information available, fill in gaps, resolve inconsistencies, and obtain formal agreement from the key stakeholders.

TABLE 7-7 STEP 2: IDENTIFY SCENARIOS

Aims	To identify a set of scenarios that illustrates the system's most important requirements.
Inputs	Consolidated inputs (as currently defined).
Outputs	Architectural scenarios.
Activities	Produce a set of scenarios that characterize the most important attributes required of the architecture and can be used to evaluate how well a proposed architecture will meet the underlying functional and quality property requirements.
Comments	A scenario is a description of a situation that the system is likely to encounter, which allows assessment of the effectiveness of the architecture in that situation. Scenarios can be identified for required functional behavior ("How does the system do X?") and for desired quality properties ("How does the system cope with load Y?" or "How can the architecture support change Z?"). We explain how to approach this step in Chapter 10.

TABLE 7-8 STEP 3: IDENTIFY THE RELEVANT ARCHITECTURAL STYLES

Aims	To identify one or more proven architectural styles that could be used as a basis for the overall organization of the system.
Inputs	Consolidated inputs (as currently defined); architectural scenarios.
Outputs	Architectural styles to consider as the basis for the system's main architectural structures.
Activities	Review existing catalogs of architectural styles, and consider system organizations that have worked well for you before. Identify those that appear to be relevant to the architecture as you currently understand it.
Comments	Using an architectural style is a way to reuse architectural knowledge that has proved effective in previous situations. This can help you arrive at a suitable system organization without having to design it from scratch and so reduces the risks involved in using new, unproven ideas. We talk more about using architectural styles in Chapter 11.

TABLE 7-9 STEP 4: PRODUCE A CANDIDATE ARCHITECTURE

Aims	To create a first-cut architecture for the system that reflects its primary architectural concerns and that can act as a basis for further architectural evaluation and refinement.
Inputs	Consolidated inputs (as currently defined); relevant architectural styles, viewpoints, and perspectives.
Outputs	Draft architectural views.
Activities	Produce an initial set of architectural views to define your initial architectural ideas, using guidance from the viewpoints and perspectives and any relevant architectural styles.
Comments	Although they may contain gaps, inconsistencies, or errors, the draft views form a starting point for the more detailed architecture work later.

TABLE 7-10 STEP 5. EXPLORE THE ARCHITECTURAL OPTIONS

Aims	To explore the various architectural possibilities for the system and make the key architectural decisions to choose among them.
Inputs	Consolidated inputs; draft architectural views; architectural scenarios, viewpoints, and perspectives.
Outputs	More detailed or accurate architectural views for some parts of the architecture.

Continued on next page

TABLE 7-10 STEP 5. EXPLORE THE ARCHITECTURAL OPTIONS *(CONTINUED)*

Activities	Apply scenarios to the draft models to demonstrate that they are workable, that they meet requirements, and that there are no hidden problems. Take any areas of risk, concern, or uncertainty that are revealed and further explore the requirements, problems, and issues. Where there is more than one possible solution, evaluate the strengths and weaknesses of each (refer to Chapter 14 for guidance on how to do this) and select the best one.
Comments	The aim of this step is to fill in gaps, remove inconsistencies in the models, and provide extra detail where needed.

TABLE 7-11 STEP 6: EVALUATE THE ARCHITECTURE WITH THE STAKEHOLDERS

Aims	To work through an evaluation of the architecture with your key stakeholders, capture any problems or deficiencies, and gain the stakeholders' acceptance of the architecture.
Inputs	Consolidated inputs; architectural views and perspective outputs.
Outputs	Architectural review comments.
Activities	Evaluate your architecture with a representative collection of stakeholders. Capture and agree on any improvements to or comments on the models.
Comments	Although each group of stakeholders will have different interests, the overall objective is to confirm that stakeholder concerns are met and that the architecture is of good quality. You may have to work hard to obtain consensus if the concerns of different stakeholders conflict with one another. We talk about this activity in Chapter 14.

TABLE 7-12 STEP 7A: REWORK THE ARCHITECTURE

Aims	To address any concerns that have emerged during the evaluation task.
Inputs	Architectural views; architectural review comments; relevant architectural styles, viewpoints, and perspectives.
Outputs	Reworked architectural views; areas for further investigation (optional).
Activities	Take the results of the architectural evaluation and address them in order to produce an architecture that better meets its objectives. This step normally involves functional analysis, the use of viewpoints and perspectives, and prototyping.
Comments	This step is done concurrently and often quite collaboratively with step 7B. The two steps feed back into step 5.

TABLE 7-13 STEP 7B: REVISIT THE REQUIREMENTS

Aims	To consider any changes to the system's original requirements that may have to be made in light of architectural evaluation.
Inputs	Architectural views; architectural review comments.
Outputs	Revised requirements (if any).
Activities	The work done so far may reveal inadequacies or inconsistencies in requirements or requirements that are infeasible or expensive to implement. In this case, you may need to revisit these requirements with stakeholders and obtain their agreement to the necessary revisions.
Comments	This step is done concurrently and often quite collaboratively with step 7A. The two steps feed back into step 5.

PROCESS EXIT CRITERIA

In the ideal world, you would continue with architecture definition until the architecture was perfect and perfectly documented in the AD. However, because architecture definition necessarily takes a high-level view of the system to be built, it's hard in practice to be confident that your architecture is the right one for the problems you are trying to solve.

The best criterion available for determining that you have finished your architecture and are ready to move into the first construction iteration is that there are no significant comments from your architectural evaluation activities, and no significant changes are therefore required to the architecture. In other words, the stakeholders all agree that the AD—or, rather, the system it documents—adequately addresses their concerns.

 PRINCIPLE Architecture definition can be considered complete once the formal review of the architectural description by stakeholders results in no significant comments or actions.

In practice, you are unlikely to achieve complete agreement, particularly when the stakeholder group is large or diverse or when requirements are complex. Usually you will finish architecture definition when most of the concerns of the more important stakeholders have been addressed and when you feel confident that the project can proceed with an acceptable level of risk. In some cases, however, you will find that some important stakeholder concerns are still outstanding when the allocated time for architecture definition ends. This is an unfortunate situation, but when time is limited, it may be unavoidable. It is essential in such cases that you prioritize your work to focus on the riskiest or most contentious areas so that at least these are resolved before you move into construction. In this way you can be relatively confident that your architecture is adequate to meet its most important challenges.

Don't forget to include yourself in the list of AD reviewers. Even if your stakeholders are happy with the architecture, if you are not, you should not consider it complete. You may have knowledge or understanding of the system that they don't, and it is your responsibility to ensure this is reflected in the architecture.

 STRATEGY Include yourself in the reviewers of the architectural description, and do not finish initial architecture definition until you are satisfied that there are no significant issues with the architecture.

It is not hard to find yourself descending into a repeating cycle of further and deeper refinement and enlargement of your AD, with the result that you never build the system or that development goes ahead without you. This worst possible outcome is to be strongly resisted. In our experience, on all but the largest projects, you should aim to complete the production of the AD in one to three months.

 STRATEGY Aim to produce an architectural description that is good enough to meet the needs of its users, rather than to strive for a perfect version that will take significantly more resources to complete without providing any real benefit to the system's stakeholders.

Of course, completion of the AD does not mean that you are no longer working as an architect. You'll be involved throughout, advising, leading, overseeing, resolving problems, revising the architecture as new knowledge emerges, and so on. This means that once the AD is baselined and placed under configuration control, it should continue to be a living document, kept up-to-date throughout the construction steps and into deployment.

ARCHITECTURE DEFINITION IN THE SOFTWARE DEVELOPMENT LIFECYCLE

Architecture definition does not replace the normal software development lifecycle but should be thought of as an integral part of it. In this section, we discuss how architecture definition fits into the common approaches to designing and building systems.

Waterfall Approaches

In the classic waterfall model, software development is viewed as a linear sequence of tasks, with each task using the outputs of the previous one as its inputs, and feeding into the next task in turn, as shown in Figure 7–4. So, for example, the functional specification provides the inputs to the design stage, the design provides the inputs to the build and unit test stage, and so on. When changes are required to the system, these feed backward to the preceding stage and possibly further up the waterfall. Although somewhat discredited as a development approach for large systems, due to its late feedback and inflexibility, the waterfall approach is still a useful and widely used model for the fundamental processes needed in a software development project.

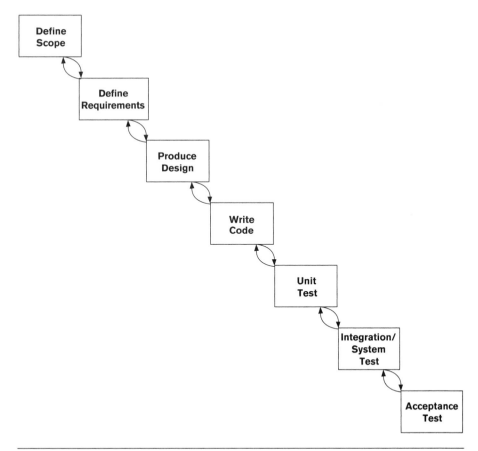

FIGURE 7–4 THE WATERFALL MODEL OF DEVELOPMENT

Architecture definition is easy to integrate with such a linear approach: It is usually viewed as a separate task early in the lifecycle (before, after, or sometimes alongside requirements definition).

Iterative Approaches

The motivation behind iterative approaches (such as Feature Driven Development and the Rational Unified Process) is to reduce risk by means of early delivery of partial functionality, as shown in Figure 7–5. Each iteration usually focuses on one area that presents significant risk because its requirements are unclear, for example, or because it is a complex or leading-edge element of the system. In most iterative approaches, the individual iterations are run as accelerated development projects in their own right, broken down into structured tasks with defined inputs and deliverables.

Typically, architecture definition would form part of the analysis phase, or it could alternatively run alongside the other tasks as an ongoing activity. Our architecture definition process is itself iterative, which dovetails quite nicely with such methods. (For the Rational Unified Process in particular, our approach fits well in its Elaboration phase.)

Agile Methods

Agile methods are a relatively recent development in software engineering. Agile methods are lightweight methods that focus on the rapid and continuous delivery of software to end users, encourage constant interaction between the customer and the software developers, and attempt to minimize the management

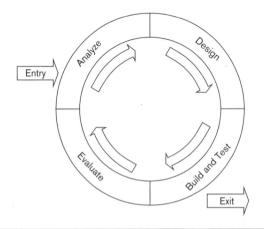

FIGURE 7–5 ITERATIVE DEVELOPMENT

overhead of the development process (in particular, a dramatic reduction in the amount of development documentation produced). Two of the best-known agile methods are Extreme Programming (XP) and Scrum.

At the time of writing, it would be fair to say that there is a fair amount of tension between software developers committed to agile methods (particularly XP) and software architects who expect to develop comprehensive ADs before embarking on detailed design and software development. Agile developers think of the architects as "bureaucratic document producers," whereas the architects think of the developers as "undisciplined hackers intent on development anarchy"; reality is probably somewhere in the middle.

Agile methods focus on delivering useful software quickly and constantly validating what is being built, both of which are positive results. On the other hand, embarking on large-scale development without understanding the problem thoroughly or having any idea where you're headed can lead to a large amount of rework that could have been avoided with more attention to early design.

From our relatively limited experience of agile methods, we suggest that they can be a good way to drive the development of each increment as you develop your system. The technical practices they encourage help create simple and reliable software that can be changed relatively easily. This can only be a good thing. As architects and developers ourselves, we suggest that architecture fits in above the construction increments, sets the context for the iterations, and helps maintain coherence and technical integrity across the system.

It's probably safe to say that the question of the relationship between software architecture and agile development will not be settled to everyone's satisfaction in the immediate future.

SUMMARY

In this chapter, we outlined a simple process of architecture definition, applicable to most software development projects, which you can use to help formulate your plans and schedules.

We started the chapter by defining the principles that our process should adhere to. It should be stakeholder-driven (of course), structured, pragmatic, flexible, and technology-neutral. It must also integrate with your existing software development lifecycle and with established best practices of software engineering.

We explained the context of the process and defined its outcomes; these obviously include specifying the architecture and producing the AD but often extend into other areas, such as better understanding of the problem being solved and management of stakeholder expectations.

We defined the essential inputs to the process: a baseline definition and stakeholder concerns. The baseline definition, which includes scope and context, must be determined and accepted at the start of the process. Stakeholder concerns, which include high-level functional and technical requirements and architectural constraints, are more likely to be discovered, elaborated, and refined as your analysis progresses.

We defined a simple, iterative process of architecture definition based on drawing up a set of architectural models, exploring some of their features in more detail, reviewing these with stakeholders, and reworking the models. Finally, we explained how this process aligns with existing development lifecycles such as the waterfall, iterative, and agile models.

FURTHER READING

Most books on software architecture include a description of some form of architecture definition process. Three books listed in the Bibliography include representative examples of different processes [GARL03, BASS03, BOSC00]. The first of these also discusses how architecture can coexist with agile processes.

A number of texts discuss the various modern software development processes, including XP [BECK00], Scrum [BEED02], Feature Driven Development [PALM02], and the Rational Unified Process [KRUC00].

The Twin Peaks model (on which we based our Three Peaks model) is described in an article in *IEEE Computer* [NUSE01].

8

SCOPE, CONCERNS, PRINCIPLES, AND CONSTRAINTS

Architecture definition can often be a voyage of discovery for both the architect and the stakeholders. At the early stages of any software development project, you will find that while the project's overall goals and objectives are probably accepted and communicated, the detail underneath is still vague. Indeed, one of your objectives as an architect is to take this detail and make it firm and ratified.

However, unless you have some idea where your boundaries are, your journey can become endless. You need a framework to work within that tells you, at a high level of detail, what you should be looking at, what you can ignore because someone else is looking at it, and what you can ignore because it is irrelevant. Without such a framework, you are likely to waste your time and the time of your stakeholders; worse still, you may end up setting misleading expectations that are hard to reverse later.

EXAMPLE Consider a situation where a government department wishes to automate the storage, retrieval, and management of official documents and brings in an architect to develop an architecture based on an off-the-shelf document management package. Work starts, and a first draft of an architecture based on the market-leading package is quickly produced.

While reviewing the architecture with stakeholders, one issue that emerges is how documents can be circulated among officials, comments recorded, and revisions approved. These capabilities are not provided by the document management package (which is not designed to solve that particular problem), so the architect starts to research ways to address these concerns. The next revision of the architecture includes a package for managing document approvals, plus software to integrate it with the original document management package. It is therefore much more complex, which significantly drives up the cost to build, deploy, and run the system.

Such an increase in overall development cost would result in the project being put on hold, but if the document revision functionality were excluded from the project scope, the architect could return to the original, more narrowly scoped design. In such a case, effective use of the terms of reference would allow the architect to get the project moving again.

One of your earliest and most important tasks, therefore, is to come up with the limits and constraints within which you will work and to ratify these with your stakeholders.

 STRATEGY If your scope and other constraints are not clear or not accepted when you start architecture definition, work with your stakeholders to define and ratify them before undertaking any more detailed analysis.

The following will fundamentally shape and define your architectural solution:

- *Business goals and drivers*: the set of fundamental issues and problems that prompted your stakeholders, especially the acquirers and users, to initiate the project
- *Architectural scope*: a definition of what is included for the architecture (i.e., should be considered by the architect) and what is excluded
- *Architectural concerns*: the requirements, objectives, intentions, and aspirations the stakeholders have for the architecture
- *Architectural principles*: principles that shape, inform, or limit your architectural design choices
- *Other architectural constraints*: standards, policies, and guidelines that also limit the project

In an ideal world, you are provided with all of these before you start the process of architecture definition. In practice, some or maybe all of them will not be given to you, or they may not be approved, or their status may not be clear. This particularly applies to your architectural principles, which tend to be more specific and which you will need to develop as you explore the architecture in more detail.

Let's look at each of these in more detail.

BUSINESS GOALS AND DRIVERS

The business goals and drivers set the context for the project and are the fundamental reason it exists. These goals and drivers are typically defined quite informally and in language that relates to one or more specific problems or potential opportunities facing the organization that has commissioned the system.

A **business goal** is a specific aim the organization has, while a **business driver** is some force acting on the organization that requires it to behave in a particular way in order to protect and grow its business.

> **EXAMPLE** A retailer may have a specific *goal* to achieve 15% of its sales via online purchases made through its Web site. A *driver* acting on the organization could be the competitive need to target its marketing to customers based on their long-term purchasing behaviors with the retailer.

It is important to gain a good understanding of the business goals and drivers because the aim of your system must be to assist the organization in meeting these challenges: If your system fails to achieve this, it won't have met the needs of your key stakeholders.

In some cases, you may be given a formal statement of business goals and drivers, probably written on behalf of the acquirers of the system. In other cases, you will need to investigate the underlying need for the system and work closely with your acquirers in order to understand the business goals and drivers. Either way, it is up to you to satisfy yourself that you understand the goals and drivers motivating the need for your system and that the system you intend to build will meet these underlying needs. This normally involves asking your key stakeholders a large number of pertinent questions to help them and you understand the goals, the drivers, and their implications.

ARCHITECTURAL SCOPE

Clear definition of scope is a vital early milestone of any system development project. You may find that the scope has already been defined for you, in which case you may limit yourself to ratifying it with stakeholders as the AD develops. If the scope is not defined, you will need to do this yourself, again based on input from your stakeholders.

Your scope definition should itemize the following information.

- The broad functional areas to be provided by the system.
- The external interfaces of the system (i.e., any data flows or control flows in or out of the system) and the external systems that communicate via these interfaces, especially where they are complex or unusual.

- Any systems to be decommissioned (switched off) or modified. Although this may not directly be your concern, you should state it up front because decommissioning a system can in some cases be as complex as writing a new one. (We return to this issue in our discussion of functional migration and data migration in Chapter 21.)
- Any data to be migrated into the new system.

It may also be useful to list some specific exclusions for clarity, although by definition anything not listed as in scope is out of scope.

What Makes a Good Scope Definition

A good scope definition has the following characteristics.

- It is fairly *brief*. One or two pages is usually sufficient; if it is necessary to provide further detail (such as a list of transactions or data items), put these in an appendix or supplementary document.
- It provides an *appropriate level of detail*. Provide too much detail and the big picture will be lost; too little detail will lead to ambiguity.
- It *states the obvious* where there is any chance this could be misconstrued. Don't be tempted to leave things out because "everybody knows that"—the odds are that some of these nuggets of information will get lost along the way.
- It *avoids any jargon* that is not widely understood. If you need to use jargon and there is any risk of confusion, provide a glossary.
- It has been *ratified* and formally *adopted* by your stakeholders. You should take it through a process of formal review, incorporate comments, and obtain sign-off from (at a minimum) the sponsor and users. It may be necessary to extend this ratification outside your stakeholder group (e.g., if changes are required to other systems).
- It is widely *disseminated* and *understood*. Make sure at this point that your stakeholders understand what they are agreeing to and realize the significance of any exclusions, caveats, or limitations.

Once accepted, the scope must be subject to change control. A change of scope down the line can have a dramatic impact on an architecture and so should not be made without an assessment that balances the benefits of the scope change against the costs of making it.

Scope definition forms the starting point of your architectural analysis (and of all other system development work). Without adequate scope definition, your project has a high probability of failure.

The Context Diagram

A context diagram presents a high-level picture of the system's boundaries and its adjacent external entities. It is often useful to produce such a diagram, if one isn't already available, to make clear the context in which your architectural analysis will take place.

EXAMPLE A clothing retailer decides to start selling its products over the Internet. The new Web site will include a detailed online catalog (drawn from an existing product database), with facilities for order acceptance, tracking, and fulfillment (i.e., shipping out the ordered products). The system should display approximate stock levels and automatically back-order out-of-stock goods. The retailer's large database of customers who order products over the telephone must integrate smoothly with the Web site.

The system needs to interact with a number of entities and systems, including:

- Customers accessing the Web site over the Internet
- The retailer's existing product database
- The retailer's existing customer database
- External systems for validating credit card details and submitting payments
- The retailer's accounts system
- The retailer's warehouse management system
- An external product distribution system

A UML-based context diagram for this system might look something like Figure 8–1.

The new system is shown in the middle of the diagram, together with the user types, systems, and data stores with which it needs to interact. Typically, such a context diagram would also be annotated with high-level information flows.

Once produced, the context diagram should be a "living" document, so keep it up-to-date with high-level changes.

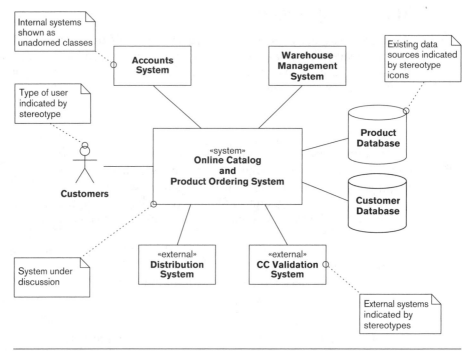

FIGURE 8-1 EXAMPLE CONTEXT DIAGRAM

ARCHITECTURAL CONCERNS

In practice, much of the information you use in your AD comes from people other than yourself. Your stakeholders are the main source of the information that shapes the architecture—their *concerns*—and because it is not possible for the architect to be an expert in everything, you may have to rely on specific business or technical expertise from subject matter experts, technology specialists, or other architects.

Your first challenge is to extract from these people the information you need, critically appraise it, consolidate it, and incorporate what you need into your AD. As if that weren't hard enough, you may find that your stakeholders don't really know what they want—or, once they realize the implications of what they are asking for, they change their minds. You will therefore have to explore their needs in more detail, helping the stakeholders revise and refine them. Where you have multiple sources of information, you may need to reconcile differences and reach consensus between conflicting stakeholders.

Let's remind ourselves of the definition of a concern that we introduced in Part I.

DEFINITION A **concern** about an architecture is a requirement, an objective, an intention, or an aspiration a stakeholder has for that architecture.

Our definition of *concern* is deliberately broad and wide ranging. On the one hand, a concern may be specific, unambiguous, and measurable. In this case, we call it a **requirement** and can use the techniques of traditional systems analysis to capture it, document it, and use it to shape the architecture. On the other hand, a concern may be vague and loosely stated but nonetheless still important to your stakeholders. Indeed, such a concern may be more important to them than the specific requirements.

EXAMPLE The retailer described in the previous example has a strong reputation for quality of service and customer responsiveness, which must be reflected in every interaction with the customer. This translates into a number of goals and aspirations for the online store.

- The values, ethos, and reputation of the retailer must be reflected in the appearance and operation of the online store and its supporting processes.
- At all times, the Web site should try to present a "human" face to the customer (even those portions of it that are fully automated).
- The online store must be easy to use by customers who have limited experience with computers and e-commerce.
- The online store must be responsive (quick to load and respond to customer actions) whether or not the customer has a fast Internet connection.
- The online store must cover all aspects of the shopping experience, including an up-to-date, browseable catalog; a secure online purchasing system; order tracking; and returns handling.

Apart from the last item, none of these can be considered formal and measurable requirements, and the last one is really a statement of scope. However, if the system does not meet these goals and aspirations, it will probably be viewed as a failure.

We can broadly classify concerns as architectural goals, functional requirements, and architectural requirements.

Architectural Goals

Architectural goals—or objectives, intentions, or aspirations—are all those concerns at the vague end of the spectrum. An architectural goal typically exhibits few of the desirable characteristics of a requirement.

- It is often expressed using imprecise language—indeed, the stakeholders may not really be clear about what they mean.

- It is unlikely to be quantifiable or measurable in any useful way, which means that there are no objective criteria for judging whether or not the goal has been met. It all comes down to gut feelings and the subjective assessments of the stakeholders.

- It usually has a strong business focus, and it is often unclear how this might translate into an architectural solution.

Unfortunately, you cannot afford to ignore architectural goals: They define the fundamental nature of the architecture and what it is supposed to achieve. However, there are a number of tactics for dealing with these goals.

- Try to turn them into requirements. For example, a goal about system responsiveness might translate into more formal statements of response time, transaction throughput, and so forth.

- Develop architectural principles that translate the goals into physical features and qualities of your architecture. For example, a goal related to ease of use might be translated into principles around a common look and feel, exception handling, and interfaces between automated and manual processes. (We will talk about principles shortly.)

- Manage your stakeholders' expectations of success, especially when goals are vague or unachievable. For example, a system developed under tight budgetary constraints that has ambitious goals for 24/7 availability is unlikely to succeed. You need to make the stakeholders understand why this is the case and work with them to develop more realistic goals.

Functional Requirements

Functional requirements are those requirements that define what the system is required to do. In our experience, it is unusual for the architect to get involved in the specification of *detailed* functional requirements. You will have been given (or will have developed) the scope statement, which should list the system's main functional areas, and you may need to explore this to the next level of detail. However, because it is uncommon for detailed functional requirements to significantly impact the architectural solution, you are unlikely to have the need (or the time) to capture any further detail for the purposes of your AD.

Of course, it is valuable to be involved in the review of detailed functional requirements as they develop, to make sure that your design is—and continues to be—compliant.

Architectural Requirements

Architectural requirements, sometimes referred to as **nonfunctional requirements**, are those that do not directly mandate functionality but still have a significant impact on the architecture. Architectural requirements typically cover system qualities such as performance, availability, or scalability.

As with functional requirements, you are unlikely to be involved in the specification of detailed architectural requirements. However, it is rare in our experience for there to be much in the way of consensus or even consideration of system qualities at this early stage in the system development lifecycle. Indeed, in many areas—internationalization, usability, accessibility—there is little consensus as to how such requirements can even be expressed or translated into system features.

You will probably have to work a lot harder to learn from your stakeholders what their architectural requirements are. You can do this by means of architectural perspectives, as we discuss in detail in Part IV of the book.

What Makes a Good Concern

The AD is primarily intended to document your architecture. However, it is often valuable to use the AD as a vehicle for recording stakeholder concerns and the other factors that led to your architectural decisions. This approach helps you explicitly demonstrate that your solution meets the needs of the stakeholders and shows where you had to make compromises because of conflicting concerns or other real-world constraints.

Concerns should be clearly stated and avoid jargon that is not understood. They are usually numbered or otherwise uniquely identified. A well-expressed architectural requirement also has the following characteristics.

- It is *traceable*, both forward and backward. In other words, the requirement can be justified backward to principles or goals, for example, and can be traced forward into architectural or design features. (We explain how to do this in the Using Principles to Demonstrate Traceability subsection.)

- It is (as far as practicable) *quantified* and *measurable*. Avoid requirements like "The system must respond quickly" or "The interface must be easy to use."

- It is *testable* in a way that objectively demonstrates whether it has been achieved.

Depending on circumstances—and timescales—it may be useful to explicitly cross-reference concerns against the key features of your architecture. For example, where there is a need for high system availability, you may choose to implement hardware redundancy in parts of your architecture.

You may choose to document concerns as part of the main AD, as an appendix, or in a separate document. Remember, however, that the primary purpose of the AD is to document the architecture—it's not intended to be a requirements specification. You probably don't want to go into much detail about concerns in the AD; you can do this later as part of functional specification and design.

As with the scope, you need to get the balance right—providing too much detail will obscure the big picture, and too little detail will lead to ambiguity.

ARCHITECTURAL PRINCIPLES

You have seen examples of principles throughout Part I and Part II, and we hope that you are beginning to appreciate their usefulness. Let's formally define them now.

DEFINITION An **architectural principle** is a fundamental statement of belief, approach, or intent that guides the definition of an architecture. It may refer to current circumstances or to a desired future state.

An appropriate use of principles is invaluable in establishing a baseline or framework for architecture definition. Principles expose stakeholders' underlying assumptions and bring them out into the cold light of day—in other words, they make the implicit explicit. They are a great way to kick off an architecture project, especially when motivation or scope are unclear. They are also useful if you suspect that there are significant but unrecognized conflicts among your stakeholders.

EXAMPLE The retailer described in the previous example wants to develop a new contact center system to deal with postal, telephone, and e-mail inquiries from its customers. However, when the hardware-sizing exercise is completed, it is discovered that the cost is way over budget because hardware replication and high-speed online backup technologies have been used to provide a very high level of system availability.

Discussion with the sponsor and users reveals that, in fact, it is only necessary for the contact center to be available for an extended working day (8 A.M. to 8 P.M.). This is encapsulated in the following principle:

> *There is no requirement now or in the medium term for the contact center to continuously be available 24/7. It will be acceptable to offer a reduced level of service (or even no service at all) for at least four hours every night.*
>
> This principle is discussed extensively with a range of stakeholders, and as a result, the hardware architecture is considerably simplified.

What Makes a Good Principle

A good principle has the following characteristics.

- It is *constructive*. It helps highlight issues, drive architectural decisions, and establish the right architectural framework.

- It is *reasoned*. It is strongly motivated by business drivers, goals, and other principles. (Indeed, we illustrate in the Using Principles to Demonstrate Traceability subsection how you can use principles to justify architectural decisions from business drivers.)

- It is *well articulated*. More than any other artifact, it is important that your principles can be understood by all stakeholders and are not open to misinterpretation (accidental or willful).

- It is *testable*. Principles are (usually) valid over the entire lifetime of the architecture, and it must be possible to determine objectively whether the principle is being adhered to.

- It is *significant*. A principle that is a truism has little value. A good test of significance is to ask whether the opposite statement could ever be true. If the statement opposing the principle is still meaningful (although obviously wrong for your circumstances), the principle is probably significant.

Let's look at an example of how a little analysis can turn a poor principle into a more useful one.

EXAMPLE An early workshop for the retailer's online store translated the goal "The online store must be easy to use by customers who have limited experience with computers and e-commerce" pretty much word-for-word into an architectural principle. However, applying the test for significance, it is clear that the opposite statement, "The online store will be hard to use," is not one that would ever make sense. As it stands, this first attempt at a principle is a truism and not of much value.

Ease of use is clearly important to the stakeholders, and further discussion reveals that this is particularly important for new customers because it is so easy for potential customers to click away to another site if they are having problems. The principle is broken down into several more specific ones, including "The sign-up process will be quick and painless and will require a minimal amount of data entry." This principle is now more reasoned (because it is supported by the rationale "This will help us win new customers") and constructive because it highlights the specific need for ease of use in the sign-up process. It is also more significant because a sign-up process that captured a lot of data might be appropriate in some other situations.

However, it is still not particularly testable: How do the stakeholders know whether they have achieved their objectives for ease of use? Some more work produces a final version of the principle, "The sign-up process will require fewer steps than that of our competitors' Web sites and will require no more data entry than they do." The principle now provides a clearer target for analysts and developers.

Principles are typically expressed in one or a few sentences in the present tense (or sometimes in the future tense if they express a desired state) in plain, jargon-free language.

Defining Your Own Principles

Although there may be some high-level principles you can pick up "off the shelf," you will likely need to develop more specific principles of your own as you explore issues in more depth. You will soon find this to be an invaluable technique in shaping and refining the architectural design.

When you first start to use them, principles may come across to you and your stakeholders as an overblown way to state the obvious, but you will recognize their usefulness the first time you start having trouble reaching consensus over one. Because principles reach right down to our core beliefs, disagreement over the wording or meaning of a principle is a sure sign of some fundamental differences among your stakeholders. It is far better to get these differences out in the open and resolve them early in the process.

It can take a lot of effort to obtain consensus on your principles, so try to get them right the first time. Revising a principle later consumes valuable time and can lead to a significant amount of architectural rework. Don't make your principles too specific: Your aim at this point is to capture the spirit and motivation of your stakeholders, rather than the details (which you will capture later).

Architects often ask, "How many principles should we define?" There is, of course, no right answer to this; you should define as many as the stakeholders need. Don't go overboard, though—if you have hundreds of principles, no one will remember them.

Using Principles to Demonstrate Traceability

One of the most powerful uses of principles is to provide traceability for your architectural decisions. In other words, you can use principles to help justify and explain particular elements or features of your architecture.

This approach relies on associating two additional pieces of information with each of your principles: its **rationale** (why it is an appropriate and valuable principle for your architecture) and its **implications** (what needs to happen in order for the principle to become reality).

Traceability comes about by linking principles together using implications and rationales. You do this as follows.

- Start with the *business drivers and goals* for the architecture. You should be able to obtain these from the definition of scope and concerns and possibly other sources too—involve your stakeholders heavily in formulating the drivers and goals.

- Use the business drivers to develop a set of *business principles*, many of which have as their rationale one or more business drivers (i.e., the business driver has as an implication the business principle).

- Use the business principles in a similar way to develop a set of *technology principles*, many of which have as their rationale one or more business principles.

- Finally, use the technology principles to develop a set of *architectural decisions*, many of which have as their rationale one or more technology principles.

Following the business drivers through to architectural decisions, via rationales and implications, helps you explain the reasoning behind your architectural decisions, as shown in Figure 8–2.

Let's illustrate this by means of a rather simplistic example.

EXAMPLE Because the retailer described previously has grown by acquisition, it now has a number of separate online catalogs in its portfolio. Each catalog fronts a separate shopping system, with its own ways of ordering goods and managing accounts. This makes life difficult for

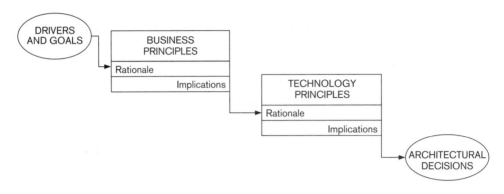

FIGURE 8–2 USING PRINCIPLES TO DEMONSTRATE TRACEABILITY

enthusiastic shoppers, who need to pay separate bills and keep each account up-to-date with changes in personal details.

The company's business strategy therefore includes the following business goal:

> **G1.** To interact with customers in a "joined-up" manner that places them at the heart of the contact process, making it easy and enjoyable for them to browse our entire portfolio and shop with us.

As a result of this, a number of business principles are accepted, including the following:

> **B1.** All customers will gain access to any information, service, or catalog via a single point of entry (the company portal).
>
> **B2.** Certain customer data items (name, address, e-mail address) are viewed as core information, and it should be necessary for a customer to update these only once for the changes to be immediately visible everywhere.

Each of these principles has goal G1 as a rationale.

After some discussion, these are driven down into the following set of technology principles:

> **T1.** Each item of core customer data will be held only once, updated in real time, and used as the authoritative source of the truth.
>
> **T2.** Any system that requires access to a core data item will retrieve it from the central data store at the time of use.
>
> **T3.** Noncore data (i.e., data that applies only to a specific service or catalog) will be managed by the system to which it pertains.

The rationales for these principles are business principles B1 and B2. An architecture is developed from these principles and includes the following elements:

D1. A central consolidated data store that manages all core customer data

D2. A messaging framework used to synchronously retrieve or update all core data

The rationales for these design decisions are technology principles T1, T2, and T3.

You can see from this simple example that the decision to deploy a central data store can be justified from business goal G1, through business principles B1 and B2, and through technology principles T1, T2, and T3.

OTHER ARCHITECTURAL CONSTRAINTS

We include in this category standards, guidelines, strategies, and policies that may all limit the architectural choices available to you.

Standards

Standards may address technology problems, such as those that define the physical mechanisms for linking computers together, or they may address business problems, such as those that define the syntax and semantics of a certain class of business messages. In any case, adopting standards usually eases the design and development process and makes it easier to integrate with other systems, now and in the future.

A large number of off-the-shelf standards are available to you.

- *Open standards* are defined and ratified by bodies such as the International Organization for Standardization (ISO), the Institute of Electrical and Electronics Engineers (IEEE), and the World Wide Web Consortium (W3C). They are generally accepted by the community at large and typically apply across a range of hardware and software environments.

- *Proprietary standards* are created and managed by commercial companies such as Microsoft, Sun, and Oracle. These usually apply only to that manufacturer's products but often gain wider acceptance because of the supplier's market dominance.

- *De facto standards* have not (yet) been ratified by an independent standards body but are widely followed. It is not always obvious which of several competing standards will ultimately be successful; in such a situation, you may want to try to isolate those parts of the architecture into a separate layer or module that can be more easily changed to comply with another standard.

- *Organizational standards* are developed for use by your organization. These may mandate the use of certain hardware or software suppliers or define standard ways to use infrastructure components such as messaging frameworks or data warehouses.

You may also have to comply with legal, statutory, or regulatory standards. Your stakeholders will be able to advise you on these, or it may be appropriate to bring in experts if the issues are complex or the consequences of noncompliance severe.

You and your stakeholders may also define local standards, which are aimed at the specific problems you are trying to solve. Although these may involve extra work up front, they will usually save you time in the long run.

You should focus on architectural-level standards while developing your AD. Coding and unit-testing standards, for example, are probably not of concern to you at this point (although they clearly are important, and you may have a hand in their formulation later).

You should ensure that compliance with standards can be tested in some way. Some standards are accompanied by programs or test suites that will demonstrate a system's compliance—if not, you may want to derive tests of your own. Again, this is not primarily your concern, but you may want to work with your developers and testers to ensure such tests are put in place, particularly if there are legal or regulatory requirements for compliance.

Guidelines and Strategies

These are less formal than standards and take the form of advice or recommended practice. Compliance with these is not mandatory, and you and your stakeholders will need to assess the need to comply in all cases.

There may be an *IT strategy* for your organization, which will impose constraints on technology choices, development approaches, and possibly architectural solutions. If an IT strategy exists, you should familiarize yourself with it and ensure that you are compliant.

Policies

Policies start to define processes that must be followed in order to meet stakeholder needs. You may need to comply with preexisting policies (security policies are a common example), or alternatively your architectural analysis may identify the need to produce some policies of your own.

CHECKLIST

- Are you clear about the fundamental business goals and drivers that have caused the key stakeholders to initiate the project?
- Is the scope of the system under consideration clearly and adequately defined?
- Has this scope been reviewed, agreed on, and signed off by relevant stakeholders, including at a minimum the acquirers/sponsors and users?
- Is the scope specified at an appropriate level of detail, balancing brevity with clarity and completeness?
- Is the scope definition internally consistent?
- Does the scope include a definition of the system's functional areas, its external interfaces, details of data to be migrated, and details of other systems to be decommissioned?
- Does the scope identify any important technology constraints, such as mandated platforms?
- Have you omitted from the scope definition any obvious statements that should be explicitly stated?
- Have you consulted all stakeholders who may be able to mandate or suggest important business and technology standards, policies, and guidelines?
- Have you documented all concerns, using simple, clear language that stakeholders can understand?
- Are all principles supported by rationales and implications? Do these ultimately tie back (via rationales) to business goals and forward (via implications) to architectural decisions?
- Have you taken into account the relevant organizational standards, policies, and guidelines?
- Have the stakeholders reviewed and ratified your concerns and principles?

SUMMARY

It is vitally important to agree on the boundaries of the architecture definition at the outset. If you don't, you are storing up problems for the future.

In this chapter, we started by describing the importance of agreeing on the system scope. As well as defining the functional areas to be provided, the scope also may have to consider external interfaces, systems to be integrated with, specialized technology capabilities, systems to be decommissioned, and data to be migrated into the new system. A good scope definition is brief, has an appropriate level of detail, states the obvious when needed, avoids jargon, and has been ratified and formally adopted by the stakeholders.

We explained that a good way to visually represent aspects of the scope is to use a context diagram. Production of such a diagram is a good way to begin your work with the stakeholders.

We explained that stakeholder concerns may be specific and measurable (in which case, we call them requirements) or may be vague and loosely stated but nonetheless still important to your stakeholders. We described how to effectively document your stakeholders' concerns.

We defined an architectural principle as a fundamental statement of belief, approach, or intent that guides the definition of an architecture. We explained how principles are extremely useful in creating a framework for architecture definition and showed how you can use principles to trace back your architectural decisions to business drivers and goals.

Finally, we considered various types of architectural constraints, such as standards, guidelines, strategies, and policies. You must take all of these into account when designing your architecture.

FURTHER READING

Many software architecture books discuss the process of setting the scope of the system; examples include Garland and Anthony [GARL03], which describes a Context viewpoint, and Bosch [BOSC00], which describes how to define the system context at the start of the architectural design process.

A number of requirements engineering books also discuss scoping systems. A particularly good example is Sommerville and Sawyer [SOMM97], which presents a clear set of guidelines around requirements capture, presentation, and ratification. Each guideline is accompanied by a cost/benefit analysis and practical suggestions on how it can be implemented.

9

IDENTIFYING AND ENGAGING STAKEHOLDERS

As we saw in Part I, the people affected by a system are not limited to those who use it. Systems are not just used: They have to be *designed and built*; they have to be *operated*; they may have to be *repaired*; they are usually *enhanced*; and, of course, they have to be *paid for*.

Each of these activities involves a number—possibly a significant number—of people distinct from the users. Each of these groups of people has its own requirements, its own interests, and its own needs from the system. We refer collectively to these people as *stakeholders*. In Part I we defined a stakeholder as follows.

DEFINITION A **stakeholder** in a software architecture is a person, group, or entity with an interest in or concerns about the realization of the architecture.

Correctly identifying stakeholders and gaining their commitment is one of the most important (yet underrated) tasks in software development. The concept of architectural stakeholder is clearly explained in the IEEE standard *Recommended Practice for Architectural Description*, and our discussion builds on theirs.

SELECTION OF STAKEHOLDERS

It is, in our experience, a subjective choice whom you select to populate your community of stakeholders. We have found, however, that casting your net more widely at the beginning is important in the long term (although in the short term, it may make your life more difficult because you will have more potentially conflicting requirements to reconcile). If you don't take stakeholders' concerns into consideration at the beginning of your development project, you can be sure that they will complain at the end, when making changes is much harder—and making architectural changes may be practically impossible.

STRATEGY The selection of stakeholders is a subjective activity; but in general, the wider the stakeholder community, the better your chances of delivering a successful product or system.

Unfortunately, there are no purely objective criteria for determining whether you have correctly identified your stakeholders. Whom you select depends on a range of factors including the goals of the system, organizational and political considerations, availability of resources, and cost and timescale constraints.

(We sometimes find, for example, that stakeholders are consulted in a spirit of openness, to demonstrate a desire to reflect a wide range of concerns, rather than an absolute need to take account of their views. There is absolutely nothing wrong with this, as long as it contributes to the success of the architecture.)

Drawing up your list of stakeholders, therefore, is a collaborative activity that sets the tone for the future direction of the project, and it is essential that you get this right. As well as ensuring that your stakeholder list is complete (we explore this issue further in the next section), there are four criteria to help make sure your list is right.

PRINCIPLE A good stakeholder in an architecture is *informed*, *committed*, *authorized*, and *representative*.

We explain each of these criteria in Table 9–1.

TABLE 9–1 CRITERIA FOR A GOOD STAKEHOLDER

Criterion	Description
Informed	Do your stakeholders have the information, the experience, and the understanding needed to make the right decisions?
Committed	Are your stakeholders willing and able to make themselves available to participate in the process, and are they prepared to make some possibly difficult decisions?

TABLE 9–1 CRITERIA FOR A GOOD STAKEHOLDER (*CONTINUED*)

Criterion	Description
Authorized	Can you be sure that decisions made now by your stakeholders will not be reversed later (at potentially high cost)?
Representative	If a stakeholder is a group rather than a person, have suitable representatives been selected from the group? Do those representatives meet the above criteria for individual stakeholders?

CLASSES OF STAKEHOLDERS

In Table 9–2, we classify stakeholders according to their roles and concerns.

Most system development projects include representatives from most if not all of these stakeholder groups, although their relative importance will obviously vary from project to project. However, if you do not at least consider each class, you will have problems in the future.

Widening your set of stakeholders leads to a tradeoff—the larger the group, the more difficult it will be to reach a consensus. Part of the architect's role is to ensure that large stakeholder communities do not become an obstacle

TABLE 9–2 STAKEHOLDER ROLES

Stakeholder Class	Description
Acquirers	Oversee the procurement of the system or product
Assessors	Oversee the system's conformance to standards and legal regulation
Communicators	Explain the system to other stakeholders via its documentation and training materials
Developers	Construct and deploy the system from specifications (or lead the teams that do this)
Maintainers	Manage the evolution of the system once it is operational
Suppliers	Build and/or supply the hardware, software, or infrastructure on which the system will run
Support staff	Provide support to users for the product or system when it is running
System administrators	Run the system once it has been deployed
Testers	Test the system to ensure that it is suitable for use
Users	Define the system's functionality and ultimately make use of it

to making progress. This requires you to actively manage the decision-making process and have a clear understanding of the relative importance of the needs of each stakeholder group. Doing this will help you defend your architectural decisions when challenged by stakeholders who feel that their needs have been ignored.

STRATEGY If you have a large stakeholder group, you need to actively manage it to ensure that its size does not impede progress. In particular, you need to balance and prioritize the needs of the different stakeholder groups, so that when conflicts occur, you can make sound, well-reasoned decisions.

It is also worth noting that, although we don't consider the architect's needs explicitly, when acting in that role you are also an architectural stakeholder. (We assume that you can represent yourself adequately to ensure that your views are taken into account!)

PRINCIPLE The architect must ensure that there is adequate stakeholder representation across the board, including nontechnology stakeholders (such as acquirers and users) and technology-focused ones (such as developers, system administrators, and maintainers).

Let's define the stakeholder classes in a little more detail.

Acquirers

Acquirers oversee the procurement of the system or product. Acquirers typically include senior management, which provides or authorizes funding for product or system development, and may also include the purchasing and legal departments, which represent the commercial interests of users in negotiations with third-party suppliers.

In a system development project, acquirers are often referred to as business sponsors, and for a product development, acquirers are likely to be senior executives from the sales, marketing, and technology groups. There may also be investor representation in this group if specific external investment is required to fund the project. In seniority terms, acquirers are usually your most important stakeholders.

Acquirers' concerns typically center around issues such as alignment with strategic objectives, return on investment, and the costs, timescales, plans, and resources involved in building and running the system. Their goals are usually value for money and efficient expenditure of resources during delivery and operation.

Assessors

Assessors oversee the system's conformance to standards and legal regulations. Assessors may come from the organization's own internal quality control or conformance departments, or they may be external legal entities.

Assessors' concerns are focused around testing (to demonstrate conformance to requirements) and on formal, demonstrable compliance.

Communicators

Communicators explain the system to other stakeholders. Internal or public trainers provide training for support staff, developers, maintainers, and so on, and technical authors create manuals for the users and administrators of the product or system. In the case of a product, the marketing department needs to communicate its key features, strengths, and benefits to potential customers.

Communicators' interests lie in understanding the rationale behind and the details of the architecture and explaining it to technical and lay audiences.

Developers

Developers construct and deploy the system from specifications; in other words, they take it through the software development lifecycle from design, code, and test to acceptance. Developers need to understand the overall architecture but also have specific concerns that focus on development issues such as build standards, choice of platform, language, and tools as well as other issues such as maintainability, flexibility, and the preservation of knowledge over time.

This category also includes development managers, who plan the development activities and lead the teams that do the work.

Maintainers

Maintainers manage the evolution of the system once it is operational. Maintainers' concerns focus on issues such as development documentation, instrumentation (facilities for operational system monitoring), debug environments, production change control, and the preservation of knowledge over time.

Suppliers

Suppliers build and/or supply the hardware, software, or infrastructure on which the system will run, or possibly they provide specialized staff for system development or operation.

Suppliers are a slightly special class of stakeholder: They are not usually involved in building, running, or using the system, but they may impose constraints due to the limitations or requirements of the products they supply. For example, a software application may mandate a particular version of the operating system to run, or may run only on certain hardware configurations, or may impose limitations on the number of concurrent connections or maximum data size. It is essential that you factor such constraints into the design of the architecture.

Support Staff

Support staff (help desk, technical support, customer service departments, and so on) provide support to users of the product or system when it is running. Support staff concerns revolve around having the information required to solve problems with users who may be communicating via telephone, e-mail, or the Internet—or in person.

System Administrators

System administrators run the system once it has been deployed. In large-scale commercial environments, system administrators play a key role because operation of the system is essential to the continuity of the business. In some scenarios, such as products aimed at the domestic PC market, the system administrators may also be the users.

System administrators may focus on a wide range of concerns, such as system monitoring and management, business continuity, disaster recovery, availability, resilience, and scalability.

Testers

Testers act as the conscience of the system development team. They systematically test the system in order to establish whether or not it is suitable for deployment and use. Although developers also perform testing, testers should be independent and do not have the same sense of ownership of the system's implementation. This, along with their specialist knowledge and experience, means that they can perform a more thorough and objective job of evaluating the system than the other stakeholders can.

Testers may be part of the same team as the developers or may be in a separate organizational unit or even a distinct organization (e.g., independent testing may be subcontracted to a specialist testing company). Wherever they are found organizationally, testers are concerned with establishing requirements, designing tests to prove whether requirements have been met, and building systems on which to run their tests.

Users

Users define the system's functionality and will ultimately make use of it. In the case of internal systems, users are internal staff who may be dealing with customers or performing back-office functions. In the case of a software product, users are the eventual purchasers of the product; here it is necessary for the product manager to represent their interests in some way, for example, by market testing. In some scenarios (e.g., e-commerce or other customer-facing systems), users may be members of the public; again, it is necessary to represent their interests secondhand.

Users' concerns obviously center around scope and functionality; however, they have operational concerns too, such as performance and security, although the architect may need to bring these to the users' attention.

EXAMPLES

We can illustrate the characteristics of these stakeholder classes by means of some examples.

An Off-the-Shelf Deployment Project

An off-the-shelf deployment project involves the selection, tailoring, and implementation of an existing software package and so involves the development of less software than a traditional system development project. However, the role of stakeholders is still vital, and many of the stakeholders from a traditional software development project are still relevant to an off-the-shelf deployment project.

EXAMPLE Company A, a manufacturer of computer hardware, wants an enterprise resource planning (ERP) system to better manage all aspects of its supply chain from ordering through delivery. Management anticipates the system being constructed from a custom off-the-shelf (COTS) package combined with some in-house development for specialized aspects of functionality. The new system must be deployed within one year, in time for a meeting where shareholders will consider future funding for the company.

Acquirers of the system include the business sponsor (senior management), who will authorize funding for the project, along with the purchasing department and representatives of IT, who will evaluate a number of potential ERP packages.

The users of the system cover a wide range of internal staff, including those who work in order entry, purchasing, finance, manufacturing, and distribution.

Developers, system administrators, and maintainers are staff members of the internal IT department, and assessors are taken from the internal acceptance test team. Communicators include internal trainers, and support is to be provided by an internal help desk (possibly in conjunction with the COTS supplier).

A Software Product Development Project

A software product is usually developed by a specialist supplier, with the development often partially funded by external investors. The intended users of the product will be in other organizations that, it is hoped, will purchase the product once it is complete. The stakeholders for such projects are often spread across a number of organizations.

EXAMPLE Company B, an educational software supplier, wants to develop a product that will be used by college lecturers to manage their schedules of classes. Company B has formed a partnership with a local college and has obtained some venture capital funding for the product. The system will run on PCs and will be inexpensive and easy to operate.

Acquirers in this case include senior management and product managers at Company B, the educational partner, and representatives from the venture capitalists.

Users of the system are college lecturers and administrative staff; note that these users do not actually exist as such because no one has yet bought the product. User representation will have to be obtained in some other way (e.g., by talking to some potential users of the product).

Developers and maintainers are product development staff from Company B, and assessors are taken from the three partner organizations. There are no real system administrator stakeholders in this example (this needs to be factored into the architecture, for example, by making the system self-managing). Support staff might be provided by Company B and/or colleges that buy the product.

Communicators include technical authors from Company B who write the user guide.

A Partnered Development

A partnered development project involves one organization using the services of another to provide systems or services it would normally provide with its own internal resources. These projects result in stakeholders who would typically be found within the acquiring organization actually being found within the external service organization. This can make it more difficult to identify and interact with these stakeholders.

> **EXAMPLE** Company C, an established financial organization, wishes to expand its presence on the Internet with the ability to market a range of financial services to members of the public. These services are aimed at residents of the country where Company C is based, as well as some international customers. Company C plans to contract out the development and operation of the system to an established Web developer.
>
> Acquirers include senior managers who will authorize funding for the project. Users include ordinary members of the public, who will access the public-facing Web site (as in the previous example, these don't exist yet), along with internal administrative staff, who will carry out its back-office functions.
>
> Developers and system administrators are staff from the Web development company. Assessors include Company C's internal accounting and legal staff, as well as external financial regulators from any country in which Company C wants to trade.
>
> Communicators and support staff are provided by Company C and/or the Web development company.

PROXY STAKEHOLDERS

We can see from the examples in the previous section that it may not be possible to identify all stakeholders until the system is developed. While some stakeholders will almost always be identifiable—particularly the acquirers and probably the users—others may not physically exist as a group. In these situations, you must identify *proxy stakeholders*. The proxy is an individual or group who predicts the concerns of the real stakeholders and ensures that they are given as much weight as other concerns.

For a new product, for example, the user stakeholders are potential customers. Your proxy user stakeholders might be the product managers from the marketing group, armed with the results of market testing, or members of the target user population willing to be involved in the product's inception.

STRATEGY When real stakeholders cannot be identified (e.g., when a user community does not yet exist), the architect should identify proxy stakeholders to represent their interests. As much as possible, the proxy stakeholders should meet the same criteria as their real counterparts.

STAKEHOLDER GROUPS

Another possible complication occurs when a stakeholder actually represents a class of person, such as user or developer, rather than an individual. It may be impossible to capture and reconcile the needs of all members of the class in the time you have available, or you may not have the stakeholders at hand (e.g., in the case of potential users of a new product in development).

A stakeholder can also be a more external group, such as a professional standards body, the company's quality assurance department, or external legal regulators. The same principle applies in this case—you need to select representative stakeholders authorized to stand in for the whole group.

 STRATEGY Where a stakeholder comprises a group, team, or organization, it is necessary to select and authorize one or more stakeholder representatives to speak for the group.

STAKEHOLDERS' RESPONSIBILITIES

Effective stakeholders fulfill the following responsibilities.

- They ensure that all of their concerns are clearly communicated to the architect.
- Representative or proxy stakeholders clearly convey to the architect all of the concerns of the people they represent.
- They make decisions in a timely and authoritative manner and stick to them.
- If the stakeholders do not have the authority to make a decision, they escalate it appropriately and obtain a decision from someone who has that power.
- They review the AD to ensure that the system meets their concerns and is—as far as they can ascertain—functionally correct.

CHECKLIST

- Have you identified at least one stakeholder of each class? If not, is the omission justified?
- Have you informed the stakeholders of their responsibilities (e.g., as defined in the previous section), and have they agreed to these?
- In particular, does each stakeholder understand the level of commitment involved, in terms of attending meetings, reviewing documents, and making decisions?
- Is each stakeholder aware of the particular role to fulfill (acquirer, user, and so on)?
- For each group of stakeholders, have you identified and engaged a suitable representative? Does this proxy have the knowledge and authority to speak on behalf of the group?
- For each stakeholder group that does not yet exist (e.g., customers for a new software product), have you identified and engaged a suitable proxy?
- If suppliers are to be included as stakeholders, are their responsibilities and (if appropriate) contractual obligations clearly understood by both sides?

SUMMARY

Understanding the role of the stakeholder is fundamental to understanding the role of architecture in the development of a software product or system. In this chapter, we showed how to select good stakeholders—those who are informed, committed, authorized, and representative—and defined a set of stakeholder classes, including the following:

- Acquirers, who oversee the procurement of the system or product
- Assessors, who oversee the system's conformance to standards and legal regulation
- Communicators, who explain the system to other stakeholders
- Developers, who construct and deploy the system from specifications
- Maintainers, who manage the evolution of the system once it is operational
- Suppliers, a special class of stakeholders who may impose constraints on the architecture due to characteristics of their products
- Support staff, who provide support to users for the product or system when it is running

- System administrators, who run the system once it has been deployed
- Testers, who test the system to ensure that it is fit for use
- Users, who define the system's functionality and will ultimately make use of it

We also discussed proxy stakeholders, who represent the interests of temporarily nonexistent stakeholders (such as the users of a new product), and explained the responsibilities of stakeholders in general.

FURTHER READING

As mentioned at the beginning of this chapter, we based our definition of stakeholders on that presented by the IEEE standard *Recommended Practice for Architectural Description* [IEEE00], which defines stakeholders in terms of an architecture definition process.

Several software architecture books [BASS03; CLEM02; GARL03] have useful discussions of the idea of an architectural stakeholder.

10

IDENTIFYING AND USING SCENARIOS

The most important goal of your software architecture is that it meets the needs of your stakeholders. In practical terms, this means that the system built based on your architectural design must be able to perform certain tasks while exhibiting certain properties (such as its performance or security) that are important to the stakeholders.

Architecture definition is inevitably a process of complex tradeoffs between competing needs. In the midst of this, it is very easy for you to lose sight of a particular system's key priorities and for these tradeoffs to start being driven by personal preferences or imagination, rather than stakeholder needs.

A good way to stay grounded when developing your architecture is to continually consider how the ideas you are developing will actually work in practice. One of the most powerful techniques we have come across is to define and apply *scenarios* to your architecture.

The idea of an architectural scenario is simple but worth defining formally nonetheless.

 DEFINITION An **architectural scenario** is a crisp, concise description of a situation that the system is likely to face in its production environment, along with a definition of the response required of the system.

A scenario can capture a particular set of interactions with its users to which the system must be able to respond, the processing that must happen at a particular point in time (such as month end), a particular peak load situation that could occur, a change that might need to be made to the system, or any other situation that the system needs to be designed to handle.

TYPES OF SCENARIOS

We can divide the possible scenarios for a system into two groups: those concerned with what the system does and those concerned with how it does it. In other words, just as with requirements, scenarios can be divided into the group of functional scenarios and the group of system quality (or nonfunctional) scenarios.

- *Functional scenarios* are nearly always defined in terms of a sequence of external events (normally derived from a system use case) that the system must respond to in a particular way. Examples include users initiating transactions, data arriving at external interfaces, temporal events (such as the end of the day) occurring, and so on. (These scenarios form the "+1" part of Philippe Kruchten's original "4+1" viewpoint approach on which we based our viewpoint set.)

- In contrast, *system quality scenarios* are defined in terms of how the system should react to a change in its environment in order to exhibit one or more quality properties. There are as many types of system quality scenarios as there are quality properties, but the more important ones tend to include security, performance, availability, and evolution (which, not coincidentally, are also our primary architectural perspectives). Examples of system quality scenarios include the ability of the system to be modified to provide a new function, to cope with a particular type of peak load, to protect critical information even if some of the security infrastructure is compromised, and so on.

USES FOR SCENARIOS

You can use scenarios in a number of ways within the architecture definition process.

- *Providing input to architecture definition*: Inspiration and ideas can come from many places. Scenarios can provide part of this input and keep the process grounded in reality by challenging you to design solutions to the specific problems the scenarios pose.

- *Evaluating the architecture*: Scenarios are a primary input into almost any process of architectural evaluation, which can range from simple credibility checks you perform in your head to heavyweight reviews using a formal process like the Architecture Tradeoff Analysis Method (ATAM). (We describe ATAM as an evaluation approach later in Chapter 14.) However, irrespective of the degree of formality you employ, scenarios drive the whole process by forcing you to consider how well the system can respond to a specific situation.

▪ *Communicating with stakeholders*: We have found that the discussion of a scenario and how the system can meet the situation described is a very useful vehicle for communicating with all types of stakeholders. A scenario tends to uncover details that formal requirements and designs have often glossed over. Reviewing with a requirements analyst how a system will settle a *particular* set of financial transactions or with a technology specialist how it will behave under a *specific* peak load condition is often much more productive than just considering the requirements or available designs (which are often simplified, generalized, and abstracted in order to make them easy to understand).

▪ *Finding missing requirements*: Another benefit of creating scenarios is that they often reveal what is missing as well as the suitability of what already exists. Considering how the system behaves in one scenario often leads stakeholders to realize that another situation they hadn't previously considered was omitted from the requirements analysis. Finding these missing requirements early can be an invaluable side effect of applying scenarios.

▪ *Driving the testing process*: Scenarios help highlight the things that are important to your stakeholders, thus providing a tremendously useful guide for where to focus testing activity. After identifying your scenarios, use them to plan the sort of testing you'll require, and make sure that the system's testers have a copy of the scenarios as a basis for their initial test plans.

IDENTIFYING AND PRIORITIZING SCENARIOS

In order to work effectively with scenarios, you need to capture a useful set and prioritize them to know where to focus your efforts for greatest effect. You can derive this information from a number of different sources.

▪ *Requirements*: Each functional requirement will suggest a functional scenario (that probably needs to be fleshed out with more specific detail), while your system quality requirements are likely to suggest behaviors (such as performance under load) that your system must exhibit.

▪ *Stakeholders*: Your stakeholders are a rich source of possible scenarios. Depending on the type and number of stakeholders, you could run a workshop to brainstorm possible scenarios, or simply meet with representatives of each stakeholder group to solicit ideas. Some stakeholder groups (such as acquirers, testers, system administrators, and maintainers) are particularly valuable sources of system quality scenarios, which are often harder to derive directly from requirements documents.

- *Experience*: There is no substitute for experience, and your own experience may well be one of the most valuable sources of possible scenarios. If you have experience in a similar domain, with similar technology, or with systems that share important characteristics with the current one, you know what was difficult and caused problems, and these situations point to useful scenarios.

Having identified a set of scenarios, you need to prioritize them, particularly if you have more than 15 or 20. With a large scenario set, it is easy to lose track of which are the most important ones to focus on. If this happens, the scenarios frequently become a hindrance to decision making because their conflicting demands simply confuse the situation.

There are a number of possible ways to prioritize your scenarios. In our experience, the two key criteria for scenario classification are the *importance* that the systems' *stakeholders* attach to the scenario and the likely *risk* that *you* consider the implementation of the scenario will involve. You need to pay significantly more attention to scenarios that key stakeholders consider crucial and that are also risky to implement than to relatively straightforward scenarios that stakeholders don't feel are that important. Scenarios that have straightforward implementations but are important to stakeholders, or those that are risky to implement but have less stakeholder value, fall somewhere between these two extremes.

Your stakeholders should be involved in the prioritization of scenarios because you are creating the architecture for them. However, as with requirements, your stakeholders normally have overlapping and conflicting interests and opinions, so the priorities they place on different scenarios will vary. You may be able to gather stakeholder representatives in a meeting to vote on scenario importance, with those getting the most votes being considered the most important. In many cases, through, this won't work, and you will need to balance the views of the different stakeholders yourself, in the same way that you often need to balance the relative priority of different requirements.

You should also consider how risky you think it would be *not* to address some of your scenarios. (You will normally do this yourself, rather than asking stakeholders to do it.) When assessing this, consider whether the overall effectiveness of the system is likely to be significantly affected by the missing scenarios. If the omission of any of your scenarios is likely to cause an appreciable difference in stakeholder satisfaction, ensure that they are prioritized accordingly.

Finally, rank your scenarios in terms of both priority and risk, so that you can focus your efforts on the high-priority, high-risk ones and spend less time worrying about the rest.

CAPTURING SCENARIOS

When capturing the scenarios for a system, we describe the functional and quality-based scenarios slightly differently.

For a functional scenario, you need to define five pieces of information.

1. *Overview*: A brief description of what the scenario is meant to illustrate.

2. *System state*: The state of the system before the scenario occurs (if significant). This is usually an explanation of any information that should already be stored in the system for the scenario to be meaningful.

3. *System environment*: Any significant observations about the environment that the system is running in, such as the unavailability of external systems, particular infrastructure behavior, time-based constraints, and so on.

4. *External stimulus*: A definition of what causes the scenario to occur, such as data arriving at an interface, user input, the passage of time, or any other event of significance to the system.

5. *Required system response*: An explanation, from an external observer's point of view, of how the system should respond to the scenario.

It is also important to give the scenario a concise, unique, and descriptive name.

EXAMPLE A functional scenario for a system that summarizes incoming data might be captured as follows.

Incremental Statistics Update

- *Overview*: How the system deals with a change to some of the existing base data.

- *System state*: Summary statistics already exist for the sales quarter that the incremental statistics refer to. The system's databases have enough space to cope with the processing required for this update.

- *System environment*: The deployment environment is operating normally, without problems.

- *External stimulus*: An update to a subset of the sales transactions for the previous quarter arrives via the *Bulk Data Load* external interface.

- *Required system response*: The incoming data should automatically trigger background statistical processing to update the summary statistics for the affected quarter to reflect the updated sales transaction data. The old summary statistics should stay available until the new ones are ready.

We have found that this stimulus–response approach works less well when trying to capture system quality scenarios. These scenarios try to illustrate characteristics that vary widely; in general, they try to show how the system responds to a change it its environment. Sometimes this change can be seen as a stimulus (e.g., being attacked), whereas in other cases (e.g., an external system slowing down or data volume increasing), we have found that viewing the change as a stimulus is rather artificial.

You need to define four pieces of information for a system quality scenario.

1. *Overview*: A brief description of what the scenario is meant to illustrate.

2. *System environment*: Any significant observations about the environment that the system is running in, such as the unavailability of external systems, particular infrastructure behavior, time-based situations, and so on. In some cases, this may also capture key facts about the system's state if the behavior specified in the scenario relies on it.

3. *Environment changes*: An explanation of what has changed in the system's environment that causes the scenario to occur. This could be infrastructure changes or failures, changes in external system behavior, security attacks, required modifications, or any of the other environment changes that require the system to possess a particular quality property in order to deal with them.

4. *Required system behavior*: A definition of how the system must behave in response to the change in its environment (e.g., how the system should respond, from a performance point of view, to a defined increase in the number of requests arriving per minute).

As with functional scenarios, a system quality scenario needs a good name.

EXAMPLE   Some system quality scenarios for the system that summarizes incoming data might be captured as follows.

Daily Data Update Trebles in Size

- *Overview*: How the system behaves when regular data volumes are suddenly greatly exceeded.

- *System environment*: The deployment environment is working correctly. The system has summary statistics in its database already. The normal data volume arriving in the daily update has been consistently between 1GB and 1.5GB. Summary processing has taken 3–4 hours in these cases.

- *Environment changes*: The daily data update on a particular day is found to be 4GB.

- *Required system behavior*: The system should process the incoming data set for a period until the period of processing exceeds the system's configurable limit for processing time. At that point, the system should stop processing the update, discard work in process, leave the previous set of summary statistics in place, and log a diagnostic message (including cause and action taken) to the operational console monitoring system.

Failure in Summary Database Instance

- *Overview*: How the system behaves when the database it is trying to write to fails.
- *System environment*: The deployment environment is working correctly.
- *Environment changes*: While writing summary statistics to the database, the system receives an exception indicating that the write failed (e.g., the database is full).
- *Required system behavior*: The system should immediately stop processing the statistics set it is working on and leave any work in progress behind. The system should log a fatal message to the operational console monitoring system and shut down.

Additional Summary Dimension Required

- *Overview*: How the system can cope with the need to extend the statistical processing provided.
- *System environment*: The deployment environment is operating normally, as initially delivered.
- *Environment changes*: The need arises to support a new statistical dimension in the summary statistics to summarize sales by type of payment option used.
- *Required system behavior*: The development team should be able to add the required processing to provide the new statistical dimension without making any changes to the overall system structure (i.e., changing any interelement interfaces or interactions) and with a total effort of fewer than 4 person-weeks.

A point worth noting from these examples is that a scenario doesn't always indicate good news, and when you create a scenario you may not have all the answers. The required failure behavior outlined in the examples isn't particularly robust, and this may not be acceptable. However, by writing this scenario, you now have a concrete case to discuss with stakeholders to help you learn what the phrase "must cope with failure conditions" in the requirements document actually means. Similarly, it isn't clear yet how the architecture would cope with the need for a new summary dimension, but you can now discuss the need for different types of evolution in a more concrete way.

APPLYING SCENARIOS

Having defined the scenarios for your system, you can apply them in a number of ways that vary greatly in their likely cost and also in the benefits you can expect to gain. This section briefly discusses the most common ways in which scenarios are applied.

Paper Models

The simplest and most common way to apply a scenario is to use it to create a paper-based model of how the system responds to the scenario. By "paper-based" we mean models like UML and data flow, whether they're created on paper, on whiteboards, in computer-based drawing tools, or in purpose-built software packages (e.g., modeling tools). The key thing about these models is that they are inert and thus can't be tested as such, only reviewed by one or more human beings. Their strength is that they are simple to understand and inexpensive to create, but their weakness is that they are only as reliable as the process used to construct and analyze them. The most common notation used for this sort of work is the UML sequence diagram.

EXAMPLE Figure 10–1, on the next page, shows how the functional scenario presented earlier might be illustrated with a UML sequence diagram.

You've probably seen and used these diagrams in a number of places in the software development lifecycle. As noted on the diagram, the boxes represent system elements that are interacting, the vertical lines represent the lifetimes of the elements (with time increasing down the page), and the horizontal arrows indicate interelement interactions and (optionally) what is returned from an interaction.

UML sequence diagrams are normally used in conjunction with an object-oriented development approach to indicate interobject interactions. This notation can usefully illustrate architectural scenarios for any kind of system—not just those built with object-oriented technology. The only requirement is that you have well-defined elements and interfaces.

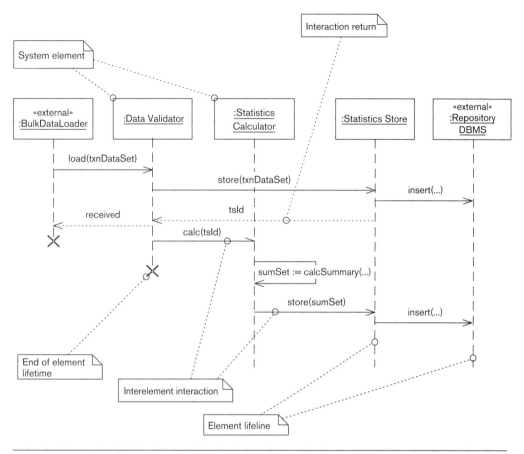

FIGURE 10-1 UML SEQUENCE DIAGRAM FOR THE INCREMENTAL STATISTICS UPDATE SCENARIO

Walkthroughs

An effective way to validate a paper-based model is to review it with a number of people and to bring the system to life with a walkthrough. In a walkthrough, someone illustrates how the system responds to the scenario by explaining each step in the process to an audience of reviewers who can ask questions.

This can be a powerful technique because the very process of walking through the system's operation in front of an audience often helps you spot flaws in your design. A problem with this technique is that for it to have much value, the audience needs to understand the system and the scenario in some detail, and it is often difficult to get people to commit the time to achieve this.

Simulations

A more sophisticated use of a scenario is to guide the development of a computer-based simulation. In complex cases, this may be cheaper or quicker than building a full-blown prototype but is usually more expensive than walking through a paper-based model. There are a number of technical options for creating simulations: spreadsheets for purely mathematical models (e.g., some performance or calculation models); certain graphical modeling tools that allow a detailed UML model to be animated; and purpose-designed simulation packages, which are often well suited to analyzing functional processes and deployment environments.

The problem with simulations tends to be that the creation of the simulation is itself a reasonably complex and costly task, yet one that often can't be directly reused later in the development process (as a prototype could, even if only as a template). There is also the question of how realistic the simulation is and how much reliance you can place on its results. On the other hand, for large-scale systems, a sophisticated simulation can be a lot cheaper than getting the architecture wrong.

Prototype Implementation Testing

A more involved way to apply a scenario is to use it to guide prototyping work so that you can satisfy yourself that your architecture will be able to meet certain goals. Building a prototype can provide you with a much higher degree of confidence that one or more aspects of your architecture will succeed. However, building prototypes is expensive and time consuming, so you can afford to do only a limited amount of it. The scenarios you identify can provide a way to focus your prototyping efforts on the high-risk areas of particular importance to stakeholders.

Full-Scale Live Testing

Finally, scenarios can provide a basis for planning real system-level tests. Because the scenarios define situations that the stakeholders have identified as particularly important to them, it often makes sense for the most important scenarios to be used as specifications of the initial system tests. These system tests often provide valuable proof for your key stakeholders that can hugely increase their confidence in the early versions of the system.

An important final point about applying scenarios is that it almost never makes sense to investigate all of your scenarios equally deeply—or at all. You may create paper models for some of them, simulate a few more, and create prototypes to investigate a couple of high-risk ones. Some of your scenarios may never be used except as a personal reality check for you and as a communication vehicle with a stakeholder or two. Focus the majority of your effort on the high-risk scenarios that stakeholders have indicated are particularly important.

EFFECTIVE USE OF SCENARIOS

Scenarios are a straightforward technique and we are confident that you will be able to apply them without any great difficulty. However, we have found the following general practices helpful in applying scenarios effectively.

Identify a Focused Scenario Set

Although scenarios are very effective, it isn't often useful to end up with dozens and dozens of them. If you consider too many at once, the net result is a lack of focus that prevents them from providing clear guidance for decision making. It is difficult to be prescriptive about the precise number of scenarios you need because it depends very much on the scale and complexity of the system. However, having more than 15 or 20 important scenarios is likely to be too many to use effectively for most systems, so work with your stakeholders to prioritize the set you end up with and focus on the riskiest and most important ones to guide decision making.

Use Distinct Scenarios

It is easy to create a number of scenarios that, although they seem different initially, are really very similar in terms of the requirements they place on the system. This leads to a situation where the cost of applying the technique increases (due to the number of scenarios that need to be created and considered) with only a marginal corresponding increase in benefits, thus reducing the effectiveness of the technique. In order to avoid this situation, revisit the scenarios you identify and consider what demands each places on the system. Where you find duplicates using this criterion, remove them; they are unlikely to provide additional significant insights into your architecture.

Use Scenarios Early

Although scenarios can be used throughout the software development lifecycle, they have the most impact when applied early, when the architecture of the system is taking shape. If you don't consider scenarios at an early stage but leave them until, say, they are needed for system testing, much of their potential benefit is likely to be lost. Of course, you may identify additional scenarios as development progresses (perhaps for testing or architectural evaluation), but do not ignore the potential benefits of applying scenarios earlier in the architectural design process. As outlined in the architecture process introduced at the start of Part II, identify the scenarios for your system as early as possible, and use them to help you focus the architecture and design activities on the most important aspects of the system.

Include the Use of System Quality Scenarios

Scenarios are often thought of in terms of *input*, *process*, and *output*, focusing on functional scenarios derived from the use cases in the functional requirements. However, this ignores the potential that scenarios have for investigating, validating, and understanding the quality properties of the system. As you identify the scenarios you are to work with, ensure that all of the system's critical quality properties are reflected in the scenarios you identify. You will often need to augment the scenarios obtained from your stakeholders with suitable scenarios reflecting the system's required quality properties.

Include the Use of Failure Scenarios

A common pitfall is that all of the scenarios you identify are positive ones that do not consider problems like missing information, overload situations, security failures, and so on. This has the undesirable effect of focusing attention on situations where everything is working and ignoring cases where things go wrong. This is often particularly dangerous when considering quality properties, where system behavior is particularly critical in failure situations. When identifying your scenarios, ensure that you consider the important failure cases and that corresponding scenarios are identified to address these.

Involve Stakeholders Closely

As the architect for your system, you are in a very good position to identify representative scenarios for the system yourself. This is very tempting to do because it is so much simpler than involving all of your stakeholders who, while providing lots of input, will complicate the process immensely. However, excluding your stakeholders from scenario identification is a dangerous decision. Although you can undoubtedly identify many scenarios yourself, the ones your stakeholders provide and the priorities they place on each may surprise you, revealing aspects of the system of which you were unaware or whose importance you hadn't realized. Make sure that stakeholders are asked to identify candidate scenarios for your system and that they have the final say (as a group) in their prioritization.

CHECKLIST

- Have you defined a wide enough range of system quality scenarios (such as security, performance, availability, and evolution)?
- Have you defined and applied a wide enough range of failure and exception scenarios?
- Have you prioritized your scenarios by stakeholder importance and risk?
- Have you reviewed and agreed on the required responses and behaviors with the appropriate stakeholders or subject matter experts?
- Have you included some scenarios that *you* think will be valuable (based on your previous experience) as well as those nominated by your stakeholders?
- Are all your scenarios cataloged and named?
- If defining a scenario helps indicate a gap or mistake in the requirements, have you made sure that this is addressed?
- If applying a scenario indicates a mismatch between required and actual response or behavior, have you revised the architectural design appropriately?

SUMMARY

Defining and applying scenarios is a powerful way to ensure that your architecture will exhibit the functionality and behavior required of it. It can also help drive out omissions and errors in the requirements and is useful when it comes to testing the system.

We defined two classes of scenarios: *functional scenarios*, which are nearly always defined in terms of a sequence of external events the system must respond to in a particular way, and *system quality scenarios*, which are defined in terms of how the system should react to a change in its environment, as a consequence of one of the quality properties it is meant to exhibit.

Scenarios are normally derived from an inspection of the system's requirements. You should also work with stakeholders to identify others (especially quality scenarios and ones that address failure situations), and you may want to identify some scenarios of your own based on your experience.

The specification of a scenario should include the initial system state and environment, external stimulus or environment changes, and the required system response or behavior.

Applying the scenario is a matter of comparing the actual, or likely, response and behavior with the requirement and addressing any gaps or mismatches. You can do this by using a paper model, a simulation, or a system prototype, or by testing the system, depending on the lifecycle stage you are in.

FURTHER READING

In the architectural context, most architecture books talk about scenarios somewhere, at least as a way to illustrate how the system is meant to work.

Some of the books that particularly talk about the use of scenarios for architecture are Clements et al. [CLEM02], where they form a key part of the evaluation approaches explained; Bass et al. [BASS03], where scenarios are used extensively to characterize quality attribute requirements; and Bosch [BOSC00], where scenarios are used to drive the architectural design process. Philippe Kruchten's "4+1" approach, where the "+1" refers to use case scenarios, was originally defined in an article in *IEEE Software* [KRUC95].

A Web search will reveal a number of vendors that can supply simulation tools and UML modeling tools that can animate a UML model, to help you investigate scenarios without building full prototypes.

11

USING STYLES AND PATTERNS

Historically, the software industry hasn't had a very good record of learning from experience. Software designers often ignore existing, proven design solutions and instead develop their own solutions to complex problems. The same can also be said of software architects, who can end up creating new designs for systems containing very familiar challenges.

One of the reasons for this state of affairs used to be a lack of easily accessible, standard solutions for common software architecture and design problems. However, during the 1990s, the design patterns movement emerged with the aim of addressing this problem. Proponents of software patterns, inspired by Christopher Alexander's work on patterns for building architecture,[1] started identifying and cataloging widely used solutions to common design problems. Today, this work has culminated in an ever-growing number of patterns available for general use.

SOFTWARE PATTERNS

The purpose of a software pattern is to share a proven, widely applicable solution to a particular design problem in a standard form that allows it to be easily reused. Software patterns should provide the following five important pieces of information.

1. *Name*: A pattern needs a memorable and meaningful name to allow us to clearly identify and discuss the pattern and, more importantly, to use its name as part of our design language when discussing possible solutions to design problems.

---

1. *A Pattern Language: Towns, Buildings, Construction,* by Christopher Alexander, Sara Ishikawa, and Murray Silverstein (Oxford: Oxford University Press, 1977). Alexander is a building architect, and his books look at building architecture, but his ideas have inspired virtually everyone in the design patterns community.

2. *Context*: This sets the stage for the pattern and describes the situations in which the pattern may apply.

3. *Problem*: Each pattern is a solution to a particular problem, so part of the pattern's definition must be a clear statement of the problem that the pattern solves and any conditions that need to be met in order for the pattern to be effectively applied. A common way to describe the problem that a pattern solves is to describe the design *forces* it aims to resolve, each force being a goal, requirement, or constraint that informs or influences the solution (such as a particular sort of flexibility needed or a particular type of interelement decoupling you want to achieve).

4. *Solution*: The core of the pattern is a description of the solution to the problem that the pattern addresses. This is usually some form of design model, explaining the elements of the design and how they work together to solve the problem.

5. *Consequences*: The definition of a software pattern should include a clear statement of the results and tradeoffs that will result from its application, to allow you to decide whether it is a suitable solution to the problem. Consequences may be positive (benefits) or negative (costs).

Let's look at a simple example of what goes into a software pattern.

EXAMPLE The widely used *Adapter* pattern is so named because it adapts the interface of a system element to a form needed by one of its clients. An outline definition of the pattern could be as follows.

The *context* of the Adapter pattern is a number of heterogeneous elements that need to be connected. The pattern solves the *problem* that arises when one system element (the client) could use the services of another system element (the target) except that the interface offered by the target element is unsuitable for use by the client. An example is a system with a .NET client that wishes to access a calculation service offered by a Java-based target. The calculation service is perfectly suitable for the client's requirements, but the client cannot call a Java-based interface and thus cannot use the service.

The *forces* include the following.

- Service interfaces should be decoupled from the underlying physical data structures and implementation algorithms.
- Services should be exposed in a way that is independent of their implementation technology.

- The adapter should provide translation only and should not perform any inherently useful functionality (this is the responsibility of the invoked service).

- Use of the adapter must not adversely affect the quality properties of the underlying service (security, resilience, performance, scalability, and so on).

The *solution* to the problem is to introduce a third system element, the adapter, sitting between the client and the target, such that it is called by the client and calls the target. The role of the adapter is simply to interpret the request from the client, transform it into the form required by the target, call the target, and transform the response into the form expected by the client. A real-world example of an adapter is an international power-plug adapter that allows, for example, electrical equipment with French plugs to be used in Denmark with Danish power sockets.

The *consequences* of using this pattern include the following.

- Decoupling of the client and target implementations allows each implementation to be varied without impacting the other. (+)

- The target can be used by different types of clients simultaneously (possibly via different adapters). (+)

- A possible reduction in efficiency could result due to the additional level of indirection between the client and target. (–)

- An increase in maintenance overhead could occur if the services provided and used change because the adapter must be changed as well as the client and target. (–)

You can find a much fuller definition of this pattern in the well-known "Gang of Four" book referenced in the Further Reading section at the end of this chapter.

STYLES, PATTERNS, AND IDIOMS

Software patterns are generally organized into three groups: *architectural styles* that record solutions for system-level organization, *design patterns* that record solutions to detailed software design problems, and *language idioms* that capture useful solutions to language-specific problems. All three types of patterns can be useful to you, although you use them in different places in the lifecycle. Before considering how to use styles, patterns, or idioms, let's define these three terms more formally. The definitions we present are all based on those defined by Frank Buschmann and his colleagues in their book *Pattern-Oriented Software Architecture*.

Architectural Styles

Architectural styles are probably the software pattern type that will be of most immediate interest to you when designing a system because they apply to system-level structures.

DEFINITION An **architectural style** expresses a fundamental structural organization schema for software systems. It provides a set of predefined element types, specifies their responsibilities, and includes rules and guidelines for organizing the relationships between them.

The key point about an architectural style is that it provides a set of organizational principles for the system as a whole, rather than for the details of one piece of the system. The solution described by an architectural style is usually defined in terms of types of architectural elements and their interfaces, types of connectors, and constraints on how the elements and connectors should be combined.

Design Patterns

A design pattern is a solution to a much more specific problem related to the structure of a particular part of a system.

DEFINITION A **design pattern** provides a scheme for refining the elements of a software system or the relationships between them. It describes a commonly recurring structure of interconnected design elements that solves a general design problem within a particular context.

A design pattern forms an input to the detailed software design of the system and guides a software designer to organize her software design units (such as classes and procedures) appropriately. The solution presented by a design pattern is defined in terms of design-level elements (such as procedures, classes, and data structures) and the structure they form when combined.

Language Idioms

Language idioms are the most specific type of software pattern, applying to situations where a particular programming language is in use.

DEFINITION A **language idiom** is a low-level pattern specific to a programming language. An idiom describes how to implement particular aspects of elements or the relationships between them by using the features of a given language.

A language idiom provides guidance to the programmer when implementing software in a specific language and is normally written to help prevent a common pitfall with the language or to illustrate a unique feature that needs to be learned. The solutions presented by language idioms are defined in terms of programming language constructs.

Patterns of all three varieties can play several helpful roles including the following.

- *A store of knowledge*: Patterns are a store of knowledge about solving a particular type of problem in a particular domain. Documenting this knowledge allows it to be shared among people solving similar problems. People can move between specialist areas more easily and work more effectively within a particular area by sharing knowledge about success and failure.

- *Examples of good practices*: A set of patterns provides examples of good design practices. You can use these examples directly, but they can also act as a guide and provide inspiration when you're solving somewhat different design problems.

- *A language*: Patterns allow designers to create and share a common language for discussing design problems. This common language helps designers relate ideas to each other easily and analyze alternative solutions to a problem. This allows for more effective communication among participants in the design process.

- *An aid to standardization*: The use of patterns encourages designers to choose standard solutions to recurring problems rather than searching for novel solutions in each case. This has obvious efficiency benefits for the design process, and reliability is also likely to increase because of the reuse that results from the application of an already proven solution.

- *A source of constant improvement*: Because patterns are generally in the public domain, you can quickly amass a lot of experience about their use. This allows rapid feedback into the pattern definition and promotes improvement over time, reflecting the experiences of its users.

- *Encouragement of generality*: Good patterns are usually generic, flexible, and reusable in a number of situations. Providing flexible and generic solutions to problems is often a goal for architects as well. Using patterns as inputs to the design process and thinking in terms of identifying design patterns within the design process can help you create flexible, generic solutions to the problems within your system.

From our point of view as architects, the real utility of design patterns in software development can be summarized in a single phrase: *reduction of risk*. The use of patterns (and ideally reusable pattern implementations) has the potential to increase productivity, standardization, and quality while reducing risk and repetition.

AN EXAMPLE OF AN ARCHITECTURAL STYLE

Having considered architectural styles in the abstract, let's continue by considering an example of a specific architectural style.

EXAMPLE   Here is a summary of the Pipes and Filters architectural style. (This is just a summary; you can find a much fuller definition in *Pattern-Oriented Software Architecture* [BUSC96].)

The *context* of the Pipes and Filters style is a system that needs to process data streams.

The style solves the *problem* of implementing a system that must process data in a sequence of steps, where using a single process is not possible and where the requirements for the processing steps may change over time.

The problem has the following primary *forces*.

- Future changes should be possible by changing or recombining steps.
- Small processing steps are easier to reuse than large ones.
- Nonadjacent steps in the process do not share information.
- Different possible sources of input data exist.
- Explicit storage of intermediate results should be avoided.
- Multiprocessing between steps should not be ruled out.

The *solution* to this problem is to divide the task into a number of sequential steps and to connect the steps by the system's data flow.

The processing is performed by filter components, which consume and process data incrementally. The input data to the system is provided by a data source while the output flows into a data sink. The data source, data sink, and filter components are connected by pipes. The pipe implements data flow between two adjacent components. The pipe is the only permitted way to connect the other components, and it defines a simple, standard format for data that passes through it, allowing filters to be combined without prior knowledge of each other's existence.

The sequence of filters combined by pipes is called a *processing pipeline*. An example of a processing pipeline appears in the informal diagram in Figure 11–1, which shows how the pieces of the Pipes and Filters style are combined. As indicated by the UML-style comments, the boxes represent the filters and the arrows represent unidirectional pipes linking the filters. Each filter performs a single task—for example, the NPV filter calculates net present value (the present value of an investment's future cash flows less the initial investment).

The *consequences* of using this style are as follows.

- No intermediate files are necessary, but they are possible. (+)
- Filter implementation can be easily changed without affecting other system elements. (+)
- Filter recombination makes creating new pipelines from existing filters easy. (+)
- Filters can be easily reused in different situations. (+)
- Parallel processing can be supported with multiple filters running concurrently. (+)
- Sharing state information is difficult. (–)
- The data transformation required for a common interfilter data format adds overhead. (–)
- Error handling is difficult and needs to be implemented consistently. (–)

You are almost certainly familiar with this architectural style from the UNIX operating system. However, it has been applied in a number

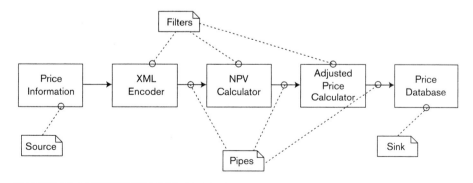

FIGURE 11–1 PROCESSING PIPELINE

of other software systems, such as Enterprise Application Integration (EAI) systems, and it is a useful system organization for a specific type of data processing problem that may occur across a number of application domains.

What does this architectural style definition tell us about systems based on it? Some of the important points are listed here.

- The system processes streams of data, rather than transactions.
- The processing can be broken into a series of independent steps.
- There is just one sort of architectural element (the filter) and one type of unidirectional connector (the pipe), and the filters must form a continuous path through the system, connected by pipes, without any cycles.
- The system doesn't need a central persistent data store.
- It should be easy to replace and reuse the system's filter elements.
- It is likely to be difficult to modify the system to address a situation where elements need to maintain or share state.
- The architect of the system will need to define and enforce an error-handling strategy because the style makes this something of a challenge.

An architectural style tells us what sort of structure a system based on it will have, in terms of the types of system elements and the structure they combine to form. The style also explains the design concerns (or forces) that led to its development and the positive and negative implications to be considered when using it.

THE BENEFITS OF USING ARCHITECTURAL STYLES

Basing your architecture on a recognizable style can have two immediate benefits. First, using a style allows you to select a proven, well-understood solution to your problems and defines the organizing principles for the system. Second, if people know that the architecture is based on a familiar style, it helps them understand its important characteristics.

In our experience, most architects do reuse good ideas they've seen before and do match previously successful solutions to the characteristics of the current problem. It's simply that we do this with varying degrees of formality and may not consider ourselves to be using architectural styles as we do it.

Most of the books documenting architectural styles assume that the styles will be used directly as generic blueprints to guide the design process. However, styles can be used during the architecture definition process in a number of ways.

- *Solution for a system design*: One of the styles you encounter may be a good solution to the particular problems you are trying to solve. In this case, you can simply adopt the style as one of the core structures of your architecture and enjoy the benefits of understanding its likely strengths and weaknesses immediately.

- *Basis for adaptation*: When considering existing styles, you may find that none of them really solve your problem, but they partially address it or address it with some limitations. In these situations, the style forms a starting point for the design process but acts as a base to be adapted to the particular constraints of the current situation. This identifies a candidate variant of the original style.

- *Inspiration for a related solution*: You may also find that none of the styles actually address the problem you are trying to solve. However, simply reading about previously identified styles and the problems they address often helps you understand the current problem in more depth so you can find a solution related in some way to the existing styles. This identifies a related candidate style.

- *Motivation for a new style*: Sometimes you are faced with a problem that does not seem to be addressed by any of the styles you have found. In this case, perhaps you are solving a problem that hasn't been widely solved before, or if it has, its solution hasn't been documented as a style. These situations often act as a spur to solve the problem in a general way and to define a new candidate architectural style capturing the resulting design knowledge.

Architectural styles tend to be quite one-dimensional, focused on solving a very specific type of problem. This means that, in all but the simplest systems, you usually need to combine a number of styles to meet the varied design problems that most systems place before you.

EXAMPLE Consider a financial trading system that needs to allow users to perform transactions but also needs to broadcast information (such as news or prices) across the system. At least two architectural styles immediately suggest themselves: the Client/Server style to allow transaction processing via central servers and the Publisher/Subscriber style to allow news and price information to be broadcast throughout the system. Another style may be needed too, such as Layered Implementation, in order to achieve portability and common use of the underlying platform. In this example, each style is needed for a distinct reason.

- The Client/Server style is present to allow secure, scalable, available transaction processing that performs well.
- The Publisher/Subscriber style is present to allow efficient, flexible, asynchronous distribution of information.
- The Layered Implementation style is present to ensure portability across deployment platforms, to ensure a common approach to the use of underlying technology, and to achieve a good level of development productivity by hiding low-level details of the underlying technology from most of the system developers.

Situations in which we need to combine styles present us with a twofold problem. First, how do we use a number of styles together and retain overall coherence in our architecture? Second, how do we know that the styles will work together and not conflict with each other?

With this problem, as with so many others in software architecture, there really is no substitute for the blend of experience, knowledge, and sound judgment that you bring to the project. Our experience with system architectures has taught us that combining styles is difficult and needs to be done carefully. In particular, the key to success is to choose one of the styles as the dominant organizing style for the system and to structure the architecture around it, introducing the other styles as subsidiary styles where they are needed to solve particular problems that the primary style cannot address by itself. Such an approach helps retain overall coherence and prompts you to consider the compatibility of the styles as you try to add the elements of the subsidiary styles to the structure imposed by the overall system organization defined by the primary style.

STYLES AND THE ARCHITECTURAL DESCRIPTION

You are likely to adopt a particular architectural style in your system because you want the system to exhibit certain qualities that the style claims to provide. Once you've chosen one or more styles to use, it is easy to forge ahead and create an architectural design based on the styles while forgetting to explain the styles you've used in the AD. When this happens, the knowledge about the styles used and why they were selected gets lost, so it is likely that, over time, the architecture will diverge from the structure suggested by the style.

In addition, many architectural styles focus on the overall functional structure of the system and will primarily affect the Functional view in the AD. However, in principle, a style could affect any of the architectural views, so explaining the styles you've used can be important to allow readers of the AD to understand the impact a style has had across the different aspects of your architecture. For these reasons, it is useful to explicitly explain the styles you have used in the AD.

We've found that there are a couple of effective ways to do this: textual commentary and model annotation. Textual commentary simply involves adding to the AD document a brief discussion of the styles you've used and why you used them, probably as an early subsection to help set the scene for the reader. Annotating your models takes this a step further and draws the reader's attention to the relationship between the generic style in use and the specific elements in the architecture. If you are using UML as your modeling notation, you can achieve this by using stereotypes to mark model elements as corresponding to particular abstract elements of the style in use. However, you need to avoid cluttering the models with a lot of extra notation, which prevents people from understanding them easily. If this starts to happen, remove the annotation from the model diagrams and just add textual notes in your explanation of the model.

COMMON ARCHITECTURAL STYLES

A few of the currently documented architectural styles that are particularly relevant to information systems architecture are briefly summarized below. You can find more information on most of these styles in the books we reference in the Further Reading section or from Internet sources.

Pipes and Filters

We defined this style as an example earlier in this chapter. The Pipes and Filters style is characterized by a single, simple element type (the filter) that processes a data stream, with instances of this type connected by simple connectors known as pipes.

Example of Use. Refer to the example illustrated in Figure 11–1.

Advantages. The style allows filter implementation to easily be changed without affecting other system elements, and it makes creating new pipelines by recombining existing filters easy. Parallel processing can also be supported with multiple filters running concurrently.

Disadvantages. Sharing state information is difficult with this style, and the data transformation required for a common interfilter data format adds overhead. Error handling is difficult and needs to be implemented consistently down the pipeline.

Common Variants. Pipes can execute in parallel rather than in sequence, or filters can have more than one entrance or exit channel.

Client/Server

This very widely used style defines a system structure comprised of two types of elements: a server that provides one or more services via a well-defined interface and a client that uses the services as part of its operation. The client and server are typically assumed to reside on different machines in a network (although this is not a requirement of the style—the client and server could be in the same operating system process).

Example of Use. This style is probably very familiar to you from mainstream IT technologies such as client/server databases.

Advantages. The advantages of the style include the centralization of complex or sensitive processing (e.g., allowing specialized hardware to be shared easily).

Disadvantages. Making the request and receiving the response between clients and servers that do not reside on the same machine introduces some unavoidable inefficiency.

Common Variants. Variants of the Client/Server style include Stateful Server (where the server is responsible for keeping track of conversational state) and Stateful Client, Stateless Server (where the client is responsible for keeping track of the state).

Tiered Computing

A development of the Client/Server style, the Tiered Computing style is widely used in enterprise information systems. A tiered system is considered to contain a number of tiers of computation, which combine to offer a service to an ultimate consumer (e.g., a human user). Each tier acts as a server for its caller and as a client to the next tier in the architecture. A key architectural principle is that a tier can communicate in this way only with the tiers immediately on either side of it; a tier is not aware of the existence of other tiers in the system apart from its neighbors. Common tiers in enterprise information systems include the following:

- Presentation (user interface)
- Business process (combining a sequence of business transactions into a service)
- Business transactions (the fundamental business operations in the system that act on business entities)

- Data access (providing governed access to business entities)
- Data storage (the databases in which the enterprise's data resides)

Example of Use. Most large enterprise information systems are organized into tiers, and a number of common application development technologies (such as J2EE and .NET) encourage this organization.

Advantages. This style allows a clear separation of concerns between tiers and provides the potential for reusability of the simpler tiers (data storage, data access, and business transactions) across a number of systems.

Disadvantages. Disadvantages of the style include the overhead of communication between the tiers and additional development complexity arising from the number of system elements that need to be developed and integrated across the tiers.

Peer-to-Peer

Often referred to as P2P, this architectural style defines a single type of system element (the peer) and a single type of connector that is a network connection (an interpeer connection). The characteristics of the connector are not important to the style, and the style has been used with a number of types of network connections.

The central organizational principle of the system is that any peer is free to communicate directly with any other peer, without needing to use a central server. Peers typically locate each other by automatically exchanging lists of known peers (although central peer lists are also used in some cases). Each peer is capable of acting as both client (when making requests) and server (when servicing requests), often being both concurrently.

Example of Use. Well-known examples of the P2P style include Internet file-swapping applications and distributed computation systems.

Advantages. P2P systems eliminate the possible point of failure that a central server represents, can be made very scalable, and are resilient to partial failures in the underlying network.

Disadvantages. Disadvantages of P2P systems include the possible partitioning of the network if no central peer list is available and the difficulty of guaranteeing a particular response from the system at any point in time.

Layered Implementation

The Layered Implementation style identifies a single type of system element: the layer. The style organizes a system's implementation into a stack of layers, with each layer providing a service to the layer above it and requesting services from the one below it. The layers are ordered by the level of abstraction they represent, with the most abstract (e.g., organization-specific operations) at the top of the stack and the least abstract (e.g., operating system–specific libraries) at the bottom. Depending on the implementation of the style, a layer may be able to communicate directly with any of the layers below it (relaxed layering) or only with the layer directly below it (strict layering).

Layers can be contrasted with the tiers in the Tiered Computing style because layers are organized based on the level of abstraction they deal with, whereas tiers are organized based on the type of service they provide. All of the layers in a particular implementation are concerned with providing a single service, but each layer is concerned with a different level of abstraction involved in providing the service. In contrast, the tiers in an implementation all operate at a broadly similar level of abstraction but are each concerned with providing a different type of service, which, when the services are combined, creates a useful system. Given this difference, tiers are often visualized as running horizontally, while layers are often visualized as running vertically. Indeed, the two styles are often combined, with each tier in the system using a stack of layers within it to organize its implementation into different levels of abstraction.

Example of Use. Communication stacks are the classic example of layered organization, but most information system technologies are organized in this way too (e.g., a locally developed utility library layered above a third-party library layered above the operating system).

Advantages. Likely advantages of this style of organization include the reuse of layers, good separation of concerns, and relatively easy maintenance due to the isolation of each layer's implementation.

Disadvantages. Disadvantages include a reduction in implementation flexibility, a reduction in efficiency when many layers need to be traversed, and the constraints that the style places on the development process (layers often need to be developed in order).

Publisher/Subscriber

The Publisher/Subscriber style grew out of a realization that client/server interactions are not suitable for all types of distributed system problems. The style defines a single system element (the publisher) that creates information of interest to any number of system elements (the subscribers) that may wish to consume it. A single type of connector, a reliable network link, is used to link the publisher and the subscribers.

The subscribers register their interest in certain information with the publisher, and when the publisher creates or changes information that subscribers have registered their interest in, the publisher notifies the relevant subscribers of the change. Depending on the implementation of the style, the notification may contain the new or changed information, or it may just be a notification of a relevant change, leaving the subscribers to query the publisher for changes themselves.

Example of Use. The Publisher/Subscriber style is widely implemented in enterprise messaging systems.

Advantages. Advantages include the flexibility to add new subscribers dynamically, the relatively loose coupling between publisher and subscribers, and the increased efficiency that comes from the subscribers not having to poll the publisher repeatedly to find new and changed information.

Disadvantages. The main disadvantage of the style is its relatively complex implementation (particularly if reliable delivery of messages is required).

Asynchronous Data Replication

While Publisher/Subscriber is normally considered to be a style that allows functional elements to exchange information, a variant of it, Asynchronous Data Replication, is a style used where information in two data stores needs to be kept synchronized (e.g., where it is replicated for performance reasons). The style has three element types: the data source, the data replica, and the replicator. The data source is a data store that owns a particular type of information, while the data replica is a separate data store that wishes to maintain a synchronized copy of some subset of the information in the source. The replicator is the element responsible for recognizing changes or additions to information in the source and performing the synchronization of the replica data store.

Example of Use. This style is widely implemented in enterprise data replication technologies, such as those supplied by the major database vendors.

Advantages. The advantages of the style include the ability to synchronize two data stores automatically and efficiently, without needing to complicate the application logic.

Disadvantages. Common problems include the latency that can occur between source update and replica update as well as the complexity of dealing with updates at the replica data store.

Distribution Tree

Another architectural style that relates to data distribution is the Distribution Tree style. This style defines three types of system elements: publishers, distributors, and consumers. The elements of the system are arranged into a tree, connected by network link connectors. A single publisher forms the root of the tree, the distributors are connected to form the intermediate nodes, and the consumers form the leaves of the tree. The publishers publish new or changed information, which the distributors then cache and distribute to their immediate child nodes. If a child node is added or restarted, it can refresh its view of the information from its parent node's cache. When the information reaches the leaf nodes of the tree, the consumer nodes consume it.

Example of Use. This style is implemented by a number of Internet push-client products.

Advantages. Distribution Tree can be scaled from small implementations to very large ones by increasing the size of the tree and its support for intermittently connected consumer nodes (such as mobile devices).

Disadvantages. Disadvantages of the style include the amount of storage required for caching and the potentially high update latency when the distribution tree becomes large.

Integration Hub

The Integration Hub style is another data-oriented architectural style, extending Asynchronous Data Replication to situations where information needs to be synchronized between a number of different systems (rather than between replica data stores).

This style defines four types of system elements: the data source, the data destination, the hub, and the adapter. The elements are organized into a cartwheel form, with the hub at the center of the wheel and the data sources and destinations at the outer edges of the spokes. Along every spoke, between hub and source or destination is an adapter (so each spoke is an adapter connected to a source or destination, radiating out from the hub). The nature of the connectors is not that important; the main characteristic to note is that the connector allows unidirectional data flow, from one end to the other.

The implementation of the hub includes a common data model for data entities of interest in the system. The adapters are responsible for translating between the common data model and the specific data models of the source or destination they connect. The sources and destinations simply supply data to or receive data from their adapters.

Information can flow between any source and destination by the data being transformed from the source's form into the common form (by the source's adapter) and then from the common form to the destination's form (by the destination's adapter). This allows routine data transfer and synchronization between systems that do not share common data models, formats, and encodings.

Example of Use. This style is widely implemented by EAI products that allow data integration between applications.

Advantages. Integration Hub allows new data sources and destinations to be added easily to the system without disrupting the existing implementation. It can also integrate sources and destinations of practically any form because a dedicated adapter hides the specifics of a source or destination.

Disadvantages. Data movement between applications will be relatively inefficient due to the amount of translation, and the imposition of a common model may mean that some information that the common model does not accommodate is lost in translation. The design of the common model can also be quite difficult.

The hub itself can become a central point of failure or a performance bottleneck if it is not designed properly. This risk can be mitigated to some extent by extending the cartwheel topology into a snowflake which links multiple hubs together.

Tuple Space

The Tuple Space style is a type of repository that allows a number of pieces of a distributed system to collaborate to share information. The two types of system elements in the style are the clients (computational elements that create and consume information) and the tuple space itself (a storage area where clients can read and write typed information tuples or records). The clients and the tuple space are connected by a client/server network connection. Clients interact with the tuple space by writing new tuples to it or requesting tuples that match simple search criteria. Clients do not interact directly. Typically the tuple space can also call back to the clients when objects they are interested in change.

Example of Use. Examples of this style include the original Linda research system (from which the style was derived) and more recent implementations such as JavaSpaces for the Java language. An application of the approach might be a price source in a banking system that allows various types of price information to be published by any number of price sources to a single tuple space and accessed from the space by any number of applications that need price information.

Advantages. The Tuple Space style provides a simple computational model, encourages loose coupling between clients, and provides good support for evolution due to the easy evolvability of the tuple space itself.

Disadvantages. Disadvantages can include the scalability limits of the tuple space element and the limited types of interaction available between system elements.

Common Variants. A more specialized version of this style known as Blackboard organizes the clients so that they collaborate to use the shared data to solve a particular problem, reading intermediate results from the blackboard, processing them, and writing the results back for other clients to process further.

DESIGN PATTERNS AND LANGUAGE IDIOMS IN ARCHITECTURE

Although it's fairly clear how you can use architectural styles because they act as a source of proven architectural design ideas, it's not necessarily as clear how design patterns and language idioms fit into the architectural design process. Given that detailed design and coding isn't your key focus, how do design patterns and language idioms contribute to your main area of work?

The answer is that design patterns and language idioms are a very important written communication path from architects to software developers. It's crucial to communicate directly by leading the team and talking face-to-face, but there are also many situations where it's important to get design constraints and guidelines on paper so that everyone can understand and consider them thoroughly. Design patterns and language idioms are a perfect mechanism for communicating design advice and constraints to a development team.

EXAMPLE Here are some typical examples of using design patterns and language idioms.

Examples of Using Design Patterns

- If you are developing a system that requires internationalization, this is an important system-wide design constraint. In order to ensure the use of a common approach to internationalization across the systems' modules, adopt or define a design pattern that illustrates how this part of a module's implementation should be performed.

- Many database applications need to use specific approaches to locking (e.g., the choice of using optimistic or pessimistic locks depending on data integrity and concurrency needs). The locking approach to use in certain situations may be an important design constraint resulting from the architectural design. Where this is the case, use a design pattern to define how database locking must be implemented.

- The evolutionary needs of the system may require that new code can be easily introduced to handle new types of data. In order to guide the design process to achieve the required flexibility, you could suggest the use of relevant design patterns like Chain of Responsibility, Reflection, or Visitor to help explain to the developers concerned the type of flexibility you need.

Examples of Using Language Idioms

■ Many modern programming languages such as Java, C++, and C# include exception-handling facilities. These facilities can be used in a number of ways, so an important architectural constraint is to standardize the exception handling. Adopt or create a language idiom that defines how the programming language's exception-handling facilities should be used, and ensure that the idiom is used throughout the system.

■ To allow a system to be easily instrumented, it can be very useful for each element to be able to return a string containing its state so that this can be written to a debug log. This is possible in most programming languages, but the mechanism available and the best way to use it varies. You can standardize this across your system by defining or adopting an idiom to be used when implementing each system element.

■ Many languages have features that need careful use to avoid subtle problems creeping in later (such as the advice to override either both or neither of Java's equals() and hashCode() methods or the need to define a copy constructor in C++ to avoid problems when using object assignment). You can help make sure that such language-specific problems don't emerge with your system by working with your senior developers to define or adopt language idioms to provide guidance in potentially problematic areas.

The identification and capture of design patterns and language idioms that are important for your system would normally be part of the activity of creating the Development view and they are normally captured as part of the common design model in that view. Practically, because this documentation can be quite large, it usually makes sense to capture patterns and idioms as part of a development standards document referenced from the AD.

CHECKLIST

■ Have you considered existing architectural styles as solutions for your architectural design problems?

■ Have you clearly indicated in your AD where you have used architectural styles?

■ Have you reviewed likely sources for possible new styles, patterns, and idioms that may be relevant to your system?

- Do you understand the design forces addressed by the patterns you use and the strengths and weaknesses of each pattern?
- Have you defined patterns and idioms to document all important design constraints for your system?
- Have you considered using design patterns and idioms to provide design guidance where relevant?

SUMMARY

Architectural styles, design patterns, and language idioms (collectively known as *patterns*) are all ways to reuse proven software design knowledge, and all three are valuable during the architectural design process. Patterns provide a reusable store of knowledge, help develop a language for discussing design, and encourage standardization and generality in design.

Becoming familiar with a range of architectural styles helps you build your design vocabulary and provides you with a library of options to consider when you meet new architectural design problems. Styles can also form the basis for further refinement and the inspiration for entirely new solutions, as well as simply being design blueprints. A good selection of relevant architectural styles for information systems already exists, and part of an architect's training is getting to know these styles and the strengths and weaknesses of each.

Patterns and idioms also help expand your knowledge of proven design solutions for more detailed problems, but they also are a valuable mechanism for recording the design constraints and guidelines that are important to achieving architectural integrity in the system's implementation.

FURTHER READING

The original book on design patterns is *Design Patterns* [GAMM95], often referred to as the "Gang of Four" or "GoF" book, which is still a definitive source of basic design patterns. A good place to start reading about patterns from the perspective of an architect is Buschmann et al., *Pattern-Oriented Software Architecture* [BUSC96] (generally known as "POSA1"). Our definitions of style, pattern, and idiom come from this book. Shaw and Garlan [SHAW96] is one of the original descriptions of architectural styles.

The Pattern Languages of Program Design conference series [PLOP95–99] has produced a large number of design-level patterns during the years it has been running. These references present the results of pattern-writing workshops at the conferences and are a rich source of useful design patterns.

More recently, Fowler has lead the creation of a book [FOWL03] containing a large number of patterns found in enterprise information systems that are likely to be of use to most information systems architects. Another recent book that contains a very valuable set of patterns focusing on the deployment aspects of large information systems is Dyson and Longshaw [DYSO04].

There are too many books of language idioms to list here, but one of the originals is Coplien's book of C++ idioms [COPL91], while more recent examples include Bloch [BLOC01] for Java.

A fair number of Web sites have appeared that contain design patterns. The speed of evolution of Web-based information sources makes it futile to attempt to present a list here, but a few of the original pattern resources are the Hillside Group, which organizes the Pattern Languages of Program Design conferences (www.hillside.net), and the patterns area of Ward Cunningham's C2 Wiki site (http://c2.com/cgi-bin/wiki?PatternIndex).

12

PRODUCING
ARCHITECTURAL MODELS

As an architect, you face the twin challenges of developing an architectural solution that effectively balances the needs of stakeholders and communicating the important details of that solution to the people who will finance, build, operate, and use it. Because we can't build the real computer system as part of the architecture definition process—just as a building architect can't construct a real house, office complex, or skyscraper while designing the building—we have to find ways to represent and analyze the system's salient features so that our different classes of stakeholders can understand them. We call these representations *models*.

 DEFINITION A **model** is an abstract or simplified representation of some aspects of an architecture, the purpose of which is to communicate those aspects of the system to one or more stakeholders.

We use models to help us cope with our inherent difficulty in coming to grips with complex concepts or ideas. An effective model, as we shall see, brings out the important aspects of an architecture while hiding unimportant distractions.

To help us put models in context within the architecture definition process, let's remind ourselves of the relationships between the main elements of the process.

- An architecture is documented in an *architectural description* (AD).
- The AD consists of one or more *views* of the architecture. (It may also include other elements, such as principles, standards, and dictionaries,

which lay the architectural foundations.) For example, an AD may include a Functional view, a Concurrency view, and a Deployment view.

- The contents of each view are based on a *viewpoint*. For example, the contents of an Operational view are based on the templates, patterns, and guidelines in the Operational viewpoint.

- Each view consists of one or more *models*. A model is a way to represent some of the salient features of an architecture that pertain to the view. For example, an Information view may include an entity-relationship model, a data ownership model, and a state transition model.

- Applying a *perspective* may lead to changes to existing models or to the creation of one or more secondary architectural models that allow a better understanding of the architecture's ability to exhibit a particular quality property. For example, the Security perspective usually involves the creation of a threat model in order to understand the security threats the system faces.

We can see from these relationships that models are central to the architecture definition process because they describe the key aspects of the system being designed. With this central role that models play in mind, let's explore how architects use models during architecture definition.

WHY MODELS ARE IMPORTANT

Although modeling isn't necessarily the most important thing that architects do, the models we create are probably the most important elements of our ADs. There are four primary reasons why we build models as part of the software development process.

1. Models help us *understand* the situations we are modeling. Building a model brings precision to our description and focuses us on the most important elements of the situation.
2. Models act as a medium for *communication*, helping us explain our thinking to others. Models reduce the amount of information the reader needs to understand, and their structure guides the reader through the information.
3. Models help us *analyze* situations by allowing us to isolate key elements and understand their interrelationships. Then we can reason about some aspect of the situation being modeled and draw conclusions about its properties.
4. Models help us *organize* our processes, teams, and deliverables as a result of the structures they reveal in the situation being modeled.

The key skill the model builder uses to achieve these benefits is **abstraction**, the process of suppressing unnecessary detail. By removing such detail from our models, we allow our stakeholders and ourselves to focus on the most important aspects of our architecture. A good model can help stakeholders understand an architecture they might not understand otherwise.

While models are certainly important to software architects, the idea of modeling isn't a new one and in fact has been with us since classical times. The ancient Greek astronomer Ptolemy taught that a central Earth was orbited by the sun, moon, planets, and stars. We now know that Ptolemy's model was wrong, but it was good enough to predict the motion of heavenly bodies to reasonable accuracy. In Renaissance times, the Polish astronomer Copernicus created the more accurate heliocentric model, in which the Earth revolved around the sun. One hundred and forty years later, Sir Isaac Newton set forth his laws of gravity and motion in *Principia Mathematica*. Newtonian mathematics survived unchallenged until Einstein published his General Theory of Relativity in 1915.

Ptolemy, Copernicus, Newton, and Einstein were all trying to describe the same phenomenon—the apparent motion of the sun, planets, and stars. None of their models were entirely correct (we'll stick our necks out here and say that someone will eventually successfully challenge Einstein, although probably not in our lifetimes!), but each of their models could be considered *good enough* for the purposes to which it was put. Indeed, Newtonian mechanics is still adequate for all but the most specialized applications even today. The lesson from these famous attempts at modeling the physical world is that no model is perfect, but even an imperfect model can provide us with useful information about the reality it is modeling. Martin Fowler captures this succinctly in his book *Analysis Patterns* when he says, "Models are not right or wrong, they are more or less useful."[1] We express this principle as follows.

PRINCIPLE Every architectural model is an approximation of reality. In other words, it is only partially accurate and partially complete.

The trick with a successful model is to make it *good enough* to achieve the purpose you have created it for, whether communicating important information to your stakeholders, analyzing a system quality, or understanding an architectural structure. This is hard, in particular because you often don't have much time to do it—the process of architecture definition is not usually allocated much time in development projects—and the situation you are trying to model may be complex, difficult, or new to you or your stakeholders.

---

1. [FOWL97, p. 2].

Remember that your models will be refined as part of the specification and design process. A rough-and-ready model that is produced early in the project and becomes established and familiar to the team over time may be more useful than something considered more fully that appears too late.

STRATEGY   Match the complexity and detail of your architectural models to the interests and skill level of your audience, the time in which you have to produce the models, and (most importantly) the way they will be used.

As a general rule, simple models are more useful in presentations to non-technical stakeholders or early in the architectural analysis to bring out some key features, while more sophisticated models are more useful as analysis, communication, and comprehension tools for you and other technical stakeholders, such as software developers.

EXAMPLE   An insurance company that has grown by acquisition has, as a consequence, a large number of systems that are connected together using a jumble of hard-to-maintain, point-to-point interfaces. Although a long-term goal of the company is to replace these systems, budget constraints mean that this may not be done for a number of years. In the meantime, someone has proposed replacing the point-to-point interfaces with a hub-and-spoke messaging infrastructure.

The architect develops some fairly sophisticated architectural models that include technology and application adapters, a message-switching hub, heterogeneous interconnectivity, and data-driven conversion rules. This has allowed her to analyze and understand the necessarily complex candidate architecture; however, she is having a hard time explaining the benefits of the proposed new architecture to the business stakeholders.

The problem is that the mass of technical detail hides the essential simplicity of the concept. The architect develops another model that fits on a single page and illustrates graphically how the current tangle of interfaces will be replaced by an architecture that is cheaper to manage, more easily adapted for new information flows or new applications, and more reliable and also suffers from fewer data quality issues. This model is far more successful with the business stakeholders.

Although producing quick back-of-an-envelope models can be helpful, you shouldn't use this strategy as an excuse for compromising the validity, consistency, and correctness of your important models—particularly ones that will be used later as a basis for the system design. Omitting details from models can lead to the dangerous situation where stakeholders believe that problems have been resolved, but in fact they are just hidden.

STRATEGY Ensure that your audience is aware of any simplifications and approximations in your model and the impact of these on their understanding of the solution.

Types of Models

When we think of an architectural model, most of us picture in our minds some sort of diagram supported by definitions of the elements it contains. However, there are many other types of models, and it is useful to broadly classify them as formal *qualitative* or *quantitative* models or informal qualitative models that we term *sketches*.

Qualitative Models

Qualitative models are analogous to the scale models and blueprints produced by building architects and structural engineers to define the structure of a new building and show how it will look in its environment. They aim to present the essence of the thing being modeled—its form and features—rather than to predict its measurable qualities. Qualitative models are extremely important to the architect and are used throughout the system lifecycle, from the early stages of architecture definition while ideas are being crystallized to late in the lifecycle when detailed aspects of the system's design need to be clarified.

DEFINITION Qualitative models illustrate the key structural or behavioral elements, features, or attributes of the architecture being modeled.

Qualitative models form the main content of the views within the AD and are also important outputs of some perspectives (such as the Security perspective mentioned earlier).

In our context, the most common forms of qualitative models are the various sorts of diagrammatic architecture models, such as a functional structure model or an information model, although we group other types under this classification, such as mock-ups, prototypes, and simulations. These all, to some extent, try to show the stakeholders how the system will look when it is built.

Historically, qualitative models have tended to be less formal than quantitative ones—in other words, they tend to adhere less strictly to rules of representation and layout—largely because the accepted rules for presenting such models (the *modeling languages*) have been on the whole weak or nonexistent. This situation is changing, however, with the advent of modeling languages such as the UML providing a standard way to represent many types of static and dynamic modeling elements. (We'll discuss this further in the Modeling Languages section.)

To get the best out of your models, therefore, you should aim for rigor, clarity, and consistency. If the modeling language you are using is insufficient for your needs, you should establish your own conventions, such as the standardized use of shape or color to represent different types of architectural element in diagrams, and stick to them faithfully in your models.

STRATEGY   Select a modeling language for your qualitative models, extend it if necessary, and follow it strictly. Make sure to provide a key or other explanation so that your audience understands the notation and conventions you are following.

Some of your models, particularly early or overview models, may be aimed at a mixed audience of business and technology stakeholders. Sometimes models are produced in response to a specific political need within an organization, such as support for a business case, in which case the models will need to fulfill a very specific set of objectives (such as accentuating the financial benefits of a new architecture in the insurance company example presented earlier).

Creating a model for both business and technology stakeholders is probably the hardest scenario you must handle. Such mixed models usually need to be less formal and rigorous than the ones aimed at more specialized groups of stakeholders. They may need to use a range of notations or none at all, and they may have to omit details the audience finds confusing—or conversely, drill down into details at certain points to highlight particular features. You can often deal with such scenarios by using a less formal type of qualitative model, a *sketch*, which we'll discuss shortly.

Quantitative Models

Quantitative models are analogous to the mathematical models of a building produced by structural and building services engineers to establish the physical characteristics of the structure, such as the required thickness of its structural elements or the number of people who will be able to comfortably enter or exit the building at peak times. The output of quantitative models is a set of metrics that predicts the behavior or other characteristics of the system. Quantitative models usually have a mathematical or statistical basis.

DEFINITION Quantitative models make statements about the measurable properties of an architecture, such as performance, resilience, and capacity.

Because they deal with system qualities instead of structures, quantitative models are usually created by applying a perspective, rather than by following the guidance in a viewpoint.

EXAMPLE A mathematical model of the capacity of a system to respond under load would represent the utilization of a hardware component by using this formula:

utilization = transaction throughput × busy time per transaction

By analyzing the utilization of hardware components, we can identify potential bottlenecks—heavily used components that slow system response—and see the effect of system changes on performance. (In fact, queuing theory, which is much more sophisticated than this example shows, can predict system response times to a reasonable degree of accuracy.)

Quantitative analysis such as capacity planning usually requires either sophisticated mathematical ability or the use of mathematical modeling tools. We return to this subject in Chapter 25 when we discuss the Performance and Scalability perspective.

Effective quantitative models are often time-consuming to create and validate, so unless you have the luxury of a lengthy architecture definition phase, your quantitative models, if you produce any at all, may have to be rough approximations. In the worst case, you may not have time to do any more than to establish confidence that your architecture will work and to understand its characteristics at a high level. However, this confidence-building work can be valuable, especially where there is uncertainty or you are breaking new ground, and such models produced early in the lifecycle can provide a useful basis on which to build more complete and accurate models later, if required.

In some cases, of course, critical quality requirements for a system make quantitative models essential. For example, if you are designing some sort of server or service-providing system for which good throughput and scalability are crucial, the creation of a performance model will be a key architectural task. In such cases, the priority of the important quantitative modeling tasks will need to be raised to the level such that sufficient time is allocated for them.

Sketches

A third kind of commonly used architectural model is a sketch, which is an informal qualitative diagrammatic model. Sketches are analogous to the artist's impressions created to help people imagine the impact of a new building without them having to understand all of the details of its structure. Sketches are inherently *informal*, by which we mean that they often incorporate diagramming elements from a range of modeling languages and methodologies—the UML, entity-relationship modeling, and so on—while strictly adhering to the rules and conventions of none of them. Sketches often make use of icons, graphics, and pictures to convey their meaning. We separate sketches from formal qualitative models to avoid any confusion between an erroneous or partially completed formal model and a deliberately informal sketch.

DEFINITION A **sketch** is a deliberately informal graphical model, created in order to communicate the most important aspects of an architecture to a nontechnical audience. It may combine elements of a number of modeling notations as well as pictures and icons.

Although they sound rather frivolous, sketches are a useful way to help your stakeholders, particularly nontechnical ones, understand the essence of your architecture. Sketches are often used during the inception phases of a system development project to explain the key features to the wider community. (This process is variously known as evangelizing or socializing the architecture.) You can also use sketches later in the development process to provide accessible, easily comprehensible overview models for less technical stakeholders in situations where the primary architectural models would be difficult for them to understand.

The inherent danger when using sketches is that their informal nature can easily introduce ambiguity into an AD and lead to confusion and misunderstanding. If a primary architectural model starts life as a sketch, you should aim to replace or reinforce it by more formally specified models as soon as you can.

MODELING LANGUAGES

Architecture Description Languages

An architecture description language (ADL) is a special-purpose notation for the sorts of models used to define the architecture of a computer system. The benefit of using an ADL is that it has been specifically designed for the creation of models at an architectural level of detail. By contrast, most general-purpose modeling notations are designed to represent much more detailed programming language structures. The architectural focus of an ADL means that you can use it to explain the architecturally significant aspects of your architecture without getting bogged down in details that are more appropriate to design work.

A number of ADLs have been proposed by research groups around the world, such as Carnegie-Mellon University, Siemens Research, and Software Research International. Some of the better-known ADLs include Aesop, UniCon, and xADL, but all of the ADLs that we are aware of are still in the research domain rather than in the mainstream. This means there is a shortage of familiar, functionally rich tools that support the use of ADLs, and your stakeholders are unlikely to understand the notation and the significance of the language elements.

The Unified Modeling Language

An alternative to using an ADL is to use a general-purpose modeling language, adapting and specializing it to suit your needs. Of the many standard notations that can be used in an AD, the most prevalent is probably the UML. As defined in the standard, the UML is "a graphical language for visualizing, specifying, constructing, and documenting the artifacts of a software-intensive system."[2] The intention behind the language is to encapsulate best practices in software design into a standard yet extensible notation. The UML provides a number of standard diagramming notations, such as use cases, class diagrams, sequence diagrams, and activity diagrams. In addition, the UML has a number of mechanisms, such as stereotyping, which allow modelers to tailor or extend the language to suit their circumstances.

The UML has some specific advantages, including the sophistication of some of its notations and its flexibility and extensibility. It is widely used, and most likely your technical stakeholders will have no trouble understanding it (although some of the more complex notations may be hard for your business stakeholders to follow). Many people are working to apply the UML to ADs and to improve its ability to be used as an ADL.

Other Modeling Languages

There are a number of domain-specific modeling languages, such as entity-relationship models for modeling data. We discuss these in more detail in Parts III and IV.

---

2. "OMG Unified Modelling Language Specification," version 1.5, p. xxviii. Accessed in January 2005 at www.omg.org/uml.

GUIDELINES FOR CREATING EFFECTIVE MODELS

Models can be expensive artifacts to produce, and it is easy to spend a great deal of time and effort creating and maintaining them. You need to be sure that your models serve a definite purpose in your AD and are effective for the uses you intend. Some helpful guidelines to follow when creating models are outlined in this section.

Model Purposefully

Make sure that every model you create has a well-defined purpose; if you're not sure what the goals of a particular model are, don't create it. Without a clear purpose for a model, it is unclear what level of detail, completeness, and formality the model should exhibit.

EXAMPLE Let us imagine that you need to consider the possible deployment options for your system. An initial deployment model created to explore deployment candidates is likely to be incomplete and at a relatively shallow level of detail. The goal of the model is simply to allow you and a few key developers to consider the options and tradeoffs involved in running your system across a number of different machines.

In contrast, if the goal is to form a basis for deployment planning and software dependency analysis, your deployment model will need to be much more detailed and reasonably complete in order for it to meet those goals. Otherwise, important aspects of deployment or software platform dependencies are likely to be overlooked. A much more thorough modeling exercise will be required to complete this model compared with the previous one because, although both models are modeling system deployment, they have quite different goals.

As you create and refine a model, continually consider its intended use so that you can create a model that will be effective at meeting its particular goals.

Address an Audience

Because different audiences often need quite different types of models or different presentations of the same model, you must also be clear about who the model's intended audience is.

EXAMPLE The information structure of a system could be represented at two different levels of detail, depending on the audience.

The system's acquirers and assessors will be interested in the information stored and processed by the system, but at a summary level where they are considering types of information rather than individual business entities.

The system's users and developers will be interested in the information stored and processed, but they will also want to know the details of the individual business entities and their attributes. The users want to be sure that the information they need is present, and the software developers need to have this level of information in order to build the system.

If a model is not targeted to a well-defined audience, there is a real danger that it will simply not be reviewed and analyzed because its readers do not feel it is relevant to them. In the example just presented, if you give a detailed data model to acquirers and assessors, they may dismiss it as "irrelevant technical detail," while users and developers may ignore a summary model because they consider it to be "too high level."

When you have identified your audience, consider the interest they have in the model, the level of detail they are likely to want, and the kinds of notation they are capable of understanding easily. This will help you develop a model that its intended audience will find useful and accessible.

The most challenging situations occur when you need to create models that are of interest to a number of different audiences (such as functional models that often have value for both software developers and the system's acquirers). In these cases, you will need to consider whether it is possible to create a single model that will be of use to all of the members of the potential audience. Often this simply isn't possible, and you will be forced to create a number of different but closely related models in order to address your different audiences (e.g., using sketches of more complex models for less technical audiences). In such cases, clearly define which model is the primary source of information and which one is derived so that you know how to resolve any inconsistencies that may occur.

Abstract Carefully

As we described at the beginning of the chapter, abstraction is the technique of omitting insignificant detail from a model or design in order to better communicate its important ideas. A key skill of modelers is achieving an appropriate and effective level of abstraction in their models.

As Ptolemy and the Greek philosophers understood, the real world is extremely complicated, and it is all too easy to be distracted from our analysis by masses of irrelevant detail. However, the Greeks also realized that we can exclude such detail from consideration without significantly affecting the accuracy of our conclusions. Indeed, it is not possible, even with the sophisticated science of the twenty-first century, to include everything in our models of the world around us.

EXAMPLE Structured development methods from the 1980s such as Structured Analysis and Design Technique (SADT) or Yourdon refer to **logical models**, which capture the essence of a system in an abstract model, without worrying about the real system elements with which it will be implemented. Once we are confident that we understand what the system will do and how it will work, we can develop a corresponding **physical model**, which is much less abstract and depicts actual hardware and software elements.

Logical models are often (though not exclusively) aimed at nontechnical classes of stakeholders, such as acquirers and users, while physical models are of most interest to builders, maintainers, and system administrators. (Indeed, the qualifiers "business" and "technology" are often used in place of "logical" and "physical," respectively.)

The dictionary definition of *abstraction* is "the act of taking away," which gives us a clear lead of how we should go about doing it. In particular, we should be clear that *abstract* does not mean "woolly" or "vague"—if anything, an abstract model may be more precise and rigorous than a more concrete one.

The key to achieving the right level of abstraction in a model is the ability to spot the essential elements as opposed to irrelevant detail. What is relevant, of course, varies hugely according to circumstances, the purpose of the model, and the needs and abilities of any interested stakeholders, so determining what to include in a model can be a pretty subjective decision.

Choose Descriptive Names

The names of elements in a model can have a significant impact on its effectiveness for communication. Your stakeholders' understanding of a model will be colored by the names of the model elements because of assumptions they draw from particular words. It is also important to choose good names because names tend to be very "sticky": Once a name has been understood and discussed, it becomes part of the common language for a project and so is very difficult to change, even if it isn't a very good name.

When initially creating a model, it is easy to give elements misleading or ambiguous names because you are still trying to understand the role and responsibilities of each element. This makes it important to keep revisiting names as you develop the model to ensure that the element names you finally choose are accurate and meaningful, helping readers of the model to easily grasp its fundamental structure and the role of each element within it.

Define Your Terms

A particular problem with graphical modeling notations is the tendency to draw the diagram that represents the structure of the model and then consider the model complete. Of course, the model isn't complete because none of the symbols on the diagram have really been defined, and the model is very open to misinterpretation. This problem isn't limited just to models created with graphical notations; it is quite common to encounter quantitative models (e.g., spreadsheet-based performance models) that are very difficult to interpret due to missing definitions of the various elements and relationships captured in the model.

As you develop a model, be sure to spend enough time carefully defining all of its elements so that their meanings, roles, and mappings to the real world are all clear and not open to different interpretations.

Aim for Simplicity

The simpler a model is, the easier it will be to use and the more likely its audience will find it effective. However, if a model is too simple, it will also fail because it no longer represents the essential features that interest the audience. You must aim for a balance somewhere between simplifying a model so far that it is no longer a valid and effective description and overcomplicating it to the point that the model is difficult to use and maintain.

Most models start out being simple and well structured, but as more detail is added and more special cases are considered, their complexity often increases significantly. Increasing a model's complexity quickly reduces its effectiveness for communication and analysis.

As your model develops and becomes more detailed and complex, continually review it yourself and ask others to do the same, in order to assess its effectiveness. If a model becomes too complex to use easily, consider replacing it with a number of simpler, related models that contain the same information but in a more accessible form.

Use a Defined Notation

Nearly all models use some form of notation to represent their content, whether it be a graphical notation, a symbolic or mathematical notation, or even program code—you have many choices. Most notations can be used in different ways, yet none of them will match your exact needs, so you will often have to extend them. The result of this is that when your stakeholders read a new model, it can be difficult to be sure what notation it is written in and what the notation means.

Without a clearly defined notation, the readers of your model must rely on their intuition and your explanation and commentary to interpret the model. The difficulty of interpreting the notation can easily become a barrier to understanding.

For every model you create, be sure to define the notation you use carefully, so that stakeholders have no doubts about its meaning and can focus on the content of the model, rather than struggling with its representation. Even with informal models like sketches, define your notation so that the sketch can be interpreted even when you are not available to explain it.

Validate Models

Models are an approximation of reality. This is what makes them valuable, allowing us to focus on important details to understand, communicate, or analyze, but it is also a potential weakness because you can never be sure whether the approximations you made have rendered the model invalid.

This aspect of models means that it is important that you continually validate your structural models for consistency and practicality and your analytical models for correspondence to the real world. You can do this via expert review, technical prototyping, and checks of your model against the real world. The important point is to validate your models often enough and thoroughly enough to be confident that they will be useful in their intended roles.

Keep Models Alive

Things change during a software development project: Requirements come and go, new constraints emerge, and priorities change. This potential for continual change is something you have to deal with in order to deliver effective systems that meet the real needs of your stakeholders.

The need to absorb changes means that you cannot expect a model developed at the start of a project and left unchanged to still reflect reality by the time the system is delivered. The challenge you face is that if your models stop reflecting reality, they soon stop being used and "die."

In order to avoid the premature demise of your models, it is important to regularly update them so they will continue to be relevant to system development. Although you do not want the maintenance of models to become a major burden that slows the project, you need to get the balance right by investing enough time and effort to keep them relevant. Scheduling a small amount of routine model maintenance activity into your weekly plans can be a useful aid for achieving this.

AGILE MODELING TECHNIQUES

Agile modeling (AM) is an approach to modeling that embraces and extends many of the points we make in this chapter. AM is based on the recognition that models are only an approximation of an ever-changing reality and therefore encourages the development of models that are just good enough. While AM applies to any of the analytical phases of software development—requirements gathering, designing, even building and testing—it is of particular interest to architects because the modeling we do is often time-constrained and must therefore be rigorously prioritized.

AM does not particularly concern itself with modeling languages per se but rather defines a set of values, principles, and practices that help you become a more effective modeler. It focuses on effective communication with stakeholders, simple solutions, early and regular feedback, and benefits gained through the knowledge of others. It defines a number of practices for effective modeling, such as developing multiple models in parallel and modeling in small increments. These principles and practices can be applied to a wide range of software projects, whether or not they are following more general agile development techniques.

You can obtain more information on AM from the Agile Alliance (see the Further Reading section at the end of this chapter).

CHECKLIST

- For each model you have produced, ask yourself the following questions.
  - Does the model have a clear purpose and audience?
  - Is the model going to be understood by its audience (business and technical stakeholders, as appropriate)?
  - Is the model complete enough to be useful?
  - Is the model as simple as possible while still being detailed enough for its purpose and audience?
  - Have you clearly defined the notation(s) used in the model?
  - Is the model well formed, that is, does it conform to the rules of the modeling language you are using?

- Do model elements have meaningful names and definitions?
- Is the model internally consistent and consistent with other models?
- Does the model have a level of abstraction appropriate to the problem to be solved and the expertise of the stakeholders?
- Does the model have the right level of detail? Is it sufficiently high-level to bring out the key features of the architecture? Does it present enough detail for a specialist audience?
- Have you provided a definition of the terminology and conventions used in the model?
- Does your model have appropriate scope? Are the boundaries clear?
- Is the model accompanied by an appropriate level of supporting documentation?
  - For quantitative models, does the model have sufficient rigor (mathematical basis) and an appropriate degree of complexity?

SUMMARY

The most important parts of any AD—and often the only things to be produced—are its models. Models are a way to represent the salient features of the system and to communicate these to stakeholders. A good model can make all the difference when helping stakeholders understand your architecture. The AD consists of a collection of views, and each view consists of a collection of models (plus other elements such as principles, standards, and dictionaries).

There are three broad classes of models, two formal and one informal. The two classes of formal models are *qualitative models* (which illustrate the key structural or behavioral elements of the system) and *quantitative models* (which make statements about measurable aspects of the system). Both are useful, although architects typically focus on qualitative models because there often isn't enough detailed information available to do any reliable quantitative analysis. The informal models are known as *sketches* and are used primarily for communication with less technical stakeholders.

A model is only an approximation of reality, and the architect must always be aware of its simplifications and approximations (and make stakeholders aware of these also).

FURTHER READING

Numerous books cover specific modeling languages, particularly the UML, and more general topics such as entity-relationship modeling, object-oriented modeling, security modeling, and performance modeling. We cite several relevant books in Parts II and III.

You can obtain information on AM from the following places.

- Agile Alliance (www.agilealliance.org)
- Ambler's site, which is devoted to it (www.agilemodeling.com)
- Ambler's book on the topic [AMBL02].

You can obtain the best and most up-to-date information on ADLs by searching the Internet.

13

CREATING THE
ARCHITECTURAL DESCRIPTION

If you follow the architecture definition process that we describe in this book, you will end up with a wide collection of material that shapes, informs, and describes your architecture: scope and context definitions, constraints, principles, requirements, scenarios, and, most important, a set of architectural views, each comprising one or more architectural models. Some of this material will be vitally important to the proper understanding of your architecture, some of it will provide useful details, and some of it may be more appropriate for other software development documentation such as the requirements definition or design specification.

Your challenge is to gather and organize the relevant material into a coherent, consistent, and complete description of the architecture, its essential features and benefits, and its underlying philosophy in a way your stakeholders can understand and accept. Let's revisit a definition we first presented in Part I.

 DEFINITION An **architectural description (AD)** is a set of products that documents an architecture in a way its stakeholders can understand and demonstrates that the architecture has met their concerns.

The purpose of the AD is to communicate the architecture to all stakeholders, throughout the system's lifetime from conception to decommissioning. The AD establishes a common understanding of the required functionality and quality properties of the entire system and ensures that the right choices are made about aspects such as scope, performance, resilience, and security.

Most important of all, the AD is often a *selling* document. It may have to present, explain, and justify ideas that are unfamiliar to its readership; convince a skeptical audience that your architectural choices are the correct ones;

and persuade stakeholders that the risks your solution brings are outweighed by its benefits.

Given all of the things you have to address in your AD, there is a temptation to bury your stakeholders under a mountain of detail. This is a mistake— the AD is intended to be a high-level view that addresses the *key* concerns and sets a stake in the ground for the rest of the project. The AD should be crisp, concise, and to the point. Otherwise, no one will read it; or if they do read it, they won't understand it; or even if they do understand it, they will not grasp the rationale behind or the implications of your key architectural decisions.

For example, UML use cases are one way to capture and annotate interactions between a computer system and its environment. Diagrams and text represent the participants (known as *actors*), the functional units, and the interactions among them. Of all the UML notations, use cases are probably the most easily understood by both technical and business stakeholders.

However, use cases are by their nature fairly local or atomic—in other words, they typically address a single interaction or a small group of related interactions. Because many architectures are so complex, an architectural model could comprise hundreds or even thousands of use cases. Although each individual use case is easy to understand, it is not possible to draw an overall picture from such a large number of individual models. Important or fundamental aspects of the system get lost in this mass of detail.

Architecturally, use cases are probably more effectively used to elaborate specific aspects of the system's functionality or to present a small selection of key interactions, rather than to represent the entire system.

PROPERTIES OF AN EFFECTIVE ARCHITECTURAL DESCRIPTION

An effective AD must balance six desirable properties: *correctness*, *sufficiency*, *conciseness*, *clarity*, *currency*, and *precision*, as shown in Figure 13–1. We discuss each of these in the following subsections.

Correctness

The most important quality of your AD is that it be right. "Right" is, of course, a subjective term, but we can define two correctness criteria that your AD must meet.

1. It must correctly represent the needs and concerns of your stakeholders. You can do this explicitly, by reflecting some of these needs back to stakeholders in the form of architectural principles, and implicitly, by presenting the features of your chosen solution. (In the latter case, you

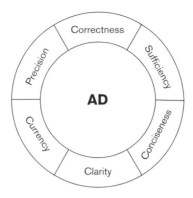

FIGURE 13-1 QUALITIES OF AN EFFECTIVE ARCHITECTURAL DESCRIPTION

need to bring out these features in some way so that the stakeholders can recognize them.)

2. It must also correctly define an architecture that will meet those needs. There are two further aspects to this: "Does the selected architecture meet the stakeholder needs?" and "Have we documented it correctly?"

Achieving this objective is, in theory anyway, straightforward—present the AD to your stakeholders, and ask them, "Is this what you need?" We talk about this in more detail in Chapter 14.

Sufficiency

Your AD must contain enough detail to answer the important questions about the architecture. In our experience, this is where most ADs tend to fall short. The structural and functional aspects of the architecture are usually addressed, but other issues may not be considered—at least not explicitly. If you haven't written down something important about your architecture because "everybody knows that," you do not have a complete AD.

If you don't include enough information in your AD, you are effectively *postponing* architectural decisions until later in the system development lifecycle. The decisions will be made anyway, but the people who make them won't have the right information, and the decisions (or their impact) won't become apparent until it's too late to do anything about them.

Of all the properties that make an effective AD, sufficiency is probably the most subjective. Your challenge is to focus on making the architecturally significant decisions and documenting them in your AD, leaving the rest to the skill and judgment of your developers.

STRATEGY Clearly document your key architectural decisions in the architectural description, and provide the rationale for any decisions that are contentious or had substantial alternatives.

If you have worked hard to identify and engage your stakeholders and have captured and agreed with all of their requirements, ensuring sufficiency should be almost automatic. If a stakeholder need is not explicitly or implicitly reflected in some element of the architecture or has not been documented in the AD, you may have a gap.

A good way to ensure sufficiency is to select appropriate viewpoints and views and to apply appropriate perspectives, as we discuss in Parts III and IV.

Conciseness

To help stakeholders grasp the key features of your architecture, your AD should focus on its important elements—in other words, the things that are *architecturally significant*—and not spend too much time on the detail.

Unfortunately, the distinction between what is and isn't architecturally significant can be very subjective. A single context diagram with a couple of pages of description is not enough; a 200-page physical data model is probably too much. You need to be somewhere in the middle. Exactly where will depend on a number of factors.

- *The capabilities and experience of your stakeholders*: If they are comfortable with the idea of stakeholder needs shaping the architecture, have a clear idea of their requirements, and are accustomed to expressing them, you may not need to put much detail into your AD.
- *The extent to which you are mandating new or unfamiliar technology*: If the bleeding-edge element of your solution is significant, you will need to spend more time explaining in your AD what the new technology does, how it works, and how the system will use it.
- *The difficulty of the problem you are trying to solve*: If your system is functionally complex or has ambitious requirements for performance or scalability, for example, you may need to explain how your architecture will meet these requirements.
- *How much time and resources you have available to produce and gain acceptance for the AD*: If you have six months to define and build your system, it is pointless to spend five months producing a perfect AD.

If you don't determine the appropriate amount of material to include in your AD, your stakeholders won't have time to read it, and you risk having them miss something important. A lengthy AD is also much harder to maintain and keep current (see the discussion in the Currency subsection).

STRATEGY Restrict your architectural description to things that are architecturally significant, and tailor the level of detail to the skills and experience of your readership, the complexity of the problem and your solution, and the time you have available to produce the architectural description.

Striking the right balance between conciseness and depth largely comes down to the experience and judgment of the architect. However, one thing is certain—a short document has a better chance of being read and understood than a very long and intricate one.

Clarity

The most challenging quality to achieve in your AD is its ability to be understood by all classes of stakeholders. At a minimum, each stakeholder should be able to understand those parts that are relevant to her.

Remember the dual purposes of the AD: to document the architecture in a way that stakeholders can understand and to demonstrate that the architecture has met their concerns. For technical stakeholders such as builders, this is fairly straightforward: They understand technology and are probably familiar with the notation (such as UML) you are using to represent it.

However, for nontechnical stakeholders, providing clarity in your AD is more of a challenge. Although most people have a basic, if vague, understanding of how computers work and what they can do, they will not appreciate the subtle ramifications of your architectural decisions without your help.

The good news is that nontechnical stakeholders require less of your AD in terms of depth and detail: just enough to grasp the main functional components and their high-level interactions. Nontechnical stakeholder concerns, as we have seen, focus more on the user experience and (indirectly) on system qualities such as response and availability. Also, terms like *database*, *server*, and even *program*, while not necessarily properly understood, are not as intimidating to the layperson as they once were.

STRATEGY Always consider your intended readership when writing parts of an architectural description, and tailor its content and presentation toward their skills, their knowledge, and the time they have available to read it.

In practice, you will aim different parts of your AD at different classes of stakeholders (indeed, that's part of what viewpoints are about). Your challenge is to make sure that these parts are all compatible with one another and with the overall design.

The physical presentation of your AD plays a big role in ensuring that stakeholders understand the aspects of the architecture that are relevant to them, grasp the significance of the architectural decisions that have been made, and are won over to its merits. Presentation is never a substitute for content, and some people are suspicious of documentation that comes across as too polished or glossy. However, good layout, clear use of language, and correct spelling and grammar will make your job of imparting architectural knowledge that much easier.

Currency

It is inevitable that your architecture will evolve over time. During development, you will find problems with your design or ways to improve it, or you may need to take on new technologies. These may result in changes to the architecture that must be reflected in the AD.

Once the architecture diverges from the AD, the AD starts to become worthless. It is no longer trusted and is no longer used as the definitive source of information about the architecture. However, you can't gauge the important properties and qualities of your architecture by inspecting source code. Your high-level, system-wide view would be lost among the detail.

The architecture will continue to evolve once your system goes live, although at a slower pace. The AD, which should be kept up-to-date with these changes as well, can play an important part later in assessing and evaluating proposed changes.

A smaller, more concise AD will, of course be easier to keep current, so this is another reason to keep your AD to a manageable size. An AD that includes too much detailed information will be in a constant state of change, while an AD that defines only the architecturally significant aspects of the system will be easier to keep current and relevant.

STRATEGY Think early in development about how the architectural description will be kept up-to-date throughout the life of the system, and try to ensure that development, operation, and support plans take this need into account.

Precision

The AD must describe the architectural structure of the system precisely, with sufficient detail to allow the system to be designed and implemented.

If you're not careful, precision can become the converse of conciseness: In other words, you can find yourself providing masses of details in your AD that are more appropriate to a design document. A number of techniques can help you here.

- Make use of abstraction and layering so that you describe things once rather than many times. (Refer to Chapter 12 for a discussion of these concepts.)
- Present detailed information in tables or lists rather than in ordinary text.
- Number requirements, principles, and other elements of the AD and refer to them by number.
- If you need to specify lower-level details, put them in appendices or separate documents rather than in the main body of the AD.
- Make plentiful use of diagrams to explain difficult concepts.
- Break down very large documents into several smaller ones by topic or by audience.

You may choose to divide your document by view—having one physical document for your Functional view, another for your Information view, and so on—or (more likely) by the type of stakeholder who will read it. In this case, you might have the following as parts of your AD:

- The benefits of the architecture extolled in an overview document aimed at the sponsor and senior management
- More functional detail in a document aimed at users
- The bulk of technical detail in one or more documents aimed at developers and other technical stakeholders

STRATEGY Aim for precision in your architectural description, but where this necessitates a large amount of detail, physically break the document into several smaller ones or put the details into appendices, so that the main document does not become too large.

GLOSSARIES

As an architect, your skills and experience—of both business and technology—tend to be, with exceptions, broad rather than deep. This means that you often end up asking your stakeholders what may seem like "obvious" questions: "What is an account?" "How does a bill of materials work?" "Why do you need to clear all your transactions at the end of the day?"

You may sometimes be surprised by the answers, and your stakeholders may find themselves thinking afresh about concepts they have taken for granted for years. You may find it valuable to capture your understanding in a glossary of terms (sometimes called a dictionary), to ensure that everyone is using the same definitions.

STRATEGY Include a glossary in your architectural description if terminology may be unclear to some readers. If possible, base the definitions on standard ones used in your organization or industry.

Glossaries have a more concrete benefit, too. As your analysis proceeds, they will feed directly into your models. Nouns translate easily into classes or entities, and verbs often translate into processes.

THE IEEE STANDARD

IEEE Standard 1471, *Recommended Practice for Architectural Description*, is one of the few—if not the only—formal standards covering the practice of software systems architecture. In its own words, it "addresses the activities of creation, analysis, and sustainment of architectures of software-intensive systems, and the recording of such architectures in terms of architectural descriptions."[1]

Clause 5 of the standard defines six recommended practices for documenting an architecture. An AD that conforms to these requirements (which include more detail than we present here) can be considered compliant with Standard 1471.

1. *Architectural documentation*: The AD must include standard control and context information, such as issue date and version, change history, and scope.

2. *Identification of stakeholders and concerns*: The AD must identify the stakeholders and their concerns (such as purpose, appropriateness, feasibility, and risks).

3. *Selection of architectural viewpoints*: The AD must identify the viewpoints used, explain the rationale for their selection, and define which viewpoint addresses each concern.

---

1. [IEEE00, p. i].

4. *Architectural views*: The AD must contain one or more views, each conforming to its corresponding viewpoint, with each view containing one or more models.

5. *Consistency among architectural views*: The AD must analyze consistency across views and record known inconsistencies.

6. *Architectural rationale*: The AD must include the rationale for choices made and describe the alternatives considered.

The motivation behind the standard is "to facilitate the expression and communication of architectures, and thereby lay a foundation for quality and cost gains through standardization of elements and practices for architectural description. . . . [I]t establishes a conceptual framework of concepts and terms of reference within which future developments in system architectural technology can be deployed."[2] If the architecture function in your organization is sufficiently mature, you should consider formal adoption of IEEE Standard 1471—and if you follow the recommendations of this book, that should not be too difficult.

CONTENTS OF THE ARCHITECTURAL DESCRIPTION

Because the experience and concerns of your stakeholders, the type and complexity of the problems you are trying to solve, and the time you have available for architecture definition vary from project to project, no two ADs are ever structured in the same way. It is difficult, therefore, to present a generic template for an AD. The contents listed in this section, while incorporating the documentation elements we discuss in this book and complying with IEEE Standard 1471, are a superset of what you are likely to produce in practice. Real-world ADs will differ from this template for a number of reasons.

- You may refer to other material (such as scope or requirements definitions) rather than summarizing it in the AD.

- You may not capture all views or apply all perspectives (you probably don't have time to do this even if you'd like to).

- You may choose to document some perspective enhancements and insights, such as more detailed security models, separately from the main document.

- Your AD may be produced by more than one person (especially if the system is large or has some complex features), which may necessitate some changes to the structure presented here.

---

2. [IEEE00, pp. 1–2].

With these caveats in mind, let's explore the different sections you may include in your ADs.

Document Control

The Document Control section clearly identifies individual versions of the AD. If there is more than one version (which will be the case on all but the simplest systems), effective document control is essential to ensure that everyone is working from the most up-to-date copy.

For the current version of the AD, Document Control normally contains the document version number, the document issue date, the document status, an overview of the changes since the previous version, document authorization, and commentary.

It is also common to include a version history (which summarizes the changes in each version, authorization, and so on) and any details on planned future versions of the AD. It may also be appropriate to include copyright, ownership, and confidentiality statements here.

Table of Contents

You can use the automated capabilities of your word processing software to generate the Table of Contents. You may want to briefly introduce the purpose and content of each main chapter, especially if your stakeholders are not familiar with this type of document.

Introduction and Management Summary

This section (which may also be called Executive Summary, Abstract, and so on) introduces the AD by doing some or all of the following:

- Describing the objectives of the AD
- Summarizing the goals of the system described
- Summarizing the scope and key requirements
- Presenting a high-level overview of the solution
- Highlighting the benefits of the solution, the risks in its implementation, and mitigation strategies

It is good practice to acknowledge your stakeholders and other sources of information here.

Depending on your audience, you may want to give an overview of the process you went through to produce the AD, particularly if there were a number of iterations, and describe the next steps (e.g., formal review of the AD).

Scope Definition

The Scope Definition section should itemize the following:

- The broad functional areas to be provided by the system
- The external interfaces of the system and the external systems that communicate via these interfaces, especially if they are complex or unusual
- Any systems to be decommissioned or modified
- Any data to be migrated into the new system

You may also want to include a context diagram and a list of principal exclusions (although by definition anything not listed in the Scope Definition section is out of scope).

Overview of Requirements and Concerns

If requirements are clearly captured and documented outside the AD, you may prefer to reference the existing documentation. Otherwise, include the following items.

- *Goals*: Briefly present the business and technology goals of the system—for example, "Reduce cost per transaction by 15%," "Streamline the ordering and fulfillment process, enabling better customer service," "Replace the legacy architecture with one that is more performant, resilient, and amenable to change," and so on.
- *Functional requirements*: List the requirements that define what the system must do. Wherever possible, requirements should be numbered (or otherwise clearly identified) and grouped by subject area. It is usually sufficient to present just a summary of these in the AD.
- *Required quality properties*: List the requirements that do not directly mandate functionality but describe how the system should work—typically covering system qualities such as performance, availability, and scalability. Again, these should be numbered and grouped by subject area.

General Architectural Principles

In this section, present the architectural principles that inform the architecture but don't fit naturally into any of the views—for example, "We buy and configure off-the-shelf software rather than build our own wherever possible."

Each principle should be numbered and should include rationale and implications. Wherever possible, tie the principles back to business drivers and forward to architectural decisions.

Views

Your AD can include sections on each of the views associated with the six viewpoints we describe in Part III. For example, the section on the Functional view could contain the following information.

- *View-specific architectural principles*: Present the architectural principles that inform the models in this view. Each principle should be numbered and should include rationale and implications, and wherever possible the principle should be tied back to business drivers and forward to architectural decisions.

- *View model(s)*: Present the models that make up the view. This includes enhanced and new models created as a result of applying perspectives. Models should be named and a brief description given of the notation and documentation conventions used (especially if these are nonstandard or extended).

- *Perspective improvements*: It may be appropriate to highlight some of the outcomes of applying perspectives to the view, namely:
  - Enhancements to view models (including new models created as a result of applying the perspective)
  - Perspective insights demonstrating that the architecture will meet its quality properties

    Alternatively, you may refer readers to an appendix for some or all of this information.

- *Application of scenarios*: Document the key scenarios that have informed the view models, here or in an appendix.

- *Commentary*: Include here any other general commentary appropriate to the view (e.g., advice and guidance to developers).

If included in the AD, sections for the Information view, the Concurrency view, the Development view, the Deployment view, and the Operational view would contain the same type of content as described here for the Functional view.

Quality Property Summary

As we described in Part I, applying a perspective leads to insights, improvements, and artifacts. Improvements (changes to view models) are documented in the section for the appropriate view. Include in this section the following:

- General insights that provide a better understanding of the system's ability to meet a required quality property
- Non-view-specific artifacts, that is, models and analyses that may be of lasting interest

It may be appropriate to provide an overview here and refer readers to an appendix for more details.

Important Scenarios

For each important scenario, record the initial system state and environment, the external stimulus, and the required and actual system behavior. Again, it may be appropriate to provide an overview here and refer readers to an appendix for more details.

Appendices

It is generally preferable to move detailed content into an appendix, which may be part of the main AD or even a separate document. This makes the important parts of the AD easier to digest but ensures that the details are not forgotten.

Almost anything can go into an appendix; here are some of the topics you may want to cover:

- References to other documents or sources of information
- A glossary of terms and abbreviations
- A stakeholder map (defining the key stakeholders, their areas of interest, key concerns, and so on)
- More detailed specification of scope, functional requirements, or quality properties

- A map between requirements and architectural features
- Explanation of any architectural styles, design patterns, and so on that you have used
- More detailed view models
- More detailed perspective models and insights
- More details on the application of scenarios
- Policies, standards, and guidelines
- Output from formal reviews of the AD
- Other supporting documentation

Consider the needs of your readership when writing the appendices. As with the rest of the AD, don't overburden them with a mass of detail that may be of little value.

CHECKLIST

- Are all key architectural decisions documented in the AD?
- Are there any key architectural decisions that you feel have yet to be made, and if so, what is your strategy for dealing with these?
- Does the AD strike an appropriate balance between conciseness and the other desirable properties (correctness, sufficiency, clarity, currency, and precision), especially given the skills and experience of your stakeholders?
- Do the sections of the AD aimed at a nontechnical audience (acquirers, users, and so on) avoid the overuse of technical jargon and define it wherever it appears?
- Do you know how the AD will be maintained once it has been accepted (during the development process and into live operation)?
- Have you reviewed the AD content suggested in this chapter (Table of Contents, Introduction and Management Summary, and so on) and included all of it that is appropriate?
- Does the presentation of the document conform to your corporate standards (if any) for such documents?
- Have you provided an accurate glossary of business or technical terms that may be unfamiliar to your readers?
- Have you considered conforming to IEEE Standard 1471 on your project or in your organization?

SUMMARY

Although every system has an architecture, not every system has an AD that effectively communicates the essence of the architecture to all of its stakeholders. A good AD will lay a solid foundation for the remaining system development work, while a poor AD may fail to address key concerns or may be ignored altogether. In this chapter, we described how you can ensure that your AD meets its goals.

An effective AD has six desirable properties: correctness, sufficiency, conciseness, clarity, currency, and precision. These properties can sometimes conflict with one another, so (as always) you have to achieve an effective balance.

Producing an AD that all stakeholders can understand is one of the greatest challenges you face. We reminded you to always consider the needs and capabilities of your readership when writing the AD. Glossaries are useful as aids for understanding and as input to more detailed modeling.

We presented a generic template for an AD that is a superset of what you are likely to produce in practice. Whichever sections you decide to include in your AD, it's important to keep the AD up-to-date during its lifetime.

Finally, in this chapter we explained the key features of IEEE Standard 1471, *Recommended Practice for Architectural Description*, and outlined its benefits.

FURTHER READING

The concept of an AD was formalized and standardized in *Recommended Practice for Architectural Description* [IEEE00].

Documenting Software Architectures [CLEM03], written by a team from the SEI, is a practitioner-oriented book that provides a great deal of useful information on writing ADs.

14

VALIDATING THE ARCHITECTURE

There is always a great sense of achievement associated with the completion of the first draft of an AD. Reaching this point normally means that you have identified possible solutions to most of the major challenges your system faces and that you have designed a candidate architectural structure for your system. However, at this point you don't actually know whether or not you have a workable architecture. Just as you don't know whether your software works correctly just because it compiles cleanly, you don't know whether your candidate architecture is sound until it has been tested, too. We term the process of testing possible architectures for a system **architectural validation**.

In the architectural validation process, you check whether you made the right architectural decisions during architecture definition and, in particular, whether you made appropriate tradeoffs between competing needs. The validation process should begin as soon as architectural decisions start to be made, and it doesn't end until a system that the stakeholders deem to be acceptable is delivered (which is the final, ultimate validation of the architecture).

Of course, conventional ADs aren't executable (in the way that a program is) and so can't be directly tested like a piece of software. However, there are a number of other useful techniques for "testing" an architecture that vary in cost, complexity, and formality, and each has its place and is appropriate in different situations and during different lifecycle stages. You will nearly always need to use a number of techniques during the system lifecycle in order to validate your architecture effectively.

Remember that although your opinion is important, you aren't the ultimate arbiter of whether or not the architecture is right. You have created the architecture to meet the needs of your stakeholders, and it is their endorsement you need. Also keep in mind as you read this chapter that architectural validation isn't a one-shot activity to be done at any one point in the lifecycle; it should be approached as a process of continual validation.

WHY VALIDATE THE ARCHITECTURE?

Let's start by considering in a little more detail why we should validate a candidate architecture as we create it. First, architectural validation is valuable because of the inevitable limitations of an AD.

- *Validating abstractions*: An AD (of the sort we talk about in this book) is an *abstraction of reality*. Many details aren't captured in the AD; if this weren't the case, the AD would lose much of its usefulness because it would be very hard to read. Validation will make sure that the abstractions you have made are reasonable and appropriate.

- *Checking technical correctness*: An AD is also *static* and can't be directly executed by a computer—it can't be tested in the same way that a piece of software can. As Bertrand Meyer has dryly noted, "Bubbles don't crash," meaning that it is easy to create models of software that look perfectly credible until someone tries to implement and test them. Only then may errors and inconsistencies become obvious, when the software fails.

Validation is also a useful process from a communication point of view.

- *Selling the architecture*: An architectural validation process can help sell your architecture to key stakeholders by showing them how it will meet their needs. Involving the stakeholders in the validation process can also help them understand the main tradeoffs that need to be made to meet the requirements and satisfy themselves that the right tradeoffs were chosen. For more technical stakeholders (such as systems administrators, testers, and developers), the validation process can act as a valuable communication vehicle, allowing them to thoroughly understand the architecture and feel some ownership of its development.

- *Explaining the architecture*: An interactive architectural validation process can often be the most effective way to engage many of the less technical system stakeholders, who may not want to read detailed ADs but need to have the key features of the architecture explained to them.

Finally, the software development process also benefits from architectural validation in a number of ways.

- *Validating assumptions*: The architectural design process involves making a lot of assumptions about a wide variety of subjects (such as priorities, speeds, space, the system's external environment, and so on). Each of the perspectives that guides design for a particular quality property aims to validate key assumptions as part of its process, but some assumptions may slip through the net. Architectural validation can guide this process and help ensure that key assumptions are tested before it is too late to change the resulting decisions.

- *Providing management decision points*: From a project management perspective, architectural validation can provide a natural framework for the key go/no-go decision points in the system development lifecycle, allowing important decisions about the system's viability to be made before too much money is spent. These project management decision points form a management decision framework that complements the technical design decision framework that results from using viewpoints and perspectives to guide architectural design.

- *Offering a basis for formal agreement*: Architectural validation can also provide the basis for formal agreement about the form of the system to be built. Using a validated AD as the basis for, say, a contract to create the software may be more effective than trying to use an initial requirements document for this purpose because of the deeper level of understanding that architecture definition and validation require.

- *Ensuring technical integrity*: Part of the architectural validation process involves ensuring compliance between the system that is built and the AD. This is an important check of the system's technical integrity and helps make sure that the right system is delivered.

In summary, architectural validation can be a valuable addition to the software development process right through the lifecycle and in particular can provide early insights into the strengths and weaknesses of various architectural options. Let's continue by considering the different types of techniques we can use for architectural validation.

VALIDATION TECHNIQUES

A number of approaches exist for validating a software architecture. They differ significantly in the cost, depth, and complexity of the validation performed, so it is important to choose the correct techniques for your particular situation.

Presentations

The simplest form of architectural validation is to present an informal explanation of the proposed architecture to stakeholders. However, simply presenting a candidate architecture to a group of stakeholders doesn't actually validate it. For any degree of validation to occur, you must carefully structure the presentation so that it engages the audience throughout and forces them to think deeply about the implications of what you are explaining.

At best, presentations can act as a useful communication and selling aid for the architecture and, at the same time, start the stakeholders thinking about the important issues. However, given the limited amount of analysis that a presentation usually allows, you should ensure that where you use presentations, you use them in conjunction with more sophisticated, rigorous techniques to achieve an effective overall evaluation.

ADVANTAGES

- Presentations are fairly quick to create and can be easily tailored to different audiences.
- A presentation is cheap and easy to do, with little or no attendee preparation required.
- You can gather feedback immediately from audience reaction and questions.

LIMITATIONS

- You get only a shallow level of analysis during a presentation meeting.
- The effectiveness of the approach relies heavily on the quality of the presentation materials, and it is easy to gain a false sense of security from a presentation that simply didn't engage the audience and make them analyze what they were hearing.
- The lack of attendee preparation usually results in a lack of time to reflect on the architecture and its strengths and weaknesses, which may result in the loss of valuable insights.

Formal Reviews and Structured Walkthroughs

Formal reviews can be an effective way to validate your AD with stakeholders, thus confirming that your understanding of their concerns is correct and allowing you to improve the design or the documentation based on their input. The formal review involves gathering a group of people to go through a document page by page, raise comments about it, discuss the concerns as a group, and agree on what actions need to be taken, if any. Formal reviews can be used for specifications or other written documents, as well as source code and other such material.

You should give each of the attendees a role before the review meeting.

- The *moderator* runs the meeting, records the actions accepted by the group, and arbitrates any disputes or disagreements.
- The *presenter*, usually the author of the work being reviewed, presents and explains it to the group. If possible, the presenter and moderator should be different people.

- The *reviewers* provide comments on the work being reviewed. Reviewers are sometimes given specific areas to consider, especially when the item under review is large or complex.

Send the item being reviewed to the reviewers a few days before the meeting, together with pointers to any background reading and instructions for the review. The moderator captures brief comments in a review record that is passed to the author after the review. The author makes the appropriate changes and returns the document to the moderator, who checks it, decides whether a second review is necessary, and signs off the review comments as having been implemented.

Minor comments (such as spelling or typographical errors) can usually be captured separately (e.g., on a marked-up copy of the document).

Structured walkthroughs are another way for a group of people to assess in detail a specification, design, or piece of code for correctness and conformance to requirements. As with formal reviews, this technique is an extremely useful method for validating a design and exposing potential weaknesses or gaps. A walkthrough usually involves stepping through one or more scenarios, exploring system behavior, and confirming that this behavior is as expected. Where problems are discovered, possible solutions can be explored by the group or put to one side for later discussion.

ADVANTAGES

- A formal review or walkthrough involves the participants much more deeply than a presentation and is likely to result in much more valuable insights.

LIMITATIONS

- A formal review or walkthrough is considerably more expensive to run than a presentation (mainly due to the cost of participant preparation).
- The results are highly dependent on the quality of preparation before the meeting.

Evaluation by Using Scenarios

Scenario-based architectural evaluation is a structured approach to evaluating how well an architecture meets stakeholder needs, in terms of the attributes (or qualities) that the architecture exhibits. The best-known scenario-based evaluation methods are probably the Architecture Tradeoff Analysis Method (ATAM) and the Software Architecture Assessment Method (SAAM), developed by the Software Engineering Institute (SEI). We describe ATAM in more detail later in this chapter.

The key concept underpinning these methods is a set of scenarios (i.e., particular situations that the system is likely to face during operation) that are important to the system's stakeholders and allow the system's properties to be estimated. Scenario-based approaches to validation contain five fundamental steps.

1. *Understand the requirements*: Review the requirements of the system again, making sure that they are well understood. Validation needs to be performed against the stakeholder requirements, and because people from outside the project usually perform an evaluation, it is important that they understand the key requirements thoroughly.

2. *Understand the proposed architecture*: As well as understanding the requirements, the evaluators need to understand the proposed architecture in enough detail to evaluate it thoroughly. They normally gain this knowledge by reading the AD and having the architecture presented to them by the architect responsible for the project.

3. *Identify prioritized scenarios*: A scenario-based evaluation method works by considering how well an architecture meets the needs of a particular scenario. Some scenarios are functional (such as "Web-site customer wishes to obtain duplicate receipt for transaction more than 6 months ago"), while others focus on a system quality (such as "During weekly consolidation processing, 400 online transactions per minute are received"). In order to ensure that the evaluation process is valid, the scenarios must reflect the interests and priorities of the stakeholders (rather than the interests of the evaluators), so the set should normally be developed in direct consultation with stakeholder representatives. The scenarios are usually prioritized (e.g., as high, medium, or low priority) to help focus attention on the more important ones during evaluation.

4. *Analyze the architecture*: The core of a scenario-based technique is the consideration of each scenario in turn, analyzing how well the architecture meets the needs of that particular situation. Doing this usually reveals possible weaknesses in the architecture, where the needs of important scenarios can't be met, and also tends to highlight places where there is conflict between different scenarios that could be comfortably met in isolation but cause problems when both need to be handled by the same system.

5. *Draw conclusions*: Having analyzed the architecture against the set of scenarios, the evaluators capture the results of the exercise in a report and draw some specific conclusions about the suitability of the architecture. If the proposed architecture cannot deal with particular scenarios or groups of scenarios, you must draw up a plan of action to address the problems.

Scenario-based techniques are not particularly complex or difficult to apply, and provided that the system is not too large or complex, the overall approach can be used effectively in an informal way. However, in more complex situations, it is important to use a more structured approach to keep control of the process and to ensure that the results are valid. Methods such as ATAM and SAAM are very valuable in these situations because they are based on a lot of existing experience and contain a lot of advice on managing the process.

ADVANTAGES

- Scenario-based approaches can provide a deep, sophisticated analysis of the strengths and weaknesses of a particular architectural approach.
- These methods lead to a more explicit understanding of the tradeoffs made in the architecture and can help explain the rationale to stakeholders.
- Scenario-based techniques help architecture teams understand the decisions they have made, why they made them, and their implications.

LIMITATIONS

- These approaches are considerably more complex and expensive to apply than simple reviews or walkthroughs.
- Because the approaches are reasonably sophisticated, training or significant preparation is required for those leading them.
- Approaches like ATAM assume that all stakeholders can participate in deep, committed, and constructive ways. If this isn't the case, the process may be of relatively little benefit.

Prototypes and Proof-of-Concept Systems

Prototypes and proofs-of-concept are most often used to mitigate technical risk (when a new or unfamiliar technology is under consideration) or to help design the user interface. For our purposes, we define a prototype as a functional subset of the system, often presented to users for feedback and validation. A **proof-of-concept**, on the other hand, is some code designed to prove that a risky element of the proposed architecture is feasible and to highlight any problems and pitfalls.

One problem with prototyping is that the risks that need to be mitigated can be quite complex. For example, a prototype may be suggested to demonstrate that an architecture can handle a large volume of transactions. In order to do this, you may have to set up a large amount of dummy data and a sophisticated simulation environment that can apply large numbers of transactions to the prototype and monitor performance. In addition, the prototype needs to be fairly sophisticated in its ability to scale in order for its results to be meaningful.

Prototyping is therefore the most expensive and time-consuming way to assess an architecture and needs careful justification. However, proving that something works by actually building it is a powerful risk-reduction mechanism.

The downstream risk with building a prototype is that the stakeholders view it as a finished system. A prototype typically has limited functionality, particularly related to error and exception handling as well as resilience, and you should normally discard it after it has served its purpose. You must clearly manage your stakeholders' expectations in this area.

ADVANTAGES

- Prototypes and proofs-of-concept can provide concrete validation of technical decisions at the point in the lifecycle when they can still be changed easily.

- Building a prototype or proof-of-concept provides an opportunity to learn about and understand the system's implementation technology, in a safe environment, before you need to use it to implement the system.

- Prototypes and proofs-of-concept can provide useful demonstrations to stakeholders to increase their confidence in the people, technology, and processes in use.

LIMITATIONS

- Prototypes and proofs-of-concept can be quite expensive and time-consuming to create, so you should use them only if a decision is important enough to justify the cost.

Skeleton Systems

The ultimate form of architectural validation is to build the system. The architectural form of this is to create a first version of the system, known as a **skeleton**, that implements the system's structure but contains only a minimal subset of the system's functionality. However, the minimal subset chosen should allow a small amount of end-to-end processing to occur, so it can prove that the system's overall structure is sound.

Unlike a prototype or proof-of-concept, a skeleton system is retained rather than discarded and becomes the basis for the construction phase, which fleshes out the skeleton with the implementation of all the required functions.

ADVANTAGES

- Skeleton systems are often the most thorough and convincing type of architectural validation possible.

- The skeleton system created is a tangible deliverable that can be used beyond the validation activity.

LIMITATIONS

- Skeleton systems are probably the most expensive form of architectural validation.
- The team creating the skeleton needs a lot of development expertise and software engineering discipline to build the skeleton system, which can be a challenge for some architecture teams.

SCENARIO-BASED EVALUATION METHODS

SAAM and ATAM are well-known examples of scenario-based architectural evaluation methods. Both of these methods were created at the SEI; SAAM is the original, simpler method, while ATAM is a more sophisticated approach developed later.

The key concept underpinning both these methods is a set of system usage scenarios that are of importance to the system's stakeholders and allow assessment of the system's properties. SAAM uses functional scenarios to evaluate how well a system will provide its key functionality and how easily it could be modified to meet likely changes. ATAM broadens this focus by using a set of quality property scenarios to test the ability of the system to exhibit its important quality properties (performance, security, availability, and so on).

We don't have space here to describe these methods in detail (although references mentioned in the Further Reading section at the end of this chapter do provide more information). Here we will briefly describe ATAM to give you an overview of the approach.

The UML activity diagram in Figure 14–1 illustrates the main steps in an ATAM architecture evaluation process. ATAM recognizes that there are two important but distinct aspects to architectural evaluation:

1. *Architecture-centric evaluation*, performed by the key project decision makers (those who created and own the architecture as well as key customer representatives—acquirers and user stakeholders, in our terminology)
2. *Stakeholder-centric evaluation*, performed by representatives from the wider stakeholder community (all those affected by the architecture)

The first half of the ATAM process (shown on the left in Figure 14–1) focuses on understanding the architecture and the decisions made to define it,

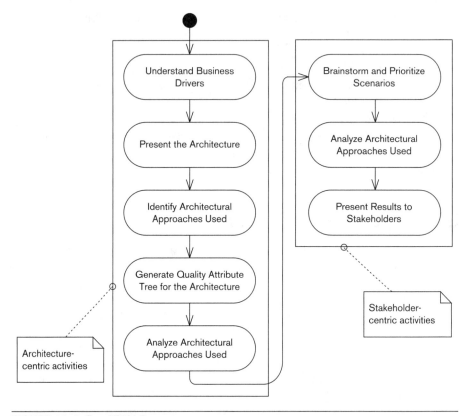

FIGURE 14-1 THE ATAM PROCESS

while the second half (shown on the right) tests the results of the first part by directly involving representatives of the entire stakeholder community.

Architecture-Centric Activities

The steps in the architecture-centric half of the process are as follows.

- *Understand the business drivers*: The members of the architecture review team (probably made up of architects, lead designers, key customer representatives, and possibly external consultants) examine the business drivers that underlie the systems' existence and make sure they understand them. This step normally consists of a business expert (perhaps the project sponsor or a business analyst) presenting the context for the system and the key business drivers to the group. Hopefully this will be a process of confirming your knowledge of the business drivers, but it may result in new insights gained from the presenter.

- *Present the architecture*: The owner of the architecture (probably you) should now present the architecture to the rest of the group. The form of the presentation isn't that important; the key is to communicate the entire architecture to the group evaluating it, in sufficient detail for them to understand it and analyze it. Due to specialization of roles, this is often the first time that many of those involved in developing the architecture will actually see and try to understand all of it. The focus of this step should be communication and understanding, rather than analyzing and evaluating, which will come later.

- *Identify the architectural approaches used*: When developing any software architecture, you make a number of high-level architectural decisions to ensure that the architecture meets certain critical goals. For example, perhaps you chose a client/server structure to allow hardware to be upgraded easily, a pipe-and-filter structure so that processing steps could easily be replaced and reused, or a cluster of machines in the deployment environment to provide resilience. ATAM terms such decisions *architectural approaches*, and this step in the process focuses on identifying the approaches used in architecture definition. Again, at this stage, don't analyze whether or not the right approaches are being used, but simply identify those in use and the reasons for each.

- *Generate a quality attribute tree for the architecture*: Having understood the drivers and the architecture, you're ready to establish the critical quality properties the system will have to exhibit and to identify scenarios to characterize each one. The output of the process is a tree of attributes, similar to the one shown in Figure 14–2.

  To create the quality attribute tree, start by listing the quality properties you think are important for your system. These are normally derived from the business drivers identified in the first step, but you may need to take into account other requirements as well. Then, for each high-level attribute you've listed, break it down to specific important areas. In Figure 14–2, the important aspect of security for this system is controlling access to its operations. For each detailed quality attribute, define at least one specific scenario that illustrates the attribute being met. Assess the scenario for its importance to the system and its difficulty of implementation, given the architecture presented in the previous steps. In the example shown in Figure 14–2, the difficulty (D) and importance (I) of each scenario is represented as high (H), medium (M), or low (L).

  The result of this process is a quality attribute tree that provides a set of scenarios with which to evaluate the architecture. The importance rating of each scenario helps focus attention on the most important aspects

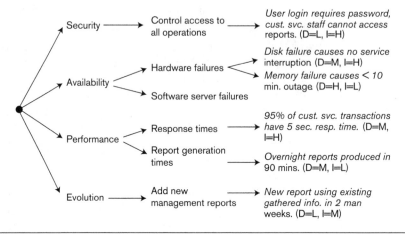

FIGURE 14-2 QUALITY ATTRIBUTE TREE

of the system, while the difficulty rating helps draw attention to areas where the architecture may need modification and improvement. Obviously, the high-importance, high-difficulty scenarios need the most attention during the rest of the evaluation process, while the low-importance, low-difficulty scenarios need the least.

- *Analyze the architectural approaches used*: In this step, the review team analyzes the architecture in more detail, in light of the quality goals, in order to establish how well it supports its required quality properties. The analysis can take a number of forms, and the authors of the ATAM process provide a fairly detailed process description for this step. Whatever approach you use, it needs to work systematically through the quality property scenarios and help you understand *how* the architecture supports the scenario and *which* architectural decisions are important to achieving it. While you do this, take special care to identify critical architectural decisions of the following types:

  - Decisions that are critical to meeting a particular quality property (termed *sensitivity points* in ATAM), such as a decision to use clustered servers to meet high-availability targets

  - Decisions that require a tradeoff between the needs of two competing quality properties (termed *tradeoff points* in ATAM), such as a decision to denormalize a database to achieve acceptable performance at the cost of more complex evolution

  This process should result in a thorough understanding (with reasoning) as to how the architecture supports (or does not support) each quality attribute scenario, a list of the sensitivity and tradeoff points in the current architecture, and a documented understanding of the risks associated with each decision.

Stakeholder-Centric Activities

This first half of the evaluation process has, in fact, performed an architectural evaluation, and the architects should now understand their architecture better and feel confident that it suits its intended purpose. However, in order to test the results of this evaluation, it is important to ensure that the criteria match the priorities of the stakeholders. The second half of the ATAM process does this by using stakeholder scenarios to test the architecture. The steps in this half of the process are as follows.

- *Brainstorm and prioritize scenarios*: Having gathered representatives of the interested stakeholder groups, explained ATAM, and summarized the steps performed so far, you can now work with the stakeholders to create a list of scenarios that *they* believe are important, both immediately and in the longer term. Have the stakeholders prioritize the scenarios to focus attention on the more important ones (a vote is often the most effective way to do this). Once the scenarios have been identified and prioritized, you can merge them into the quality attribute tree.

- *Analyze the architectural approaches used*: This step is analogous to the same step on the architecture-centric side but considers how the architectural approaches support (or don't support) the *new* scenarios the stakeholders have identified. Ideally, these new scenarios will be similar to the set identified by the architecture team, and this step will simply be a confirmation of the previous analysis. In reality, this step quite often sets "a cat among the pigeons" as the architecture team realizes that the architecture won't be able to meet some scenarios that are important to stakeholders. As in the corresponding architecture-centric step, you should identify sensitivity and tradeoff points.

- *Present the results to the stakeholders*: Finally, you present the results of the evaluation back to the stakeholders so that they understand how the architecture is going to support their scenarios. Your presentation should also highlight sensitivity and tradeoff points to help stakeholders understand how important, say, the new clustered server environment is in meeting *their* scenarios and, similarly, why meeting, say, a security requirement means that a usability requirement will have to be compromised. This step is an important communication and selling activity, helping the stakeholders feel ownership of *their* architecture and hopefully gaining their confidence in and support for the architecture team's work.

Although this is no more than a thumbnail sketch of the ATAM process, we hope it is enough to give you a flavor of what it is and how it works.

VALIDATION DURING THE SOFTWARE LIFECYCLE

Validation shouldn't be thought of as a single activity, performed at a particular point in the development lifecycle, but should be treated as an ongoing task that continually assesses the system's architecture as it is being developed. Having said this, not all validation activities apply equally well at each lifecycle stage, so you need to choose carefully the approaches used. Figure 14–3 illustrates where the different validation approaches typically fit into the software lifecycle.

When you are defining scope and exploring options for the architecture, the emphasis is on the following validation techniques, which help you make sound architectural decisions.

- *Presentations*: The proposed architecture should be widely presented as early as possible. Presenting the architecture to different stakeholders is cheap and easy to do and helps you validate the fundamental assumptions you're making about the role and nature of the system.
- *Reviews and walkthroughs*: As the architecture starts to emerge, organize more formal reviews of parts of it with stakeholders particularly affected by the decisions being made. For example, as soon as the system's

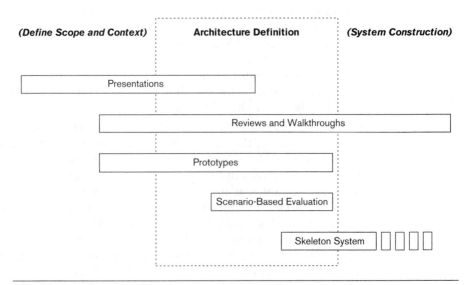

FIGURE 14-3 VALIDATION APPROACHES AT DIFFERENT POINTS OF THE LIFECYCLE

deployment platform is designed, have a formal review of it with the groups in the organization that are responsible for providing the IT infrastructure on which you plan to rely. As soon as the system structure starts to emerge, review it with the testers to make sure that they understand the scale and scope of testing required and that the proposed architecture actually is testable. The key point here is to start holding reviews as soon as there is anything to review, rather than waiting until the complete "perfect" AD has been completed. It's best to get the bad news as early as possible, and formal reviews can provide some confidence that the major decisions you're making are valid.

- *Prototypes*: Build prototypes of parts of the system in order to support technical decision making and to better understand the technologies included in the architecture.

During the detailed architecture definition process, the focus of validation moves to understanding the strengths and weaknesses of the proposed architecture and ensuring that it is suitable for the system being built. The techniques used in this phase include the following.

- *Reviews and walkthroughs*: When an AD is available, you can perform formal reviews and walkthroughs to gain general consensus that the architecture is feasible, suitable for the proposed system, and free of major problems (as far as people can tell). The completion of these reviews is a suitable point to get formal agreement (possibly in the form of a sign-off) that the architecture is acceptable to the system's important stakeholders.

- *Prototypes*: Build prototypes in order to resolve technical concerns that emerge during the architecture definition process and to validate particular architectural decisions.

- *Scenario-based evaluation*: In order to provide a deeper understanding of the system's attributes (such as performance, security, maintainability, and functionality), you can apply a scenario-based evaluation technique once a reasonably complete AD is available. Such an evaluation allows a more sophisticated level of analysis than a simple review or walkthrough, while still being achievable within a short timeframe and at a reasonable cost.

- *Skeleton system*: As soon as the AD is available, the architecture team, working with the lead designers, can create a skeleton implementation of the system to demonstrate how it will work and also to provide a development environment in which the full development of the system can take place. A skeleton system implementation can be a powerful proof point for many stakeholders, proving that the architecture really can provide the facilities needed, as well as demonstrating some directly useful deliverables as early as possible.

Another good point for validation comes later in the development life-cycle, when most of the important parts of the system are being or have been developed, with the focus now on the consistency of the AD and the architecture as realized in the system. The techniques of most use during system construction are as follows.

- *Reviews and walkthroughs*: Work closely with the development team to review the implementation as it is taking shape, acting as consultant and mentor and advising how best the architecture should be interpreted. Ideally, you will be able to work as part of the development team, but you might work external to it. In either case, it is important to perform continual reviews so that the implementation actually reflects the architecture. Then when problems are found, you can modify the architecture to address them, rather than just letting the implementation drift away from the architecture described in the AD.
- *Skeleton system*: As development progresses, the skeleton system will be fleshed out with the implementation of the system and so over time become a full implementation. Ensure that every development iteration adds working, useful functionality to the system.

RECORDING THE RESULTS OF VALIDATION

It's important to clearly and formally record the validation results to avoid misunderstandings about the problems found and the resulting decisions or changes. Failing to do this can lead to useful architectural improvements being ignored or getting lost, and in turn, this can often lead to a significant reduction of the stakeholders' confidence in the architecture and the architect.

There are many ways to record validation results, each with advantages and limitations. We find the following approaches useful.

- *Meeting minutes*: Recording the progress of meetings is a standard business technique that, if done accurately, can provide a definitive record of discussions and their results. The problem with meeting minutes is that they are hard to take properly, and often the important points are swamped by details that are not that significant later. The difficulty in taking good minutes can also lead to different groups of people writing a number of subtly different sets of minutes, which people use later as ammunition to win arguments. Given these problems, it's not very surprising that many people view meeting minutes with a certain amount of suspicion.

- *Decision logs*: A more focused approach to recording validation results is to use a decision log, which records decisions as they are made, along with their rationale and an identification of who made and agreed on them. A decision log can be kept in a spreadsheet, a word processor document, a collaborative Web site, or even a purpose-built software tool. Their great advantage is simplicity, although they do need to be carefully maintained and can suffer from a lack of context, which is often important later when understanding decisions.

- *Review records*: Using a well-defined approach to reviews or walk-throughs should result in problems and possible resolutions being documented in a reasonably standard form.

- *Evaluation reports*: Evaluation reports document the outcomes of architectural evaluation exercises in a standard, structured way to make them useful to the architect and stakeholders. This ensures that you won't lose the benefits of the exercises and lessons learned.

- *Document sign-off*: The normal way to record agreement with a particular decision or architecture is to gain a formal sign-off of a document, recording the agreement with its content. This can often be necessary if there is some form of contractual agreement required or if the agreement of certain key stakeholders is needed to progress past a particular project checkpoint. For you as the architect, it can also be quite reassuring to have a signature to approve a particular course of action. However, bear in mind the limitations of relying on document sign-off to prove stakeholder satisfaction—it really doesn't prove that the signer understood the content and is unlikely to guarantee that building the system will result in happy stakeholders.

CHECKLIST

- Have you planned how your software architecture will be validated throughout its development?
- Have you identified suitable validation techniques for use at each stage of the lifecycle? Do you know when you will use each?
- Have you allocated time and resources for validation and rework?
- Are the system's stakeholders ready and willing to engage in the validation process? If not, have you started to try to persuade them to participate?
- Are the architects suitably trained to perform architectural validation (e.g., presentation skills, soft skills for stakeholder interaction, specific technique skills such as inspections, ATAM, or SAAM)?

- Have you considered using experts from outside the immediate project team (perhaps other architects elsewhere in your organization) to provide independent validation?
- Have you defined a mechanism whereby decisions arising from reviews can be tracked and monitored to ensure that the appropriate changes are made to the architecture?

SUMMARY

Software architecture can't be executed like a piece of software, so we need to find other ways to test it. Architectural validation is the process of testing a software architecture for its fitness for purpose and for the presence of possible defects. This validation uses different techniques to test different aspects of the architecture at different stages during the lifecycle.

Some of the more important techniques for architectural validation include presenting the architecture to stakeholders, performing reviews and walk-throughs, using more formal scenario-based architectural evaluation techniques, building throwaway prototypes and proofs-of-concept, and creating early skeleton versions of the real system. Each of these techniques applies to different stages of the lifecycle, and they all come with different advantages and limitations.

You should treat the activity as a continual process of validation and improvement, running alongside architectural design, rather than as a one-shot review that the architecture must pass.

FURTHER READING

Not many books or articles about architectural validation are aimed at practitioners. A couple of notable exceptions are Clements et al. [CLEM02], which is a thorough and practical guide to applying the SEI's scenario-based techniques, including ATAM and SAAM, and Gilb and Graham [GILB93], which is a comprehensive guide to running formal reviews ("inspections").

A useful, accessible, academic article on architectural evaluation is Dobrica and Niemela [DOBR02], a paper that reviews a number of approaches to architectural evaluation and analysis (including SAAM and ATAM), explaining the similarities and differences between them.

PART III

THE VIEWPOINT CATALOG

15

INTRODUCTION TO THE VIEWPOINT CATALOG

Part III is a catalog of our six core viewpoints: Functional, Information, Concurrency, Development, Deployment, and Operational. As we said in Part I, while this taxonomy is not unique, we believe it does a good job of partitioning the AD into a manageable number of sections, while ensuring a widespread coverage of concerns.

For convenience, in Table 15–1 we reiterate the viewpoint taxonomy we presented originally in Part I.

Figure 15–1 shows the relationships between views created using these viewpoints.

For each viewpoint, we present the following details:

- The most important *concerns* addressed by the viewpoint, with an identification of the stakeholders who are most likely to be interested in its views
- The most important *models* you might build to present the views, together with the notations used and the activities for building them
- Some *problems and pitfalls* to be aware of and risk-reduction techniques for mitigating against these
- A *checklist* of things to consider when developing the viewpoint and when reviewing it to help ensure correctness, completeness, and accuracy

Because of space limitations, we can present only an overview of some complex and detailed topics. Most of the chapters in Part III could easily expand into entire books in their own right. Our objective is to get you started, and to that end, each viewpoint chapter includes a number of references to sources of further information.

TABLE 15-1 VIEWPOINT CATALOG

Viewpoint	Definition
Functional	Describes the system's functional elements, their responsibilities, interfaces, and primary interactions. A Functional view is the cornerstone of most ADs and is often the first part of the description that stakeholders try to read. It drives the shape of other system structures such as the information structure, concurrency structure, deployment structure, and so on. It also has a significant impact on the system's quality properties such as its ability to change, its ability to be secured, and its runtime performance.
Information	Describes the way that the architecture stores, manipulates, manages, and distributes information. The ultimate purpose of virtually any computer system is to manipulate information in some form, and this viewpoint develops a complete but high-level view of static data structure and information flow. The objective of this analysis is to answer the big questions around content, structure, ownership, latency, references, and data migration.
Concurrency	Describes the concurrency structure of the system and maps functional elements to concurrency units to clearly identify the parts of the system that can execute concurrently and how this is coordinated and controlled. This entails the creation of models that show the process and thread structures that the system will use and the interprocess communication mechanisms used to coordinate their operation.
Development	Describes the architecture that supports the software development process. Development views communicate the aspects of the architecture of interest to those stakeholders involved in building, testing, maintaining, and enhancing the system.
Deployment	Describes the environment into which the system will be deployed, including capturing the dependencies the system has on its runtime environment. This view captures the hardware environment that your system needs (primarily the processing nodes, network interconnections, and disk storage facilities required), the technical environment requirements for each element, and the mapping of the software elements to the runtime environment that will execute them.
Operational	Describes how the system will be operated, administered, and supported when it is running in its production environment. For all but the simplest systems, installing, managing, and operating the system is a significant task that must be considered and planned at design time. The aim of the Operational viewpoint is to identify system-wide strategies for addressing the operational concerns of the system's stakeholders and to identify solutions that address these.

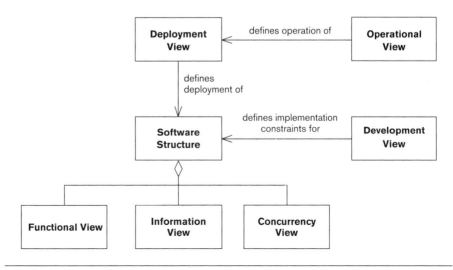

FIGURE 15-1 VIEW RELATIONSHIPS

16

THE FUNCTIONAL VIEWPOINT

Definition	Describes the system's runtime functional elements and their responsibilities, interfaces, and primary interactions
Concerns	Functional capabilities, external interfaces, internal structure, and design philosophy
Models	Functional structure model
Problems and Pitfalls	Poorly defined interfaces, poorly understood responsibilities, infrastructure modeled as functional elements, overloaded view, diagrams without element definitions, difficulty in reconciling the needs of multiple stakeholders, inappropriate level of detail, "God elements," and too many dependencies
Stakeholders	All stakeholders
Applicability	All systems

The Functional view of a system defines the architectural elements that deliver the system's functionality. The view documents the system's functional structure—including the key functional elements, their responsibilities, the interfaces they expose, and the interactions between them. Taken together, this demonstrates how the system will perform the functions required of it.

The Functional view is the cornerstone of most ADs and is often the first part of the description that stakeholders try to read. (Too often, it is also the only view of the architecture produced.) It is probably the easiest view for stakeholders to understand. The Functional view usually drives the definition of the other architectural views (Information, Concurrency, Development, Deployment, and Operational). You will almost always create a Functional view and will often spend most of your time defining and refining it.

As with all of the other views, the challenge when defining the Functional view is to include an appropriate level of detail. Focus on what is architecturally significant—in other words, what has a visible impact on stakeholders—and leave the rest to your designers.

CONCERNS

Functional Capabilities

Functional capabilities define what the system is required to do—and, explicitly or implicitly, what it is not required to do (either because this functionality is outside the scope of consideration or because it is provided elsewhere).

On some projects, you will be given an approved requirements specification at the start of architecture definition, and you can focus in the Functional view on showing how your architectural elements work together to provide this functionality. If you aren't given a good-quality requirements specification, the onus falls on you, before you proceed any further, to document and obtain high-level agreement on what the system must do.

External Interfaces

External interfaces are the data and control flows between your system and others.

Data can flow inward (usually resulting in an internal change of system state) and/or outward (usually as a result of internal changes of system state). A control flow may be inbound (a request by an external system to yours to perform a task) or outbound (a request by your system to another to perform a task).

Interface definitions need to consider both the interface syntax (the structure of the data or request) and semantics (its meaning or effect).

Internal Structure

In most cases, you can design a system in a number of different ways to meet its requirements. It can be built as a single monolithic entity or a collection of loosely coupled components; it can be constructed from a number of standard packages, linked together using commodity middleware, or written from scratch; its functional needs can even be met by Web services provided by systems external to the organization.

The internal structure of the system is defined by its internal elements, what they do (i.e., how they map onto the requirements), and how they interact with each other. This internal organization can have a big impact on the system's quality properties, such as its availability, resilience, ability to scale, and security (e.g., a complex system is generally harder to secure than a simple one).

Design Philosophy

Many of your stakeholders will be interested only in what the system does and the interfaces it presents to users and to other systems. Other stakeholders will be interested in how well the architecture adheres to sound principles of design. Technical stakeholders want a sound architecture because a well-designed system is easier to build, operate, and enhance. Other stakeholders—particularly acquirers—want this because it is faster, cheaper, and easier to get a well-designed system into production.

The design philosophy will be underpinned by a number of design qualities such as those listed in Table 16–1.

TABLE 16–1 DESIGN QUALITIES

Design Quality	Description	Significance
Separation of concerns	To what extent is each internal element responsible for a distinct part of the system's operation? To what extent is common processing performed in only one place?	High separation results in a system that is easier to build, support, and enhance but may adversely impact performance and scalability compared with a monolithic approach.
Cohesion	To what extent are the functions provided by an element strongly related to each other?	High cohesion is logically sensible and tends to result in simpler, less error-prone designs.
Coupling	How strong are the element interrelationships? To what extent do changes in one module affect others?	Loosely coupled systems are often easier to build, support, and enhance but may suffer from poor scalability compared with a monolithic approach.
Volume of element interactions	What proportion of processing steps involve interactions between elements as opposed to within an element?	Communicating between certain types of elements can be an order of magnitude more expensive (in terms of processing time and elapsed time), and significantly less reliable, than performing an operation within a functional element.
Functional flexibility	How amenable is the system to supporting functional changes?	Systems that are designed to be easy to change are usually harder to build and typically don't perform as well as systems that are less adaptable.
Overall coherence	Does the architecture "look right" when decomposed into elements?	If the architecture doesn't look right, this may indicate underlying problems and may also make it harder for stakeholders to understand.

TABLE 16-2 STAKEHOLDER CONCERNS FOR THE FUNCTIONAL VIEWPOINT

Stakeholder Class	Concerns
Acquirers	Primarily functional capabilities and external interfaces
Assessors	All concerns
Communicators	All concerns, to some extent
Developers	Primarily design philosophy and internal structure, but also functional capabilities and external interfaces
System administrators	Primarily design philosophy and internal structure
Testers	Primarily design philosophy and internal structure, but also functional capabilities and external interfaces
Users	Primarily functional capabilities and external interfaces

Stakeholder Concerns

Typical stakeholder concerns for the Functional viewpoint include those listed in Table 16–2.

MODELS

Functional Structure Models

The functional structure model typically contains the following elements.

- *Functional elements*: A functional element is a well-defined part of the runtime system that has particular responsibilities and exposes well-defined interfaces that allow it to be connected to other elements. At its simplest level, an element is a software code module, but in other contexts it could be an application package, a data store, or even a complete system.

  In general, it is not appropriate to model underlying infrastructure as functional elements, unless that infrastructure performs a functionally significant task, independent of the other functional elements. Infrastructure that simply supports the operation of the functional elements should normally not be shown in the Functional view; it is best considered in the Deployment view.

- *Interfaces*: An interface is a well-defined mechanism by which the functions of an element can be accessed by other elements. An interface is defined by the inputs, outputs, and semantics of each operation offered and the nature of the interaction needed to invoke the operation.

- *Connectors*: Connectors are the pieces of your architecture that link the elements together to allow them to interact. A connector defines the interaction between the elements that use it and allows the nature of the interaction to be considered separately from the semantics of the operation being invoked. The nature of the interactions between elements can be intimately bound up in how they are connected.

    The amount of consideration you need to give connectors depends on your circumstances. At one extreme, you can just note that one element connects to another. At the other extreme, a connector can be modeled as a type of element in its own right. As always, focus here on what is architecturally significant.

- *External entities*: External entities can represent other systems, software programs, hardware devices, or any other entity that your system communicates with. They are obtained from your system context definition, and each appears in the functional model at the far end of an interface.

The functional structure model does not contain entities like processes or threads that define how code is packaged and executed. Therefore, the Functional view does not constrain how the functional components are packaged to allow their deployment and execution—this is the domain of the Concurrency view.

NOTATION You can use a number of techniques to represent the Functional view in a model.

- *UML component diagrams*: Using UML for a Functional view has a number of advantages, including its widespread comprehension and its flexibility. The main UML diagram you will use for the Functional view is a component diagram, which shows a system's elements, interfaces, and interelement connections.

EXAMPLE Figure 16–1 shows the typical elements in a UML component diagram. The system consists of two internal elements, Variable Capture and Alarm Initiator, interacting with one external element, Temperature Monitor. Variable Capture exposes one interface, Variable Reporting, which is invoked by Temperature Monitor, and Alarm Initiator exposes one interface, Limit Condition, which is invoked by Variable Capture. Variable Reporting is tagged with information that tells us it is an XML remote procedure call, over the HTTP protocol, and that at most ten concurrent invocations can exist at one time.

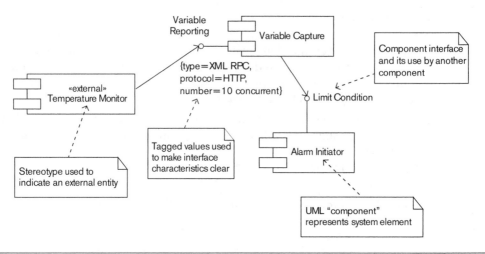

FIGURE 16-1 EXAMPLE OF A FUNCTIONAL STRUCTURE IN UML

You represent each of the system's elements and external entities with a UML component icon, annotated with its name and any stereotype needed to make the nature of the element clear. (Stereotypes allow you to extend the semantics of standard UML in a logical and consistent way to meet your individual circumstances.) One common stereotype used is <<external>>, which indicates that the icon refers to an external entity, rather than a system element. Another is <<infrastructure>>, which indicates an infrastructure element of the system that has a distinct functional role.

UML interface icons attached to a system element represent the interfaces it exposes. We have found the small "lollypop" interface icon is more effective in the Functional view than the larger stereotyped class icon. In order to differentiate between different types of interfaces, sets of tagged values may be associated with interfaces that are not of the standard type for the system. The values used must be standardized for each system depending on its characteristics. Indicating the type of interface, the protocol used to access it (if any), and the number of concurrent users allowed provides a good basis for interface classification.

Once you have identified elements and interfaces, you can illustrate interelement communication via the interfaces with arrows, as described in the following example.

EXAMPLE The UML component diagram shown in Figure 16–2 is an example of using UML to document the functional structure of a simple system. The system under consideration provides a Web storefront

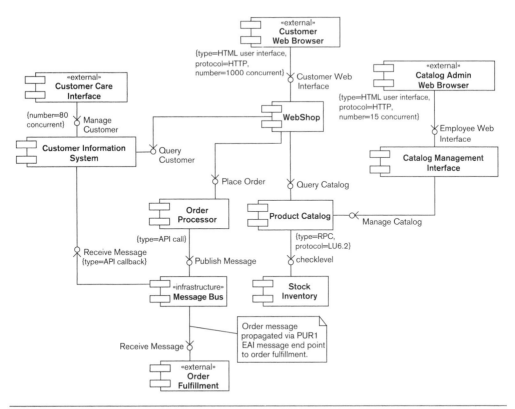

FIGURE 16-2 EXAMPLE OF A UML COMPONENT DIAGRAM

(called the WebShop) for customers to use when purchasing items from an online catalog that fits into an existing enterprise software environment. (To save space, we have omitted the detailed descriptions of the system components and their interfaces, but obviously these would be crucial information for a real model.)

The model shows that the system communicates with four external entities: the Web browsers of the three main user types (customers, customer care representatives, and catalog administrators) and an external system (the order fulfillment system). Our system is composed of six main functional components and a piece of functional infrastructure—a message bus that links the Order Processor, the Customer Information System, and the external Order Fulfillment system.

Customers order from the WebShop, which interacts with the Product Catalog, the Order Processor, and the Customer Information System. The catalog administrators maintain the product catalog via their Web-based interface, while the customer care representatives maintain the customer information via a dedicated interface client program (the Customer Care Interface). When the stock level of a particular item in the catalog is needed, the Product Catalog accesses this information from the Stock Inventory (which already exists).

We also have some insights into the nature of the intercomponent interactions. We know that up to 1,000 customers, 80 customer care representatives, and 15 catalog administrators may access the system simultaneously. We also note that the interaction between the Product Catalog and the Stock Inventory components takes place using a specific protocol (presumably due to preexisting technology). We can assume for this example that the unadorned intercomponent communication takes place via some form of standard remote procedure call (which we will assume has been clearly defined elsewhere).

Having said this, one of the interesting points to note about this model is how much is *not* obvious from the diagram. The responsibilities of the components aren't clear, the details of their interfaces aren't clear, and the details of how the components interact aren't clear. This impresses on us the need to complete the textual descriptions that underpin the diagram and the need to understand the system via a number of models rather than just one (e.g., intercomponent interactions can be shown via system scenario modeling, as we described in Chapter 10).

- *Other formal design notations*: UML is not the only well-defined design notation suitable for software development. A number of structured notations (such as Yourdon, Jackson System Development, and the Object Modeling Technique of James Rumbaugh) have been successfully applied to software development problems for many years, and you should consider the use of any well-defined notation that is suitable for describing your system. The problem with using any of the notations developed for software design is that they tend to be fairly weak at describing the concepts (such as large-scale elements, interfaces, deployment options, and so on) that are important to architects.

- *Boxes-and-lines diagrams*: Many architects use a functional structure diagram drawn by using a simple boxes-and-lines notation. Such a diagram should show just the functional elements and their interfaces and should link the elements to the interfaces they use with a clear graphical device (typically an arrow, possibly with some annotation) that indicates the use of a connector.

EXAMPLE The boxes-and-lines diagram shown in Figure 16–3 gives an alternate, less formal, possibly more user-friendly representation of the system described in the previous example.

In this model, we have defined our own notation. Functional elements are represented by using rectangles and the links between them by using lines, with arrows indicating the direction(s) of information flow. External user-facing interfaces are represented by using an icon meant to look like a computer monitor, and external back-end systems are represented by using rectangles with rounded corners. Data stores are represented by an icon that looks like a disk drum, and functional interfaces (the Internet, the message bus) are represented by a cloud icon. The scope of the system is those elements within the dotted rectangle.

The benefit of the boxes-and-lines diagram is that nontechnical stakeholders, particularly business users and sponsors, may find it easier to understand. Such a model can be an invaluable tool in selling the features and benefits of the system to these stakeholders without getting bogged down in technical detail. Often you may use the boxes-and-lines diagram as a front for more detailed, rigorous UML models.

Although the boxes-and-lines diagram may be less formal than a UML model, you shouldn't use this as an excuse for being less rigorous. In particular, early in architecture definition, you should define a standard notation for your diagrams—and make sure you stick to it. Try to develop icons that give an indication of the underlying purpose of the elements modeled (e.g., the disk-drum icon shown in Figure 16–3 is often used to model data stores).

You should always support any such model with a definition of its elements and the interfaces between them, presented in a standardized way.

- *Sketches*: You can create a less formal feel for the view by using a sketch, that is, by introducing an ad hoc notation as required to represent each of the aspects of the view that are significant for your system. The use of a sketch is often required to effectively communicate essential aspects of the view to nontechnical stakeholders. The problem with this approach is that it can lead to a poorly defined view and confusion among stakeholders. As with the boxes-and-lines diagram, you can get around this by using a sketch to augment a more formal view notation (such as UML) and using different notations for different stakeholder groups.

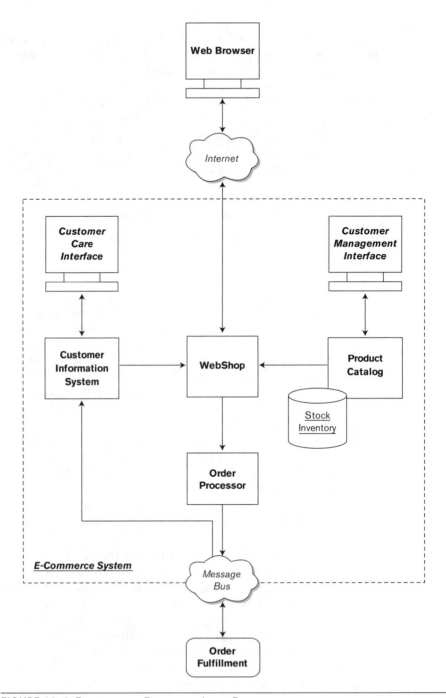

FIGURE 16-3 Example of a Boxes-and-Lines Diagram

Representing procedure-oriented element interactions is relatively straightforward, but modeling message-oriented interactions (such as those found where elements are connected via publish/subscribe messaging systems) can be significantly harder.

We used to model message-oriented interfaces by showing the message distribution mechanism (typically a piece of message-oriented middleware) as a functional element and connecting the various message source and destination elements to it. This does get the point across, but it's difficult to discern the overall message flow in the system. An alternative approach, suggested in Garland and Anthony [GARL03], uses ports to model message-oriented interactions between system elements.

The notion of ports comes from the real-time systems community, where a port is an abstract representation of the source or destination of messages. This approach of representing message-oriented interactions via a separate modeling primitive is a nice approach and helps make the messaging within the system clear.

EXAMPLE An example of Garland and Anthony's approach is shown on the next page in the UML model in Figure 16–4.

This diagram illustrates part of a notional system in a financial institution where prices are calculated by one system element (the Price Calculator) and distributed to the other system elements via asynchronous messages. The small boxes (labeled "Prices") attached to the system elements represent ports. The one attached to the Price Calculator is an output port (it creates messages), and the ones attached to the other elements are input ports (they receive messages). The name on each port indicates the type of message that flows over that connection. (An element may be involved in a number of separate message-oriented interactions.) Finally, the arrowheads indicate the direction that the messages propagate (and so implicitly distinguish output and input message ports).

When the message-oriented interactions are illustrated by using a separate notation, they can be combined with procedure-oriented element interactions on a single diagram without fear of confusion. The only possible problem we see with this approach is that the use of ports isn't core UML and isn't widely understood in the information systems community, so it may need to be explained to avoid confusion.

You can also use such a technique to model higher-level messaging systems, such as those that implement Enterprise Application Integration architectures.

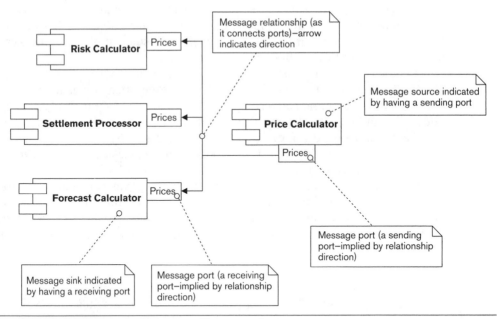

FIGURE 16-4 EXAMPLE OF A MODEL FOR MESSAGING INTERACTIONS

Remember that a Functional view should describe only the system's functional elements. If you need notational items to represent deployment, concurrency, or other aspects of the system, your Functional view has become overloaded.

ACTIVITIES

Identify the Elements. You can identify the functional elements by following these steps.

- Work through the functional requirements, deriving key system-level responsibilities.
- Identify the functional elements that will perform those responsibilities.
- Assess the identified set against the desirable design criteria.
- Iterate back to refine the functional structure until you judge it to be sound.

Of course, some elements may be defined for you already (e.g., software libraries, software packages, preexisting systems or subsystems), in which case the process for these elements is one of understanding rather than identifying and designing.

Refining the set of functional elements involves applying one or more refinements to the functional structure.

- *Generalization*: Identifying some common responsibilities across a number of elements and introducing a number of more general elements that can be reused across the system to perform these tasks. Generalization is often important as part of a larger enterprise or product-line architecture to allow reuse of software assets across a number of similar products or systems.

- *Decomposition*: Breaking a large, complex element into a number of smaller subelements. For large systems, you will often need to break the top-level functional elements into more manageable subsystem-level elements to allow them to be designed and built, breaking down large elements into smaller ones.

- *Compression*: Replacing a number of small functional elements with a larger element that includes all of the functions of the smaller ones. Compression is typically used when a large number of small but similar functional elements have been identified. In such cases, it often makes sense from an architectural perspective to replace the smaller elements with a single large element that can factor out the commonality between the smaller ones and reduce the amount of interactions the system requires.

- *Replication*: Replicating either a system element or a piece of processing. An example is data validation, where you identify a validation element for incoming data and then replicate it across a number of the system's external interfaces.

If you are using an architectural style to guide your design process, the process is slightly different because it will involve creating an instantiation of the style such that the system-level responsibilities are assigned to elements of the style. This activity is closely related to the next step—assigning responsibilities to the elements.

We don't talk about the element identification process in a lot of detail in this book because there are many ways to do it, and the correct method to use depends on the type of system and the software development approach you are using. (Procedural, object-oriented, and component-based approaches all influence component identification in different ways.) See the Further Reading section at the end of this chapter for some sources that discuss element identification.

Assign Responsibilities to the Elements. Once you have identified candidate elements, your next activity is to assign clear responsibilities to them—that is, the information managed by the element, the services it offers to other parts of the system, and the activities it initiates. You may have done this in the previous step; if not, complete it here.

EXAMPLE   Table 16–3 assigns responsibilities to two of the elements for the e-commerce system described in earlier examples.

Design the Interfaces. The services offered by your elements need to be accessed via well-defined interfaces. The definition of an interface must include the operations that the interface offers, the nature of the interface (messaging, remote procedure call, Web service, and so on), and the input, outputs, preconditions, and effects of each operation.

A good approach to consider when developing element interfaces is Design by Contract, an interface design method originally created by Bertrand Meyer for developing interfaces in object-oriented systems. This approach involves defining interfaces via "contracts" that use preconditions, postconditions, and invariants to precisely define operation behavior and relationships.

The appropriate notation for interface definition depends on the nature of your architecture (considering factors such as the likely implementation technology, the background of the development team, and the kinds of interfaces that need to be described). The following are some common interface definition notations.

- *Programming languages*: Interfaces can be defined directly by using a programming language to define the operation signatures along with text and/or language assertions to define the operation semantics. This approach is simple but ties you to the style, assumptions, and limitations of the particular programming language. Because the focus of programming languages is at a level well below that of architecture, this may not be

TABLE 16–3 EXAMPLES OF ELEMENT RESPONSIBILITIES

Element	Responsibilities
WebShop	• Present customers with an HTML-based user interface they can access with a Web browser. • Manage all state related to the customer interface session. • Interact with other parts of the system to allow customers to view the catalog and stock levels, buy goods, and view their customer information.
Customer Information System	• Manage all persistent information about customers of the system. • Provide a query-only interface that can be used to retrieve information held on a particular customer that should be visible to that customer. • Provide an information management programmatic interface that can be used to create customer information management applications. • Provide an event-driven message-handling interface to accept details of orders placed by customers and the state changes of those orders.

ideal, particularly if you're using multiple technologies. This approach works particularly well for programming libraries or other situations where the system is really a single, large programming artifact.

- *Interface definition languages*: Specialist interface definition languages have been developed to support mixed-language distributed systems technology (so there is one for CORBA, one for COM, and so on). These languages are independent of implementation technology and tend to offer simpler facilities than programming languages do, more suitable for large-scale interelement communication. Provided that your interested stakeholders can read (or be taught to read) them, these languages offer a good option for defining operation signatures. Unfortunately, none of them offer facilities for defining operational semantics, but they can be used in conjunction with natural language or specialist languages like Object Constraint Language (OCL) to achieve this.

- *Design notations*: Software design notations like UML can be used very successfully for interface definition, particularly if more advanced features (like OCL) can be used for the definition of operational semantics. However, UML's interface definition language is aimed at defining the operations of an object-oriented language class, so in an architectural context it may make sense to use UML and OCL with an interface definition language for operation signature definitions, to encourage the creation of suitable interfaces.

- *Data-oriented approaches*: Interfaces can also be described purely in terms of messages that are exchanged. Examples of this type of interface definition include interfaces accessed via messaging systems and interfaces defined in terms of XML document exchange (e.g., those defined for systems built using Web services). This approach works well for interfaces that have few operations (often just one called "process") but have complex structured data forming the operation parameters.

Whatever notation you use to describe interfaces, remember that an interface is significantly more than just a simple definition of how you call the operations. An interface definition must accurately communicate the pre- and postconditions of each operation and how the operations should be combined in order to perform a useful function (preferably with examples). Anything less than this is likely to cause significant problems during system integration.

EXAMPLE Here is an example of part of the interface definition for a simple `manage_customer` interface for the Customer Information System element in Figure 16–2.

```
Customer_Information_System::manage_customer
```

Interface Type

CORBA RPC, accessed via IIOP protocol.

Interface Signatures

```
typedef struct customer {
  ...
} customer_t ;
typedef unsigned long cust_id_t ;
typedef sequence<cust_id_t> cust_id_list_t ;

interface manage_customer {

   /* Operations */
   cust_id_t add_customer(new_customer customer_t)
             raises invalid_customer ;
   void del_customer(cust_id_t customer_id)
     raises no_such_customer ;
   void mod_customer(cust_id_t  customer_id,
                   customer_t updated_customer)
     raises no_such_customer, invalid_customer ;
   /* Queries */
   customer_t get_customer(long customer_id)
     raises no_such_customer ;
   cust_id_list_t get_customers_by_postal_code(
                   string postal_code) ;
   ...
}
```

Operation Definitions

```
manage_customer.add_customer
```

Description: This operation adds a new customer to the customers known to the system. The customer details are defined by the information passed as a parameter.

Precondition: The first name, surname, address line 1, town, postal code, and home phone number fields in the `customer_t` parameter supplied must not be null.

Postcondition: A new customer is added to the system, its information being taken from the `new_customer` parameter. A unique ID is allocated for this customer and returned as the return value of this operation.

...

Examples of Usage

Scenario 1: Adding a New Customer

Assemble the information for the new customer (at least, first name, surname, address line 1, town, postal code, and home telephone number).

Call the `get_customers_by_postal_code()` operation with the new customer's postal code.

If the return list isn't empty, retrieve each matching customer using the `get_customer()` operation and check the surname and home telephone number against the details of the new customer. If there is a match, this may be a duplicate customer.

If this is not a duplicate customer, call the `new_customer()` operation, passing it the new customer details in a `customer_t` structure. The ID assigned to the new customer will be returned if the operation is successful.

. . .

Check the Functional Traceability. The requirements documentation for your system will have defined a number of functions that the system has to offer. You should carry out a traceability check to ensure that all functional requirements have been met by the proposed functional structure. Such an analysis often reveals missing or incomplete functions in the functional structure model. The traceability analysis is usually presented as a table of functional requirements cross-referenced against functional model elements.

Walk through Common Scenarios. It can be extremely valuable and illuminating to walk through common system usage scenarios with your stakeholders, using the Functional view to illustrate how the system will behave in each case. In such a walkthrough, you should explain how the system's elements would interact in order to implement the scenario. Often, architectural weaknesses or misunderstandings as well as missing elements are identified as part of such a process. Such a walkthrough can form part of a larger architectural assessment exercise such as that introduced in Chapter 14.

Analyze the Interactions. Given the impact that excessive interelement interactions can have, it is useful to analyze the chosen structure from the point of view of the number of interelement interactions taken during common processing scenarios. In most cases, choosing a functional structure that minimizes such interactions results in a well-structured system with cohesive, loosely coupled elements. It is typically an important step toward an efficient and reliable system. When performing interaction analysis, you need to make tradeoffs to ensure that reducing interelement interactions does not result in a distorted system structure with undesirable redundancy or inappropriate element partitioning.

Analyze for Flexibility. Successful systems are always under pressure to change. Given this reality, as early as possible you should consider how flexible your architecture is in the face of change. The functional structure of a system is often one of the primary factors affecting the flexibility of information systems. It's useful to work through some "what if" scenarios that reveal the impact of possible future changes on your system. A common problem at this point is that the changes implied by the change analysis conflict with those suggested by the interaction analysis. Therefore, it is important that you trade off these two factors during architectural evaluation in order to find the right balance for your system.

PROBLEMS AND PITFALLS

Poorly Defined Interfaces

Many architects define their elements, responsibilities, and interelement relationships well, yet totally neglect their interface definitions. Defining interelement interfaces clearly can often be something of a chore. However, it is one of the most important tasks you can perform for the system. Without good interface definitions, major misunderstandings will occur between subsystem development teams, leading to a range of problems from obviously incorrect behavior to subtle, occasional system unreliability.

RISK REDUCTION
- Define your interfaces clearly and as early as possible.
- Review them frequently to ensure that they are clearly understood.
- Do not consider element definition complete until interfaces have been designed.
- Make sure that interface definitions include the operations, their semantics, and examples where possible.

Poorly Understood Responsibilities

It is easy to become very focused on a couple of key scenarios and to consider the functional elements only in this context. If you don't state explicitly the responsibilities of the elements (and don't perform traceability analysis), a lot of confusion can remain over *exactly* what each functional element is meant to do. This often leads to problems later: Either functionality is missing because it fell between the gaps or functionality is duplicated because two subsystem development teams both thought that a piece of functionality was their responsibility.

RISK REDUCTION

- Ensure that element responsibilities are formally defined as early as possible.

- Do not allow the development process to drift into element design without element responsibilities being formally defined, reviewed, and approved.

- Make sure that all implementers understand where their boundaries are (and why they are there).

- Make sure that all requirements have been mapped to the elements that implement them.

Infrastructure Modeled as Functional Elements

In general, you should not model underlying infrastructure as functional elements. Adding infrastructure elements to the Functional view simply makes it more confusing without adding useful information. Infrastructure can normally be hidden inside the functional elements; the Deployment view defines the infrastructure in more detail.

However, sometimes a piece of infrastructure does actually play a significant architectural role in its own right. In such cases, you may choose to model the infrastructure as one or more functional elements in this view—otherwise, the view is incomplete. For example, consider a software package that implements a message bus that the elements use to send messages to each other. In this case, the message bus is providing the critical functional responsibility of routing messages between elements, and the functional structure doesn't make any sense without it. In contrast, an underlying remote procedure call technology component (such as an application server) need not be modeled as a functional element because it does not directly alter the system's functional structure (although it certainly will appear in other views as part of the underlying infrastructure).

RISK REDUCTION

- Avoid modeling underlying infrastructure elements as you develop your initial element model. Focus on functional elements that solve part of the problem the system is going to address.

- Question the need for any elements that do not have names related to the domain of the problem being addressed.

- Address specific infrastructure issues in another view (typically, a Deployment view).

Overloaded View

The Functional view is the cornerstone of the AD and is often the primary structuring device. However, beware of letting it become *all* the views rather than just the central view. It is often tempting to overload the Functional view with the intent to make things clearer by adding deployment or concurrency information or other aspects of the architecture to this view. If you decide to use a compound view, make this an explicit decision. Don't allow the Functional view to simply creep into being an overloaded description of many aspects of the system. Such a description is very unlikely to be easy to understand and therefore is of limited use.

EXAMPLE Figure 16–5 shows an example of what we mean by view overloading.

This model has a number of problems (even assuming that good textual descriptions are used to back up the diagram to form a complete model). The first problem is that we don't know what the notation means. It's obviously related to UML, but various bits and pieces of ad hoc notation have been added: the dashed line from the Socket Library box to the Web Server box, the dotted lines within the Server Node(s) box, and so on. This means that we don't really know what the diagram means and will have to ask the architect who drew it. We can probably discern enough for ourselves to continue, although some problems remain.

- The system provides a salesperson with an interface to allow something (perhaps a holiday or flight) to be booked.
- A number of server-side components (presumably Enterprise Java Beans, given the name used) implement something on a server computer. However, we don't know what components exist, just that (presumably) there is a group of them.
- The server components appear to be implemented by using a utility library that in turn uses a calendar library (presumably for specialist calendar processing for dates). This implies that a layered model is planned for the component design.
- A number of processes run on the server computers: one for the Web server, one for the application server, and one for the Oracle database management server. (We're interpreting the dotted lines as operating system processes.)

We can discern this sort of information from the model (and presumably could untangle the notation if we could talk with the architect); the

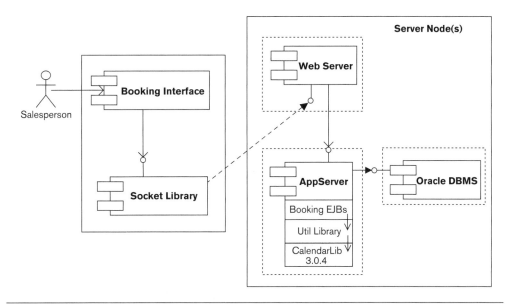

FIGURE 16-5 VIEW OVERLOADING

real problem is the overloading of the diagram. Even in our initial understanding of it, we need to consider functional structure, deployment across machines, concurrency, software design constraints, and so on. These are separate concerns, at different abstraction levels, of interest to different stakeholders. The result is that none of the concerns are addressed very clearly, and this model probably can't be used with any of our stakeholders apart from developers and testers (and even they will probably need more detail about each of their concerns).

The overloading of the model is probably also one of the reasons that the notation is confusing. It is very hard to overload a diagram's function and not end up with notational confusion because of the need to represent a number of unrelated concepts together on one diagram.

RISK REDUCTION

- Remove everything from your Functional view except for the functional elements.

- Create other views, based on the other viewpoints we define in this book, to describe the other aspects of your architecture.

- Develop the other views in parallel and cross-reference between views to illustrate other aspects of the architecture. (We talk about this in Chapter 22.)

Diagrams without Element Definitions

When developing models that are inherently structural in nature (such as the functional structure model), there is a tendency to draw the diagram representing the model's structure and then to move on to something else without really defining the entities shown in the model. Defining each of the model elements carefully can be a tedious process, but unless this is done well, the model is meaningless.

RISK REDUCTION

- Define each element as it is added to the model, and review the definitions with your stakeholders to check that the definitions are clear and accurate.
- Do not consider the model complete until every element has a good definition.

Difficulty in Reconciling the Needs of Multiple Stakeholders

The central role of the Functional view means that most stakeholders are interested in it. This can cause you significant problems when formulating the view—how do you create a view description that means something to all of these different types of stakeholders? End users, developers, system administrators, and all of the other groups have specific interests and needs, and you often need to communicate with each in a different way. It is often difficult to identify a single model or notation suitable for use with all of these parties.

RISK REDUCTION

- Use different modeling languages with different stakeholders. In general, stakeholders break into two major groups—technical stakeholders and nontechnical (business) stakeholders.
- You can communicate effectively with the technical stakeholders by using your primary architectural models (such as the functional structure model). Some explanation of notations may be required, but on the whole a technical stakeholder will understand these models.
- The nontechnical stakeholders are unlikely to understand your primary architectural models, so you'll need to create simplified models for them, derived from the primary models. We have found that a less technical notation (such as the sketches we described in Chapter 12) with brief textual annotation is often a more effective communication medium here.

Inappropriate Level of Detail

A common question when creating the Functional view is when to stop. If the process of functional analysis becomes too detailed and ends up defining too many layers of elements, you are starting to act as a software designer as well as an architect. Obviously, there is no simple solution to this problem—it depends on the context.

RISK REDUCTION

- Our experience suggests that if you have to define more than two or three levels of elements, assuming a limit of about eight to ten functional elements at the top level, you may have a problem. So, if possible, keep your level of detail below this limit.

- Another danger sign can be the inclusion in the Functional view's models of details about the workings or internal structure of functional elements. If your system is very large, modeling it as a group of systems rather than working down into the elements would make the problem tractable.

"God Elements"

Software designers often see object-oriented designs that have a single huge object in the center of the design, with lots of small objects attached to it. This situation is often dubbed the "God object" problem. The underlying problem in such cases is usually an inappropriate partitioning of responsibilities between design elements—the large object (often called "Manager") is really the entire program, and the small objects are often just data structures that this object uses. A very similar problem can exist in ADs, particularly if you consolidate too zealously (perhaps as a result of interaction analysis).

This problem leads to a situation where the system is hard to maintain because the God element is terribly complex and difficult to understand. It also results in this one component's characteristics dominating the quality properties that the system exhibits. It becomes difficult to solve related problems like performance, reliability, or scalability because they all involve changing this one system element.

EXAMPLE The UML element diagram in Figure 16–6 illustrates the sort of structure that often suggests the presence of a God element in your system.

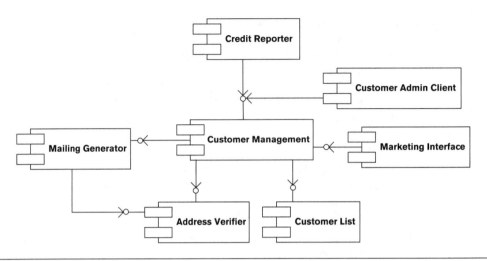

FIGURE 16-6 A GOD ELEMENT

> In this situation, the Customer Management system element appears to exhibit the major characteristic of a God element, namely, nearly all interelement interactions involve it. From this structure, it is likely that the Customer Management element contains too much of the system's functionality and has dependencies with too many of the system's elements. Repartitioning the system into a set of elements with more evenly distributed functionality would make sense.

RISK REDUCTION

- Aim for a broadly even distribution of system-level responsibilities between your major elements. As a guideline, if you find more than 50% of your system's responsibilities concentrated in less than 25% of your functional elements, you may be heading toward a number of large elements and your system will lack cohesion, be difficult to develop, and be resistant to change.

Too Many Dependencies

The converse to the God object problem is static object diagrams that look like a number of spiders fighting for control. Complex interactions between elements make the system harder to design and build and may lead to a solution that is hard to change and performs poorly.

RISK REDUCTION

- This problem can often be the symptom of too many small elements in the system—practicing some judicious compression may help you resolve it.

- In general, a system element should only need to be aware of the existence of a couple of other elements in order to perform its functions. If any of your elements need to use services from more than 50% of the other elements in the system, consider revising your functional structure.

CHECKLIST

- Do you have fewer than 15–20 top-level elements?

- Do all elements have a name, clear responsibilities, and clearly defined interfaces?

- Do all element interactions take place via well-defined interfaces and connectors that link the interfaces?

- Do your elements exhibit an appropriate level of cohesion?

- Do your elements exhibit an appropriate level of coupling?

- Have you identified the important usage scenarios and used these to validate the system's functional structure?

- Have you checked the functional coverage of your architecture to ensure it meets its functional requirements?

- Have you considered how the architecture is likely to cope with possible change scenarios in the future?

- Does the presentation of the view take into account the concerns and capabilities of all interested stakeholder groups? Will the view act as an effective communication vehicle for all of these groups?

FURTHER READING

Many software architecture books focus on the functional aspects of architecture, and the subject is (rightly) central to those that take a broader view. In addition to the many books we mentioned in Parts I and II, the following are relevant to the concepts we introduced in this chapter.

Clements et al. [CLEM03] is a detailed, thorough, and practical guide to documenting various architectural styles. In the context of this chapter, the discussions of overloading views and documenting the various styles of interfaces are particularly pertinent. Garland and Anthony [GARL03] describes how to go about designing the software architecture for large-scale information systems; the approach we suggest for modeling message-oriented element interactions comes from this book. The techniques we outline for element identification are based on the architectural "unit operations" described in Bass et al. [BASS03], where they are described more fully.

Many good books explain UML and how to use it to produce rigorous ADs [FOWL00; CHEE01; DSOU99]. Checkland [CHEC99] presents an approach to understanding real user requirements, using an informal diagrammatic approach called the "rich picture" (analogous to our description of sketches) to help communicate with end users.

Meyer [MEYE00] is the definitive reference on Design by Contract (and much more related to object orientation), while Mitchell and McKim [MITC02] provides a nice, concise, practitioner-oriented introduction to the approach. Wirfs-Brock et al. [WIRF90] is one of the original books on responsibility-driven design, while Shaw [SHAW94] is one of the first written attempts to explain why connectors between elements are just as important to model as the elements themselves.

17

THE INFORMATION
VIEWPOINT

Definition	Describes the way that the architecture stores, manipulates, manages, and distributes information
Concerns	Information structure and content; information flow; data ownership; timeliness, latency, and age; references and mappings; transaction management and recovery; data quality; data volumes; archives and data retention; and regulation
Models	Static data structure models, information flow models, information lifecycle models, data ownership models, data quality analysis, metadata models, and volumetric models
Problems and Pitfalls	Data incompatibilities, poor data quality, unavoidable multiple updaters, key matching deficiencies, poor information latency, interface complexity, and inadequate volumetrics
Stakeholders	Primarily users, acquirers, developers, and maintainers, but most stakeholders have some level of interest
Applicability	Any system that has more than trivial information management needs

The ultimate purpose of any information system is, of course, to manipulate data in some form. This data may be stored persistently in a database management system, in ordinary files, or in some other storage medium such as flash memory, or it may be transiently manipulated in memory while a program executes.

Nowadays, many organizations possess massive amounts of information on their customers, their products or services, their own internal processes, and their competitors. Although some of this information may be hard to access, inconsistent, and inaccurate, it still represents a substantial asset—one that, if correctly used, can bring substantial benefits. We see this often, in large systems integration projects that attempt to bring together information from a variety of sources to produce a consolidated customer view, an integrated view of the supply chain, or an accurate financial picture.

Formal data modeling and design can be a long and complex process. As an architect, you can do data modeling only at an architecturally significant level of detail. You need to focus on those aspects of the data model where getting it wrong would affect the system as a whole rather than just a part of it. Your task is to develop a complete but high-level view of static information structure and dynamic information flow, with the objective of answering the big questions around ownership, latency, references, and so forth.

You use the Information view to answer, at an architectural level, questions about how your system will store, manipulate, manage, and distribute information.

CONCERNS

Information Structure and Content

The structure and content of the information that the information system manages is clearly a huge concern for any information system. Your challenge as an architect is to focus on the right aspects of information structure and to leave the details to the data modelers and data designers.

Typically, you should focus on a relatively small number of data items (entities, classes, and so on) and the relationships among them. Deciding which entities are important depends on the problems you are trying to solve and the concerns of your stakeholders. However, you should bear the following in mind when selecting the data items of interest.

- Focus on a small number of entities that your stakeholders view as significant or meaningful. Primarily consider your user stakeholders, but also take into account the concerns of other stakeholder types such as maintainers.
- Focus on data-rich entities, rather than ones that have few attributes (e.g., type entities are typically less important in architectural data models). Choose entities that:
  - Are fundamental to the nature of the concerns being addressed
  - Are significant to the users or other stakeholders
  - Have a complex or poorly understood internal structure
  - Are heavily used or volatile (the contents are expected to change frequently)
- In the early stages of developing your models, try to focus on abstract rather than physical data, and keep the models simple. Don't worry too

much about formal modeling techniques such as relational database normalization at this point.

- Your early models should typically align with and be driven by the system's functionality, and you should be concerned less with physical considerations such as location or ownership (although we address these issues and others in this chapter).

Information Flow

Just as important as the static information structure is the way that information moves around the system and is accessed and modified by its elements. The important questions here include the following.

- Where is data created and destroyed?
- Where is data accessed and modified?
- How do individual data items change as they move around the system?

As with information structure, information flow is typically considered at a high level only as part of architecture definition. In any case, because you will have only a high-level data model to work with, you won't be able to drill down into too much detail here.

Because the main purpose of most systems is to process information, information flow is often analyzed within Functional rather than Information views. This is acceptable as long as you don't end up with a small number of complex, overloaded models that are hard to understand—and as long as you make sure that the data-specific concerns discussed in this chapter are also addressed.

Data Ownership

In many architectures, particularly those that involve the integration of new and/or existing systems, data is physically distributed across multiple data stores and accessed in different ways. This situation, while often unavoidable, creates all sorts of problems.

- Which copy of a particular data item is the most up-to-date one?
- How do you keep synchronized any data held in multiple places?
- What validation and business logic should be applied to the modification of data, and what assumptions can be made about data that has been validated elsewhere?
- If the same data item can be modified in several places, how are conflicts reconciled?

EXAMPLE An insurance company employs a large number of workers who visit customers at home to sell them financial products. The company maintains a central database of customers and prospects, an extract of which is downloaded to each salesperson's laptop when visiting the office. Whenever a sale is closed at a customer's home, the information is stored in a holding area on that laptop until it can be uploaded to the central database later.

The company opens a call center that allows customers to update their details and also offers limited capabilities to sell products. This leads to an increase in the number of complaints.

- Details stored on laptops are sometimes overwriting more recent data on the central database and vice versa.

- New customers who phone the call center find that there is no record of their details because the laptop where they are stored has not yet been synchronized.

- Sometimes, uploads from a laptop fail because the central database implements more up-to-date, stringent business validation logic.

In order to address these problems, the architect first has to agree with the business stakeholders on some general rules about how to deal with update conflicts and failures (e.g., recent updates always override older ones). These rules are then coded into the application, at considerable time and cost.

A useful way to analyze these problems and develop architectural strategies to handle them is to develop a model of data ownership. The data owner (or master) of a data item is the system or data store that contains the definitive, up-to-date, validated value of that data item. The data owner always has the correct value for that data and can act as the final arbiter where any data disputes occur.

By defining the owner of each data item, you can ensure that your data consumers are always working with the right data and that your data producers always write it to the correct place. Where this is not possible in practice, you can analyze potential conflicts and inconsistencies and then develop strategies to deal with them.

EXAMPLE A national system for registering motor vehicles operates from a number of semiautonomous regional centers. Each center is responsible for registering vehicles purchased in that region. Each vehicle must be allocated a unique number, but conflicts could arise because there is no real-time communication between the regional centers. (In data ownership terms, each center is a creator of the vehicle registration number data item.)

The problem is resolved by partitioning the data ownership, that is, by allocating to each center a separate, distinct range of numbers to assign to vehicles purchased in its area. Care must be taken to ensure that the ranges will never overlap. This is done by making each range far larger than the anticipated number of cars to be registered: The North center is given the range 1 to 100 million, the West center 101 million to 200 million, and so on.

A by-product, incidentally, of your data ownership analysis will be a high-level definition of some of your system's interfaces. Where one system is a data owner and another is a data consumer (or maintains a copy of that data), some sort of interface is required between them. You can use the interface definitions to cross-check the models in your Information view against the models in your Functional view. Any interface derived from data ownership rules should also exist as a process flow between the two participants.

Timeliness, Latency, and Age

If your data is held in a single data store and always accessed synchronously in real time, you do not need to worry about timeliness, latency, and age. Unfortunately, many information architectures do not work this way, and it is inevitable that some scenarios involve data that is old or out-of-date, if only by a few minutes.

EXAMPLE A commodity brokerage accepts a number of feeds from information sources that provide up-to-date pricing and volume information, as well as news stories relevant to the commodities being traded. The feeds are all channeled through a single gateway application that sorts, filters, and distributes the information to appropriate subscribers.

A catastrophic hardware failure renders the gateway unavailable for several days. When it comes back online, the subscribers are flooded with several thousand price messages that, because they are several days old, are of no interest to the recipients.

The gateway is modified so that after a failure, it discards messages that are older than a certain configurable age. Another failure occurs (a change of hardware supplier is called for), and the algorithm discards all messages more than one day old. Unfortunately, some vital news reports are also discarded along with the out-of-date prices.

The gateway is modified a second time, to take account of the message type as well as the age before discarding a message.

In this example we have separate *information providers* (the external systems that provide pricing and volume information) and *information consumers* (the internal users who make use of it). Because the process of information transfer from provider to consumer takes a finite (and possibly long) time, discrepancies can occur. If the time lag cannot be reduced to zero, you need to work with stakeholders to develop nonautomated solutions to the problems that may arise from inconsistent data.

The time lag between the visibility of information to providers and to consumers is expressed by means of **latency**, the length of time between the data item being updated at the data source and the updated value being available to all parts of the system.

You may also need to take into account the age of some data items (the time since the data item was last updated by its data source). A system that disseminates information on volatile stock prices, for example, may not be interested in prices that are hours or even minutes old. You may be able to discard this information because it is no longer needed.

You should identify key points where time-based inconsistencies can arise and, with the help of your stakeholders, develop strategies to handle them, such as the following.

- Tag important data items with a "last updated" date and time.
- Warn users when data may be outdated.
- Hide or discard data that may be too old.
- Reduce latency by means of faster interfaces or direct access to data sources.

References and Mappings

Whether data is managed by using relational entities or objects and classes, every piece of data needs a unique identifier or key that distinguishes it from others of similar type (e.g., customer number, machine serial number, or ISBN number). In relational database terminology, this is called a **primary key**; in object-oriented programming, the term **object ID** is often used; a more useful general term (which does not assume any underlying information model) is **reference**.

Where data is spread over multiple repositories, identifiers often become an issue. Different systems may use different mechanisms to identify the same data item, and these mechanisms will need to be reconciled at points where data exchanges occur. Because key assignment can be a volatile activity (consider a sales system where many new orders are created per second), you will need to keep this reconciliation process up-to-date with new information as it arrives.

EXAMPLE A newspaper captures sports information submitted by journalists along with results and scores that arrive electronically. The paper collates the information and publishes daily league tables for individual competitors and teams. Although the paper's own central database allocates identifiers to each competitor and team, most of the information sources refer to them only by name—and in the case of foreign competitors, these names are not always spelled correctly.

The database is suffering some significant data quality issues. Scores and results are sometimes allocated to the wrong player or team, phantom teams with spellings similar to real ones are created regularly, siblings' results are often allocated to the wrong person, and some results fail to be loaded at all.

Transaction Management and Recovery

Transaction management is so fundamental to the operation of modern relational databases that its significance in the architectural context can easily be forgotten. A classic example, which we repeat here, illustrates the importance of transaction management.

EXAMPLE A bank customer uses an automated teller machine to transfer $500 from her checking account to her savings account.

The bank uses two data stores, CHECKING and DEPOSIT, to manage these two different types of accounts. The transfer is implemented as two updates: a withdrawal of $500 from CHECKING, and a corresponding deposit of $500 into DEPOSIT, as shown in Figure 17–1.

It's essential that either both of these updates complete successfully or neither of them do. For example, the transaction might not go ahead if the customer doesn't have sufficient funds in her checking account. If only one of the transactions completes, either the customer or the bank would lose money.

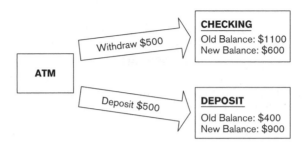

FIGURE 17–1 TRANSACTION MANAGEMENT FOR FUNDS TRANSFER

A **transaction** is a sequence of data updates that occur as an atomic unit—that is, either all updates are accepted and written to permanent storage or none of them are. Transaction management ensures the right outcome by *committing* updates (writing them permanently to disk) only if all updates can be successfully applied. Transaction management will *roll back* (undo) all of the updates if one of them fails.

Transaction management across multiple systems is complicated to design, build, and operate, requiring complex techniques such as two-phase commit or compensating transactions. Such techniques can impose a heavy burden on processing power, leading to increasing latency and response time, and you should use them only where absolutely necessary.

Data Quality

The quality of a particular data item is the extent to which the current value of that data item agrees with the correct value in the real world. Poor-quality data can have a significant impact on an organization's ability to carry out its operations. If you don't have accurate data about your customers, for example, you risk annoying them, losing them, or even being sued by them. (Given all this, it is still a surprise how many systems manage to survive on data that is incomplete, incorrect, or outdated.)

EXAMPLE A mail-order furniture company has created a marketing database from customer orders and requests for brochures or quotations. It uses this customer database to phone customers about special offers and to try to persuade them to buy more of the company's products.

Unfortunately, the data in the marketing database has been cobbled together from a number of sources and is therefore outdated and inaccurate.

Moreover, a number of customers have asked not to be cold-called, but these requests have not always been transferred from the spreadsheet where they're managed into the marketing database.

As a result, many customers receive cold calls who do not want them, or are offered products they already own, or are offered unsuitable products (e.g., those that are too expensive). This creates a significant amount of dissatisfaction among existing and potential customers, leading to bad publicity and possibly to lost sales.

Data quality becomes an issue for you as an architect in cases where the system makes use of data from a variety of sources, particularly when some of these are external to your sphere of influence. If your data quality is variable, you must consider such issues as the following.

- How will data quality be assessed (especially where data is frequently updated)?
- What minimum data quality criteria must be met?
- How will these criteria be enforced?
- How will poor-quality data be improved? Will this be done in an automated way, or will it require manual intervention?
- Can good-quality data be corrupted by data of lesser quality? (For example, a customer address is updated, but the postal code is omitted.) If so, should this be prevented or checked?
- Is it possible for information quality to degrade as it flows around the system?

The answers to these questions will have implications for the architecture. For example, it may be necessary to develop or deploy automated tools for monitoring or assessing data quality or for repairing poor-quality data. If repairing data needs some human intervention, you may have to set up a holding area where data can sit until it has been manually repaired.

Data Volumes

The volume of data that a system needs to manage or process can have a fundamental impact on its architecture. A system developed to handle megabytes or gigabytes of data will probably be structurally different—and possibly even functionally different—from one that has to manage terabytes of data. As data volumes increase, your architecture comes up against various physical, technical, and operational limitations:

- The amount of data that can physically be addressed by operating systems and programs
- The amount of data that can be stored on disk and tape devices and other media
- The time required to move data from one location to another (backup, e.g., for extract and load, regular updates, and so on)
- The maximum capacity of communication networks and integration hubs to transmit information
- The time taken to complete large batch jobs

You also need to consider the rate at which volumes are likely to grow over time, so that your architecture can accommodate future as well as current needs. We discuss this issue further in Chapter 25.

Archives and Data Retention

In many systems, it is becoming rare for data to be deleted; it may be kept for legal reasons or for historical analysis. Although disk storage is now relatively inexpensive, even enterprise disk architectures cannot expand indefinitely, and sooner or later your data will grow to a point where you run out of room. Then you will need to archive older, less useful data to some other storage medium such as high-capacity magnetic tapes.

You must define carefully the scope of data to archive. It obviously can't be data that is still needed to support any production activities, nor should it be data that is likely to be useful for regular analysis. Data is usually selected on the basis of age combined with business rules to determine its usefulness.

Your archiving strategy can have a significant impact on your architecture.

- Archiving large volumes of data may make some systems fully or partly unavailable for significant periods of time.
- Your physical disk sizing needs to take into account the length of time that data will be retained.
- You may need to define the processes that move production data to archive media.
- There may be an impact on the network infrastructure if archive storage is remote.

Don't try to add archival capabilities as an afterthought. Design your architecture from the beginning in such a way that archiving is a natural part of the information lifecycle.

Regulation

You may need to consider in your information architecture a number of types of legal regulations. Specific classes of systems, particularly in the financial area, are more or less closely regulated by governmental or autonomous bodies, such as the Securities and Exchange Commission in the United States or the Financial Services Authority in the United Kingdom. These regulations may impact your information architecture in many ways, having implications related to accuracy, security, data retention times, and even the scope of data that must be held.

In Europe, particularly, and to a lesser extent in the United States, strong legislation around personal privacy and data security may also have an impact on your information architecture. In recent years, the threat of cyberterrorism has led to legislation requiring information to be retained and possibly made available to government security agencies. This may also need to be factored into your architecture. We consider this point further in our discussion of the Regulation perspective in Chapter 28.

Stakeholder Concerns

Typical stakeholder concerns for the Information viewpoint include those listed in Table 17–1.

TABLE 17–1 STAKEHOLDER CONCERNS FOR THE INFORMATION VIEWPOINT

Stakeholder Class	Concerns
Acquirers	Concerned with preserving and safeguarding the value of the organization's information assets, so the following are key (although not always recognized as such): • Data quality and archives • Data retention
Assessors	Typically focus on regulation and data quality
Communicators	Rarely focus on detail on the information architecture, but may find a background understanding of the key principles and strategies helpful
Developers and maintainers	Interested in how the data architect's models will translate into real databases and (real-time, batch) information interfaces
System administrators and support staff	Interested in how these real-world system components will be managed and supported
Users	Concerned with functional aspects of the information architecture (e.g., data ownership, references and mappings, and regulation) and user-visible qualities such as timeliness, latency, and age; data quality; and transaction management and recovery.

MODELS

Data modeling is probably the best-served area of information systems in terms of established, rigorous, and generally understood analysis and modeling techniques. The three most important types of models are the following:

1. *Static data structure models*, which analyze the static structure of the data
2. *Information flow models*, which analyze the dynamic movement of information between elements of the system and the outside world
3. *Information lifecycle models*, which analyze the way data values change over time

We discuss these models in this section—particularly how they are used in the architectural context—and briefly describe some other types of models you may find useful, such as data ownership models, data quality analyses, metadata models, and volumetrics models.

Static Data Structure Models

Static data structure models analyze the static structure of the data: the important data elements and the relationships among them.

Entity-relationship modeling is an established technique of data analysis that, unlike many other systems analysis techniques, has a solid mathematical foundation. Data items of interest are referred to as **entities**, and their constituent parts are called **attributes**. The semantics of the data defines the static **relationships** among entities. Each relationship has a **cardinality**, which defines how many instances of one of the entities can be related to an instance of the other.

EXAMPLE A library stores a number of *books* for its *members*. Members *check out* books for a period of time, after which they are renewed or returned. Each book has one or more *authors*, who receive a fee each time a book is checked out. The fee is paid to the author via the book's *publisher*.

Each of the italicized terms in this description is represented as an entity in the entity-relationship model. Attributes of the model include book title, author name, ISBN number, and publisher name and address.

Class models perform a role similar to that of entity-relationship models but for the object-oriented world. They model data items (**classes**), their constituent data parts (**attributes**), and the static relationships among them (**as-**

sociations). It is possible to use class model notation to model relational entities by omitting the behavioral aspects from the model.

Class models also document the behavioral aspects of a system, such as interfaces and methods, and features specific to object-oriented analysis, such as inheritance.

EXAMPLE In the previous example, classes would be modeled for *books*, *members*, *authors*, and *publishers*. Methods would provide the necessary functionality for *checking out* books.

NOTATION There are a number of similar notation styles for documenting entity-relationship models. Figure 17–2 shows an entity-relationship diagram in the Structured Systems Analysis and Design Methodology (SSADM) style for the library example.

A UML class model for the same example would look something like Figure 17–3.

ACTIVITIES Formal data modeling includes a wide range of activities.

- A process called *normalization* reduces the model to its purest form, in which there is no repeated, redundant, or duplicated information. It is rare for relational models to be taken beyond third-normal form, and from the architect's perspective it is often more useful (although less rigorous) to model some data unnormalized.

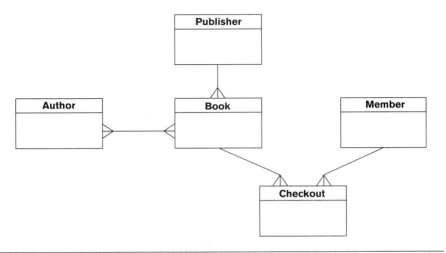

FIGURE 17–2 ENTITY-RELATIONSHIP DIAGRAM FOR THE LIBRARY EXAMPLE

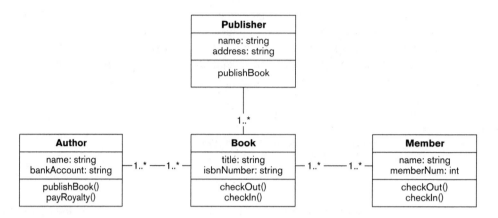

FIGURE 17-3 UML CLASS MODEL FOR THE LIBRARY EXAMPLE

- *Domain analysis* looks at attributes (fields) of data items and the rules that define their permissible values. For example, a customer number may always be a 10-digit integer with the last digit being a check digit, or a telephone number is always a country code followed by a dialing code and a number. Domain analysis is important in schema design but is usually too detailed for an AD.

- Techniques such as *structural decomposition* or *aggregation* are used to derive class models. Structural decomposition involves breaking an element into smaller coherent pieces, while aggregation is the reverse process—creating a new element by combining other, similar elements.

Unfortunately, static data structure models are not easily decomposed into levels of detail—for entity-relationship diagrams in particular, it is, in theory, "all or nothing." In practice, you do not have time to produce a hundred- or maybe thousand-entity data model as part of your architecture. The way to approach this is to focus on a small number of the most important entities/classes and the relationships among them.

You can usually omit from your model detail such as intersection entities (replace these with nonnormalized, many-to-many relationships, as we did in the entity-relationship diagram shown in Figure 17–3 between author and book) and type entities (such as product type).

As a very general guideline, if you have more than about 20 entities, or if your entity-relationship diagram won't easily fit on a single page, you have probably presented too much detail. In this case, you need to either remove some less important entities from the model or use partitioning and/or decomposition to simplify the overall picture.

Information Flow Models

Information flow models analyze dynamic movement of information between elements of the system and with the outside world.

These models identify the main architectural elements and the information flows between them. Each flow represents some data transferred from one component to another—in other words, a data interface. Associated with each flow is a direction, the scope of the data transferred, volumetric information, and (in a physical model) the means whereby data is exchanged, whether it is a transfer of flat files or a real-time exchange of XML messages.

EXAMPLE A publisher supplies *lists of newly published books* to libraries in a PDF document that is mailed to librarians monthly. When a library receives a book, it is accompanied by an *electronic delivery note* in the form of an XML file, which is imported directly into the library's book management system. When books are checked out and back in, the *new state* is recorded by means of bar-code readers. When a book is disposed of, it is manually *marked as deleted* in the system by a PC application that accesses the database directly.

Each italicized term represents a data flow into, out of, or around the system.

As with static information modeling, you should aim to keep your information flow models high-level and simple. It is not necessary to provide much detail at the architectural stage. Fortunately, most notations support this naturally through decomposition.

Information flow modeling is most useful for data-intensive systems, and it complements the modeling of process flow (see Chapter 16), which is often more appropriate to processing-intensive systems. In practice, you usually do only one or the other, depending on the nature of the system, the skills of the architect, and on the interests of the key stakeholders.

NOTATION There are a number of information flow notations from classic systems analysis, such as Gane and Sarson or SSADM data flow diagrams, although these are as much about process as about information flow. Figure 17–4 shows an example of a data flow diagram.

The following notation is used in the diagram.

- Large rectangles represent processes that manipulate data.
- Narrow open rectangles represent data stores (logical or physical collections of information).

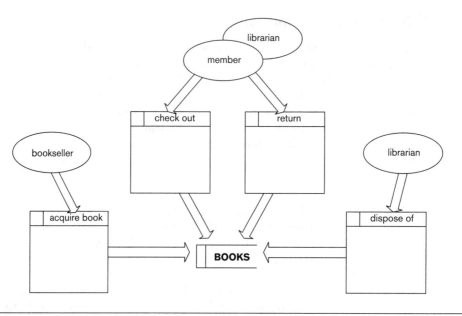

FIGURE 17-4 Data Flow Diagram for the Library Example

- Arrows represent data flows.
- Ellipses represent external entities (people or other systems that interact with this system).

The diagram conveys several pieces of information.

- Members and the librarian provide information to the check out and return processes.
- A bookseller provides information to the acquire book process.
- The librarian provides information to the dispose of process.
- All this information is written to the BOOKS data store.

UML version 1 does not directly support this type of analysis, although it is possible to use sequence diagrams to represent information flow for particular processes.

ACTIVITIES Information flow models are typically created through a process of stepwise refinement, with the big flows being considered first and then broken into further detail where necessary.

You can use your data ownership model, if you have one, to cross-check against the information flows required to maintain data integrity where ownership is distributed (as discussed earlier).

Information Lifecycle Models

Lifecycle models analyze the way data values change over time.

Entity life histories model the transitions that data items undergo in response to external events, from creation through one or more updates to final deletion. A life history can be a useful cross-check to ensure that there is processing to deal with all of the life events associated with an entity. In particular, it can help you ensure that entities are created in a controlled manner and that all entities have a means of deletion.

EXAMPLE A book is created when it is *published* (as far as the library system is concerned, anyway). The book is then *acquired* by the library and repeatedly *checked out* and *returned* until it is finally *disposed of*.

Each italicized verb in this description is an event in an entity life history for a book.

State transition models (or *statecharts* in UML terminology) model the overall changes in a system's state in response to external stimuli. This is a useful way to model systems whose interactions with the outside world are unpredictable or do not conform to standard patterns. A statechart models the system as a finite state machine (FSM). An FSM always has a current state, which is the sum total of the data it holds. When an external event occurs, the FSM changes deterministically to another state and may also instigate some special processing as a result of the change.

EXAMPLE A book is initially *published*; it is then *acquired* by the library, and once on the shelves it alternates between being *available for loan* and *checked out*, until it is *disposed of*.

Each italicized term represents a state of a book.

NOTATION An entity life history is usually represented by using some sort of tree structure, with nodes for each event and branches to represent iteration, selection, and so forth, as shown in Figure 17–5.

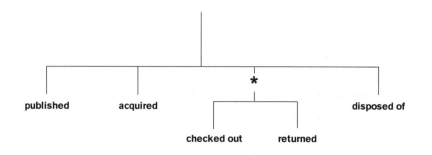

FIGURE 17–5 ENTITY LIFE HISTORY FOR THE LIBRARY EXAMPLE

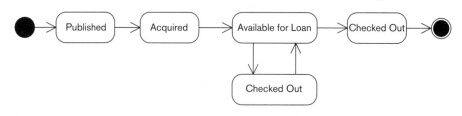

FIGURE 17–6 UML STATE DIAGRAM FOR THE LIBRARY EXAMPLE

A UML state diagram uses railroad tracks to represent the possible state transitions of an object, as shown in Figure 17–6.

ACTIVITIES Lifecycle models are derived through an understanding of the system's functional requirements, by identifying all the significant events and understanding the data impact of each.

Other Types of Information Models

DATA OWNERSHIP MODELS Data ownership models define the owner for each data item in the architecture. In this context, "data item" typically means entity (table) or, occasionally, attribute (field), although more complex partitions can be modeled. Of course, in practice, life is never this simple, and you may have to model a number of different classes of data ownership, such as:

- Owner or master, which holds the definitive value for that data item
- Creator, which creates new instances of that data item
- Updater, which modifies existing instances of that data item
- Deleter, which deletes existing instances of that data item

- Reader, which can read but not change instances of that data item
- Copy, which holds a read-only copy of that data item
- Validater, which performs validation on the data item to ensure that it meets business rules
- A combination of these

At its simplest level, data ownership can be modeled by using a grid, with systems and data stores along one axis and data items along the other. Each cell in the grid defines the ownership class of that data item, as shown in Table 17–2.

It may be useful to develop a *trust and permissions model* to define which systems, under which circumstances, are allowed to modify which data items. For example, an external system that provides data updates in a weekly batch might be trusted less than one managed and monitored internally, might require further validation before updates are accepted, or might be constrained to updating only noncritical data values.

In practice, you may not be able to avoid having more than one creator/updater/deleter for a data item (although it is useful to try to define a single data owner). This particularly occurs when valuable data is held in legacy systems. Where two systems can modify the same piece of data, you need to develop *conflict resolution strategies*, such as the following, to ensure that business rules are followed and that information is left in a consistent state.

- Always accept the latest update.
- Maintain multiple copies of the same data item, tagged with their sources.
- Maintain a history of data changes rather than just the latest version of the data.
- Trust one system more than another, so that system's updates take priority.
- Create more complex rules depending on the data changed and the nature of the change.

TABLE 17–2 EXAMPLE OF A DATA OWNERSHIP GRID

System	Customer	Product	Order	Fulfillment
Catalog	None	Owner	None	None
Purchasing	Reader	Updater	Owner	Creator
Delivery	Copy	Reader	Reader	Updater
Customer	Owner	Reader	Reader	Reader

- Record multiple values and require manual intervention to fix the conflict.
- Reject conflicting updates altogether.
- Use a combination of these strategies.

Although you are unlikely to define detailed rules as part of your AD, it is important to provide sufficient advice and guidance for your designers.

DATA QUALITY ANALYSIS From the architectural perspective, your data quality analysis will focus on defining *sources* of poor-quality data and *principles and strategies* for dealing with this data. Possible strategies include the following.

- *Ignore poor-quality data*: This approach is suitable when poor-quality data is not an issue or when the cost of repairing data far outweighs the benefit of improving it.

> **EXAMPLE** An Internet search engine manages a database of many hundreds of millions of URLs. At any one time, a small proportion of these will no longer be valid because pages have been renamed or Web sites removed. However, it is not cost-effective for the search engine to regularly clean up its database to remove these links.

- *Automatically fix poor-quality data*: There are a number of tools available to do this, depending on the type of data.

> **EXAMPLE** You can use tools that will repair or complete addresses or telephone numbers, based on databases of postal codes or telephone dialing rules.

- *Discard poor-quality data*: This may be the best approach where the cost of bad data far outweighs the cost of not having the data at all.

> **EXAMPLE** A company receives bulk mailing lists of variable quality from an external supplier, which it uses to send out marketing material to potential customers. For about 10% of the data, postal codes are missing, invalid, or do not correspond to the mailing address. Such records are discarded because the company is penalized by the postal service if too much of its outgoing mail is incorrectly or incompletely addressed, and material sent to these addresses is unlikely to arrive anyway.

- *Deal with poor-quality data manually* (in other words, get users to fix it): This is a very costly approach, however, and you must consider how poor-quality data will be identified and how it will be forwarded to users for correction.

Be aware that there may be legislative requirements for data quality (e.g., some countries charge penalties for maintaining or using incorrect data on members of the public). We consider this point further in our discussion of the Regulation perspective in Chapter 28.

METADATA MODELS Metadata is "data about data." Metadata consists of rules that describe and prescribe data items of interest—entities, attributes, relationships, and so forth. Metadata originated in the study of geospatial data and has had an increased profile in recent years following the growth of the World Wide Web and various initiatives around business-to-business communication.

ISO Standard 11197-3 defines metadata as "the information and documentation which makes data sets understandable and sharable for users."[1] Metadata may address a number of aspects of the data it describes, such as:

- Data format (syntax)
- Data meaning (semantics)
- Data structure
- Data context (the relationships among data items)
- Data quality

Many organizations are beginning to develop enterprise-wide metadata models; if these are available to you, they can form an extremely valuable input to your Information view. In addition, there are a number of cross-industry metadata models being developed under the auspices of groups like the Dublin Core Metadata Initiative.

Metadata models are closely allied to the other types of data models we have described, particularly data structure models that include some elements of metadata (field attributes, relationships, and so on). Most metadata models take the form of structured (or unstructured) text, but some more formal notations are available, in particular those based around XML.

Some automated tools can extract metadata from large databases. Although these are to some extent in their infancy, they can be extremely useful, especially when dealing with legacy systems whose data internals may not be well understood.

---

1. [ISO96, p. vii].

Volumetric Models Volumetric models look at current and predicted data volumes. These can range from a few simple calculations on a scrap of paper to sophisticated statistical models to complete online simulations of systems.

You can develop a simple volumetric model by estimating the numbers of instances of each entity and multiplying these by the size of each instance (the sum of the sizes of each attribute). You should then apply a technology-dependent scaling factor to cater for physical storage overheads such as indexes, pointers and data framentation. You can enhance the model by applying predicted growth rates or estimating the volatility of each entity (the proportion of the instances which change per unit time).

Problems and Pitfalls

Data Incompatibilities

At their simplest, data incompatibilities arise because different systems encode field-level information in different ways.

- One system may use Y and N for Boolean values, while another uses 1 and 0, or hex FF and 00.
- One system may use standard ISO abbreviations such as FR or DE for countries, while another has its own numeric encoding.
- One system may record monetary amounts in euros, while another uses the local currency in which the transaction took place.
- One system may record amounts by volume, another by weight.

These sorts of problems are usually fairly easy to resolve. Much more problematic, however, are incompatibilities between business models.

Example An architecture is required to integrate a telephone billing system with another system used to manage prospects, sales, and marketing promotions. A telephone customer may have several phone lines or may charge calls on a single line to different charge codes; for this reason, the billing system is based on the concept of a telephone account. Even worse, some accounts may be held jointly by several customers (especially business accounts), and some others (such as public emergency phone lines) have no real customer at all.

The sales system is concerned solely with customers (and more importantly, prospective customers). However, the system needs to know

> about these customers' existing accounts, as well as other details such as payment history and usage, in order to avoid trying to sell customers something they already have.
>
> The business models for these systems are fundamentally incompatible, and a lot of work is going to be needed to develop an architecture that successfully brings them together.

Incompatible business models can usually be reconciled only by using what may turn out to be fairly complex processing. In the example, you would probably have to develop a subsystem or service that was responsible for maintaining the links between customers and their accounts. This service would have to be updated (possibly in real time) when customers or accounts were created, deleted, or updated, or when the links between them were changed. It would own and manage the information itself and provide that data on demand to any other architectural element that required it.

Such a service would sit at the core of the architecture, being accessed by many other architectural elements, with ambitious targets for performance, scalability, and availability. This service would need to be very carefully designed, built, and tested.

RISK REDUCTION

- Develop a common, high-level model of the data structure, the key data attributes, and their domains, and validate it against all parts of the system (internal and external).
- Review your model with the business to ensure that it reflects reality.
- Focus on a small number of critically important attributes, rather than trying to model everything.
- Don't forget to include external entities in your model (e.g., if you exchange data with other organizations).
- Consider developing a data abstraction layer on top of data sources to hide the incompatibilities from other parts of the architecture.

Poor Data Quality

If the actual data is inconsistent, inaccurate, or incomplete, it doesn't matter how good your data model is—you will face big problems when your system goes into operation.

In fact, the real problem is not necessarily poor data quality but *unexpectedly* poor data quality. If you know that some data will be inadequate, you can develop strategies early to deal with it and successfully manage the expectations of your stakeholders in this area.

RISK REDUCTION

- Validate your key assumptions about data quality early (e.g., "All products can be uniquely identified by using a common key").
- Make sure that you understand what data is important and what data is less important (your stakeholders, primarily users, can tell you this), then focus on the important data.
- Make use of commercially available data quality tools to analyze the quality of existing data.
- Identify the places where poor quality data can appear, and develop strategies for dealing with it, such as rejecting poor-quality data, marking it as suspect, or attempting to fix it.

Unavoidable Multiple Updaters

When creating distributed architectures, we all strive to achieve models whereby each data item is updated in one place and one place only. Unfortunately, in the real world this ambition cannot always be realized, for a number of reasons: Legacy systems cannot easily be changed, data may be sourced from outside the organization, or there may be limitations imposed by geography or politics.

As we have seen, multiple creators or updaters can have a significant impact on the architecture, and resolving such problems is not always easy. From the architectural perspective, you need to be aware of where this can happen so that you can take suitable measures to mitigate the risks.

RISK REDUCTION

- Ensure that your data ownership model is complete and accurate and that all data items with multiple updaters are identified.
- Determine with your stakeholders (primarily your users) which of these multiple updaters are important, and focus on these.
- Understand where inconsistencies through multiple updaters can arise and locate the crunch points where incompatible data items meet.
- Develop strategies for resolving these, such as always overriding old updates with newer ones, or maintaining two copies of data and resolving problems manually.

Key-Matching Deficiencies

Where you are bringing together data from multiple systems, key-matching problems almost inevitably arise, as we saw earlier. These may not become apparent until you get into detailed design—by which time it is very expensive to change the architecture—or, even worse, once the system is running.

RISK REDUCTION

- Make sure that you have identified keys for all entities, and satisfy yourself that these keys are compatible across the architecture.
- At all points where data from different systems comes together, ensure that you have the means to map keys from one system to the other.
- Wherever possible, go for common keys and standardized ways of modeling data.

Poor Information Latency

Poor latency typically arises from overly complex architectures or architectures that are not designed to handle the volumes of data they are presented with. You may also have latency issues that are outside your control. For example, data may arrive from an external source only once a week, or updates may need to be applied in batches overnight because of the limitations of a legacy system.

As with data quality, poor latency becomes an issue only if it is *unexpectedly* poor. By identifying expected latency early, you can identify problem areas and develop strategies to deal with them.

RISK REDUCTION

- Where there is distance or complexity between information providers and information consumers, ensure that you predict, as best you can, what the information latency will be.
- Where latency is significant, review this with your stakeholders to determine whether it is a concern.
- Better still, obtain agreement on realistic latency requirements for all data items up front, and validate your model against these.

Interface Complexity

If two systems need to transfer information between themselves, one bidirectional interface needs to be built. For three systems, three interfaces are needed; for four systems, six. In general, if your architecture comprises n systems, each of which needs to exchange information with every other, you need to build $n(n-1)/2$ interfaces, as shown in Figure 17–7.

Even though it is unlikely that every system in your architecture needs to exchange information with every other, once you have more than a handful of

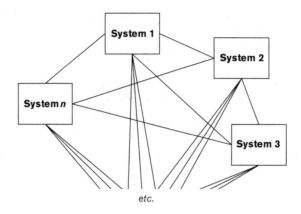

etc.

FIGURE 17-7 INTERFACE COMPLEXITY

systems, the number of interfaces required becomes unmanageable. Change the interface definition for any one of your n systems, and $n-1$ interfaces need to be redesigned, recoded, tested, and deployed. This represents a significant burden for developers and often acts as a barrier to change.

RISK REDUCTION

- Where interface requirements are complex, consider applying an architectural style called the *integration hub*. In this model, all systems are linked once via a specialized adapter to one central integration hub. The adapter performs system-specific translation, and the hub handles message routing, resilience, and more specialized functions such as publish and subscribe, acknowledgment, and guaranteed delivery. An example is shown in Figure 17–8.

  The advantage of this approach is that if a system changes, often only the adapter for that system needs to be modified. Furthermore, specialized code for routing, resilience, and so forth has to be implemented only once, in the central hub. (A disadvantage is that the central hub is a single point of failure and can constrain throughput.) There are many off-the-shelf, configurable integration hub products.

  Integration hubs and similar architectures form part of the wider topic of Enterprise Application Integration, a full consideration of which is outside the scope of this book. (See the Further Reading section at the end of this chapter.)

Inadequate Volumetrics

A system designed to handle a thousand updates per day is unlikely to cope well when faced with a million updates per day. Unless you are clear about

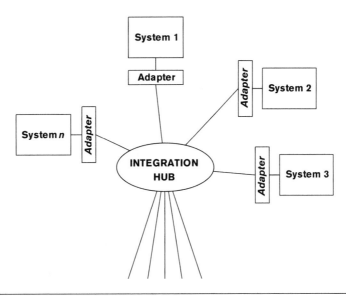

FIGURE 17-8 EXAMPLE OF AN INTEGRATION HUB

the volumes of data the system is expected to handle, you have little chance of designing an appropriate architecture. (We address the issue of volumetrics in more detail in Chapter 25.)

RISK REDUCTION

- Make sure that data volumes are captured, reviewed, and approved by your stakeholders.
- Make sure that volumes are realistic. If the stakeholders convey doubt or vagueness about this, pursue the issue, and if in doubt, increase them to allow for the margin of error.
- Make sure that your data volumes cover all scenarios—not just the on-line day, for example, but also the overnight processing and peak periods such as the end of the year or holiday processing.
- Make sure that there is an effective translation of business volumes into physical ones. For example, a single business transaction, such as placing an order, may result in several physical transactions, such as decrementing stock levels, posting account records, assigning compensation to sales staff, and arranging delivery of the ordered item.
- Make sure that your data volumes take future expansion into account.
- Prototype your data stores and the access to them for the expected volumes you do have.

CHECKLIST

- Do you have an appropriate level of detail in your data models (e.g., no more than about 20 entities)?
- Are keys clearly identified for all important entities?
- Where an entity is distributed across multiple systems or locations with different keys, are the mappings between these keys defined? Do you have processes for maintaining these mappings when data items are created?
- Have you defined strategies for resolving data ownership conflicts, particularly where there are multiple creators or updaters?
- Are latency requirements clearly identified, and are mechanisms in place to ensure these are achieved?
- Do you have clear strategies for transactional consistency across distributed data stores, and do these balance this need with the cost in terms of performance and complexity?
- Do you have mechanisms in place for validating migrated data and dealing appropriately with errors?
- Have you defined sufficient storage and processing capacity for archiving? And for restoring archived data?
- Has a data quality assessment been done? Have you created strategies for dealing with poor-quality data?

FURTHER READING

The literature on information architecture per se (as opposed to data design techniques or specific data management technologies) is sparse, almost nonexistent.

Fortunately, data modeling, and particularly relational modeling, which underpins much that we do, has a strong theoretical grounding, so there is a plethora of books on the subject. The classic of the genre, which is still being updated, is probably Date [DATE03]. Other good general books include Elmasri and Navathe [ELMA99] and Kroenke [KROE02].

Kim [KIMW99] looks at some of the newer techniques such as object-oriented databases. Redman [REDM97] provides a detailed discussion of the issues around data quality and how to develop strategies for data quality analysis and improvement.

Enterprise Application Integration architectures are covered in a large number of books, such as Linthicum [LINT03] and Ruh et al. [RUHW00].

You can find further information on metadata modeling in ISO Standard 11197-3 [ISO96] and on the Internet.

A vast number of books (too numerous to mention here) cover specific relational database products (e.g., Oracle, SQL Server, DB2, Sybase) and tools and technologies for application development, systems management, and integration.

18

THE CONCURRENCY VIEWPOINT

Definition	Describes the concurrency structure of the system, mapping functional elements to concurrency units to clearly identify the parts of the system that can execute concurrently, and shows how this is coordinated and controlled
Concerns	Task structure, mapping of functional elements to tasks, interprocess communication, state management, synchronization and integrity, startup and shutdown, task failure, and reentrancy
Models	System-level concurrency models and state models
Problems and Pitfalls	Modeling of the wrong concurrency, excessive complexity, resource contention, deadlock, and race conditions
Stakeholders	Developers, testers, and some administrators
Applicability	All information systems with a number of concurrent threads of execution

Historically, information systems were designed to operate with little or no concurrency, running via batch mode on large central computers. A number of factors (including distributed systems, increasing workloads, and cheap multiprocessor hardware) have combined so that today's information systems often have little or no batch mode operations.

In contrast, control systems have always been inherently concurrent and event-driven, given their need to react to external events in order to perform control operations. It is natural, then, that as information systems become more concurrent and event-driven, they start to take on a number of characteristics traditionally associated with control systems. Similarly, it is unsurprising that, in order to deal with this concurrency, the information systems community has adopted and adapted proven techniques from the control systems community. Many of these techniques form the basis of the Concurrency viewpoint.

The Concurrency view is used to describe the system's concurrency and state-related structure and constraints. This involves defining the parts of the system that can run at the same time and how this is controlled (e.g., defining how the system's functional elements are packaged into operating system processes and how the processes coordinate their execution). To do this, you need to create a process model and a state model: The process model shows the planned process, thread, and interprocess communication structure; the state model describes the set of states that runtime elements can be in and the valid transitions between those states.

Once you have created concurrency and state models, you can use a number of analysis techniques to ensure that the planned concurrency scheme is sound. The use of such techniques is typically part of creating a Concurrency view, too.

It's worth noting that not all information-based systems really benefit from a Concurrency view. Some information systems have little concurrency. Others, while exhibiting concurrent behavior, use the facilities of underlying software packages (e.g., databases) to hide the concurrency model actually in use.

EXAMPLE Data warehouse systems tend to be batch loaded overnight and accessed from a number of desktop machines. These systems do exhibit concurrent behavior—multiple clients can request information from the data warehouse concurrently. However, such a system will typically rely on the underlying database management system to handle all of the concurrency for it (in any way it chooses). Therefore, the process model used is of little architectural significance, and you have little or no control over it. The interesting aspects of the concurrency relate much more to the design of the physical data model and should be handled there.

In contrast, however, many of today's information systems are inherently event-driven, reactive, concurrent systems. This is particularly the case when considering infrastructure such as middleware products. Systems of this type typically sit idle until an external event occurs and then process the event. Given that many external events can occur simultaneously and that the interarrival time of such events may be lower than the time taken to process them, this kind of information-based system is inherently concurrent, with many operations being executed at once.

EXAMPLE Consider an e-commerce system that uses a message-based approach to processing transaction requests. In such a system, when a request arrives, it is translated into a message that is queued for the appropriate functional element that can process it. In order to prevent message queues growing too long and to make efficient use of processing resources, the processing element will need to process a number of messages concurrently. In this case, there may be a large number of concurrent operations within the functional element, each one needing access to shared resources.

The Concurrency view is extremely relevant to systems that exhibit this kind of behavior. Use of the Concurrency view allows the concurrency design of such systems to be made explicit and helps interested stakeholders understand concurrency constraints and requirements. It also allows you to analyze the system to avoid common concurrency problems such as deadlocks or bottlenecks.

CONCERNS

Task Structure

The most important aspect of creating a Concurrency view is establishing the system's process structure, which identifies the overall strategy for using concurrency in the system and the set of processes across which the system's workload is partitioned. The process structure also defines how the functions of the system are distributed across the set of processes identified. It may be necessary to consider the use of operating system threads within processes or to abstract away from individual processes and consider groups of similar processes instead.

Note: Throughout this chapter, the word *task* is used as a generic term to describe a processing thread—whether it is a single operating system process, one thread within a multithreaded process, or some other software execution unit. Where the difference is significant, the terms *process* and *thread* are specifically used.

The aspects of the system's task structure that this view needs to address depend very much on the kind of system you are dealing with.

EXAMPLE A complex, small-footprint system may have only one or two operating system tasks but may need to use a very complex thread model to meet its efficiency and responsiveness goals. In this case, the focus of the task structure activity needs to be at the thread level.

A large enterprise system may be comprised of literally hundreds of concurrent processes, many containing dozens of threads. In this sort of system, the task structure activity needs to be at the level of groups of similar processes in order to focus on the architecturally significant aspects of the concurrency.

Mapping of Functional Elements to Tasks

The mapping of functional elements to tasks can have a significant effect on the performance, efficiency, resilience, reliability, and flexibility of your architecture, so this needs careful consideration. The key question to address is which functional elements need to be isolated from each other (and so placed in separate processes) and which need to cooperate closely (and so need to run within the same process).

Interprocess Communication

When functional elements reside within a single operating system process, communication among them is relatively simple because of their shared address space. While some coordination may be required (see the Synchronization and Integrity subsection), you can use any number of data structures to pass information among them. Similarly, a number of easily used control mechanisms (such as the procedure call and variants of it) can transfer control among elements as needed.

In contrast, when elements reside in different operating system processes, communication among them becomes more complex. This complexity increases if the processes also reside on different physical machines.

A number of interprocess communication mechanisms can be used to link elements in different processes, including remote procedure calls, messaging, shared memory, pipes, queues, and so on. Each has its own strengths, weaknesses, and constraints, and inappropriate use of these mechanisms can cause problems at the system level (e.g., queue latency causing response time problems). In order to deliver a system with an acceptable set of quality properties, the Concurrency view needs to consider and identify the set of interprocess communication mechanisms that will be used to provide the interelement communication required by the system's functional structure.

State Management

In many systems, the runtime state that system elements may be in is important to the correct operation of the system. These systems tend to be event-driven and exhibit a high degree of concurrency.

For these systems, a concern of the Concurrency view is to clearly define the set of states that each functional element of the system can be in at runtime, the set of valid transitions between those states, and the causes and effects of the interstate transitions. Such careful state management is a major factor in ensuring reliability and correct behavior for most concurrent systems. Again, if you are using a formal architectural style, it may define how the system's runtime state should be handled.

Note that this concern refers to the state of the runtime elements of the system. Another type of state management important to many information systems is the set of valid states and transitions for their core persistent information (business objects). However, this is a distinct concept of state, and we refer to persistent object state models as *lifecycles* to avoid any confusion between the two. Object lifecycles are discussed in Chapter 17 about the Information viewpoint.

Having said this, it is quite reasonable to consider state management in the Functional view—after all, the state of functional elements is what we're considering. However, our experience is that the design of the system's state management usually fits better in the Concurrency view. Those systems where state is important are usually those where concurrency is important too, and considering system-level state usually involves the consideration of the concurrency around it as well.

Synchronization and Integrity

As soon as more than one thread of control exists in the system, it is important to ensure that concurrent execution cannot result in corruption of information within the system. This concern applies at a number of levels in the system, from a shared variable within a multithreaded module at one end of the scale to critical corporate transaction data in shared data stores at the other.

An important concern for the Concurrency view to address is how concurrent activity will be coordinated so that the system operates correctly and maintains the integrity of the data within it.

Startup and Shutdown

When you have more than one operating system process in your system, startup and shutdown of the system can become more complicated to manage. Intertask dependencies may mean that tasks need to be started and stopped in very specific orders so that if some tasks fail to start, others will not be started. The system startup and shutdown dependencies are an important part of your concurrency design and need to be clearly understood by developers, testers, and administrators.

Task Failure

When functional elements reside in different processes or run on different threads, dealing with element failure becomes significantly more complex. This is because an element in one task cannot rely on another task being available when it needs to communicate with it, whereas when an element calls another one in the same task, it knows the element will be there. Your concurrency design needs to take into account this added possibility of failure and ensure that the failure of one task doesn't bring the entire system to a halt. In order to address this concern, you need a system-wide strategy for recognizing and recovering from task failure.

Reentrancy

Reentrancy refers to the ability of a software element to operate correctly when used concurrently by more than one processing thread. This is primarily a concern for software developers when designing their software elements. From an architectural perspective, reentrancy is an important constraint for certain elements, so the architecture must clearly define which modules need to be reentrant and which don't.

EXAMPLE   If you are developing an e-mail server, the ability to support a great deal of concurrency is likely to be a key concern. Without this, it will be hard to use the e-mail server for large user populations who will want to send and receive e-mail simultaneously. You can take a number of approaches to achieve such concurrency, but for the sake of argument, let's assume that you have decided to implement the server by using a single operating system process and many (perhaps hundreds) of concurrent operating system threads running within it: some sending e-mail, some receiving e-mail, and some managing the server's internal state.

In this sort of environment, it is crucial to decide which of the elements of your system have to be reentrant and which don't. Any element involved in sending and receiving e-mail (e.g., a name resolution library that translates e-mail domains to network addresses) will need to be reentrant to ensure that it can be used simultaneously by many sending and receiving threads. Without such a guarantee, the name resolution library could be the source of many subtle problems later if its internal state could be corrupted by concurrent access.

The reentrancy needs of your architecture can also affect which third-party software elements you can use within the system and where you can use them.

TABLE 18-1 STAKEHOLDER CONCERNS FOR THE CONCURRENCY VIEWPOINT

Stakeholder Class	Concerns
Administrators	Task structure, startup and shutdown, and task failure
Communicators	Task structure, startup and shutdown, and task failure
Developers	All concerns
Testers	Task structure, mapping of functional elements to tasks, startup and shutdown, task failure, and reentrancy

Stakeholder Concerns

Typical stakeholder concerns for the Concurrency viewpoint include those shown in Table 18–1.

MODELS

System-Level Concurrency Models

The Concurrency view maps the functional elements onto runtime execution entities via a concurrency model. The concurrency model typically contains the following items.

- *Processes*: In this context, the term *process* refers to an operating system process, that is, an address space that provides an execution environment for one or more independent threads of execution. The process is the basic unit of concurrency in the design of the system. At the architecture level, the processes are normally assumed to be isolated from each other so that if one process wants to affect the execution of another, it must use an interprocess communication mechanism.

- *Process groups*: At the architecture level, it can often be useful to group individual processes so that a collection of closely related processes can be considered as a single entity at the system level. This can provide a useful abstraction that allows less important concurrency concerns to be deferred until subsystem design. An example is a database management system (DBMS). The important point from the system level is that the DBMS is a functional unit, accessed via well-defined interfaces, which runs in its own process or group of processes. However, the details of the exact number of processes it uses (e.g., how many logging processes run within the DBMS) and the function of each are almost certainly irrelevant to the architecture—indeed, this will probably be decided by a technical specialist later in the design process. Using a process group in this situation makes it clear that a group of related processes will be used but defers the details of the set until later. The other common use for process groups is simply as a hierarchical structuring technique for large or complex systems that contain many processes. All of the processes may need description, but the use of process groups can make the process model easier to comprehend.

▪ *Threads*: In this context, the term *thread* refers to an operating system thread, that is, a thread of execution that can be independently scheduled within an operating system process. Threads are known as *lightweight processes* by some operating systems. At the level of system architecture, threads can often be ignored, with the details of their use being the responsibility of subsystem designers (perhaps with you guiding their use via design patterns in the Development view). For some systems, you do want to model the use of threads in at least some parts of the system. Threads are normally represented in process models via a decomposition of a process.

▪ *Interprocess communication*: When processes are running, they are assumed to be isolated from each other so that one process cannot change anything in another process. However, in most concurrent systems, processes do need to interact in order to coordinate their execution, request services from each other, and pass information among themselves. They achieve these interactions via a number of interprocess communication mechanisms, which are the connectors in the system's runtime architecture.

The mechanisms available vary depending on the underlying technology platforms in use. However, interprocess communication mechanisms generally fall into one of these groups.

- *Procedure call mechanisms* are all some sort of variation on an interprocess function call and are usually based on some form of remote procedure call or some sort of message-passing operation.
- *Execution coordination mechanisms* allow two or more processes (or threads) to signal to each other when certain events occur. Coordination mechanisms include semaphores and mutexes and are typically limited to coordination between processes or threads running on the same physical machine.
- *Data-sharing mechanisms* allow a number of processes to share one or more data structures and access them concurrently (possibly coordinating this access via coordination mechanisms). Data-sharing mechanisms include shared memory, distributed tuple spaces (like Linda and JavaSpaces) and simple, traditional mechanisms such as client/server databases and shared file storage.

As the architect, you need to specify the interprocess communication mechanisms used with some care because their selection can significantly affect the quality properties (such as performance and reliability) that the system exhibits. It is also important to note that the interprocess communication mechanisms you choose must be compatible with the element interfaces defined in the Functional view. If one functional element uses an interface from another functional element and the two are mapped to different processes, the processes must be linked by an interprocess communication mechanism that can support the constraints of the interface being used.

NOTATION You can represent the Concurrency view in a number of ways. Some of the more common notational approaches include UML, other formal notations, and informal notations, which we describe briefly here.

- *UML*: UML does not have particularly strong concurrency modeling facilities built into it but does include the notion of an active object that can be stereotyped as a process or as a thread. The problem for the architect is that you normally don't want to consider objects, just coarser-grained entities such as components. The solution to this is to use simple objects (defined only by their names) to represent the processes and threads and to nest threads inside processes and components inside both. One complication if you do use this approach is that many UML tools will not let you nest objects on your diagrams. If this is a concern, consider using a stereotyped package instead of a stereotyped object. You may also need to consider adding a process group stereotype, depending on the level of concurrency model you need to represent.

   Simple examples of interprocess communication, like remote procedure calls, can be represented by using standard UML intercomponent associations, with arrowheads indicating the direction of communication (and possibly using tagged values on the association to make the communication mechanism clear). More complex forms of interprocess communication (shared memory, semaphores, and so on) can be represented quite effectively by introducing further stereotypes and showing associations between the components in the tasks and the interprocess communication mechanisms they use.

   Figure 18–1 shows an example of UML being used for a concurrency model.

   This model shows how the system is implemented by using three processes (a client, a statistics service, and a statistics calculator) along with a process group to implement the Oracle DBMS instance. The concurrent activity between the Statistics Accessor and Statistics Calculator components needs to be coordinated because they are in different processes;

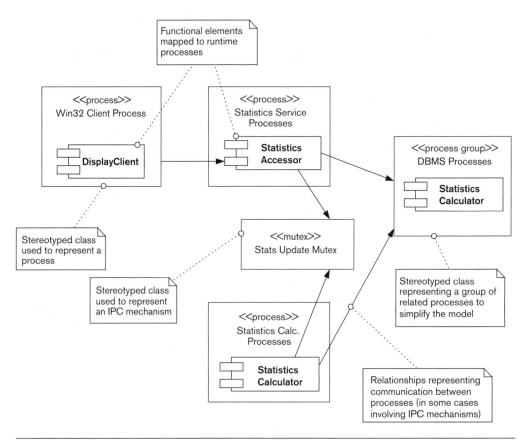

FIGURE 18-1 CONCURRENCY MODEL DOCUMENTED BY USING UML

a mutex is used to achieve this. The illustrated scenario is very simple, and there is little or no architecturally significant thread design in this model. Figure 18–2 shows a more involved model with more architecturally significant threading.

The concurrency model shown in Figure 18–2 illustrates a case where the process structure is very simple, namely, two processes that communicate via a socket stream. However, the thread structure in the DBMS Process instance is architecturally significant, and its structure and interthread coordination strategy needs to be documented and explained. The model shows that there is a single thread containing the Network Listener component, which communicates with between 1 and 40 threads that contain the four main query processing components via an interprocess communication queue. The Disk IO Manager component is hosted on its own thread, and there may be up to 10 instances of this

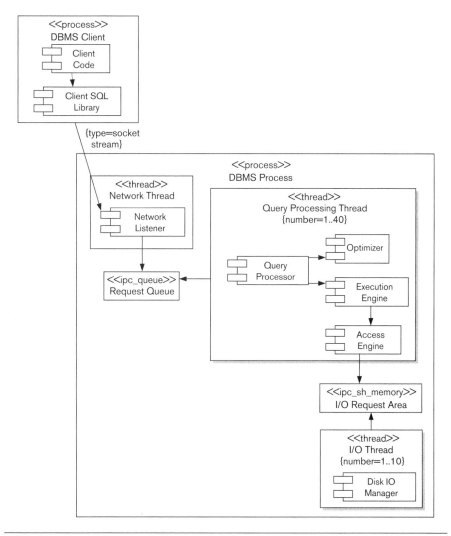

FIGURE 18-2 THREAD-BASED CONCURRENCY MODEL

running. The Access Engine component communicates with the Disk I/O Manager instances via the shared memory mechanism.

■ *Formal notations*: The real-time and control systems research community has created a number of concurrency modeling languages that allow the creation of process models. A number of these languages, such as LO-TOS, Communicating Sequential Processes (CSP), and the Calculus for Communicating Systems (CCS), are formal and represented textually. Most of these languages are mathematical and fairly abstract, and they aren't widely understood or used in information system development. While this doesn't mean they can't be useful, we have yet to come across a large-scale industrial application of them to information systems. The problem with using these languages tends to center around the need to teach them to the interested stakeholders and their focus on abstract concurrency analysis (such as deadlock analysis) rather than concrete mapping of functional elements to tangible executable entities (such as operating system processes).

- *Informal notations*: In our experience, by far the most common notation used to represent process models is an informal one, created by the author of the model. Given the relatively small number of object types in a process model, an informal notation invented for the problem at hand often works very effectively as a communication tool as long as it is explained well enough. The notation needs to capture processes, process groups, threads, and the set of interprocess communication mechanisms in use. As long as the notation to represent each of these components is well defined, an informal notation often has much to recommend it. In particular, the notation can be kept simple and avoids the potentially awkward process of bending a general-purpose notation like UML to represent the model being described. The risk with informal notations is that people can misunderstand the model because they don't know the notation.

ACTIVITIES

Map the Elements to the Tasks. The first and most fundamental task when creating your process model is to work out how many processes you need and to decide which functional elements will run in which processes. In some cases, this is a very straightforward process—each functional element ends up being a process (or perhaps a process group). In other cases, there is a complex N:M mapping between functional elements and processes, with some elements partitioned between processes and other elements running in shared processes. The important point about this mapping is that you should introduce concurrency only where it is actually required. Concurrency adds complexity to the system and adds significant overhead to interelement communication when it must cross process boundaries. Therefore, add more processes to your system only if you need them for distribution, scalability, isolation, or other reasons guided by the requirements for your system.

Determine the Threading Design. The term *threading design* refers to the process of deciding on the number of threads to include in each system process and how those threads are to be allocated and used. In most cases, threading design is not something that the architect needs to get directly involved in—this is usually the job of the subsystem designers. However, you may get involved in designing and specifying general threading approaches or patterns that should be used at various points in the system in order to meet the system's required quality properties or to ensure consistency across the implementation.

Consider the Approach to Shared Resources. As soon as concurrency is introduced into the system, you must carefully consider how to share resources between concurrent threads of execution. Resource sharing is considered in some other parts of the architecture too (notably, the Information view), and the two activities might be best tackled as a single task. This isn't a book on concurrent computing, so we don't have space to discuss all of the options and potential pitfalls to consider when sharing resources. The simplistic advice is simply that whenever a resource (such as a piece of data in memory, a file, a database object, or a piece of shared memory) is shared among two or more concurrent threads of execution, it must be protected from corruption. This is usually achieved with some form of locking protocol. Like threading design, the details of resource sharing are rarely architecturally significant. Your role in relation to this is to ensure that suitable resource-sharing approaches are used where necessary and that the approach used is suitable in the overall context of the system and does not produce unacceptable side effects for the system as a whole.

Assign Priorities to Threads and Processes. Some tasks in your system may be more important than others. If you have tasks of different importance running on one machine, you need to control their execution so that the more important work gets done before the less important work. The normal method for achieving this is to use the facilities of the underlying operating system to assign priority levels to the different threads and processes. All modern operating systems provide this feature in roughly the same way. Tasks are explicitly or implicitly given runtime priorities. When the operating system's thread scheduler is choosing tasks to run, it considers the higher-priority tasks before the lower-priority ones, thus getting the important work done first. If you can avoid assigning explicit priorities to threads, in general do so—processing priorities can add a lot of complexity to your process model and can introduce subtle but serious problems. However, sometimes you can't avoid it. In these cases, keep the assignment of priorities as simple and as regular as possible, and analyze and prototype your approach to make sure that you aren't introducing problems worse than the one you're trying to solve.

Analyze Deadlocks. Having introduced concurrency into the system, you have also introduced the risk of the entire system grinding to a halt in unexpected ways. Wherever you have concurrency in the presence of shared resources, you always have the possibility of deadlock. In order to avoid this problem, You should check for deadlock if your system requires complex concurrency involving shared resources. You can use a number of modeling techniques for deadlock analysis, such as Petri Nets, which allow you to create a model of your processing threads and shared resources and then analyze the model to catch potential deadlock situations. With experience, it is also usually possible to perform effective deadlock analysis through careful, informal consideration of your concurrency model.

Analyze Contention. Wherever you have a number of tasks and shared resources, you almost always find contention. Contention occurs between tasks when more than one task requires a shared resource concurrently. The introduction of coordination mechanisms (like mutexes) inevitably introduces contention when workloads are high. If contention rises beyond a certain point, the system will slow dramatically, and little useful work will get done. In order to avoid this during normal operations, you need to analyze your shared resources from this point of view. The basis of the technique is to identify each of your possible contention points. Then, for each, estimate the likely number of concurrent tasks contending for the resource and how long each will need the resource for. This allows you to establish the likely wait times that each task experiences at each point and then to estimate how such contention will affect your processing times and throughput. Repeating the exercise for different workloads allows you to estimate the maximum theoretical workloads your system can possibly support.

State Models

A state model is used to describe the set of states that a system's runtime elements can be in and the valid transitions between the states. The set of states and transitions for one runtime element is known as a **state machine**, and the collection of all of the interesting state machines for your system forms the overall state model.

Usually, you will find that each system task identified in the concurrency model will have one or at most a few functional units mapped to it that are effectively in control of the task. These functional units normally have the system's interesting state models associated with them. If you create a state model, be sure to focus on these system elements so that the state model describes only architecturally significant information. You don't need to capture all of the state machines inside all of the system's elements; the AD needs to describe only state that is visible at the system level, not state that is hidden inside the system's elements.

An important decision to make before you start creating the state model is the set of semantics you want to use in your state machines. Modern state modeling notations (in particular, UML's statechart, discussed later) allow you to introduce a mind-boggling degree of complexity. You need to use such notations carefully if you want to produce a comprehensible model.

A basic state machine in the state model would normally contain the following types of entities.

- *State*: A state is an identifiable, named, stable condition during a runtime functional element's lifetime. States are normally associated with waiting for something (an event) to occur or performing some sort of operation.

- *Transition*: A state transition defines an allowable change in state, from one state to another, following the occurrence of an event. From a modeling point of view, transitions are normally considered to occur in zero time and so cannot be interrupted.

- *Event*: An event is an indication that something of interest has happened in the system (and is normally recognized by an operation being invoked on an element or a time period ending). Events are the triggers that cause transitions between states to occur.

- *Actions*: Actions are atomic (noninterruptible) pieces of processing that can be associated with a transition (so an event causes the transition to occur, and then an action is executed as part of the state transition).

More sophisticated state modeling notations allow additional modeling elements such as *guards* (Boolean conditions governing state transitions), *activities* (long, interruptible items of processing that can be associated with states), and *hierarchical states*.

NOTATION State models are typically represented by using a graphical notation derived in some way from the classic state transition diagram. The most popular variant in use today is probably the UML notation for representing state, the *statechart*. At the end of this subsection we briefly discuss other graphical notations as well as some nongraphical ones, but first we focus on UML's statechart.

- *UML*: A statechart is a flexible notation that can be used in a number of different ways at differing levels of sophistication. Deciding which parts of the notation to use is an important step before getting too far into the modeling process. Figure 18–3 shows a simple UML statechart for the Query Processor element we presented earlier in Figure 18–2.

    This statechart shows the basic notation for a UML statechart, with two normal states and the use of start and end pseudostates to indicate how the element's lifecycle begins and ends. The two normal states are linked with a pair of transitions showing how the element can move between these states. Each of the transition arrows is annotated with an event name and an action name to define how the transition is triggered and what happens as a result of the transition occurring. The event and action normally correspond to operations on the element.

    Note that the statechart shown in Figure 18–3 probably doesn't need to be included in the AD because it doesn't appear to be architecturally significant. The details of how the Query Processor element arranges its internal state don't seem to affect the rest of the system, so these details should be eliminated from the AD and captured in the appropriate software design documents. In fact, our experience is that it is often better to

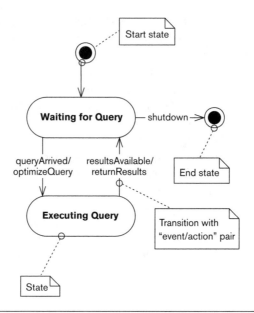

FIGURE 18-3 SIMPLE STATECHART FOR THE QUERY PROCESSOR ELEMENT

leave detailed state modeling to the subsystem design teams rather than to spend much time considering it at an architectural level.

A more sophisticated (and arguably more architecturally significant) example of a statechart is shown in Figure 18–4.

This example illustrates more of the UML statechart notation, in particular, composite and concurrent states. This diagram represents the state machine for a system element that is some sort of calculation engine. It has a single top-level state (Running) that is entered when the element is started and exited when a shutdown event is received (the reset() action is performed as part of that transition).

The Running state has been decomposed into four substates that comprise the business of running this element: Waiting for Data, Calibrating Metrics, Calculating, and Distributing Results. The transition arrows indicate the possible transitions between states (along with the events that cause the transitions and the actions that will be executed).

The Calculating state is interesting because it is a concurrent state, as you can see from the dashed line that bisects it. This means that while in the Calculating state, the element is actually in two concurrent substates (Calculating Values and Calculating Risk). When the activity associated with these states completes, the transition from the states is taken, and when both are complete, the element can leave the Calculating state.

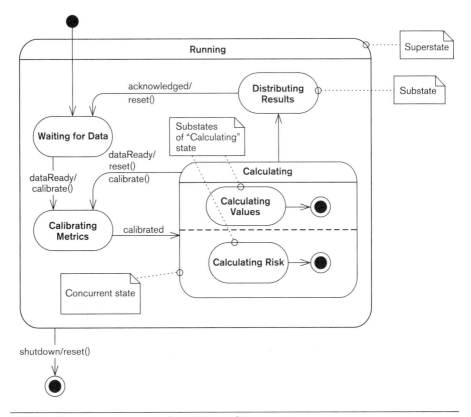

FIGURE 18-4 COMPOSITE AND CONCURRENT STATECHART

There appear to be two architecturally significant aspects to this state machine.

- If new input data becomes ready when the element is in the Calculation state, in-progress results are discarded (by executing the `reset()` action), and calculation starts again. In contrast, if this occurs while results are being distributed, the distribution process is not interrupted.
- No matter the state of the element, if a shutdown event is received, all processing immediately stops, the state is reset, and the element exits.

Of course, whether or not these facts are architecturally significant depends on the situation. However, we can make a reasonable argument that these facts are visible at the system level and thus can affect or be relied on by other system elements, and therefore, these facts need to be captured as part of the architecture.

An interesting point to note about the UML statechart is that its ability to show hierarchical state composition allows you to express architectural constraints on state models without needing to define the entire model. The statechart in Figure 18–5 illustrates this point.

This statechart distills one of the architecturally significant features from the statechart in Figure 18–4, namely, that a shutdown event must be immediately responded to in any running state and a reset of the element performed as part of shutdown. In effect, this documents an architectural constraint that the designer of the corresponding part of the system must respect; but while clearly defining this constraint, the statechart leaves the details of the lower-level states to the subsystem designer.

- *Other graphical notations*: In addition to UML, many other graphical notations exist for modeling state. Some of the better-known ones include simple state transition diagrams, Petri Nets, SDL, and David Harel's original Statecharts. All of these notations have strengths and weaknesses when compared to each other and to UML statecharts, and they are worth considering if UML statecharts cause you problems. However, the standardization of and wide familiarity with UML statecharts means that in general they should probably be your first choice. The Further Reading section at the end of this chapter contains some references to information about these notations.

- *Nongraphical notations*: In principle, the graphical notations can all be represented in a textual form (and indeed many graphical state modeling notations do define an equivalent textual form). Similarly, a number of primarily textual formalisms for modeling and analyzing state can be represented in a graphical form (for an accessible example, look at the Finite State Processes language). A textual state model can be useful when the model needs to be processed in some way by machine, but for human readers it is almost always better to use a graphical notation where possible.

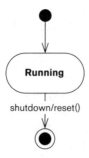

FIGURE 18–5 ARCHITECTURAL CONSTRAINT STATECHART

ACTIVITIES

Define the Notation. Before starting to create your state model, spend some time working out your needs for the modeling notation and defining how you will use your chosen notation.

Identify the States. The core activity when creating a state model is to work out what states your system elements can be in and the processing (if any) associated with each state. Beware of accidentally modeling activities as states; this is a common modeling mistake. If in doubt, try considering your state machine as a UML activity diagram. If you can do this, you have probably modeled activities rather than states. When performing state identification at the architectural level, focus on the states that are visible from outside the element and thus have a system-wide effect.

Design the State Transitions. Once you know what states your elements can be in, design a set of transitions that allows them to move between the states correctly. For each transition, clearly identify how the transition is triggered and any (atomic) actions that must be performed as a side effect of traversing it. Make sure that the events and actions you identify can be supported by the operations and state of the element for which you are designing a state machine.

PROBLEMS AND PITFALLS

Modeling of the Wrong Concurrency

When considering the concurrency design of a system, it is easy to get bogged down in the details of the internal concurrency and state design of each element. It's not part of your job as an architect to design detailed thread models that define how individual threads in a server will be allocated, used, and freed, along with all of the coordination between them. Remember that your role is to concentrate on the system rather than all of the details of each element. The concurrency that you should be concerned with is the architecturally significant concurrency, that is, the overall concurrency structure, the mapping of functional elements to that structure, and the system-level state model. You may also be involved in specifying common approaches such as design patterns that need to be used for the concurrency within elements, but in general you should not need to design all of the details—this will only distract you from the system-level problems (which are often quite enough to worry about).

RISK REDUCTION
- Focus on architecturally significant aspects of concurrency.
- Involve the lead software developers as early as possible so they can work on the more detailed aspects of this problem.

Excessive Complexity

Simplicity should always be an aim when designing a system. Simple designs are easier to create, analyze, build, deliver, and support. However, this is particularly important when considering concurrency because it is fundamentally difficult to understand. As we have seen, the price of complex concurrency can be very high at design time, implementation time, and beyond. More software engineering hours have probably been wasted on reworking problematic concurrency than on almost anything else. Simplicity in your concurrency approach will have a major positive impact on the amount of effort required to deliver and support your system.

RISK REDUCTION

- Be sure that all of the concurrency you introduce is justified in terms of stakeholder benefits.
- When designing state models, use the simplest subset of notation possible to capture your state machines in order to encourage a simple state model.

Resource Contention

Resource contention usually manifests itself as excessive activity in small, specific parts of the system (colloquially known as *hot spots*). Careful and early analysis of the concurrency model for potential contention can help you avoid such problems, but in reality, as soon as one resource contention point is eliminated, the next one will emerge. Therefore, tackling resource contention is normally a process of reducing the contention to an acceptable level.

RISK REDUCTION

- Analyze your system as it is being designed to spot resource contention as early as possible, and design around it. Use your usage scenarios to predict which parts of the system are likely to encounter high levels of concurrency, and focus your attention in these regions.
- Reduce contention by decomposing locks on large resources into a number of finer-grained locks, thus reducing the amount of time locks are held.
- Consider alternative locking techniques such as optimistic locking that reduce the time locks are held.
- Eliminate shared resources where you can.
- If possible, reduce the amount of concurrency you need around problematic contention points.

Deadlock

Deadlock occurs when a thread requires access to a resource that has already been locked by another thread. Like resource contention, you can often avoid deadlock through early and thorough analysis of the system. Danger points are those parts of the system where different types of processing threads need access to a number of the same resources. Where you find potential deadlock points, you will probably need to redesign the system to avoid the problem.

RISK REDUCTION

- Where possible, ensure that resources are always allocated to tasks in a fixed order.

- Attempt to isolate parallel threads in such a way that deadlock between them is impossible.

- Certain commercial products that use locks (such as database management systems) provide significant assistance with handling deadlock—in most cases, recognizing it and breaking it by terminating one or more of the problematic transactions. These technologies can be very useful when dealing with deadlock, but their use often needs to be carefully designed into the system so that such deadlock recovery actions are handled correctly.

Race Conditions

A race condition is problematic behavior that results from unexpected dependence on the relative timing of events. It usually occurs when two or more tasks are attempting to perform the same action concurrently. The tasks race for the resource, and the first one to reach the appropriate point in the program code wins and performs the action.

Race conditions are only problematic when they are unplanned because the system has not been designed to cope with more than one task performing the action concurrently. In these cases, information can be corrupted or lost, and the system can behave in unpredictable ways. A classic example is a system-wide data structure in an operating system process that a number of threads can update. If multiple tasks try to update the data structure concurrently (e.g., to increment a counter indicating the number of requests accepted), the resulting value will be undefined and very likely incorrect.

RISK REDUCTION

- Ensure that there are no unprotected, shared system-level resources that can cause race conditions.

- Automatically introduce protection mechanisms for all potentially shared resources.
- Ensure that the definition of each element interface clearly states whether or not the interface is reentrant.

CHECKLIST

- Is there a clear system-level concurrency model?
- Are your models at the right level of abstraction? Have you focused on the architecturally significant aspects?
- Can you simplify your concurrency design?
- Do all interested parties understand the overall concurrency strategy?
- Have you mapped all functional elements to a process (and thread if necessary)?
- Do you have a state model for at least one functional element in each process and thread? If not, are you sure the processes and threads will interact safely?
- Have you defined a suitable set of interprocess communication mechanisms to support the interelement interactions defined in the Functional view?
- Are all shared resources protected from corruption?
- Have you minimized the intertask communication and synchronization required?
- Do you have any resource hot spots in your system? If so, have you estimated the likely throughput, and is it high enough? Do you know how you would reduce contention at these points if forced to later?
- Can the system possibly deadlock? If so, do you have a strategy for recognizing and dealing with this when it occurs?

FURTHER READING

The area of concurrency has been studied and written about widely, although not many books consider it from an architect's perspective.

A good overview of concurrency in general (albeit with a Java-specific slant) and a good introduction to modeling and analysis appears in Magee and Kramer [MAGE99]; this book also introduces the Finite State Processes language mentioned earlier. Unfortunately, Cook and Daniels [COOK94] is out of print; however, it is well worth tracking down a copy as it contains a particularly good discussion of using statecharts to model object state. You can find a lot of good UML-specific advice about state modeling in Rumbaugh et al. [RUMB99], which is organized as a reference so it's easy to find definitions of the various UML elements involved.

Each of the visual formalisms has its own following and literature. Girauld and Valk [GIRA02] is a relatively academic text that explains how to apply Petri Nets to the analysis of concurrency characteristics, while the SDL Forum Society Web site [SDL02] is a good starting point for finding out more about SDL. A fairly recent reference on CSP is Roscoe [ROSC97]; the definitive book on CCS is still Milner [MILN89]; and the original reference for statecharts was Harel's paper [HARE87]. You can find an introduction to JavaSpaces in Freeman et al. [FREE99], while a rich source of design patterns for concurrent and network-oriented systems is Schmidt et al. [SCHM00].

19

THE DEVELOPMENT
VIEWPOINT

Definition	Describes the architecture that supports the software development process
Concerns	Module organization, common processing, standardization of design, standardization of testing, instrumentation, and codeline organization
Models	Module structure models, common design models, and codeline models
Problems and Pitfalls	Too much detail, overburdening the AD, uneven focus, lack of developer focus, lack of precision, and problems with the specified environment
Stakeholders	Software developers and testers
Applicability	All systems with significant software development involved in their creation

A considerable amount of planning and design of the development environment is often required to support the design and build of software for complex systems. Things to think about include code structure and dependencies, build and configuration management of deliverables, system-wide design constraints, and system-wide standards to ensure technical integrity. It is the role of the Development view to address these aspects of the system development process.

This viewpoint is relevant to nearly all large information system projects because almost all of them have some element of development, whether it is configuring and scripting off-the-shelf software, writing a system from scratch, or somewhere between these. The importance of this view depends on the complexity of the system being built, the expertise of the software developers, the maturity of the technologies used, and the familiarity that the whole team has with these technologies.

You need to focus here on issues, concerns, and features that are architecturally significant. You should view your work as a starting point for the more detailed design work that will be performed as part of the software development phase.

CONCERNS

Module Organization

The large systems you are likely to encounter as an architect may be built from hundreds of thousands of lines of source code spread over thousands of files. Source files are normally organized into larger units called **modules** that contain related code (such as the code to implement a library or coherent piece of functionality). Arranging code in such a logical structure helps developers understand it and work on it without affecting other modules in unexpected ways.

When working with a complex module structure, you need to identify and thoroughly understand the dependencies between the modules to avoid ending up with a system that is difficult and error-prone to maintain, build, and release.

Common Processing

Any large system will benefit from identifying and isolating common processing into separate code units. For example, standardizing how the system logs messages and handles configuration parameters can significantly simplify its administration.

The Development view helps ensure that the areas of common processing are identified and clearly specified. You will typically do this only in outline form, adding further refinement and detail as development progresses.

Standardization of Design

Most systems are developed by teams of software developers rather than individuals. Standardizing key aspects of design provides critical benefits to the maintainability, reliability, and technical cohesion of the system (and saves time, too). You can achieve design standardization by using design patterns and off-the-shelf software elements.

Standardization of Testing

Standardization of test approaches, technologies, and conventions helps ensure a consistent approach to testing and speeds up the testing process. Key concerns include test tools and infrastructure, standard test data, approved test approaches, and test automation.

Instrumentation

Instrumentation is the practice of inserting special code for logging information about step execution, system state, resource usage, and so on that is used to aid monitoring and debugging. Because instrumentation can have an adverse impact on performance, it should be possible to switch off this capability, alter the level of detail at which messages are logged, and possibly even use build tools to remove the instrumentation code altogether.

System messages can be logged to a system console, a file, or a message service, and metrics on system usage can be logged to a file or a database for later analysis.

Codeline Organization

The system's source code needs to be stored in a directory structure, managed via some form of configuration management system, built and tested regularly, and released as tested binaries for further testing and use. The way that all of this is achieved is normally termed the **codeline organization** for a system, the **codeline** being a particular version of a set of source code files with a well-defined organization, usually building to form a particular version or variant of the system.

Ensuring that the system's code can be managed, built, tested, and released is crucial to achieving a reliable system—particularly when you're using iterative development and many releases are necessary. As an architect, you may wish to specify, in outline form at least, how this is to be done.

Stakeholder Concerns

Typical stakeholder concerns for the Development viewpoint include those shown in Table 19–1.

TABLE 19-1 STAKEHOLDER CONCERNS FOR THE DEVELOPMENT VIEWPOINT

Stakeholder Class	Concerns
Developers	All concerns
Testers	Common processing, instrumentation, and possibly codeline organization

MODELS

Module Structure Models

The module structure model defines the organization of the system's source code, in terms of the modules into which the individual source files are collected and the dependencies among these modules. It is also common to impose some degree of higher-level organization on the modules themselves to avoid having to enumerate many individual dependencies.

Once you have identified a set of modules into which you can organize the source files, you can use the common architectural approach of grouping modules at similar abstraction levels into layers. You can then organize these layers into a dependency stack from the most abstract or highly functional (conceptually at the top) down to the least (at the bottom). You can then define interlayer dependency rules to avoid unwanted dependencies between modules at very different abstraction levels. Typically, software in a module communicates only with other modules at the same layer or in the layers directly above and below it (although there are often exceptions to this rule for performance or efficiency reasons).

In some situations (e.g., when separate module structures are needed for client and server elements), you may need a number of such models. In other cases (e.g., when developing an extension to a monolithic application package), a module structure model is less useful.

NOTATION A module structure model is often represented as a UML component diagram, using the package icon to represent a code module and dependency arrows to show intermodule dependencies. If you require higher-level module organization, you can show module grouping by the use of enclosing packages annotated with suitable stereotypes.

Another common alternative is a simple boxes-and-lines diagram that shows the layers, their relative ordering, and the components within them.

EXAMPLE Figure 19-1 shows an example of using UML to document a module structure model.

This layer model shows a module organization with three layers, each layer being represented by a stereotyped package. The system's modules are shown as UML packages within the layers.

The model shows that the domain layer depends on the utility layer, which in turn depends on the platform layer (i.e., the domain-layer components can access only the utility-layer components, and so on).

However, you can also see that nonstrict layering has been used in this system because all of the domain-layer components depend on facilities provided by the Java Standard Library component rather than accessing its facilities via intermediate utility components. (In contrast, the domain-level components cannot access the JDBC Driver component.)

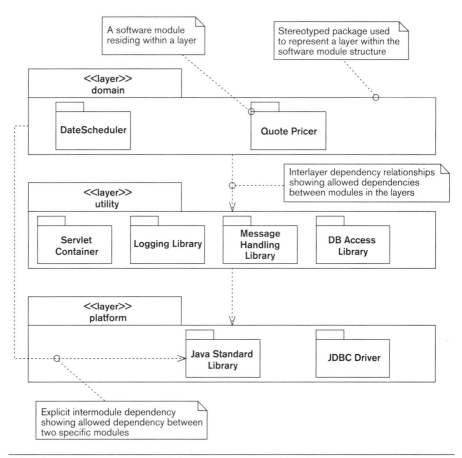

FIGURE 19–1 EXAMPLE OF A UML MODULE STRUCTURE MODEL

ACTIVITIES

Identify and Classify the Modules. Group the source code for the system into a set of modules, and (optionally) classify them—by abstraction or other criteria—into a higher-level organization.

Identify the Module Dependencies. Identify a clear set of dependencies between the modules (or the higher-level groups) so that everyone involved in the design and construction of the system can understand the impact of making changes.

Identify the Layering Rules. If a layered approach is to be used, you need to design a set of rules to be followed with respect to the layers. Can modules call modules only in their own layer and the one above or below, or do you want a less rigid rule in order to meet system quality properties such as performance and flexibility?

Common Design Models

To maximize commonality across element implementations, it is desirable to define a set of design constraints that apply when designing the system's software elements. Such design constraints are valuable for two principal reasons.

- You can reduce risk and duplication of effort by identifying standard approaches to be used when solving certain types of problems.
- Commonality among system elements helps increase the system's overall technical coherence and makes it easier to understand, operate, and maintain.

A common design model has the following three important pieces.

1. A definition of the *common processing* required across elements, such as:
   - Initialization
   - Termination and restart of operation
   - Message logging and instrumentation
   - Internationalization
   - Use of third-party libraries
   - Processing configuration parameters
   - Security (e.g., authentication or encryption)
   - Transaction management
   - Database interaction

   These aspects of your software element designs can benefit greatly from using a standard approach across all system elements. Identifying and defining common processing is a key architectural task that directly contributes to the overall technical coherence of the system.

2. A definition of *standard design approaches* that should be used when designing the system's elements. These start to emerge when (having defined the functional structure) you think ahead a little about how the subsystems might be implemented. When you see situations where the same sort of processing is performed by different elements or where you know that the implementation of a certain aspect of an element will have a system-wide impact, you should consider whether you need a standard design approach. When identifying a common design approach, you must define what the approach is, where it should be used, and why it should be used. In other words, it is a special sort of design pattern.

3. A definition of what *common software* should be used and how it should be used. This may be the result of making other higher-level decisions (e.g., selecting an access library for your chosen database) or identifying a reusable component (e.g., a third-party message-logging library or a locally developed graphical user interface element) that can save you development time and reduce risk. In either case, your common design model needs to clearly identify what common elements should be used, where they should be used, and how they should be used.

As with the module structure model, you may need to define different design constraints for different parts of the system. In any case, as an architect, you are only starting a task that will continue throughout the design and build.

NOTATION The common design model is a partial design document, and as such, the notations it uses are those of software design—usually a combination of text and more formal notation such as UML.

The following example shows some possible design constraints from a common design model.

EXAMPLE Here is an example of a common design model.

Common Processing Required
  a. Message Logging
   - All components must log human-readable messages.
   - Messages must be logged at one of the following levels: Fatal, Error, Warning, Information, Debug.
   - Components should log messages at all five possible logging levels.
   - Logging should be achieved via a standard library (as defined later) to standardize destination, format, configuration, and so on.

  [. . .]

b. Internationalization

- All user- and administrator-visible strings must be stored in message catalogs so that hard-coded strings are not present in source code.
- Parameters must be inserted into internationalized strings using position-independent placeholders to avoid problems with ordering across languages.
- Locale-sensitive information (dates, times, currency strings, and so on) must be formatted according to the current locale in force, and default formats should not be used.
- Strings logged at debug level or for other purely internal use should not be internationalized but should be hard-coded in the source code.

[. . .]

Standard Design

a. Internationalization

- For internationalization of locale-sensitive resources (primarily strings), use an external resource catalog to store resources outside the source code files. This means that all strings must be extracted from a message catalog before they can be used in a program (e.g., to write a log message).
- As the server software is being written entirely in Java, the internationalization implementation will use the Java Platform's native internationalization facilities: the resource bundle, the formatting classes in the `java.text` package, and the `Locale` class.
- The relationships between these different elements of the internationalization technology are as follows. [. . .]
- *[You would place a definition of a design pattern for using the Java internationalization facilities here.]*

[. . .]

Standard Software Components

a. Message Logging

- All message logging must be performed using the standard `CCJLog` package, which is part of the standard build environment.
- The `CCJLog` package must be used in a standard way, which is documented as a code sample in the `src/server/sample/logging/CCJLog` source directory.

[. . .]

ACTIVITIES

Identify Common Processing. Identify *what* common processing is required, *where* the processing is required (in all elements or just some?), and *how* the common processing should be performed.

Identify the Required Design Constraints. Establish whether any common processing should be standardized and whether critical aspects of subsystem design will have a negative system-wide impact if not designed in a certain way. If you find such situations, consider whether you can impose a design constraint that will resolve the problem, and, if so, add it to the list.

Identify and Define the Design Patterns. Document a set of mini design patterns that clearly define the constraints. The constraints are defined in terms of the software design that needs to be followed, the applicability of the constraint (i.e., where to use it), and the rationale for the constraint (to allow those following it to understand its role).

Define the Role of Standard Elements. Consider whether you have any standard software elements that can be shared among subsystems. You will often identify such standard elements when considering the system's common processing. If you find standard elements, clearly define their roles and how they should be used.

Codeline Models

Although you certainly don't want to be dictating the minutiae of the software developers' lives, you do need to ensure that there is order rather than chaos when it comes to the organization of the system's code.

The key things to define are the overall structure of the codeline, how the code is controlled (usually via configuration management), where different types of source code live in that structure, and how it should be maintained and extended over time (in particular, how any concurrent development of different releases should work). A codeline model normally needs to capture the following essential facts:

- How code will be organized into source files
- How the files will be grouped into modules
- What directory structure will be used to hold the files
- How the source will be built to form releasable binaries
- What type and scope of tests will need to be run regularly and when they should be run
- How the source will be released for testing and use
- How the source will be controlled using configuration management (including any use of branching, change sets, and so on) to coordinate multiple developers working on it concurrently

Defining these aspects of the development environment is an important part of achieving reliable, repeatable build and release processes. The information you provide through your model will help prevent confusion and frustration as developers work together.

In situations where development of the system will be distributed among different teams or among members of teams working at different locations, addressing this concern becomes even more important. You may have to take into account factors such as different time zones or even the different languages spoken by development staff.

Depending on the skill and experience of the developers, you may be comfortable leaving the majority of this work to your design team; at the other extreme, you may want to specify this in some detail.

NOTATION In principle, you can represent the codeline model by using structured notations like UML. However, our experience of trying this suggests that it often isn't worth the bother. A simple approach based on text and tables with a few clear diagrams to explain the conventions used should suffice.

ACTIVITIES

Design the Source Code Structure. Design the overall structure of the directory hierarchy to be used to store your system's source code. This must be flexible enough to provide easy maintenance but simple enough that developers know where their source files should live.

Define the Build Approach. To achieve a reliable system build process, you need to mandate a common approach across the system. A build and release specialist may do this for you, but the build approach does need careful design. Whatever approach you use, it must make it possible to easily build the system automatically and also allow developers to use central or local copies of the latest build.

Define the Release Process. Having completed a clean build of the system, you need to release the resulting work products (binaries, libraries, generated documentation, and so on) for testing and use. To ensure that this process is reliable and repeatable, you must design a clear process, preferably automated. Again, specialists may do the design for you, or you may need to do it yourself. It is particularly important to be clear about the build validation (such as automated test suite execution) that needs completion before release.

Define the Configuration Management. To ensure repeatability and technical integrity, you must use a common approach to configuration management. Its definition should encompass the tools to be used, the configuration structures (such as variants, branches, and labels) to be used, and the process for managing the deliverables under configuration control.

Problems and Pitfalls

Too Much Detail

Most software architects are experienced software designers, which means that you probably have a lot of background knowledge related to the process of software design and implementation. The danger that stems from this is the temptation to use the Development view to define low-level details about the system's implementation that are really the concern of the designers and implementers.

Risk Reduction

- Minimize the number of design constraints you identify. Identifying too many is often counterproductive and causes problems as developers try to shoehorn their elements into the space left by a number of different constraints (or simply ignore them).
- Carefully review everything you describe in the Development view, and question whether it is architecturally significant. If not, eliminate that detail from the Development view.

Overburdened Architectural Description

A problem related to having too much detail is the question of where to put the contents of the Development view (particularly in the common design model). For a complex system, the common design model can require a significant amount of text, and given that it is aimed at a specialized group of stakeholders, it can seem out of place in the main AD document.

Risk Reduction

- Capture the details of the system-wide design constraints in a separate document specifically aimed at the software developers, and then summarize the constraints required and their rationale in a short section of the AD. This allows interested stakeholders to satisfy themselves that the design constraints have been considered, without needing to understand the details of these constraints.

Uneven Focus

We all have a tendency to focus on things that we understand and find interesting. This can lead to a situation where, for example, the design patterns to be used for network request handling are discussed in minute detail, but the initialization processing required of each element is hardly considered at all.

RISK REDUCTION

- Try to step back from the system and consider all of the aspects of software development that need to be defined at an architectural level.
- Find specialist expertise to advise you in areas you aren't familiar with.

Lack of Developer Focus

Always remember that the primary (and often only) customers of the Development view are the software developers and testers working on your project. The Development view must answer their questions and be relevant to their concerns. If it isn't, it will almost certainly be ignored.

RISK REDUCTION

- Involve the developers and testers in defining the Development view.
- Delegate aspects of the view's development to senior software developers when possible, to give the software development team ownership of the aspects of the architecture that affect them.

Lack of Precision

Because the Development view has to cover many aspects of the software development, and because you are unlikely to have expertise in all of them, lack of precision is a risk. Developers might misinterpret imprecise descriptions or, if they cannot understand the descriptions, might ignore them altogether.

RISK REDUCTION

- This problem often occurs when an architect knows that it is important to define some aspect of the system but knows little about it and thus simply states that it needs to be performed. When defining the Development view, make sure to review its contents early with the software developers and testers to check that the view's definitions are precise enough.
- Do not be afraid to make use of the knowledge of subject matter experts where your experience is limited—you are not expected to be an expert in everything!

Problems with the Specified Environment

Keeping up-to-date with new and emerging technologies takes a lot of time. It is particularly hard to get reliable information on how mature those technologies are and how appropriate they might be for your architecture.

This imposes the risk of specifying aspects of the Development view based on out-of-date (or perhaps just incorrect) knowledge and assumptions, which can lead to later problems in development or live operation and damage your credibility with developers.

RISK REDUCTION

- Make sure you specify technology and techniques you really know about, or get trusted, expert advice from subject matter experts to help make the relevant decisions.
- Delegating research and design of aspects of the Development view to members of the software development team can help alleviate this problem while having other positive side effects, such as giving the software developers a heightened sense of ownership of the system.

CHECKLIST

- Have you defined a clear strategy for organizing the source code modules in your system?
- Have you defined a general set of rules governing the dependencies that can exist between code modules at different abstraction levels?
- Have you identified all of the aspects of element implementation that need to be standardized across the system?
- Have you clearly defined how any standard processing should be performed?
- Have you identified any standard approaches to design that you need all element designers and implementers to follow? If so, do your software developers accept and understand these approaches?
- Will a clear set of standard third-party software elements be used across all element implementations? Have you defined the way they should be used?
- Is this view as minimal as possible?
- Is the presentation of this view in the AD appropriate?

FURTHER READING

Many books discuss the use of design patterns in software development, the original book being, of course, Gamma et al. [GAMM95]. This topic is explored further in Coplien et al. [PLOP95–99].

You can find discussions of configuration management, release processes, and so forth in Bays [BAYS99] and Leon [LEON00].

20

THE DEPLOYMENT VIEWPOINT

Definition	Describes the environment into which the system will be deployed, including the dependencies the system has on its runtime environment
Concerns	Types of hardware required, specification and quantity of hardware required, third-party software requirements, technology compatibility, network requirements, network capacity required, and physical constraints
Models	Runtime platform models, network models, and technology dependency models
Problems and Pitfalls	Unclear or inaccurate dependencies, unproven technology, lack of specialist technical knowledge, and late consideration of the deployment environment
Stakeholders	System administrators, developers, testers, communicators, and assessors
Applicability	Systems with complex or unfamiliar deployment environments

The Deployment view focuses on aspects of the system that are important after the system has been tested and is ready to go into live operation. This view defines the physical environment in which the system is intended to run, including the hardware environment your system needs (e.g., processing nodes, network interconnections, and disk storage facilities), the technical environment requirements for each node (or node type) in the system, and the mapping of your software elements to the runtime environment that will execute them.

The Deployment viewpoint applies to any information system with a required deployment environment that is not immediately obvious to all of the interested stakeholders. This includes the following scenarios:

- Systems with complex runtime dependencies (e.g., particular third-party software packages are needed to support the system)
- Systems with complex runtime environments (e.g., elements are distributed over a number of machines)

- Situations where the system may be deployed into a number of different environments and the essential characteristics of the required environments need to be clearly illustrated (which is typically the case with packaged software products)
- Systems that need specialist or unfamiliar hardware or software in order to run

In our experience, most large information systems fall into one of these groups, so you will almost always need to create a Deployment view.

CONCERNS

Types of Hardware Required

The Deployment view must clearly identify the types of hardware the system needs and the role each type plays. This includes general-purpose hardware to execute the main functional elements of the system, storage hardware to support databases, hardware that allows users to access the system, network elements required to meet certain quality properties (such as firewalls for security), specialist hardware (such as cryptographic accelerators), and so on.

This involves identifying the general types of hardware required and mapping each of your functional elements to one of the hardware types. In effect, this is a logical model of the hardware your system requires. Then, when you have defined what each piece of hardware does, you can think about the details of exactly what hardware elements you need.

Specification and Quantity of Hardware Required

This concern, which follows from the previous one, addresses the specific details of the hardware that will need to be procured and commissioned in order to deploy the system—in effect, a physical model of the hardware your system needs.

This is a separate concern from the previous one because it is much more specific and of interest to different stakeholders. For example, developers are interested in whether the deployment platform will use Intel or Sun SPARC servers, whether the servers will run Linux or Sun Solaris, and what general processing resources will be available to them. However, system administrators are interested in the details of the specific machines that need to be procured and commissioned in order to create your runtime environment.

Be specific when considering the specification and quantity of hardware you need. If specific models of equipment are required, you need to clearly identify them and record their specifications for easy reference. If specific models aren't required, you should still be precise where needed.

Third-Party Software Requirements

All information systems make use of third-party software as part of their deployment environment—even if only an operating system. Many information systems make use of dozens of third-party software products, including operating systems, programming libraries, messaging systems, application servers, databases, data movement products, Web servers, and so on. Although these third-party products are extremely valuable, using them incurs additional complexity that needs to be managed.

Your Deployment view should make clear all of the dependencies between your system and any third-party software products. This ensures that the developers know what software will be available for them to use and that the system administrators know exactly what needs to be installed and managed on each piece of hardware.

Technology Compatibility

Each software and hardware element in your system may impose requirements on other technology elements. For example, a database interface library may require a particular operating system network library in order to function correctly, or a disk drive may require a particular type of controller in the machines that will access it.

Furthermore, if you use a number of pieces of third-party technology together, there is always the danger of uncovering incompatible requirements. For example, your database interface library may require a certain version of the operating system, while a graphics library you want to use isn't supported on that version. Such incompatibilities have a habit of emerging late in the testing cycle and causing a lot of disruption—so if you consider them early, you will avoid problems later.

Network Requirements

Your Functional and Concurrency views define the functional structure of your architecture and make it clear how its elements interact. Part of the process of creating the Deployment view is to decide which hardware elements host each of these functional elements. Because elements that need to communicate often end up on different machines, some of the interelement interactions can be identified as network interactions.

One of the concerns the Deployment view addresses is the set of requirements the system places on its underlying network as a result of these network interactions. This view needs to clearly identify the required links between machines, the required capacity and reliability of the links, and any special network functions the system requires (load balancing, firewalls, encryption, and so on).

Network Capacity Required

In our experience, software architects need to get less involved in specifying network capacity than in identifying the processing and storage hardware because the network is normally provided by a group of specialists who design, implement, and operate the network for an entire organization. However, this group needs to know how much network capacity your system requires and the type of traffic you need to carry over the network. In order to provide this information, you must calculate and record the amount and type of network traffic that needs to be carried over each intermachine link in the proposed network topology.

Physical Constraints

Software architects and software engineers are lucky when compared to our colleagues working in other engineering disciplines. Normally, we don't have to worry that much about physical constraints because software has no weight, has no physical size, requires no storage space, and so on. However, when taking a system-level view, physical constraints suddenly become important again.

Considerations such as desk space for client workstations, floor space for servers, power, temperature control, cabling distances, and so on may seem relatively mundane. However, if someone doesn't consider them, your system simply won't be deployed. There is no point in specifying four monitors for each workstation in order to create an incredibly powerful user interface if your users have desk space for only two. Similarly, if there isn't enough floor space in your data center for your servers, they aren't going to get installed.

Stakeholder Concerns

Typical stakeholder concerns for the Deployment viewpoint include those shown in Table 20–1.

TABLE 20-1 STAKEHOLDER CONCERNS FOR THE DEPLOYMENT VIEWPOINT

Stakeholder Class	Concerns
System administrators	Types, specification, and quantity of hardware required; third-party software requirements; technology compatibility; network requirements; network capacity required; and physical constraints
Developers	Types and (general) specification of hardware required, third-party software requirements, technology compatibility, and network requirements (particularly topology)
Communicators	Types and specification of hardware required, third-party software requirements, and network requirements (particularly topology)
Testers	Types, specification, and quantity of hardware required; third-party software requirements, and network requirements
Assessors	Types of hardware required, technology compatibility, and network requirements

MODELS

Runtime Platform Models

The runtime platform model is the core of this viewpoint. This description defines the set of hardware nodes that are required, which nodes need to be connected to which other nodes via network (or other) interfaces, and which software elements are hosted on which hardware nodes.

A runtime platform model has the following main elements.

- *Processing nodes*: Each computer in your system is represented by one processing node in the runtime platform model. This allows you and other stakeholders to see what processing resources are required for the system. For situations where many similar machines are required (e.g., Web server farms), you can use a summary notation (such as UML's shadow notation) to simplify the diagram, but make sure that the number of nodes required is still clear.

- *Client nodes*: You also need to represent client hardware, but probably in less detail than the main processing hardware. You may have less control over client hardware than server hardware, and if this is the case, you need only represent the types and quantities of client machines required rather than the precise details of each. If you have special needs for presentation or user interaction hardware (e.g., touch screens, printers), this is specified as part of the client hardware.

- *Online storage hardware*: This defines how much storage is needed, how it is partitioned, what it is used for, and whether or not processing takes place close to its associated stored data. The storage hardware could be disk devices within a processing node or dedicated storage nodes such as disk arrays. Make the distinction between the two types clear so that the physical impact of separate storage nodes on the deployment environment is understood. You need to include the capacity (and possibly speed) of each type of storage hardware in the model.

- *Offline storage hardware*: Despite the ever-growing capacity of online storage hardware, many systems that deal with a lot of information still require offline storage (archives) as well. Somehow the problems always grow faster than the hardware capacity. Offline storage will also probably be required to allow backup of information held online. You need to ensure that there is sufficient capacity, that the hardware is fast enough to complete archive and retrieval in an acceptable time, and that there is sufficient network bandwidth between it and the online storage. The type, capacity, speed, and location of your offline storage hardware all need to be included in your models.

- *Network links*: Your model needs to capture the essential connections required by your system (rather than your ideas on how the network will be built from specific network elements). It is sufficient at this point to show the links between your hardware nodes; you'll capture more details about the network, such as internode bandwidth requirements, in the network model (described next in this chapter).

- *Other hardware components*: You may need to consider specialist hardware for network security, user authentication, special interfacing to other systems, or specialist processing (e.g., for automated teller machines).

- *Runtime element-to-node mapping*: The final element of this model is a mapping of the system's functional elements to the processing nodes where they execute. How to go about defining this mapping depends on how complex your concurrency structure is. If you have a Concurrency view, you can map the operating system processes identified in that view to the processing nodes. If you don't have a Concurrency view, you can map functional elements from the Functional view directly to processing nodes (and in this case, presumably the details of the operating system processes in use aren't architecturally significant).

This runtime platform model is typically captured as a network node diagram that shows nodes, storage, the interconnections required between the nodes, and the allocation of the software elements between the nodes.

NOTATION Common notations used for capturing the runtime platform model include the use of UML, traditional boxes-and-lines diagrams, and textual notations. Each of these options is outlined in this subsection.

- *UML deployment diagram*: You can use a UML deployment diagram to document a runtime platform model. This diagram shows computing nodes with software elements inside them and associations between the nodes representing the required communication links. Associations between the elements can also be used to indicate interelement dependencies. Figure 20–1 shows an example of a simple runtime platform model that maps functional elements straight to processing nodes and is represented as a UML deployment diagram.

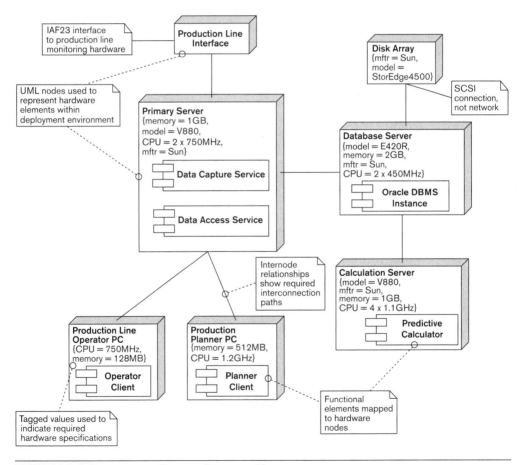

FIGURE 20–1 EXAMPLE OF A RUNTIME PLATFORM MODEL

UML does not associate detailed semantics with the nodes or associations and does not provide different types of each. Therefore, effective use of this diagram type normally relies heavily on stereotypes, tagged values, and comments in order to distinguish between different types of nodes and links. A runtime platform model such as this needs to be augmented by plain text descriptions of each of the major elements, clearly defining their important attributes.

- *Boxes-and-lines diagram*: Given the lack of precision in the basic UML deployment diagram, many architects choose a simple boxes-and-lines notation for Deployment views. Boxes are used to represent nodes and elements, with arrows for interconnection, annotating this as required in order to make the meaning of each diagram element clear. With such an approach, you need to carefully define the diagrammatic elements used to avoid causing any confusion for the reader. This notation is easier to draw with drawing tools that don't support UML, and it is more comprehensible to nontechnical stakeholders.

- *Text and tables*: Reference information such as required hardware specifications is best represented by text that is organized into tables for easy, unambiguous reference.

ACTIVITIES

Design the Deployment Environment. You typically start by identifying the key servers in the system and the key client hardware (assuming that you need to supply or specify the clients), and then you identify the network links between these nodes. With this done, you have the backbone of your deployment environment. The rest of the process is normally elaboration, adding special-purpose hardware (e.g., disk storage, cryptographic accelerators, or nodes for redundant capacity) as required and specifying the hardware specification and software requirements for each node along with the required specification of any interconnections.

Map the Elements to the Hardware. Once you have a proposed deployment environment, you need to find a home in it for each of your functional (software) elements. In reality, this is an iterative process where mapping the software elements to hardware resources may suggest changes in the deployment environment design (or newly identified deployment environment options may suggest new alternatives for software element locations). The main challenges here relate to managing dependencies, ensuring enough machine capacity is available, and trading off the advantages of separated versus colocated elements (e.g., security versus performance). Refer to Chapters 24 and 25 for more depth on these topics.

Estimate the Hardware Requirements. This activity normally starts with some initial estimation before initial deployment environment design, followed by an iterative process of refinement as architecture and design progresses.

The resources you need to estimate include processing power, memory, disk space, and I/O bandwidth for each processing node.

Conduct a Technical Evaluation. In order to design and estimate the deployment environment, you may need to perform a number of technical evaluation exercises such as prototype element development, benchmarks, and compatibility tests. For example, you may wish to create a representative prototype system to ensure that your application server, object persistence library, and database all work smoothly together and to check the transaction throughput you can achieve.

To ensure a representative test, identify the key attributes of your application (size, type of processing, and so on), and make sure you include all of this in your technical evaluation.

Obtaining time and resources for technical evaluation is often a problem. We have found that arguing for evaluation resources in terms of risk management is often the most effective way to deal with this.

Assess the Constraints. It is rare for architects to be left to define a Deployment view without any external constraints. The constraints you encounter may be formal standards, informal guidelines, or simply implicit constraints that you know exist. However the constraints are expressed, you need to review your proposed deployment environment design to ensure they are met.

Network Models

In the interests of simplicity, the runtime platform description does not typically illustrate the network in any detail. If the underlying network is complex, it is usually described in a separate (but related) network model.

In our experience, the network is usually designed and implemented by networking specialists rather than the software architect. However, it is important that you provide the networking specialists with a clear specification of the network you are expecting. This description must indicate which nodes need to be connected, any specific network hardware (such as firewalls or routers) you are expecting to be present, and the bandwidth requirements and quality properties required from each part of the network. As such, this model is normally a logical or service-based view of what you require of the network, rather than a physical view that specifies its individual elements. In the case of software product development, such a model is a valuable specification for customers planning the deployment of your software.

The primary elements of a network model are as follows.

- *Processing nodes*: The processing nodes represent your system elements that use the network to transport data. This set of nodes should match the set from the runtime platform model, but here they are abstracted to simple elements that have just network interfaces.

- *Network nodes*: In most cases, the network nodes indicate a type of network service that you expect to be available (such as firewall security, load balancing, or encryption).

- *Network connections*: The network connections are the links between the network and processing nodes. They are elaborated to include the characteristics of the service you expect the link to provide (most typically bandwidth, but perhaps quality of service or other network services).

This description is typically represented as an annotated network diagram, which can really be thought of as a network-oriented specialization of the runtime environment diagram. In cases where your network requirements are very simple, you can describe the network sufficiently by elaborating on the runtime platform model, rather than creating a separate network model. However, given the critical dependency that most of today's systems have on the underlying network, a separate network model is a useful tool to focus attention on this aspect of the system.

Figure 20–2 shows a simple example of a network model for the runtime platform we depicted earlier in Figure 20–1. This diagram would be augmented with textual descriptions for each of the major elements.

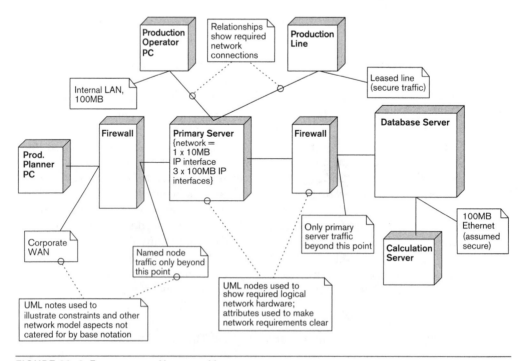

FIGURE 20–2 EXAMPLE OF A NETWORK MODEL

NOTATION Common notations used for capturing the network model include the use of UML and traditional boxes-and-lines diagrams. These options are briefly discussed in this subsection.

- *UML deployment diagram*: UML's deployment diagram is a useful base notation for a network model. However, as with the runtime platform description, you will probably need to heavily annotate it to make your intentions clear.

- *Boxes-and-lines diagram*: For reasons similar to those discussed earlier, the network model is often drawn using an informal notation.

ACTIVITIES

Design the Network. The network design is typically handled separately from that for the computer hardware because different specialists are involved. From your point of view, this is a process of sketching what you need from the network (in terms of connections, capacity, quality of service, and security). This results in what is effectively a logical rather than physical network design. Your logical network design then becomes a specification for a specialist network designer to take further.

Estimate the Capacity. Part of designing your logical network is to estimate the capacity you need between each node. Precision isn't that important at this stage, but a realistic estimation of the magnitude of the traffic that must be carried is important. You can estimate the capacity figures by combining peak transaction throughput and a rough approximation of the size of messages required to carry the transaction's information; the result is normally combined with a judicious scaling factor to allow for inevitable overheads and prediction inaccuracies.

Technology Dependency Models

In some cases, you may choose to manage the dependencies within your development or test environment by bundling your elements and the software they rely on into one deployment unit. However, in many cases this simply won't be possible for reasons such as efficiency; cost, licensing, or flexibility. If this is the case, you need to manage the dependencies in your deployment environment.

Technology dependencies are usually captured on a node-by-node basis in simple tabular form. The software dependencies are typically derived from the Development view, where you define the environment used by the software developers. You can also derive hardware dependencies from test or development environments, but in many cases you have to rely on manufacturer specifications and some judicious testing to confirm them.

TABLE 20-2 SOFTWARE DEPENDENCIES FOR THE PRIMARY SERVER NODE

Component	Requires
Data Access Service	Solaris 8.0.2 Sun C++ 4.1.2 libraries
Data Capture Service	Solaris 8.0.2
	Sun C++ 4.1.2 libraries
	Oracle OCI libraries 8.1.7.3
Sun C++ 4.1.2	Solaris patch 1534567
	Solaris patch 1538367
Oracle OCI 8.1.7.3	Solaris optional module SUNWcipx
	Solaris patch 1583956

EXAMPLE Table 20–2 shows an example of software dependencies for the Primary Server node in our example from Figure 20–1.

From this table, it is possible to see that this node in the system needs a particular version of Solaris with three patches and one optional module installed, as well as a particular version of an Oracle product and a particular version of a set of language libraries.

In simple cases, it may be possible to use the Development view contents rather than listing dependencies in this view. However, in more complex cases, it is unlikely that the Development view contains the detail required to fully define the software dependencies for each node in the system.

NOTATION A technology dependency model is often best captured by using a simple text-based approach, but it can sometimes benefit from the use of some simple graphical notations. Both of these options are briefly discussed in this subsection.

- *Graphical notations*: One way to capture software dependencies is to extend your runtime platform model to add an indication of the software stack required on each machine to support the system elements executing there. In simple cases, this can be a useful elaboration of the runtime platform model. The problem with this is that complete and accurate software dependency stacks on each node can clutter the runtime platform model to the point where it is no longer usable—in this case, you should record this information separately.

- *Text and tables*: Dependencies are almost always captured as simple text tables. It is important to capture the exact requirements for third-party software (e.g., detailed version numbers, option names, and patch levels).

ACTIVITIES

Analyze the Runtime Dependency. This is usually a manual exercise to work through your system elements, identifying the dependencies they have and then repeating this process for each of the third-party elements. You normally derive the runtime dependencies from documentation supplied with each piece of third-party technology you are using and your own build and test environment requirements. With this done, you can clearly define the third-party elements you need for each processing node in the system.

Conduct a Technical Evaluation. In order to correctly document dependencies, you may need to do some prototyping or technical investigation.

Intermodel Relationships

For complex systems, a Deployment view contains two or three closely related models rather than a single model. We have found that the three models described earlier tend to be used by different stakeholders at different times. Senior staff in the groups responsible for deployment refer to the runtime platform model early in the project, a specialist networking group consults the network model, and system administrators use the technology dependency model during more detailed installation planning close to deployment. For this reason, we've found it valuable to present each separately.

A good way to consider these models is as a set of informal layers, with the core of the view being the runtime platform model. You can think of the network model as a lower-level layer supporting the runtime platform by elaborating on the details of the network required. Think of the technology dependency model as a more detailed layer on top of the runtime platform that defines the software and hardware installation requirements on each machine in the deployment environment.

In an ideal world, a software architecture tool would allow you to create a single model for yourself and then extract different aspects of it automatically as required. However, we aren't aware of any such tool in the commercial area.

Figure 20–3 illustrates this relationship between the models within the Deployment view. The runtime platform model is the core of the view, with the network model providing more details of the network underpinning the system and the technology dependency model providing more detail about the hardware and software installed on each node to provide the runtime environment.

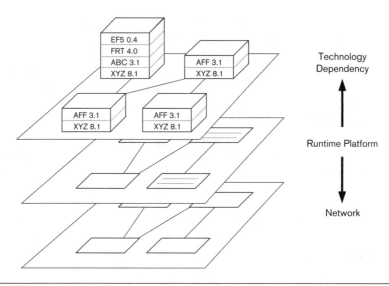

FIGURE 20-3 MODELS IN THE DEPLOYMENT VIEW

PROBLEMS AND PITFALLS

Unclear or Inaccurate Dependencies

Large-scale computing technology tends to be fairly complex, and it often has many explicit and implicit dependencies on its runtime environment that, if not met, cause runtime problems. This difficulty is compounded by the fact that most of these dependencies are invisible and can't be checked easily— you may not discover that you have the wrong version of a utility library until your database server fails to start.

"You need Oracle and Solaris" or "It uses SPARC hardware" are pretty common dependency statements. For all but the smallest systems, these are too vague to allow safe deployment of the system. You should specify which versions are required, whether any optional parts of the products are needed, whether any patches are required, and so on. With the complexity and flexibility of enterprise software products today, you need to be very clear what is required and what isn't.

RISK REDUCTION

- Capture clear, accurate, detailed dependencies between your software elements and the runtime environment in the Deployment view.
- Capture dependencies between third-party software and the runtime environment it needs.

- Perform compatibility testing to ensure that the dependencies between the elements are correct.
- Use existing, proven combinations of technologies where the dependencies are well understood.

Unproven Technology

Everyone wants to use the newest and coolest technology—and understandably so, as it often has the potential to bring great benefits. However, because its characteristics are unknown, using technology that you don't have experience with brings significant risks: functional shortcomings, for example, or inadequate performance, availability, or security.

RISK REDUCTION

- As much as possible, use existing software and hardware that you can test before committing to its use.
- When you must use new technology (or technology new to you), get advice from people who have used the technology before.
- Create realistic, practical prototypes and benchmarks to make sure that technologies work as advertised.
- Perform compatibility testing to ensure that new technologies work well with existing technologies.

Lack of Specialist Technical Knowledge

Designing a large information system is a complex undertaking that requires a huge amount of specialist knowledge about many different subjects. No one person can possibly be an expert on all of the technologies you may need to use. This is why we use teams of people to develop systems and why some people specialize in particular technologies, allowing them to advise others.

Given the number of technologies used in many systems, it can be difficult to assemble a project team with expertise in all of the technologies required. This can lead to a situation where you end up relying on vendor claims for products rather than proven knowledge and experience.

RISK REDUCTION

- Bring specialist knowledge into your team so that you have mastery of all of the key technologies you need to use to deliver your system. If you don't need the knowledge full-time, hire trusted and experienced part-time experts as needed.

- Obtain external expert review of your architecture to validate your assumptions and decisions.
- Obtain binding contractual commitments from your technology suppliers where possible.

Late Consideration of the Deployment Environment

The deployment environment is where your system hits reality. We've seen problems in some projects when the system is designed from a purely software-oriented perspective and the deployment environment is considered only when the software is complete. Remember that an inappropriate deployment environment can make an otherwise good system totally unusable.

The deployment environment also often affects how the software is designed and implemented, and this can be expensive to change. For example, if plans change and you need to use a group of small machines rather than a single large machine to host your server elements, this could have a significant impact on the architecture of your server software, a change that would be expensive to make late in delivery.

RISK REDUCTION

- Design your deployment environment as part of architecture definition rather than as part of a separate exercise performed after the system has been developed.
- Obtain external expert review of your architecture to get early feedback before you spend too much time or money.

CHECKLIST

- Have you mapped all of the system's functional elements to a type of hardware device? Have you mapped them to specific hardware devices if appropriate?
- Is the role of each hardware element in the system fully understood? Is the specified hardware suitable for the role?
- Have you established detailed specifications for the system's hardware devices? Do you know exactly how many of each device are required?
- Have you identified all required third-party software and documented all the dependencies between system elements and third-party software?
- Is the network topology required by the system understood and documented?

- Have you estimated and validated the required network capacity? Can the proposed network topology be built to support this capacity?

- Have network specialists validated that the required network can be built?

- Have you performed compatibility testing when evaluating your architectural options to ensure that the elements of the proposed deployment environment can be combined as desired?

- Have you used enough prototypes, benchmarks, and other practical tests when evaluating your architectural options to validate the critical aspects of the proposed deployment environment?

- Can you create a realistic test environment that is representative of the proposed deployment environment?

- Are you confident that the deployment environment will work as designed? Have you obtained external review to validate this opinion?

- Are the assessors satisfied that the deployment environment meets their requirements in terms of standards, risks, and costs?

- Have you checked that the physical constraints (such as floor space, power, cooling, and so on) implied by your required deployment environment can be met?

FURTHER READING

A great deal of literature describes specific deployment technologies; unfortunately, little of it discusses how to design a realistic and reliable system deployment environment. Some software architecture books [CLEM03; GARL03; HOFM00] contain explanations of how to document deployment views. Dyson and Longshaw [DYSO04] includes a number of patterns appropriate to the Deployment view.

21

THE OPERATIONAL VIEWPOINT

Definition	Describes how the system will be operated, administered, and supported when it is running in its production environment
Concerns	Installation and upgrade, functional migration, data migration, operational monitoring and control, configuration management, performance monitoring, support, and backup and restore
Models	Installation models, migration models, configuration management models, administration models, and support models
Problems and Pitfalls	Lack of engagement with the operational staff, lack of backout planning, lack of migration planning, insufficient migration window, missing management tools, lack of integration into the production environment, and inadequate backup models
Stakeholders	System administrators, developers, testers, communicators, and assessors
Applicability	Any system being deployed into a complex or critical operational environment

Considerable effort is spent defining the architecture and design of today's large systems. However, it is rare in our experience to find a system for which comparable consideration is given as to how the system will be controlled, managed, and monitored. The aim of the Operational viewpoint is to identify a system-wide strategy for addressing the operational concerns of the system's stakeholders and to identify solutions that address these.

For a large information system, the Operational view focuses on concerns that help ensure that the system is a reliable and effective part of the commissioning enterprise's information technology environment. For a product development project, the Operational view is more generic and illustrates the *types* of operational concerns that customers of the product are likely to encounter, rather than the concerns of a specific site. This view also identifies the solutions to be applied throughout the product implementation to resolve these concerns.

Of all the views you create for your AD, the Operational view is often the one that is least well defined and needs the most refinement and elaboration during the system's construction. This is simply because many of the details that the Operational view considers are not fully defined until design and construction is well under way. However, considering the issues described in this chapter as early as possible will save you a lot of time and effort later.

Concerns

Installation and Upgrade

Installation and upgrade can range from the development team installing and configuring software elements on customer-specific hardware to the ultimate users of the system obtaining hardware and software from a number of sources and performing installation, integration, and configuration themselves.

The other major area of variability is whether this is a pure installation or whether a previous version of your system is already installed, making the installation of the current version actually an upgrade. Upgrade can be significantly more complex than installation due to the need to respect existing data, configuration settings, the state of running elements, and so on. However, the use of iterative development approaches means that upgrade, rather than installation, is the norm, so you need to master it.

As an architectural concern, installation is less about the design of detailed procedures and plans and more about ensuring that the system can be installed or upgraded in a way that is acceptable to stakeholders. This involves working with technical specialists to understand the installation processes, software developers to ensure their elements can be easily and reliably installed, and system administrators to assure a practical, low-risk installation approach.

Functional Migration

Functional migration is the process of replacing existing capabilities with the ones provided by your system. This usually means migrating users of an older system to use your new system. Your migration approach may comprise one or more of the following:

- A *big bang* where the migration occurs irrevocably at a single point in time (often over a weekend)

- A *parallel run* where new and old versions of a system are used side by side until confidence in the new system is high enough to allow switching off the old one

- A *staged migration* where parts of a process or an organization are moved to a new system one by one, to manage the risk and cost of the migration activity

As an architectural concern, migration is centered on two issues—*risk* and *cost*. The big bang approach, for example, can be the cheapest because it requires no replication of resources, but it can be extremely risky because there is no easy recovery route if the migration goes wrong. Other approaches can be extremely expensive (because they require duplication of resources and the implementation of costly processes to ensure that systems run together in lockstep) but reduce risk.

Data Migration

Most if not all system developments involve some element of data migration— that is, loading data from existing systems into the new one(s). A goal of a data migration exercise is almost always to automate as much as possible, particularly where large volumes of data are involved. Where migrated data is very old, of variable quality, or poorly modeled, data migration may be extremely complex.

Data migration software is typically viewed as utility software with a limited life, rather than as a system requiring long-term support. This does not mean that it is of any lesser quality, but it may consist of a collection of automated software, semiautomated procedures, and manual intervention to deal with exceptions (such as missing data or data in unexpected formats). This also adds to the complexity of the process.

Nowadays, systems that manage hundreds of gigabytes or terabytes of data are not uncommon, and this presents its own migration challenges. Massive data stores are far more likely to include data that does not conform to business rules and therefore requires exceptional processing (possibly manual intervention). It can take days or weeks to extract data from or load data into massive data stores, and it is important that you do not underestimate the time required to reorganize databases, create indexes, and so on.

Fortunately, you can also make use of a wide range of Extraction, Transformation, and Load (ETL) tools that will help you automate this process. Many ETL tools allow you to define transformation rules visually and provide facilities for accessing a wide range of different physical formats, performing standard transformations, and monitoring and analyzing the results.

Another frequently overlooked problem occurs when you are migrating data from a live system that is continuing to be updated while you migrate from it, as discussed in this example.

EXAMPLE A government tax office has a very large database of taxpayers that it is migrating into a new system. The database is updated through end-user screens in tax offices throughout the country.

The architect predicts that extracting all of the data from the database will take between three and five days. The data must be sorted, which will take another day, and will then be loaded into the new system, which will take ten days. Finally, indexes must be created on the new system, which takes another day. The overall elapsed time to migrate is over two weeks, during which time the original system is estimated to have received 100,000 updates, as shown in Figure 21–1.

Special code has to be written to capture these updates as they occur and to apply them to the new system once the bulk of the data has been migrated into it, so that the extract is complete.

In short, data migration may be a significant piece of work in its own right, and you should manage it the same way as any other development project, with requirements, design, build and test, and acceptance—and, of course, architecture. Many of the architectural principles described in this book apply equally well to such a migration subproject, although the success criteria are different. In a migration project, it is the successfully migrated

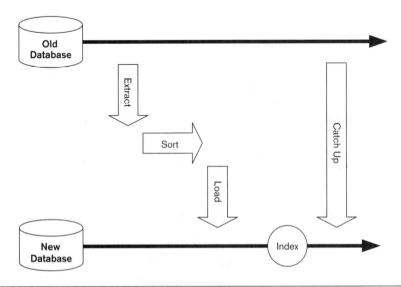

FIGURE 21–1 DATA MIGRATION FROM A LIVE SYSTEM

data that has to be accepted, rather than the software, which will be discarded once migration is complete.

Operational Monitoring and Control

Once a system is running in its production environment, it will require some amount of routine monitoring, to ensure that it is working correctly, and some routine control operations, to keep it working that way (startup, shutdown, transaction resubmission, and so on).

Some systems need little monitoring or control—for example, a file server that needs only direct operational control when it fails or fills up. Others may need quite a lot—for example, a large financial reconciliation system that accepts data feeds from a variety of sources and may need routine monitoring and control to identify and rectify communication link and data reconciliation failures.

The amount of monitoring and control needed depends on the likely number and variety of unexpected operational conditions the system is likely to encounter in production. However, the development of monitoring and control facilities can be a major effort in itself, so you may have to balance stakeholder needs in this area against cost and time. You also need to consider the system's deployment environment to make sure that the solutions you identify are appropriate.

Configuration Management

Many of the elements that make up your deployment environment will have their own configuration parameters. Databases, operating systems, middleware products, and of course your own software elements may all require detailed, specific configuration for the system to operate correctly. You may also need to make coordinated sets of changes to these configurations on a regular basis (the canonical example being a switch from online to batch mode and back again every 24 hours). Managing a number of separate element configurations can rapidly become complex enough to be a major source of operational risk for the system.

The discipline of configuration management aims to address this problem. Configuration management encompasses the processes and technologies to group, modify, and track element configuration parameters in a reliable and predictable manner.

The process of operational configuration management tends to be a fairly specialist job, handled by the system administration groups that run the production systems. From the architectural perspective, addressing this concern involves understanding the operational configuration your system requires and ensuring that it is possible to achieve it in a way that will be accepted by the interested stakeholders.

Performance Monitoring

The process of understanding and improving system performance is known as *performance engineering*, which we discuss in Chapter 25. However, the basis of all performance engineering work is *measurement*, so performance monitoring is an important concern for most systems. Your system needs to be able to capture, present, and store accurate quantitative performance information.

Production system administrators are often the first people who need to recognize and respond to a performance problem. You need to involve them in this process as early as possible to make sure they can work with the proposed solution.

In Chapter 25, we discuss in more detail the kinds of metrics needed for performance engineering and how you can capture and report them.

Support

End users, support staff, and maintainers have an interest in the type and level of support needed, who will provide that support, and the channels through which it will be delivered. As well as the system itself, support may be needed for the associated hardware infrastructure (computers, printers, and the network).

Backup and Restore

As we saw in our description of the Information viewpoint in Chapter 17, data is an extremely valuable asset to any organization and should be protected and "insured" the same way that its other assets are. Processes to do this should be carefully designed, built, and executed and should also be regularly tested to ensure they are still working correctly.

EXAMPLE One of us visited a trade organization many years ago that ran its membership database on a stand-alone UNIX system. The system administrator faithfully backed up the database to tape every night but, unfortunately, because the output of the process was not captured to a log file, nobody realized that the tape drive was broken and no data was being written. Only when the inevitable happened and a disk failed did the soon-to-be-unemployed system administrator realize that he had a shelf full of blank tapes. The organization had to recreate its membership database from paper records, which was a slow, painful, and costly process.

You shouldn't forget the restore side of the equation, either. As a minimum, restoring data should leave it in a transactionally consistent state (i.e., with all updates entirely committed to the restored database or not recovered at all). You will need to consider the amount of data lost as a result of the restore; at a minimum, this will be any transactions that are active at the time of failure but may include a lot more, particularly if backups can be done only when the system is offline.

If your data is distributed, this problem becomes much harder. Although a failure in any one program will affect only that program's data, the data may then become inconsistent with the rest of the system; you need to develop strategies to deal with this. Typically, the solution involves recovering or recreating the lost data, either manually or (preferably) automatically. In some cases, it may be more appropriate to revert the rest of the system to the older state.

A significant complication for backup and restore planning is the fact that, in many situations, transactional consistency must extend across a system's entire distributed data set, as shown in the next example.

EXAMPLE A university maintains academic records for all its students in a number of databases. The main database stores results for each exam taken by each student, while a consolidated database turns these into an overall score for each student based on exam success, as shown in Figure 21–2.

A database corruption means that the Exam Results database has to be restored from its latest clean backup, which is almost three months old, and the results for the last three months rekeyed into it. Although the Student Scores database is unaffected by the corruption, special actions must be taken to prevent this manually recovered data from filtering into the Student Scores database and corrupting its data. As a result, it could take several weeks to repair the damage due to the corruption of one database.

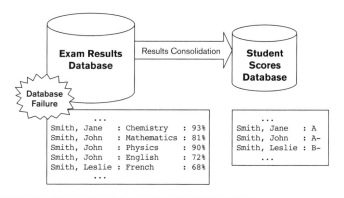

FIGURE 21–2 EXAMPLE OF BACKUP AND RECOVERY

TABLE 21-1 Stakeholder Concerns for the Operational Viewpoint

Stakeholder Class	Concerns
Assessors	Functional migration, data migration, and support
Communicators	Installation and upgrade, functional migration, and operational monitoring and control
Developers	Operational monitoring and control and performance monitoring
Support staff	Functional migration, data migration, and support
System administrators	All concerns
Testers	Installation and upgrade, functional migration, data migration, monitoring and control, and performance monitoring
Users	Support

If your system contains data distributed over a number of data stores, you must ensure that your Operational view takes this into account when considering backup and recovery.

Stakeholder Concerns

Typical stakeholder concerns for the Operational viewpoint include those listed in Table 21-1.

Models

The Operational view consists of models that illustrate how the system will be put into production and kept running effectively once it is there.

Bear in mind that for most enterprise systems, each of these models can be quite large and involved. When this is the case, it's sensible to summarize the model in the AD and reference a fuller model in another document, to avoid making the AD too large and unwieldy.

Installation Models

Moving a system from its development environment to its production environment is a critical part of the system's lifecycle. Your AD needs to demonstrate that it is possible for a system built using this architecture to be installed (and upgraded) in a practical way.

The installation model should discuss installation and/or upgrade as needed for your system. This model needs to help the reader understand:

- What needs to be installed or upgraded to move the system into production
- What dependencies exist between the various groups of items to be installed and upgraded
- What constraints exist on the process to perform the installation and/or upgrade for the system
- What would need to be done to abandon and undo the installation and/or upgrade if something goes seriously wrong

The AD doesn't need to include a complete installation and upgrade plan—that information goes into a different document produced later in the development lifecycle. Instead, the installation model provides your view of the requirements and constraints the architecture imposes on installation and upgrade. The installation model in your initial AD is likely to contain only an overview of your installation strategy (because the details of what needs to be installed aren't fully known at that time), but you will be able to elaborate and refine this model as construction of the system progresses.

NOTATION The best notation to use for an installation model really depends on the situation and what the primary stakeholders (the system administrators) are familiar with. In our experience, an approach using text and tables is often the best way to communicate this information.

Simple lists work well for laying out and defining the elements of the installation problem. In simple cases, cross-reference tables can describe dependencies, while more involved dependencies are usually effectively addressed with the use of dependency diagrams.

ACTIVITIES

Identify the Installation Groups. Start by considering what elements of your architecture need to be installed and/or upgraded, and identify groups of them that can be handled together. For each group, define which elements it contains and the approach that will be used to install or upgrade that group.

Identify Any Dependencies. Technical dependencies often exist between different parts of a complex system during installation, so that the installation process has to proceed in a specific order. Identify the dependencies that exist between your installation groups to reveal these constraints.

Identify Any Constraints. Consider the overall installation process and the different ways it could be achieved. Other than the ordering dependencies you considered in the previous activity, does your architecture impose any further constraints on the process? (For example, do you need to start one element after it is installed so it can generate code or data needed to install the next one? Do you need to restart one of the machines during installation?)

Design the Backout Approach. Consider what would need to be done to undo any of the installation tasks you have identified. In particular, identify anything that would be complex or time-consuming to undo.

EXAMPLE This example shows an installation model for a rental-tracking system, based on the results of the activities just described.

Installation Groups

- *Win32 Desktop Client*: Contains all of the software in the W32CLIENT component. Installation shall be via InstallShield automatic installer, remotely executed via management tool.
- *Database Schema*: Contains all DBMS schema definitions and data abstraction stored procedures. To be packaged as simple SQL scripts and installed using a custom written Perl script.
- *Web Interface*: Contains the server-resident user interface components (the WEBINTERFACE component). Installation will be by manual administrative action, copying files into IIS directories according to written instructions.
- *Rental-Tracking Service*: Contains the .NET assemblies that implement the services called by the Web and Win32 interfaces (the RENTALTRACKER component). Installation will be by manual administrative action, copying files into IIS directories according to written instructions.
- *Reporting Engine*: Contains the .NET assemblies that implement the summary reporting engine. Installation will be by manual administrative action, copying files into IIS directories according to written instructions.

Dependencies

- Win32 Desktop Client, Web Interface, Rental-Tracking Service, and Reporting Engine depend on Database Schema.
- Win32 Desktop Client and Web Interface depend on Rental-Tracking Service.
- Web Interface depends on Reporting Engine.

Constraints

- *Win32 Desktop Client*: A restart of the client machine will be required during this installation process.

Backout Strategy

This is the first release of the software, so backout is reasonably straightforward and consists simply of uninstallation. For each installation group, the following action will be required.

- *Win32 Desktop Client*: Run the installer with an `uninstall` flag.
- *Database Schema*: A custom Perl script will be supplied to remove all objects created during the installation.
- *Web Interface*: Manual administrative action will be required. The supplied instructions will list the files to be removed.
- *Rental-Tracking Service*: Manual administrative action will be required. The supplied instructions will list the files to be removed.
- *Reporting Engine*: Manual administrative action will be required. The supplied instructions will list the files to be removed.

Migration Models

If a migration process is required, the migration model needs to illustrate the strategy that will be used. Again, a complete plan is not called for in the AD, but rather a succinct definition of the strategies to be employed. This model should allow its reader to understand:

- What overall strategies can (or will) be employed to migrate information and users to the system
- How the new system will be populated with information from the existing environment
- How information in the new and old environments will be kept synchronized (if required)
- How operation could revert to the old system if serious problems emerge with the new one

As with the installation model, the migration model should focus on the requirements and constraints that the current architecture places on the detailed migration process that will be developed later.

NOTATION A migration model is usually documented by using text and tables because no suitable, widely accepted graphical notations are available. Some informal diagrams may help illustrate data migration and synchronization, and particularly complex data migration may require some form of data model to illustrate the transformations involved.

ACTIVITIES

Establish Possible Strategies. Assess your architecture and the existing system(s), and establish which migration strategies (i.e., big bang, parallel run, staged migration) are possible, how each would work, and the tradeoffs among them.

Define the Primary Strategy. In some situations, you will simply define the options and someone else will decide which approach to use (e.g., if you're developing a product and different customers want to migrate different ways). In other cases, you will be tasked with the responsibility of defining which strategy best meets the needs of your stakeholders and making it happen.

Design the Data Migration Approach. Having identified a strategy to use, you need to decide how to populate the system with all of the information in the existing system(s). This doesn't mean you need to spend days mapping fields between databases, but it does mean you have to understand the problem well enough to choose an appropriate approach for the data migration and determine how long it is likely to take and what tasks and resources might be required.

Design the Information Synchronization Approach. Some situations call for information to be synchronized between the old system(s) and the new one. This is particularly the case when using the parallel run migration strategy because information in the old system(s) may continue to be updated after the new system goes live. If synchronization is required, it may be unidirectional (just into the new system) or bidirectional (information changes need to be migrated from new to old as well as old to new). Your task is to identify an overall approach that will allow the required degree of synchronization to be performed within the operational constraints of your environment.

Identify the Backout Strategy. Being able to back out to an existing system (if available) is an attractive risk-reduction option for live operation. The problem is that it isn't always clear how such a backout would work, or if it is even possible (e.g., reverse data migration may not be practical due to the design of the new system). You need to decide whether a backout strategy involving the old system(s) is required and, if so, how it could work.

Configuration Management Models

You may need to create a configuration management model if your system requires complex, regular reconfiguration (e.g., reconfiguring parts of the system to handle different types of workloads according to a calendar-based schedule). This model must explain to its reader:

- The groups of configuration items in the system and how each is managed
- The dependencies that exist among the configuration groups

- The different configuration value sets required for routine system operation (and why each is required)
- How the different sets of configuration values will be applied to the system

The aim is to create a model of the system configuration management problem (rather than identifying lots of individual configuration values). This allows those responsible for system configuration management to understand the problem and plan their solution for it.

Like the installation model, this model is unlikely to be complete in your early AD but can be elaborated and refined as construction of the system progresses and the details of the configuration items required become known.

NOTATION This model is often quite simple and best documented by using text and tables. In more complex cases, it is usually best treated primarily as a data model, and a data-modeling notation, such as entity-relationship diagrams or UML, is a useful addition to the textual description.

ACTIVITIES

Identify the Configuration Groups. Consider all of the configuration values your system requires and break them into cohesive groups with as few intergroup dependencies as possible. This allows you to abstract the problem of managing the individual values to the level of managing large groups as a single unit (think of them as clumps of values). Name each group, explain its purpose, and explain how the configuration group would be managed (how values are defined, collected, applied, and so on).

Identify Any Configuration Group Dependencies. Having identified the groups of configuration information in your system, you can clearly identify and record any dependencies among them. For example, if changing the configuration of your database management system means reconfiguring the operating system, or adding more instances of one of your elements means changing the application server configuration, record these as intergroup dependencies. Identifying these dependencies allows you to start understanding the problem of reconfiguring your system in production.

Identify Configuration Value Sets. Consider your system during its routine operational lifecycle, and establish how many configurations your system will need during it. Define the characteristics of each value set, and identify the configuration groups that change between different configurations. For each set you identify, define its purpose and when it needs to be applied. This allows assessment of the operational impact of your architecture's configuration needs.

Design the Configuration Change Strategy. Once you have identified the configuration your system needs and the changes you need to make to it, design an approach to achieve this in your intended production environment.

Again, rather than focusing on the minutiae of the administration process, you need to identify a practical overall approach that the production administrators of your system will accept.

EXAMPLE This example shows a configuration management model for the rental-tracking system we described earlier.

Configuration Groups

- *DBMS Parameters*: The SQL Server 2000 parameters that control the initialization, operation, and performance characteristics of the database. These are managed via SQL scripts, applied by database administrators.

- *IIS Parameters*: The IIS parameters that control the initialization, operation, and performance characteristics of the server. These are managed by using a set of JScript scripts that will be supplied with the system.

- *Reporting Engine Options*: The Reporting Engine parameters that control what is summarized and when summaries are computed. These are managed as a set of configuration files read by the component.

Configuration Dependencies

- When the IIS Parameters are set to allow more connections, the DBMS Parameters must be changed to allow for the possible increase in load.

- If the Reporting Engine Options are set for more aggressive summary activity, the DBMS Parameters must be set to allow for an increased amount of data cache being required.

Configuration Sets

- *Standard*: Normal configuration for planned system workload of up to 1,200 concurrent users with the Reporting Engine producing level 1 summary statistics every 6 hours.

- *High Volume*: Configuration to be applied when high client volume is expected. Increases capacity to 2,000 concurrent users and switches off routine operation of the Reporting Engine.

- *Month End*: Configuration to be applied during the last 2 days of the month, limiting concurrent usage to 800 users and allowing the Reporting Engine to run continually to produce complete summary statistics.

Configuration Change Strategy

The configuration sets will be applied as follows.

- The DBMS will be manually reconfigured first, by the database administrator running a single script that sets the parameters for the desired configuration set. (This could involve a DBMS restart.)
- Next, the Reporting Engine Options will be changed by altering the Engine's configuration file parameter and restarting it.
- Finally, the IIS configuration set will be applied by an administrator running the appropriate JScript script and restarting the IIS engine.

Administration Models

When your system is running in its production environment, it will require some degree of administration to monitor it and keep it running smoothly. The administration model is the section of your AD where you define the operational requirements and constraints of your architecture and the facilities it provides for administrative users.

The administration model must define the following items.

- *Monitoring and control facilities*: In order to support your system's administrators, you may need to provide some monitoring and control facilities as part of your architecture. This may involve custom utilities and features and/or integration into an existing management environment. It can be as simple as a basic message log or as complex as a full-blown integration with a management or monitoring infrastructure. You need to clearly define the facilities you are going to provide, how these address the problem, and whether any limitations in these facilities could constrain their applicability or usefulness.

- *Required routine procedures*: You should also review the architecture you have designed and identify any administrative work that needs to be performed on a regular basis or that may be required in exceptional circumstances. Depending on the system, this can be as basic as a weekly backup and a monthly health check, or it can be a set of complex procedures performed on a round-the-clock basis to keep a critical high-volume system running at peak efficiency. For each procedure, you need to define its purpose, when it is performed, who performs it, and what is involved in performing it. In most cases, you should cross-refer to the relevant monitoring and control facilities provided.

- *Likely error conditions*: Any complex system can suffer unexpected failures due to internal or external faults. From simple situations such as disks filling up to sudden failures of the underlying network causing a cascade of problems, many error conditions that occur can require administrative intervention to rectify them. Some of these conditions are independent of your architecture and are caused by underlying platform failures. The administrators of your system will probably already be experts at diagnosing and recovering from these failures. However, you cannot expect them to understand the possible error conditions that are unique to your architecture, and you need to explain these carefully to help administrators understand the conditions they may need to recover from. Your description should include when the condition can occur, how to recognize it (referencing relevant monitoring facilities provided), how to rectify it (referencing relevant control facilities provided), and possible further failures the condition could trigger.

- *Performance monitoring facilities*: A specialist subset of system monitoring is the ability to monitor the performance of the system. The difference between operational monitoring and performance monitoring tends to be how the data is used. Operational monitoring usually reports by exception and produces little or no output data when everything is going well. In contrast, performance monitoring facilities are usually designed so that performance information can be extracted and analyzed routinely to allow system performance to be tracked over time. We talk more about performance activities in general in Chapter 25. In an administration model, you need to explain the types of performance measures you will make available and how administrators or developers will extract and analyze the information when required.

An important point to note is the strong degree of cross-reference between the administrative facilities you define in this model and the common design model in the Development view. In the Operational view, you define the facilities you will provide for the administrative stakeholders. The Development view needs to define the common processing required across all of the system's elements in order to actually achieve those facilities.

NOTATION The primary customers of the administration model are system administrators, who may not be software developers by training. We have found that the right notation for this model is nearly always text and tables augmented with a few informal diagrams where needed. Extensive use of more formal notation such as UML is less appropriate for this model.

ACTIVITIES
Identify the Routine Maintenance Required. Consider your system running in its production environment and create a list of the types of operational

tasks that will need to be performed to keep the system running smoothly. For each task type, define who needs to perform it, when it needs to be performed. and how it should be performed.

Identify Your Likely Error Conditions. Analyze your architecture by considering its primary usage scenarios, and work out what is likely to go wrong during the operational lifecycle (elements failing, data stores filling up, systems running out of memory or other runtime resources). Make sure you think about the ones related to administration and maintenance as well as the ones that end users would be aware of—it is often harder to plan for failures during larger-scale administrative scenarios (such as data maintenance). Identify the classes of error conditions that can occur, what causes them, and how they can be rectified to get the system running again. You should also try to estimate the likely availability impact of the failure to ensure that you can recover the system in a time acceptable to your stakeholders. You may want to consider the error conditions that could occur if routine maintenance *isn't* performed, so that the importance of this maintenance is understood.

Specify Any Custom Utilities. Routine and exceptional procedures may require system-specific utilities to allow administrators to perform them efficiently. Such utilities can range from very simple database or operating system scripts to significant pieces of software in their own right. Consider whether any such utilities are required, and specify any you need.

Identify the Key Performance Scenarios. Some of your architectural usage scenarios will be much more important than others from a performance perspective (look for the scenarios that support time-critical business processes, involve a high workload, are executed very frequently, or are required by key stakeholders). Extract these scenarios from the overall system usage scenarios.

Identify the Performance Metrics. Consider the key performance scenarios and identify metrics that will allow you to measure the performance achieved for each and to analyze where the system spends most of its time and resources. In order to abstract the problem, it may be more useful to identify classes of metrics rather than individual ones. Make sure that you record what each metric or class identified actually means and what it is used for.

Design the Monitoring Facilities. Having established the operational tasks and performance metrics required, you can design monitoring facilities to be used across the system to provide routine system monitoring and error condition recognition and to gather performance metrics from the system's elements. This design will be at the outline level, to be fleshed out later during the development increments of the lifecycle. However, at this stage you should provide enough detail to clarify what needs to be done in each system element to provide the administration facilities required.

EXAMPLE   This example shows an administration model for the rental-tracking system.

Monitoring and Control

The monitoring and control facilities are as follows.

- *Server Message Logging*: All server components will write information, warning, and error messages to the Windows Event Log of the machine they are running on.
- *Client Message Logging*: The client software will log messages if an unexpected error is encountered. The log will be written to the hard disk of the client machine for later manual retrieval.
- *Startup and Shutdown*: No system-specific startup and shutdown facilities will be provided because the software will run in the context of the IIS and SQL Server 2000 servers, and their facilities are considered to be sufficient.

Operational Procedures

Routine operational procedures are as follows.

- *Backup*: Operational data in the SQL Server database will need to be backed up. This will involve backing up the transaction logs every 15 minutes and backing up the application's databases every day. Details of this procedure will be left to the database administrators.
- *Pruning of Summary Information*: The Reporting Engine does not remove the summary reporting information it creates. This information is left in place and is available to users of the Win32 client interface. Database administrators will need to monitor the performance of the Reporting Engine and the management reporting aspects of the Win32 client components and manually prune the summary information when its volume starts to impact performance. A written procedure will be supplied to explain how the pruning should be performed.

Error Conditions

The error conditions that administrators should be expected to handle are as follows.

- *Database Out of Log Space*: If transaction volume rises above a certain point, it is possible that the transaction log will fill. This will

cause the system to suspend operation. Database administrators
will need to recognize log space problems and manually back up
the logs to free space. If this happens routinely, the backup interval
for the transaction logs should be reduced.

- *Database out of Data Space*: If the database runs out of data space,
  the system will stop operating. Again, database administrators will
  need to recognize this condition and either prune the summary information (see above) or add more data space to the system. A
  written estimate of the amount of space required for various volumes of workload will be provided.

- *IIS Failure*: If the IIS server fails, the system will completely fail,
  and Win32 clients will lose contact with the server. Administrators
  need to recognize this condition and restart IIS. The system will recover automatically once IIS is restarted. The Win32 clients will automatically reconnect once the server is available again.

Performance Monitoring

No application-specific performance monitoring facilities are planned.
System performance monitoring should be achieved by using the following facilities.

- *SQL Server 2000 Counters*: The SQL Server 2000 product allows a
  wide range of performance counters to be collected via the Windows 2000 Server's Performance Monitor application. These
  counters should be used to assess the volume of workload on the
  database and the time taken for the application's transactions to
  complete.

- *IIS/ASP.NET Counters*: IIS Server and ASP.NET produce a wide
  range of performance counters to be collected via the Windows
  2000 Server's Performance Monitor application. These counters
  should be used to assess the number of Web requests being ser-
  viced and how long it is taking to service them.

- *.NET Counters*: The .NET runtime allows a wide range of performance counters to be collected via the Windows 2000 Server's
  Performance Monitor application. These counters should be used
  to establish the amount of non-Web-request workload that the application is performing and how long it is taking to perform the
  operations.

Support Models

Once your system is running in production, at least some of the system's stakeholders are likely to need help using or operating it, and other parties will need to provide assistance to them. The support model should provide a clear abstraction of the support that will be provided, who will provide the support, and how problems can be escalated between parties when searching for a resolution. This means defining the following in your support model.

- *Groups needing support*: The model must clearly define the groups of stakeholders that will require support, the nature of support they need, and the appropriate mechanisms for delivering that support.
- *Classes of incidents*: The model must also define what sort of support incidents are likely to be encountered and what sort of response is reasonable to expect in each case. The definition of each class of incident should clearly state the characteristics of an incident in that class, typically in terms of operational, organizational, or financial impacts.
- *Support providers and responsibilities*: Each type of support incident needs to be handled by at least one support provider, who must accept responsibility for resolving the incident. The model should capture who the support providers are and their responsibilities for incident resolution.
- *Escalation process*: A serious incident often requires a number of different support providers to resolve the situation because it is too complex or specialized for a single provider to handle. Your model should define how incidents are escalated between support providers and the responsibilities of each when this happens. This will help ensure that incident resolution does not stall because of confusion over responsibilities or a lack of expertise by a particular provider.

As with the other models for the Operational view, the focus of the support model should be to provide an overview of the support problem and a strategy for its solution rather than the definition of detailed procedures.

NOTATION This model needs to be understood by a number of different technical and nontechnical stakeholder groups. The majority of the model should normally be a text-and-tables definition of the support to be provided, with some flow diagrams (such as UML activity diagrams) where required to make the information flow and decision-making processes clear.

ACTIVITIES
Identify the Supported Groups. Identify the groups of stakeholders who will need support, the type of support they will need, and the possible avenues through which that support could be provided.

Identify the Support Providers. Decide who will be providing support to your stakeholders. For each provider (which will probably be an organization), define the support they provide and how they provide it.

Identify Any Incidents Requiring Support. Consider the types of incidents that could trigger the need for assistance by each of your groups of supported stakeholders, and characterize the incident type by likely frequency and severity.

Map the Providers, Incidents, and Groups. Decide which support providers will resolve which incident types for which stakeholder groups, and ensure that each provider can offer suitable support.

Plan the Escalation. Consider your groups of support providers, and identify which of them may need to escalate problems to other support providers. Define the escalation paths that should be used between providers and the responsibilities of each provider when this happens.

EXAMPLE This example shows a support model for the rental-tracking system.

Supported Groups

- *Web Users*: People using the Web interface to book or manage their rentals may need support if there are problems with the site or if they have difficulties using the Web interface. Few assumptions may be made about this group, and the primary support channel should be e-mail, with telephone backup.

- *Win32 Users*: Internal users using the Win32 client may need help with a range of problems including usage issues, system problems, and PC support. Their primary support channel is assumed to be telephone, although they may be prepared to receive support via e-mail.

- *Windows Administrators*: The administrators of the server machines are technically sophisticated and will require assistance only in unexpected failure scenarios. They will need to receive immediate assistance via telephone as well as query resolution via e-mail.

- *Database Administrators*: The database administrators are technically sophisticated and will require assistance only with unfamiliar database behavior. They will need to receive immediate assistance via telephone as well as query resolution via e-mail.

Support Providers

- *Web Services Help Desk*: This organizational group is responsible for resolving all support incidents raised by users of the Web interface. They provide support via e-mail and telephone, 6 days per week, 20 hours per day.

- *IT Help Desk*: This organizational group is responsible for resolving all support incidents raised by users of the Win32 client interface. They provide support via e-mail and telephone and can often provide direct assistance at the end user's desk as well. Support is provided during normal business hours.

- *DBA Group*: This organizational group is responsible for resolving all support incidents related to database management systems. They provide support via e-mail and telephone. Support is normally provided during normal business hours, with the option of using on-call staff outside this period.

- *Windows Administrators*: This organizational group is responsible for resolving all support incidents related to IIS, .NET, and Windows 2000 Server and underlying hardware. They provide support via e-mail and telephone. Support is provided during normal business hours, with the option of using on-call staff outside this period.

- *Microsoft Support*: This is an external organization (the Microsoft Corporation's Support division) that is responsible for assisting with the resolution of support incidents caused by a fault or usage problem with the SQL Server 2000, Windows 2000 Server, or IIS products. They provide support via e-mail, newsgroups, Web sites, fax, and telephone. Support is provided 24 hours per day, every day.

- *Development Team*: This is the organizational group that developed the system originally and maintains it on an ongoing basis. They are responsible for resolving any incident that other support providers cannot resolve. They provide support via e-mail, telephone, and site visits during normal business hours, with the ability to reach on-call staff during other times.

Support Incidents and Resolution

- *Web Usage Difficulties*: This class of support incident covers any situation where a user of the Web interface is having problems using the system that are not caused by failure or malfunction of a system component. These incidents should be resolved in a single interaction with the Web Services Help Desk, either by phone or e-mail. The impact on the organization should be minimal.

- *Win32 Usage Difficulties*: This class of support incident covers any situation where a user of the Win32 client interface is having problems using the system that are not caused by failure or malfunction of a system component. These incidents should be resolved in a single interaction with the IT Help Desk, either by phone or e-mail. The impact on the organization should be minimal.

- *End-User System Errors*: This class of support incident covers any situation where a user of the system encounters a problem caused by failure or malfunction of a system component. These incidents should be resolved within 1 working day. The user should interact entirely with staff of the IT or Web Services Help Desk, who will manage problem resolution and deal with other support providers as required. The impact on the organization should be moderate and should not threaten business operations beyond inconvenience.

- *Slow End-User Performance*: This class of support incident covers any situation where end users complain of unacceptably slow performance. These incidents should be resolved within 3 working days. The user should interact entirely with members of the IT or Web Services Help Desk, who will manage problem resolution and deal with other support providers as required. The impact on the organization should be moderate and should not threaten business operations beyond inconvenience.

- *Database Corruption*: This class of support incident covers any situation where the database system reports internal corruption. These incidents should be resolved within 2 hours (although, realistically it is recognized that they could return; however, the original incident should be resolved within 2 hours). The DBA Group is responsible for recognizing and resolving these situations. The impact on the organization should be moderate, but business operations will be interrupted while the problem is resolved.

- *Database Failure*: This class of support incident covers any situation where the database system needs to be recovered from backups. These incidents should be resolved within 4 hours. The DBA Group is responsible for recognizing and resolving these situations. The impact on the organization may be severe during this period, with business operations being interrupted for the whole period of the incident, but should not continue beyond the resolution of the incident.

- *IIS or Windows 2000 Server Failure*: This class of support incident covers any situation where the IIS Server, underlying operating system, or underlying hardware suffers a failure. These incidents should be resolved within 1 hour. The Windows Administrators are responsible for recognizing and resolving these situations. The impact on the organization may be severe during this period, with business operations being interrupted for the whole period of the incident, but should not continue beyond the resolution of the incident.

Escalation

The escalation process is as follows.

- Users of the Web interface will report problems to the Web Services Help Desk.
- Users of the Win32 client interface will report problems to the IT Help Desk.
- The Help Desks will report system problems to the Windows Administrators.
- The Windows Administrators will report database problems to the DBA Group.
- The Windows Administrators will report other problems to the Development Team.
- The Windows Administrators, DBA Group, and Development Team will report problems with Microsoft software to the Microsoft Support organization.

In each case, the organization accepting the incident must provide the reporter with a unique identifier for the incident and record the reporter's description of it. If the problem is not immediately resolved, the organization accepting the incident must provide the reporter with information on resolution status within 75% of the target resolution time.

PROBLEMS AND PITFALLS

Lack of Engagement with the Operational Staff

In many organizations, a gulf exists between the development staff members who build systems and the operational staff members who deploy and administer them. This can be a significant problem if you want to achieve a smooth, incident-free system rollout.

RISK REDUCTION

- The best solution to this problem is to engage early with the operational groups, stressing how valuable their contribution is. Operational staff often have a legitimate grievance with software developers because systems are frequently passed on to them with very little thought given to operational requirements.
- Use an explicit Operational view to help avoid this situation.

Lack of Backout Planning

Many systems we've seen don't have real backout plans. In fact, many commercial software products don't have graceful recovery mechanisms to cope with situations like failed upgrades. Without a good backout plan, you are relying on a perfect rollout for your entire system, which experience suggests is somewhat optimistic.

RISK REDUCTION

- Make sure that your system can be backed out of its production environment by defining a clear procedure and reviewing it.

Lack of Migration Planning

Many information systems replace a manual system, a previous automated system, or an earlier version of themselves, but many systems are developed without a good migration plan. Migration planning isn't glamorous or, in many cases, even interesting, but without it, you are unlikely to achieve a smooth system deployment.

RISK REDUCTION

- Make sure you understand the migration needs of your architecture as early as possible.
- Address migration needs in your AD.

Insufficient Migration Window

In our experience, data migration *always* takes longer than anticipated, typically because the data does not conform to the level of quality and consistency expected of it and because of the problems associated with handling and manipulating large volumes of data.

RISK REDUCTION

- Consider how you will deal with data errors and inconsistencies.
- Develop processes for accepting migrated data, and make sure your stakeholders have bought into them.
- In your hardware sizing models, factor in the storage requirements for transitional data.
- Include adequate elapsed-time contingency in your migration plan.
- Factor in the time needed to reorganize databases, create indexes, and so on.
- Where you are migrating data from live systems and the migration time is substantial, create strategies for reconciling any data updates made during the migration period.

Missing Management Tools

Most software developers (and, in fact, many architects) are very focused on the business of building new software. However, successful software spends most of its life in production, not development. This mismatch between focus and lifecycle often manifests itself as a lack of operational facilities, which can result in a system that is difficult to monitor and control. Software developers can monitor or control the system by using primitive tools (operating system commands or simple scripts) because of their detailed knowledge of its internal workings. Operational staff often don't have this knowledge and need more sophisticated tools to automate the required operational procedures. Without such tools, the system is unlikely to be managed well.

RISK REDUCTION

- Understand the needs of your administration stakeholders as early as possible and involve them in the development of the Operational view.
- Ensure that administrators' needs are addressed with standard, system-wide facilities.

Lack of Integration into the Production Environment

Most information systems are deployed into some sort of existing production environment, even if it is a simple or informal one. Unfortunately, it's common to find that a new system doesn't work with the environment. This can be quite a problem for operational staff who need to learn new interfaces or tools or even totally new ways to manage the system.

RISK REDUCTION

- Make sure that you understand the existing environment and its integration needs early in your system design.

- Involve experts who understand the target production environment as early as possible, and get their advice on how it works and the type and level of integration needed.

Inadequate Backup Models

Backup and restore processes can fail quite spectacularly, and you don't want to find out about problems in your model when you are desperately trying to recover important data.

RISK REDUCTION

- Do not be tempted to skimp on this area or omit it from consideration entirely.

- Incorporate backup and restore as a central part of your architecture rather than trying to add it afterward.

- Make sure that your backup scheme includes all the information you need for data recovery.

- Estimate how long backup and recovery will take, and perform some practical testing under realistic conditions.

- Make sure that your model describes how data will be restored as well as backed up.

- Consider how to maintain data consistency across multiple data stores when you have to recover one of them to an earlier state.

- Consider a "belt-and-braces" approach to backup. For example, many end-user systems—especially older, mainframe-based ones—write copies of updates received from clients to an audit and recovery area as well as to the main database. This means that if the database is damaged, it is possible to replay these transactions into the database in order to get it in synch again.

CHECKLIST

- Do you know what it takes to install your system?
- Do you have a plan for backing out a failed installation?
- Can you upgrade an existing version of the system (if required)?

- Do you know how information will be moved from the existing environment into the new system?
- Do you have a clear migration strategy to move workload to the new system? Can you reverse the migration if you need to? How will you deal with data synchronization (if required)?
- Do you know how the system will be backed up? Are you confident that the approach identified will allow reliable system restoration in an acceptable time period?
- Are the administrators confident that they can monitor and control the system in production?
- Do the administrators have a clear understanding of the procedures they need to perform for the system?
- How will performance metrics be captured for the system's elements?
- Can you manage the configuration of all of the system's elements?
- Do you know how support will be provided for the system? Is the support provided suitable for the stakeholders it is being provided for?
- Have you cross-referenced the requirements of the administration model back to the Development view to ensure that they will be implemented consistently?
- Is the data migration architecture compatible with the amount of time available to perform the data migration? Are there catch-up mechanisms in place where the source data is volatile during the data migration?

FURTHER READING

Little or no existing literature deals with the operational aspects of a system from the perspective of a software architect. Although there are many books on installing and managing specific pieces of technology, we have found very few books that examine the principles that underpin reliable production systems operation.

We are aware of some books that at least partially address this area [GOOD99; VOSS89; WYZA99]. Also, Dyson and Longshaw [DYSO04] includes a number of patterns useful in the Operational view.

22

ACHIEVING CONSISTENCY ACROSS VIEWS

The use of views addresses one of the biggest challenges you face as an architect: to represent a large and complex system in a way your stakeholders can understand. A view is a way to portray those aspects or elements of the architecture that are relevant to the concerns the view intends to address—and, by implication, the stakeholders for whom those views are important.

Without views, you end up with a single, all-encompassing model that tries (and usually fails) to illustrate all of the aspects of your system. Such a model is complex, uses a mix of notations, and is too hard for anyone to understand—never mind appreciate the subtleties, nuances, and implications of your architectural choices.

However, the problem with partitioning the representation of your architecture through using views is that it is difficult to ensure consistency between them—in other words, ensuring that the structures, features, and elements that appear in one view are compatible and in alignment with the content of your other views. This consistency is a vital characteristic of your AD—without it, the system will not work properly, will not achieve its design goals, and may even be impossible to build.

Unfortunately, although some design tools can simplify the process of creating your models, we are not aware of any currently available tool that will automate such consistency checking to the extent that you need it to. The use of formal modeling languages such as UML only partially addresses this problem, and the tools that support these languages typically provide only basic features for checking one model for consistency against another. And, of course, if you are using an informal notation or one you have developed for your specific situation, the problem is even worse.

Ensuring consistency between views therefore largely comes down to the skill, thoroughness, and diligence of the architect and (to a lesser extent) the stakeholders. We have found the following strategies helpful in achieving interview consistency.

- *Focus on consistency from the outset*: We saw that trying to apply quality properties after the fact doesn't work—good performance, availability, and resilience have to be designed into your solution from the start. Similarly, it is no good waiting until your models are nearly complete to determine whether they are consistent with one another: More likely than not, they won't be, and you will be faced with a significant piece of rework and additional review.

- *Enumerate model elements*: Assigning each significant model element a unique identifier simplifies the process of asking such questions as, "Is element 3 from Model B consistent with element 5 from Model D?"

- *Ensure that consistency checks are a formal part of reviews*: Consistency should be one of the criteria you use to review models and other architectural documentation. This means both *internal consistency* (Is this part of the model consistent with other parts of this model?) and *external consistency* (Is this model consistent with other models that make up the AD?).

RELATIONSHIPS BETWEEN VIEWS

Although all of the views are obviously interrelated, in practice there are *strong* dependencies only between *some* of the views. The UML class diagram in Figure 22–1 shows the most important of these dependencies. The relationships illustrate a strong dependency, which implies that if something changes at the end of the arrow, a change will probably be required at the start of the arrow.

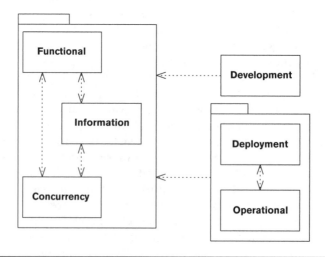

FIGURE 22–1 DEPENDENCIES BETWEEN VIEWS

Conversely, if there's no dependency between two views, changing something in one is unlikely to itself necessitate a change in the other. (So changing a Development view element, for example, does not in itself imply any changes to the Functional models—unless you are changing it for a reason not to do with development, of course.)

Note that if you don't develop a particular view—for example, if you encapsulate the concurrency aspects of the architecture in the Functional view, rather than in a separate Concurrency view—it is still useful to apply the checklists presented in this chapter for that view, to ensure that you have addressed its most important concerns.

FUNCTIONAL AND INFORMATION VIEW CONSISTENCY

Goal: To ensure that the functional and information structures are compatible and that nothing is missing in one that is required by the other.

- Does every nontrivial functional element in the Functional view that needs persistent data have corresponding data elements in the Information view?

- Does every nontrivial data element in the Information view have at least one element in the Functional view that is responsible for the maintenance of that data?

- If information flows are described in the Information view, are they consistent with the interelement interactions in the Functional view?

- If the Information view requires specific functional features (e.g., distributed transaction support, redundant logging of updates, and so on), are these features addressed in the Functional view?

- Do the data ownership models in the Information view align with functional structure in the Functional view?

- If the data ownership characteristics are complex (e.g., multiple creators or updaters), do the functional models reflect the requirements for maintaining distributed data consistency?

- If there are significant issues around the maintenance of distributed identifiers (keys), do the functional models include features to address these problems?

- If the architecture has significant data migration and data quality analysis aspects, are there functional elements for these in the Functional view?

- If the functional structure has loose coupling as an architectural goal, is this reflected (as far as possible) in the static information structure?

FUNCTIONAL AND CONCURRENCY VIEW CONSISTENCY

Goal: To ensure that the functional elements are all mapped to a task that will allow them to execute and that the interelement interactions are supported by interprocess communication mechanisms if required.

- Is every functional element in the Functional view mapped to a concurrency element (a process or thread) responsible for its execution in the Concurrency view?
- If functional elements are partitioned into separate processes, are suitable interprocess communication mechanisms used to allow all of the interelement interactions shown in the Functional view?
- If multiple functional elements are packaged into a single process, is it clear which element controls the process?

FUNCTIONAL AND DEVELOPMENT VIEW CONSISTENCY

Goal: To ensure that all of the functional elements are mapped to a design-time module and to ensure that the common processing, test approach, and codeline specified are all compatible with and can support the proposed functional structure.

- Does the code module structure include all of the functional elements that need to be developed?
- Does the Development view specify a development environment for each of the technologies used by the Functional view?
- If the Functional view specifies the use of a particular architectural style, does the Development view include sufficient guidelines and constraints to ensure correct implementation of the style?
- Where common processing is specified, can it be implemented in a straightforward manner over all of the elements defined in the Functional view?
- Where reusable functional elements can be identified from the Functional view, are these modeled as libraries or similar features in the Development view?
- If a test environment has been specified, does it meet the functional needs and priorities of the elements defined in the Functional view?
- Can the functional structure described in the Functional view be built, tested, and released reliably using the codeline described in the Development view?

FUNCTIONAL AND DEPLOYMENT VIEW CONSISTENCY

Goal: To ensure that each of the functional elements is correctly mapped to its deployment environment.

- Has each functional element been mapped to a processing node to allow it to be executed?
- Where functional elements are hosted on different nodes, do the network models allow the required element interactions to occur?
- Are functional elements hosted as close as possible to the information they need to process?
- Are functional elements that need to interact extensively hosted as close together as possible?
- Are the specified network connections sufficient for the needs of the interelement interactions that will be carried over them (in terms of capacity, reliability, security, and so on)?
- Is the hardware specified in the Deployment view the most efficient solution for hosting the specified functional elements?

FUNCTIONAL AND OPERATIONAL VIEW CONSISTENCY

Goal: To ensure that each of the specified functional elements can be installed, used, operated, managed, and supported.

- Does the Operational view make it clear how every functional element will be installed (and upgraded if necessary)?
- If migration is required, does the Operational view make it clear how migration will occur to every functional element that needs it?
- Does the Operational view explain how each functional element will be monitored and controlled in the production environment?
- Does the Operational view explain how the configuration of each functional element will be managed in the production environment?
- Does the Operational view explain how the performance of each functional element will be monitored in the production environment?
- Does the Operational view explain how each functional element will be supported in the production environment?
- Are the approaches that the Operational view specifies for installation, migration, monitoring, control, and support the simplest set that will support the needs of the system's functional elements?

INFORMATION AND CONCURRENCY VIEW CONSISTENCY

Goal: To ensure that the concurrency structure of the system does not cause data access problems and that the proposed information structure is compatible with the concurrency structure.

- Does the concurrency design imply concurrent access to any of the system's data elements? If so, have the data elements been protected from concurrent access problems?
- When functional elements are packaged into operating system processes, is the data they require still available to them?
- If functional elements that share data elements are packaged into different operating system processes, has a suitable interprocess data-sharing mechanism been defined?

INFORMATION AND DEVELOPMENT VIEW CONSISTENCY

Goal: To ensure that the proposed development environment can provide the technical resources required to develop the data management aspects of the system.

- Does each data management technology identified in the Information view have development tools and the environment defined for it?
- Does the sizing of the development environments and test data platforms reflect the data volumes created in the Information view?
- If the Information view defines a significant migration data aspect, are there development tools and environments defined to support this?
- If the Information view defines external data components (e.g., for existing systems or external systems under construction), does the Development view take this into account (e.g., the creation of stub environments, realistic test data, and so on)?

INFORMATION AND DEPLOYMENT VIEW CONSISTENCY

Goal: To ensure that the proposed deployment environment provides the resources required to support the defined information structure.

- Does the Deployment view include enough storage (of the appropriate types) to support the information storage approach specified by the Information view?

- If separate storage hardware is used, does the Deployment view specify sufficiently fast and reliable links from the storage to the processing hardware?
- Does the Deployment view reflect the requirements for backup and recovery as addressed by the Information view?
- If large volumes of information need to be moved, is sufficient bandwidth available so that this can be achieved without critically impacting the operation of the system?

INFORMATION AND OPERATIONAL VIEW CONSISTENCY

Goal: To ensure that the system's information structure can be installed, used, operated, managed, and supported.

- Does the Operational view make it clear whether specific installation steps are required for the system's data management technology?
- If migration is required, does the Operational view make it clear how data migration will occur?
- Does the Operational view explain how the data management technology will be monitored and controlled in the production environment?
- Does the Operational view explain how the configuration of the data management technology will be managed in the production environment?
- Does the Operational view explain how the performance of the data management technology will be monitored in the production environment?
- Does the Operational view explain how the data management technology will be supported in the production environment?

CONCURRENCY AND DEVELOPMENT VIEW CONSISTENCY

Goal: To ensure that the concurrency structure specified in the Concurrency view can be built and tested in the development environment specified by the Development view.

- If the concurrency structure is complex, are sufficient design patterns specified in the Development view to guide its implementation?
- Does the codeline defined in the Development view support the packaging of the system's functional elements into the operating system processes specified by the Concurrency view?

- Does the test approach defined in the Development view support testing of the concurrency structure specified in the Concurrency view?
- Does the development environment defined in the Development view allow development and testing of the concurrency structure specified in the Concurrency view?

CONCURRENCY AND DEPLOYMENT VIEW CONSISTENCY

Goal: To ensure that the system's runtime tasks are correctly mapped to execution resources.

- Is every operating system process mapped to a processing node to allow it to run?
- Can the interprocess communication facilities used in the Concurrency view be implemented on and between the processing nodes specified in the Deployment view?
- Are the processing nodes specified in the Deployment view sufficiently powerful to host the processes mapped to them from the Concurrency view?
- Is every processing node in the Deployment view fully utilized by the processes mapped to it?

DEPLOYMENT AND OPERATIONAL VIEW CONSISTENCY

Goal: To ensure that the deployment environment described in the Deployment view can be installed, used, monitored, managed, and supported.

- Does the Operational view define how each of the elements in the deployment environment will be installed?
- Does the Operational view describe how each of the elements in the deployment environment can be monitored and controlled?
- Does the Operational view make it clear which monitoring and control facilities already exist, which can be bought, and which must be developed?
- Can each of the elements in the deployment environment be supported in the organization?

PART IV

THE PERSPECTIVE CATALOG

23

INTRODUCTION TO THE
PERSPECTIVE CATALOG

P art IV is devoted to descriptions of a number of perspectives. We describe the perspectives listed in Table 23–1 in detail, with a chapter devoted to each. We have chosen to explore this set of perspectives more thoroughly because we have found that the quality properties addressed by them are crucial to most information systems.

We outline the perspectives listed in Table 23–2 in the final chapter of Part IV. We have chosen to explore these perspectives more briefly than the others for reasons of space and because, although they are often important, we have not found them as universally applicable as the ones listed in Table 23–1.

For each perspective, we present the following details:

- The perspective's *applicability to views*—that is, which of your views are most likely to be impacted by applying the perspective
- The most important *concerns* the perspective addresses
- A description of *activities for applying the perspective* to your architecture
- The key *architectural tactics* to be considered as possible solutions when your architecture does not exhibit the required quality properties the perspective addresses
- Some *problems and pitfalls* to be aware of and risk-reduction techniques for mitigating against these
- *Checklists* of things to consider when applying the perspective and when reviewing it, to help ensure correctness, completeness, and accuracy

As in our viewpoint catalog, we present only an overview of some complex and detailed topics. Our objective is to provide the fundamental information in

TABLE 23–1 PERSPECTIVES DESCRIBED IN DETAIL

Perspective	Desired Quality
Security	The ability of the system to reliably control, monitor, and audit who can perform what actions on what resources and to detect and recover from failures in security mechanisms
Performance and Scalability	The ability of the system to predictably execute within its mandated performance profile and to handle increased processing volumes
Availability and Resilience	The ability of the system to be fully or partly operational as and when required and to effectively handle failures that could affect system availability
Evolution	The ability of the system to be flexible in the face of the inevitable change that all systems experience after deployment, balanced against the costs of providing such flexibility

TABLE 23–2 PERSPECTIVES DESCRIBED IN BRIEF

Perspective	Desired Quality
Accessibility	The ability of the system to be used by people with disabilities
Development Resource	The ability of the system to be designed, built, deployed, and operated within known constraints around people, budget, time, and materials
Internationalization	The ability of the system to be independent from any particular language, country, or cultural group
Location	The ability of the system to overcome problems brought about by the absolute location of its elements and the distances between them
Regulation	The ability of the system to conform to local and international laws, quasi-legal regulations, company policies, and other rules and standards
Usability	The ease with which people who interact with the system can work effectively

each area, so each perspective chapter also includes references to a number of sources of further information.

As we said in Part I, there are many possible perspectives that could apply to a particular architecture, and it is not usually feasible to consider all of them in the context of all of the views. Not every perspective is relevant to every view, or even to every system, and there will be instances where you don't need to consider some of the perspectives at all. The key to getting the most out of them is to consider to what extent each perspective is important to your architecture and to tailor your approach accordingly.

24

THE SECURITY
PERSPECTIVE

Desired Quality	The ability of the system to reliably control, monitor, and audit who can perform what actions on these resources and the ability to detect and recover from failures in security mechanisms
Applicability	Any systems with publicly accessible interfaces, with multiple users where the identity of the user is significant, or where access to operations or information needs to be controlled
Concerns	Policies, threats, mechanisms, accountability, availability, and detection and recovery
Activities	Identify sensitive resources, define the security policy, identify threats to the system, design the security implementation, and assess the security risks
Architectural Tactics	Apply recognized security principles, authenticate the principals, authorize access, ensure information secrecy, ensure information integrity, ensure accountability, protect availability, integrate security technologies, provide security administration, and use third-party security infrastructure
Problems and Pitfalls	Complex security policies, unproven security technologies, system not designed for failure, lack of administration facilities, technology-driven approach, failure to consider time sources, overreliance on technology, no clear requirements or models, security as an afterthought, security embedded in the application code, piecemeal security, and ad hoc security technology

Many factors drive today's need for information systems security, including the increasing trend to distribute systems, the use of public networks (particularly the Internet) as part of system infrastructure, the rising interest in interorganizational computing (such as that envisaged by Web services), and other less technical reasons such as the increasing interest the media and the public have shown in computer security. All of these factors point to the fact that today your system's stakeholders are likely to be more interested in the security of the system than they would have been only a couple of years ago.

We define *security* as the set of processes and technologies that allow the owners of resources in the system to reliably control who can perform what actions on particular resources. The *who* refers to the people, pieces of software, and so on that form the set of actors in the system who have a security identity; security specialists normally call such actors *principals.* The *resources* are the parts of the system considered sensitive (i.e., those to which access must be controlled) such as data elements and operations. The *actions* are the operations that the principals in the system will want to perform on the resources (e.g., read them, change them, execute them, and so on), as shown in Figure 24–1.

The resources, principals, and actions that need to be considered are often very specific to the system. An Internet service provider is likely to have a totally different set of security concerns compared with those of a military intelligence organization, which will be different again from an enterprise implementing an internal information system that allows dialup access to its employees. However, in all these cases, security is still the business of allowing the right levels of access to the right resources to the right people.

It is also important to recognize that security is not a simple process of "being secure" or not. Rather than a binary state, security is really a process of risk management that balances likely security risks against the costs of guarding against them. Bear this in mind to help you set realistic assumptions in the minds of your stakeholders and to make intelligent tradeoffs that address the real security risks your system faces.

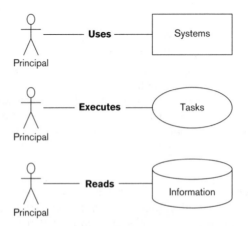

FIGURE 24–1 PRINCIPALS, ACTIONS, AND RESOURCES

TABLE 24–1 APPLICABILITY OF THE SECURITY PERSPECTIVE TO THE SIX VIEWS

View	Applicability
Functional	The Functional view allows you to clearly see which of the system's functional elements need to be protected. Conversely, the functional structure of the system may be impacted by the need to implement your security policies.
Information	The Information view also helps you see what needs to be protected—in this case, the sensitive data in the system. Information models are often modified as a result of security design (e.g., partitioning information by sensitivity).
Concurrency	The Concurrency view defines how functional elements are packaged into runtime elements like processes. Security design may indicate the need to isolate different pieces of the system into different runtime elements, and if so, this will affect the system's concurrency structure.
Development	You may identify guidelines or constraints that the software developers will need to be aware of in order to ensure that the security policy is enforced. You need to include these guidelines or constraints in (or reference them from) the Development view.
Deployment	The security design may have a major impact on the system's deployment environment. For example, you may need security-oriented hardware or software, or you may need to change previously assumed deployment arrangements in order to address security risks.
Operational	Enforcing security policy is not just a matter of adding advanced technological features to a system. How the system is operated once it is in production will have a major affect on its security. The Operational view needs to make the security assumptions and responsibilities extremely clear, so that these aspects of the security implementation can be reflected in operational processes.

APPLICABILITY TO VIEWS

Table 24–1 shows how the Security perspective affects each of the views we discussed in Part III.

CONCERNS

Policies

The security policy for a system defines the system's security needs. It defines the controls and guarantees that the system requires for its resources and identifies which principals (or groups of principals) should be granted which types of access to each resource (or type of resource) within the system. A security policy can be considered the security specification for a system, as it defines the set of security-related constraints that the system should be able to enforce.

A typical security policy defines the information access policy in terms of the different types of principals the system contains (e.g., clerks, managers, administrators) and, for each type of information (e.g., payroll records, customer details, invoice information), what sort of access each principal group requires (e.g., whether they can view the information, change it, delete it, share it). The policy also should define information integrity constraints that must be enforced, such as the integrity rules and checking required in data stores and protection of messages from unauthorized changes.

Threats

While the policy defines the security constraints the system requires, the threats the system faces are the possible ways the security constraints might be breached by an attacker who wishes to avoid them. Explicitly considering the security threats the system faces allows you to identify security enforcement mechanisms that can then counter these threats. Adding security mechanisms to a system is never free and often adds significantly to the complexity and cost of the system, while often reducing its usability and making it more difficult to operate in production. Therefore, it is important to select mechanisms according to the threats faced, to ensure that all of the chosen mechanisms are applied to counter realistic, credible security threats to the system.

Common threats to information systems include password cracking, network attacks that exploit software or configuration vulnerabilities, and denial-of-service attacks as well as nontechnical, social-engineering attacks that try to trick authorized users of the system to perform operations on behalf of the attacker.

Mechanisms

The security mechanisms in a system are the set of technologies, configuration settings, and procedures required to enforce the rules established by the security policy. Information systems security is a relatively mature field, and many proven security technologies already exist to act as mechanisms in an information system. Examples of commonly used security technologies include user name and password authentication, single-sign-on systems, virtual private networks to secure network links, database access control systems, and SSL/TLS encryption for client/server connections.

Your challenge as an architect is to select the right set of technologies from the wide array available and to apply them appropriately for the particular system you are building. In particular, it can be difficult to safely combine a number of these different technologies, along with system-wide security configuration settings and a set of secure operational processes, to create a truly secure end-to-end system.

Accountability

Accountability is the means of ensuring that every action can be unambiguously traced back to the principal who performed it.

In centralized server-based systems, the notion of auditing is a common mechanism used to ensure accountability. In distributed systems, cryptographic message signing is typically used to prove that a message originated from a particular principal (a form of accountability also known as nonrepudiation).

Availability

Availability is often thought of as a purely operational consideration, but in fact it also has a relationship to security. Ensuring that potential attackers of your system cannot block its availability with denial-of-service attacks is an important part of your security design.

Designing a system for availability involves thinking about planned and unplanned outages that can occur due to the nature of the system itself; designing a system to avoid outages as a result of an external attack involves thinking about risks that can occur as a result of the environment in which the system resides (such as who can access the system and how). Availability security is an area that has rapidly gained importance as systems have started to be routinely connected to public networks like the Internet.

Detection and Recovery

System security is never perfect, and if a system is attractive enough to an attacker, it is almost inevitable that some sort of security breach will occur eventually. This means that an important security concern is the ability of the system to detect security breaches and recover from them. Addressing this concern is unlikely to be a purely technical matter but is more likely to involve people and processes as well as the technology required to spot a security breach and react to it appropriately.

ACTIVITIES: APPLYING THE SECURITY PERSPECTIVE

The activity diagram in Figure 24–2 illustrates a simple process for applying the Security perspective. In this section, we describe the activities in this process.

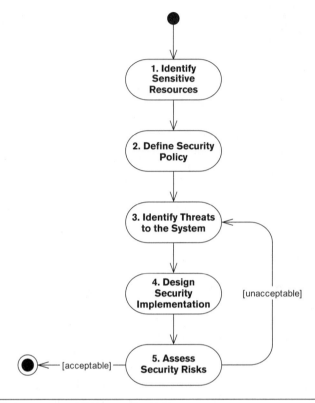

FIGURE 24-2 APPLYING THE SECURITY PERSPECTIVE

Identify Sensitive Resources

Before considering *how* to secure your system, you need to establish *what* needs to be secured. All of the security for your system needs to be driven from this key concern, which you should consider as early in the system's lifecycle as possible.

The information you gather about the security-sensitive resources feeds into all of the other security-related decisions you make.

NOTATION A simple text-and-tables approach is normally sufficient, although you may choose to annotate one of the diagrammatic models of the architecture (typically in the Functional or Information views).

ACTIVITIES
Classify Sensitive Resources. Using the Functional and Information views as primary inputs, along with any security requirements information avail-

able, decide what the sensitive resources in the system are—typically, functional operations and data items. For each type of sensitive resource, define the reasons the resource is sensitive, who should be considered its owner, and the type of access controls required for the resource.

EXAMPLE Table 24–2 shows a simple example of documenting some of the sensitive resources that might appear in an e-commerce ordering system.

If you're fortunate enough to have comprehensive security requirements defined for you, the sensitive resources may have already been identified. In many cases, though, you will need to do this yourself, in conjunction with

TABLE 24–2 EXAMPLE OF SENSITIVE RESOURCE IDENTIFICATION

Resource	Sensitivity	Owner	Access Control
Customer account records	Personal information of value for identity theft or invasion of privacy	Customer Care Group	No direct data access
Descriptive product catalog entries	Defines what is for sale and its description; if changed maliciously, could harm the business	Stock Management Group	No direct data access
Pricing product catalog entries	Defines pricing for catalog items; if maliciously or accidentally modified, could harm business or allow fraud	Pricing Team in Stock Management Group	No direct data access
Business operations on customer account records	Needs to be controlled to protect data access and integrity	Customer Care Group	Access to individual record or all records by authenticated principal
Descriptive catalog operations	Needs to be controlled to protect data access and integrity	Stock Management Group	Access to catalog modification operations by authenticated principal
Pricing catalog modification operations	Needs to be controlled to protect data access and integrity	Pricing Team	Access to price modification operations by authenticated principal, with accountability of changes
. . .	. . .	. . .	. . .

interested stakeholders (such as auditors and managers of the groups owning the information). Useful sources of input information for this exercise include organizational security policies and relevant external regulations, as well as the opinions of interested stakeholders.

When performing this exercise, be sure that everyone (including yourself) understands exactly what is included in each group of resources as well as the identity of the group's owner and the type of security required for the resources in the group.

Define the Security Policy

Having identified the system's sensitive resources and the threats against them, you should be able to define a security policy (also sometimes called a *trust model*) for your system. The security policy is the basis for the security implementation in the system. This model identifies *who* will be trusted with *what* access to *which* system resources (and any constraints on this access such as limiting it to certain times or days of the week), the *integrity* guarantees required within the system, and the *accountability* required when sensitive resources are accessed.

Ideally, you will have a complete, unambiguous, straightforward security policy defined for you by the system's main stakeholders that you can just check and review before proceeding. Alternatively, if it's like every system we've worked on, you'll have nothing of the sort, in which case you need to get a written, approved definition.

The policy definition should normally be defined in terms of groups of resources and principals (often based on organizational unit and role) rather than enumerating lots of specific cases. Also remember that this is a policy, not a design, so it needs to define what access will be provided to whom rather than defining how this will be achieved.

Work to make the security policy as simple and general as you can, with as few special cases as possible. A straightforward policy model allows the simplest possible implementation of enforcement mechanisms and makes it more likely that the model will get enforced correctly.

The other vital quality of a security policy model is precision. This model is an important deliverable for your system, and it should be approved by all the important stakeholders. If the model isn't precise, each group of stakeholders will interpret it differently, according to their own interests, assumptions, and desires. This is bound to lead to problems when implementing the policy.

NOTATION A security policy is normally defined by using a simple text-and-tables approach to create a structured document. Tables are particularly valuable when defining groups of resources and principals and showing the types of access allowed.

ACTIVITIES

Identify the Principal Classes. In order to make defining the security policy more manageable, start by grouping your principals into classes you can treat as groups for security policy purposes. Partition the principals into sets based on the types of access they require to different types of sensitive resources.

Identify the Resource Classes. Partition the system's sensitive resource types into groups that you can treat together for access control purposes. (The resource types come from identifying the sensitive resources, as described earlier.)

Identify the Access Control Sets. For each resource class, define the operations that can be performed on members of that class and the principal classes that should be allowed to access each operation on the class.

Identify the Sensitive Operations. Consider any system-level operations that are independent of the system's managed resources (such as administrative operations), and define which principal classes should be allowed to access these operations.

Identify the Integrity Requirements. Consider any situations in the system where information is or could be changed, and identify the set of integrity guarantees required for that information.

EXAMPLE Table 24–3, on the following page, shows part of the result of defining the security policy for an e-commerce system.

Seven different classes of principals have been identified (including unauthenticated Web-site users) and six classes of sensitive resources. Only data administrators are allowed access to data directly; all other users can only execute business operations. Data administrators can also execute business operations (on the basis that they can simulate their occurrence anyway by changing data), but all of their activity is audited. The other classes of principals have been allocated just enough privileges in order to perform their roles in the system.

Identify Threats to the System

In a perfect world, we could now stop and simply publish the list of sensitive resources and the security policy, and everyone would voluntarily follow the policy. However, the reason we need security is that we can't necessarily trust everyone, so we need to identify the possible threats to the security policy. Identifying threats provides a clear definition of what in the system needs to be protected and what it needs to be protected from. This makes it clear which threats you are aware of and can try to guard against and also (implicitly) the threats you have not considered.

TABLE 24–3 EXAMPLE OF AN ACCESS CONTROL POLICY

	User Account Records	Desc. Catalog Records	Pricing Records	User Account Operations	Desc. Catalog Operations	Price Change Operations
Data administrator	Full with audit	Full with audit	Full with audit	All with audit	All with audit	All with audit
Catalog clerk	None	None	None	All	Read-only operations	None
Catalog manager	None	None	None	Read-only operations with audit	All	All with audit
Product price administrator	None	None	None	None	Read-only operations	All
Customer Care clerk	None	None	None	All	Read-only operations	None
Registered customer	None	None	None	All on own record	Read-only operations	None
Unknown Web-site user	None	None	None	None	Read-only operations	None

The result of this process is termed a *threat model*, which builds on the initial list of sensitive resources and should provide a thorough analysis of the threats you think the system is subject to, the impact of the threat being realized, and the likelihood of the threat occurring.

To create a threat model, you ask a number of key questions about your proposed system.

- Who is likely to try to infringe the security policy?
- How will they try to do so?
- What are the attacker's main characteristics (such as their sophistication, motivation, resources, and so on)?
- What are the consequences of the policy being breached in this way?

Explicitly identifying threats allows specialists from outside your project to provide assistance by reviewing the model and advising you about potential threats that have not been considered at all or threats that may have been incorrectly characterized in the model. Be sure to have it widely reviewed so that you can be confident you have considered all likely threats. The threat model also allows you to systematically consider the set of security facilities your system needs.

NOTATION The threat model is normally presented by using a text-and-tables approach to create a structured document. A graphical alternative is to use an attack tree, which provides a structured, graphical notation to categorize and illustrate the threats a system faces and the likely probability of each occurring.

EXAMPLE An attack tree is a useful approach for representing the threat model for your system. The technique is based on the Fault Trees technique used in safety-critical systems design to analyze possible failure modes. In the security domain, you can take a similar approach to represent possible attacks on your system.

An attack tree represents the possible attacks your system may face in order for an attacker to achieve a particular goal. The root of the tree is the goal the attacker is trying to obtain, and the branches of the tree classify the different types of attacks the intruder could attempt in order to obtain the goal.

Attack trees can be represented graphically (as a tree structure with nodes and links) or textually as a "dotted decimal" hierarchy (like nested subheadings in a technical document). The latter form is often more practical because attack trees can get very large as all possible attacks are considered, which can make the graphical form difficult to draw and comprehend.

Here is a possible attack tree for the goal of extracting customer credit card details from an e-commerce Web site.

Goal: Obtain customer credit card details.
1. Extract details from the system database.
   1.1. Access the database directly.
      1.1.1. Crack/guess database passwords.
      1.1.2. Crack/guess operating system passwords that allow database security to be bypassed.
   1.2. Access the details via a member of the database administration staff.
      1.2.1. Bribe a database administrator (DBA).
      1.2.2. Conduct social engineering by phone/e-mail to trick the DBA into revealing details.

2. Extract details from the Web interface.

   2.1. Set up a dummy Web site and e-mail users the URL to trick them into entering credit card details.

   2.2. Crack/guess passwords for user accounts and extract details from the user Web interface.

   2.3. Send users a Trojan horse program by e-mail to record keystrokes/intercept Web traffic.

   2.4. Attack the domain name server to hijack the domain name and use the dummy site attack from 2.1.

   2.5. Attack the site server software directly to try to find loopholes in its security.

3. Find details outside the system.

   3.1. Conduct social engineering by phone/e-mail to get customer services staff to reveal card details.

   3.2. Direct a social-engineering attack on users by using public details from the site to make contact.

An attack tree should be created for each of the possible goals that an attacker may have for breaching your system's security. Once you have an attack tree, you can analyze each threat it contains to establish whether the system's security neutralizes the threat.

ACTIVITIES

Identify the Threats. Consider the security threats your system faces from the perspective of the sensitive resources within it, the possible access to these resources that potential attackers might wish to gain, the main characteristics of the potential attackers, and the types of attacks they are likely to carry out.

Characterize the Threats. Characterize each threat in terms of the resources that would be compromised if the attack were successful, the result of this compromise, and the likelihood of the attack occurring.

Design the Security Implementation

Once you understand the sensitive resources and threats, you can consider the technical security design for the system. The goal of this step is to design a system-wide security infrastructure that can enforce the system's security policy in the face of the risks identified in the threat model. In this step, you consider using specific security technologies such as single-sign-on systems, network firewalls, SSL communication link security, cryptographic technology, policy management systems, and so on.

This design process results in a number of design decisions you should incorporate in the architecture. These decisions affect a number of architectural structures, including those likely to be described in the Functional, Information, Deployment, and Operational views.

NOTATION As the outputs of this step are a set of design decisions to be reflected in the architectural views, the notation used for the technical security design depends on the notation used in each view. You may also produce some form of overall security design model, which is typically captured by using a software design notation such as UML (similar to its use in the Functional viewpoint).

EXAMPLE Based on the attack tree shown in the previous example, some of the security measures you might consider for the e-commerce system include the following:

- Isolating the database machines from the public network by using network firewall technology
- Isolating the security-sensitive parts of your system from the public network by using network firewall technology
- Analyzing the paths into your system to check them for possible vulnerabilities
- Arranging penetration testing to see if experts can find ways into your system
- Identifying an intrusion detection strategy that would allow security breaches to be recognized
- Training administration and customer service staff (in fact, probably all staff) to avoid social-engineering attacks and to abide by strict privacy protection procedures for customer information
- Designing your site so that a minimal amount of user information (ideally, none) is publicly viewable
- Designing your site so that sensitive information (e.g., credit card numbers) is never shown in full (e.g., display just the last four digits to allow legitimate users to identify their cards in lists)
- Constantly reminding users of security precautions they should take (e.g., not revealing passwords to anyone, including your staff; checking URLs before entering information; and so on)

It is interesting to note how much of a typical security implementation does not involve security technology directly but is about making sure that people act in a secure manner.

Activities

Design a Way to Mitigate the Threats. For each of the previously identified threats to sensitive resources, design a security mechanism to address the threat. This may include modifying existing architectural decisions, applying one or more security technologies, and designing procedures and processes for the system's operation and use.

Design a Detection and Recovery Approach. Bearing in mind that the security mechanisms you identify are unlikely to be foolproof, design a system-wide approach to detecting violations of the system security policy and recovering from them. This will typically include technical intrusion detection solutions, internal system checks and balances to reveal unexpected inconsistencies, and a set of processes for regularly checking the system for intrusions and reacting to any discovered. Good solutions for intrusion detection are available as proven commercial and open source software packages; however, deciding how to use the packages and design the processes around them are still system-specific activities.

Assess the Technology. One way to address a threat is to use a piece of security technology to provide a security mechanism. This activity involves assessing which candidate security technologies are suitable for addressing a particular threat in a particular context. This includes generic assessment (e.g., checking reliability, ease of use, and so on) as well as context-specific assessment (e.g., checking that the proposed technology can be operated by the system's administrators and is efficient enough to meet the system's performance and scalability goals).

Integrate the Technology. Once you have decided which security technologies to apply to your system, the other important activity is deciding how you will integrate them with the primary system structure and with other security technologies. It is important to spend some time designing the integration approach carefully, to avoid possible security loopholes creeping in due to the unexpected side effects of an ad hoc integration approach.

Assess the Security Risks

No security system is perfect. The process of implementing system security is a balancing act: You balance the risks you believe you face against the cost of implementing solutions for those risks and the costs you may face if the risks occur.

Having designed a security infrastructure for your system, you now need to reevaluate the risks to consider whether your proposed security infrastructure has achieved an acceptable cost/risk balance. If so, your Security perspective is complete. If not, you need to return to a consideration of the threat model and redesign the security infrastructure in order to achieve an acceptable cost/risk balance.

TABLE 24-4 EXAMPLE OF RISK ASSESSMENT

Risk	Estimated Cost	Estimated Likelihood	Notional Cost
Attacker gains direct database access.	$8,000,000	0.2%	$16,000
Web-site flaw allows free orders to be placed and fulfilled.	$800,000	4%	$32,000
Social-engineering attack on a customer service representative results in hijacking of customer accounts.	$4,000,000	1.5%	$60,000
. . .	. . .	. . .	. . .

NOTATION The risk assessment delivers a record of the set of risks, the estimated likelihood of each risk occurring given the design of the system, and the notional cost (i.e., the estimated cost adjusted for the probability of occurrence) that each risk implies. This information is usually best presented with a simple tabular form.

EXAMPLE Table 24–4 shows an example, using a tabular presentation style, for a couple of the risks facing our e-commerce system.

A risk presentation in this form allows us to focus on the risks with the highest notional costs (i.e., those that have the highest risk of loss and greatest likelihood of occurrence).

ACTIVITIES

Assess the Risks. The single activity in this step is a process of risk assessment. For each risk in your threat model, reevaluate its likelihood of occurrence given the planned security infrastructure, and compare this against the security needs you established earlier in the process. Assess whether this is an acceptable level of security risk for your particular system's situation.

ARCHITECTURAL TACTICS

Apply Recognized Security Principles

The field of computer security is relatively mature for a rapidly evolving, high-technology discipline. There is an established body of knowledge, developed and applied by an identifiable professional security community with its own principles, standards, norms, and culture.

This community of researchers and practitioners has established a number of widely accepted and commonly applied principles that are considered important to establishing security within a system. Some of the more important principles include the following.

- *Grant the least amount of privilege possible*: Always grant security principals the smallest set of privileges they require in order to perform their tasks. Consider varying the set of privileges a principal has over time if certain sensitive tasks are executed only intermittently.

- *Secure the weakest link*: The security of a system is only as strong as its weakest element, so understanding the weakest link in your security is an important step toward understanding how secure your system really is. The weakest link could be technological (an unsecured network link), procedural (allowing easy access to a data center), or human (people who write down their passwords). Identify and secure the weakest links in your system's security until you achieve an acceptable level of security risk.

- *Defend in depth*: If you examine physical security systems, you'll find that they rarely rely on just one security measure. Just as medieval castles had moats, drawbridges, and strong walls, banks have alarms, vaults, security guards, surveillance systems, and multiple locks on important doors. These are examples of the principle of defense in depth, where a series of defenses provides a greater level of security than a single technique could. Defense in depth is particularly relevant to computer systems, given that many of the security technologies we use may themselves have hidden flaws and that we are also susceptible to human and procedural failures. Rather than relying on one security measure to counter each threat to your system, consider possibilities for layering defenses to provide greater protection.

- *Separate and compartmentalize*: Attempt to clearly separate different related responsibilities so that authority for each can be assigned to different principals if required, and compartmentalize responsibilities for different parts of the system so that they can be controlled individually. This makes it easier to control access securely and means that a successful attack on one part of the system does not immediately compromise it entirely. Good examples are separating the "security override" privilege from the "alter audit trail" privilege (with the audit trail being used to record use of the "security override" privilege) and implementing separate security configuration and mechanisms for each major subdivision of a system.

- *Keep security designs simple*: Security professionals often say that complexity is the enemy of security. Complexity in a system is difficult to deal with and makes it very difficult to analyze the system to assess its security, which makes problems more difficult to understand and rectify when you find them. Systems with stringent security requirements need to be simple enough to make it possible for them to be secured and verified.

▪ *Don't rely on obscurity*: Some years ago, it was common for the details of secure systems to be kept secret in an attempt to make them more difficult to attack. An example of this was hiding security secrets, such as cryptographic keys, in obfuscated (and undocumented) computer code for which the source was kept secret. The problems with this approach are that it assumes the attackers aren't smart enough to work past the obscurity and that it may prevent external experts from assessing the real level of security provided. The conventional wisdom in today's security community is total disclosure, where the system is designed assuming that potential attackers know it as well as its implementers do. This principle avoids the system's security becoming dependent on hiding secrets, which is often extremely difficult to do.

▪ *Use secure defaults*: Many systems we have encountered include inherently insecure default settings and behaviors, including empty default passwords, permissive default access control lists, network ports open by default, and so on. Such behavior is very likely to result in real security threats, particularly when exhibited by packaged software products, which are often installed by users who are not familiar with them. Ensuring secure default behavior makes a real contribution to practical systems security.

▪ *Fail securely*: Another common problem found in many real systems is insecure failure mode behavior, where the system is reasonably secure during normal operation but becomes insecure when things go wrong. Examples include audit trails that suspend auditing if the audit logs run out of space, systems that drop back to insecure mode processing if security negotiation fails, unprotected recovery consoles that appear after crashes, and so on. System failures are inevitable occasionally, so make sure that if your system fails, it does so securely.

▪ *Assume external entities are untrusted*: Within your system you should be able to exert a great deal of control over the security environment and the principals within it. This is not the case for external entities who access the system. Ensure that all external entities are totally untrusted until proven otherwise to avoid accidental security breaches in unexpected cases.

▪ *Audit sensitive events*: Most systems include a number of key security-related events that, if abused, could compromise the security system. Common examples include resetting passwords, assigning powerful roles, and manipulating audit trails. These sensitive events need to be securely audited so that their use can be monitored. This principle often places a number of constraints on your deployment structure to ensure that a reliable audit trail can be implemented.

Make sure that you understand these commonly accepted principles and apply them as appropriate to your system's security. In the Further Reading section at the end of this chapter, we recommend a number of background references that can provide much more detail on these subjects.

Authenticate the Principals

Authentication is the reliable identification of each of the principals who can use the system. These principals could be people, computers, pieces of software, or anything else in the system that has a security identity. Nearly all system security depends on being able to identify the various principals in the system reliably.

Implementing authentication involves reliably binding a unique name of some sort to each principal who can use the system. A wide variety of authentication technologies exist to allow you to identify the principals in your system, including user names with passwords, public/private key systems (such as X.509 digital certificates), and hardware token technologies (such as smart cards). Off-the-shelf products known as single-sign-on systems allow you to delegate the entire system-wide authentication process to them (which is particularly useful in mixed technology environments such as those with both UNIX and Windows authentication). Each of these technologies has its place, but each tends to be suited to different environments and security needs, so you need to select the right ones for your system.

The key decision to be made is how every principal in your system is uniquely identified, via a mechanism that is secure enough to address the particular risks your system faces. You should bear in mind that you may need to use different principal authentication technologies for different principal types, and in some cases, principals may need to be identified by more than one authentication technology (e.g., users in a corporation may have separate digital certificates, Windows networking logins, Oracle database logins, and Lotus Notes logins). Where multiple logins are necessary, we strongly recommend some form of single-sign-on technology as a unifying layer on top of the different underlying systems. People simply can't remember more than a couple of passwords, and forcing them to remember more will result in passwords written on notes stuck to terminals!

What is critical at the architectural level is that every principal can be reliably identified when required and that the system you use is simple and usable enough that the system's users will not try to work around it.

Authorize Access

Once you have identified the principals, authorization involves restricting and enforcing what those principals are permitted to do within the system. Conceptually, you define lists of principals and their permitted actions for each controlled resource in the system. This usually involves assigning principals to roles and groups so you can treat them as homogeneous populations. Then you can define permitted actions on resources for the roles and groups in the system.

Most enterprise software technologies already include some form of access control that allows you to limit access to resources based on user identity and credentials (such as group membership). In addition, software developers can code explicit security checks into their software when they implement the system.

In many systems, your key problem as the architect is how to create a coherent access control system from this patchwork of separate, often incompatible authentication and authorization technologies. For system security to be manageable and effective, the system architecture needs to include a clearly defined approach to enforcing principal authorizations, particularly if multiple candidate authorization systems are available in the system's environment.

A solution to this problem can be the use of purpose-built standard access control products. These software packages (such as IBM Policy Director or Entrust GetAccess) allow access to many sorts of resources to be controlled through a single product that interfaces to a variety of authentication systems. At the other extreme, including a simple homegrown access control manager in your system's architecture may be sufficient.

Ensure Information Secrecy

Secrecy is the means of ensuring that only owners of information (or those with whom they choose to share it) can read that information.

Secrecy can be partially achieved by using authorization appropriately, to prevent access to stored information that a principal is not authorized to access. However, access control is rarely sufficient, and it usually needs to be combined with other techniques in order to achieve the secrecy required.

Traditional information systems were highly centralized, with huge information vaults held on central computers. The information was tightly controlled by access control systems (typically as part of database management systems) and was accessible only via custom applications running on terminals directly connected to the central computer.

In contrast, today's information systems are highly distributed, with many computers communicating in order to implement the functions of the system. This means that information can be much less secure than with a traditional centralized system—particularly if public networks are used for communication and the different parts of the system are within different organizations.

One of implications of this shift is that sensitive information needs to be protected once it moves outside the authorization controls of the database servers where it resides. Ensuring secrecy of information outside databases normally involves the use of cryptography, to encrypt information in such a way that only principals who have access to a particular key can decrypt it and read it. In reality, the inherent complexity of cryptography means that it is typically implemented by securing network links through the use of communications protocols that include cryptographic protection, like SSL/TLS.

From the architect's point of view, the snag with this neat picture is that extensive use of cryptography in your system is not without cost. It will add significant complexity to many aspects of the system (cryptographic key management alone is a complex problem), and it also tends to have high computational costs, burning up precious computing resources that could be dedicated to useful functional processing. It can be difficult to apply cryptography correctly so that the system is actually secure. It is significantly more complex than just using server certificate–based SSL to identify your servers because this leaves your system open to any number of alternative attacks (such as intercepting information elsewhere in the system once it has been decrypted).

In general, use your threat model to identify where information needs to be protected, and use the minimum amount of cryptography that leaves your system acceptably secure.

Ensure Information Integrity

Integrity is the name given to the concern of ensuring that information is protected from unauthorized change (particularly during message transmission).

Implementing integrity in most information systems also involves the application of cryptography. We would like the recipients of messages sent over a network to be able to satisfy themselves that they have received each message unchanged and that no one has tampered with it. Ensuring integrity of information usually involves the application of cryptographic hash functions. Hash functions are cryptographic operations that use a secret key to compute a large numeric value for a block of information. They allow the recipient of that block to ensure that the information has not been changed since the hash value was computed. However, useful as this is, the same caveats mentioned for secrecy also apply to integrity, in particular that it adds both complexity and runtime overhead to the system and so needs to be used judiciously.

Ensure Accountability

Many systems require some or all of their users to be accountable for their actions. In some systems (such as certain financial and medical systems), legal requirements mandate user accountability for key operations. There tend to be two distinct forms of accountability required in information systems: *auditing* and *nonrepudiation* of messages.

Auditing is usually used in situations where secure central servers execute the system's primary operations. These servers can record logs of operations performed by the system's users, which can later be used to establish how a particular situation occurred.

In distributed systems without centralized servers, auditing is less relevant (due to the lack of a secure store for the audit trail). The related requirement in such systems is nonrepudiation, the ability to definitively identify a message's creator in a way that she cannot plausibly deny. A common solution to this problem is to use digital signatures on messages that can be generated only by someone with access to the corresponding digital certificate's private key.

Both of these approaches come with their own costs. Auditing has a runtime performance penalty associated with it, as well as management and storage overhead for the records created. Digital signatures are computationally expensive to create and verify, and they can be complex to administer because they require all of the principals in the system to have a unique digital certificate. We are also ignoring other important complexities such as certificate management and revocation and the difficult problem of ensuring that technically sophisticated users do not compromise other users' digital certificates.

Once again, your role as an architect is to balance the cost of these accountability mechanisms against the risks you think your system faces, applying these techniques where the threat model indicates they are really needed.

Protect Availability

When thinking about system availability, it is natural to focus on hardware reliability, software replication, failover, and so on. Such approaches are an important piece of the availability puzzle, as we discuss in Chapter 26 on the Availability and Resilience perspective. However, there is an easily overlooked security aspect related to availability: protecting your system from hostile attacks that aim to reduce its availability.

Such attacks, known as *denial-of-service (DoS) attacks*, have been the subject of increasing interest in the last few years as systems have started to expose their network interfaces to public networks like the Internet. DoS attacks can range from something as simple as forcing a user to be locked out by repeatedly using an incorrect password with her login,[1] to sophisticated

---

1. This doesn't sound like a terribly serious attack until you consider time-sensitive systems such as online auctions. This attack has allegedly been used on a number of occasions at Internet auction sites to prevent users bidding on (and so raising the prices of) items that the attacker wishes to buy. Other systems can also be vulnerable to similar DoS attacks—for example, a battlefield system isn't much use if an attacker can lock out all of its users simply by bombarding it with credible user names and random passwords.

network attacks using custom software that overloads systems, to physical attacks such as attempting to interrupt a system's power supply.

Work to understand the possible DoS threats your system faces and the impact of any of the threats occurring. This will probably require working with security specialists who understand this area in detail. Once you understand the threats, their costs, their likelihoods, and the potential approaches to protect against them, you need to decide the right level of protection for your system by balancing these factors. Be aware, however, that protecting your system from network DoS attacks can be tremendously difficult, and for most systems you may simply have to accept some level of risk of such an attack occurring.

Integrate Security Technologies

Almost inevitably, when you design the security implementation, you will need a number of different technologies in order to fulfill all of the requirements. Similarly, security normally needs to be implemented across a number of distinct parts of your system. Given this situation, you need to make an early design decision about how to achieve end-to-end security in the system. Implementing a large number of unrelated security technologies is highly undesirable because it introduces complexity and the likelihood of creating security vulnerabilities at the boundaries of each technology.

Part of your role in the security design of the system is to ensure that security is implemented consistently and that the different pieces of the technology are put together to form a complete, integrated security system. This will be particularly important if you're using security consultants from a number of sources (such as different product vendors) who will all focus on their own part of the security puzzle.

Provide Security Administration

Administration is a weakness of many existing security systems, particularly where complex policies need to be enforced or where there is a need to cope with the sort of large user populations found in today's global organizations. This problem can become even more awkward when you need to combine a number of security technologies in order to implement the security policy.

As part of architecture definition, you need to ensure that the planned security implementation can be administered effectively (this will form part of the Operational view). Without good administration, security policy is likely to be ignored simply to "get the job done." Complex security administration facilities can also lead to security loopholes caused by administrators who are unaware of the full ramifications of their actions. Remember to involve key stakeholders when considering security administration. Your system administrators will be able to provide a lot of feedback about the acceptability of the administration facilities available—testers too often have a perspective on this because they need to reproduce large security configurations automatically to allow reliable, repeatable testing of the security facilities.

Use Third-Party Security Infrastructure

Many of today's infrastructure technologies (such as J2EE and .NET servers, enterprise directories, and e-mail servers) provide a number of standard security functions. Also, specific security infrastructure technologies (such as enterprise access control products) are available that can provide security services to applications. These technologies offer an alternative to the traditional approach to implementing application security—namely, embedding policy enforcement in the application code.

In general, using external security infrastructure is simpler than coding it directly; after all, someone else has done a lot of the work already. This approach is often much more flexible, too. Rather than needing to change program code when the security policy changes, it is often possible to change the configuration of the infrastructure element—a process that can be achieved by the administrators without involving software developers. Most importantly, a security infrastructure product is likely to provide more reliable security than application-specific code because it is more widely used and has been written by software developers with specialized interest and training in system security.

We strongly recommend adopting a security approach of pushing as much of your policy enforcement into the underlying infrastructure of your system as possible. We suggest this for three reasons: simplicity, flexibility, and reliability. Security infrastructure products hide much of the complexity of integrating different security systems. They should also provide some degree of abstraction over individual mechanisms, allowing the mechanisms to be changed more easily. Finally, widely deployed infrastructure products have been widely tested, analyzed, and understood, increasing their reliability when compared with custom solutions.

PROBLEMS AND PITFALLS

Complex Security Policies

Security policies have a habit of starting out simple and well-defined but becoming complex, full of special cases, and poorly understood as they are reviewed by more and more stakeholders. Implementing system security is difficult during the best of times. If the security policy is not a simple and regular rule set, this job becomes much more difficult during both development and system operation, and the likelihood of flaws in the security implementation is much higher.

Risk Reduction

- Make sure that the security policy is as simple as it can be—make functional, performance, and other tradeoffs if appropriate in order to achieve this goal.
- If policies appear to be very complex, consider partitioning the security-sensitive resources or the principals in different ways to make the policy simpler.

Unproven Security Technologies

There are many security technologies available for implementing your security infrastructure. They range from simple, very well understood technologies such as user names and passwords to large-scale, sophisticated systems in their own right such as many public/private key cryptography implementations.

However, whatever technology you use, your system's security is only as strong as its weakest link. A single weak element in your security infrastructure has the potential to make the rest of the infrastructure irrelevant. The weakness in an element can come from an inherent design or implementation flaw in the underlying product, a mistake made in its application, or indeed a mistake made in operating the technology.

Risk Reduction

- Err on the side of caution when selecting your security technology—such technology needs to be well understood and proven in operation before you can consider it a sound choice for a generic piece of infrastructure.
- If you don't have practical experience with a particular technology, find someone who does have such experience to guide you. (And don't assume that everything the vendor says is true!)

System Not Designed for Failure

As any architect knows, things go wrong in the process of designing, building, and operating information systems. Therefore, system elements are often created to fail in certain ways in order to minimize the impact of a particular failure. This is often a sound approach. It allows the system to continue being used (possibly with reduced function) while one or more pieces of it are being fixed. However, when considering security, this is not always the best approach.

To illustrate this, consider the failure of a security element that controls access to a sensitive resource. If the element is unexpectedly unavailable, the high-availability approach to design might suggest that the default behavior in such cases is to simply allow access until the security element is fixed. However, this obviously isn't the right thing to do from a security perspective.

Similar but much more subtle examples of this problem can happen when un-expected errors occur and security has not been considered while designing the relevant error-handling code.

RISK REDUCTION

- Design your security infrastructure to cope with failure in a safe way from the beginning so that unexpected element failures do not open se-curity loopholes in the system.

- Ensure that your security infrastructure is configured to fail securely if unexpected situations occur.

- When reviewing your architecture in failure scenarios, be sure to check what impact the failures have on the system's security.

Lack of Administration Facilities

An important but often neglected part of designing security infrastructure is to ensure that it can be effectively administered when the system is in produc-tion. Your testers may also have administration needs to ensure that they can reproduce large-scale test scenarios effectively.

Two common problems in this area include administration tools that can be used only for simple test cases (rather than for the thousands of users who can be found in real systems) and the use of a patchwork of administration tools that need to be carefully combined in order to manage the system. Such a situation will likely result in loopholes in security policy enforcement as ad-ministrators struggle to use inadequate tools to control access.

RISK REDUCTION

- Review your architecture to ensure that its administration facilities are adequate for the expected size of the user population and the complexity of the security policy.

- Make sure that the administration facilities you are planning to provide are acceptable to the administrators and operators who will have to use them.

- If possible, make sure that administrative security operations can be per-formed by using one task-driven interface, rather than requiring the use of a number of tools to perform a single task. If many steps are required, the likelihood of omission or error is much higher.

Technology-Driven Approach

A problem we have seen with the security design of some systems occurs when the available technology drives the security design process. You can tell that you have this sort of problem when you inquire whether the designers have considered security yet and you get the reply, "Oh yes—we're secure, we use SSL." In such situations, although security technology is deployed, you often have no idea whether it addresses the system's security needs.

RISK REDUCTION

- Drive your security design by the resources that need to be protected, the security model that needs to be implemented, and the security threats that the system faces.
- Avoid designing your security architecture around specific pieces of security technology. Don't incorporate security technology that is not justified by the security needs of your system.

Failure to Consider Time Sources

A number of security mechanisms rely on checking the passage of time (e.g., product license timeouts and password expirations). These mechanisms assume that a reliable source of time is readily available. Although the specifics of the mechanisms and the time source they need differ, they all share the characteristic that if the time source is compromised, the mechanism is ineffective.

RISK REDUCTION

- Identify the security mechanisms that require accurate time and the characteristics of the time they need (such as accuracy, absolute or relative, universal or time zone, and so on).
- Incorporate enough secure time sources in your system to meet the needs of your security mechanisms.
- Make sure you understand what will happen if a secure time source is unavailable or is compromised.
- Protect secure time sources against likely threats (using mechanisms such as calling back to secure servers, using external time servers or dedicated hardware devices, using operating system access controls to the time source, and so on).

Overreliance on Technology

It is often said by security luminaries like Bruce Schneier[2] and others that security is a process, not a product. Yet you can often find system designers

---

2. *Cryptogram,* February 15, 2002, www.schneier.com/crypto-gram-0202.html—in reference to Microsoft security.

placing great reliance on particular security products to keep their systems secure. Although you certainly do need to use good third-party security products to secure your system, you need to use them intelligently as part of an overall security design that encompasses all of the different aspects of your system.

At a recent security conference, an executive of a security product company pointed out that "there is no way you can buy anything, subscribe to anything and say you are 100% secure."[3] This is sound advice, coming from someone actually in the IT security industry.

RISK REDUCTION

- Use your threat model to drive your security design. Addressing these tangible threats will help you design a system that is secure, rather than a system that just uses security technology.

- Design a sound set of operational procedures to avoid human error exposing the system to security threats.

No Clear Requirements or Models

It is common for systems to have no clear, well-defined security requirements and no formal security models at all. The problem with these systems is that you simply don't know if they are secure because you don't know what "secure" means. Security is an area where it isn't possible to be confident that you have met the needs of the stakeholders without firm requirements and formal models. Security can't be seen, and most stakeholders won't test it. You'll find out that you have problems only when the security is breached—at which point you can be pretty certain that the stakeholders won't think their needs are being met.

RISK REDUCTION

- Drive the security design process by using threat and security policy models. Developing these models will help define requirements because they focus the stakeholders' minds on what is valuable, what is likely to be attacked, and what the impact of such attacks would be.

- Use plenty of concrete examples when discussing security with stakeholders. Security is an abstract area that requires some lateral and imaginative thinking in order to be effective. Examples will help your stakeholders think clearly about what they need.

---

3. Arthur Wong, CEO and founder of Security Focus, speaking at RSA Conference 2002, as reported on cnn.com, February 25, 2002, http://archives.cnn.com/2002/TECH/internet/02/25/2002.security.idg/.

- When identifying your architectural scenarios, consider those related to security as well as to functionality, performance, evolution, and so on. Thinking through security-related scenarios can help identify and clarify important security requirements.

Security as an Afterthought

Because stakeholders often don't think about security requirements explicitly, these requirements don't always get mentioned in the initial requirements analysis. This can lead to the problem where security has to be added to the system at some point during (or even after) development. At best, this is likely to be an expensive and painful process involving a lot of rework. At worst, it won't be possible to introduce the required security without changing the system in some way that upsets a stakeholder group.

RISK REDUCTION

- Start considering the system's security as soon as you start developing its functional and information structure. This will allow you to understand the security needs early in the lifecycle and make sure that the system you design can be secured.

Security Embedded in the Application Code

A problem observed in a number of systems occurs when the code that enforces the security model is found sprinkled throughout the application itself. As explained earlier, the problems with this approach include reduced reliability, the difficulty of changing the security model being enforced, and the likelihood of introducing security errors in your system.

RISK REDUCTION

- Push as much of the security technology as possible into your underlying infrastructure elements.
- If security does need to be in application code, apply good software engineering judgment to encapsulate as much of it as possible in a single place.

Piecemeal Security

To be effective, security needs to be considered on a holistic basis, throughout the system. A problem seen in many systems is security being applied to parts of the system but not to others. For example, highly sensitive data is encrypted during transmission but not when stored. This may or may not be a problem depending on the sensitivity of the data and the threats the system is likely to have to withstand. Your role is to make sure that security is implemented everywhere it is needed as revealed by the threat model—not just in the places that immediately spring to mind.

RISK REDUCTION

- The use of an architecture-driven development process will help address this risk. Make sure that you keep considering the architecture and particularly its security as a whole, rather than as a set of separate parts.

Ad Hoc Security Technology

Computer security is a specialized field with its own culture, standards, processes and background. Security engineers (the people who build security technology and secure systems) tend to have a lot of specialized training and experience. Similarly, cryptographers (the people who study and create ways to encrypt and decrypt data) tend to have advanced degrees in cryptography. Despite this, many software developers without this specialized background fancy themselves as amateur security engineers or cryptographers and decide to create some or all of the security technology in their systems.

In general, we suggest that this is a bad idea—creating truly secure technology is harder than it looks, and without specialized training, most of us can't do it reliably. Given the integrated nature of security, the consequences of one piece of weak security technology can be pretty catastrophic.

RISK REDUCTION

- Use proven, widely accepted security technology from established providers wherever possible, and get expert help with its use and deployment.

- Make sure you find out what previous users of the possible technologies thought of it and how the security community as a whole rates it.

- If you have to create your own technology, engage expert assistance to help you systematically develop it.

CHECKLISTS

Checklist for Requirements Capture

- Have you identified the sensitive resources contained in the system?
- Have you identified the sets of principals that need access to the resources?

- Have you identified the system's needs for information integrity guarantees?
- Have you identified the system's availability needs?
- Have you established a security policy to define the security needs for the system, including which principals are allowed to perform which operations on which resources and where information integrity needs to be enforced?
- Is the security policy as simple as possible?
- Have you worked through a formal threat model to identify the security risks your system faces?
- Have you worked through example scenarios with your stakeholders so that they understand the planned security policy and the security risks the system runs?
- Have you reviewed your security requirements with external experts?

Checklist for Architecture Definition

- Have you addressed each threat identified in the threat model to the extent required?
- Have you used as much third-party security technology as possible?
- Have you produced an integrated overall design for the security solution?
- Have you considered all standard security principles when designing your security infrastructure?
- Is your security infrastructure as simple as possible?
- Have you defined how security breaches will be identified and how to recover from breaches?
- Have you applied the results of the Security perspective to all of the affected views?
- Have external experts reviewed your security design?

FURTHER READING

You can find a short but thorough and very readable introduction to the main concepts of information systems security in a recent magazine article [LAMP04]. A much deeper but still quite readable introduction to the process of building secure systems and processes appears in Anderson [ANDE01]; this book provides a comprehensive introduction to many important security topics, as well as being an entertaining read, full of interesting stories from the security field. A more specific background text aimed at information systems architects is Hardman et al. [HARD01], which explains how to build secure enterprise information systems using Enterprise Java Beans and CORBA technology. In addition to detailed information on security specifics for these technologies, the book includes some useful background and puts the facilities in the context of an overall security process.

A well-known, generally respected, and always colorful figure in the security field is Bruce Schneier. Two of his books that offer useful background are his introduction to cryptography [SCHN95], which provides a good nuts-and-bolts introduction to cryptographic technology for software engineers, and his later book [SCHN01], which moves beyond his initial technology-focused approach and explains how technology will never provide a complete solution to security problems. This second book is worth reading to understand just how complex the security field is and how broad effective security solutions need to be.

Two good, practical security books aimed at software developers are Viega and McGraw [VIEG02] and Howard and LeBlanc [HOWA02]. Both books explain how to construct software that is secure by design rather than by accident or buzzword compliance. Chapter 5 in the former book also presents and explains a practical and simple set of security principles. The Fault Trees approach, which forms the basis of the attack trees we introduced in this perspective, is explained in Leveson [LEVE95].

TABLE 25-1 APPLICABILITY OF THE PERFORMANCE AND SCALABILITY PERSPECTIVE TO THE SIX VIEWS

View	Applicability
Functional	Applying this perspective may reveal the need for changes and compromises to your ideal functional structure to achieve the system's performance requirements (e.g., by consolidating system elements to avoid communication overhead). The models from this view also provide input to the creation of performance models.
Information	The Information view provides useful input to performance models, identifying shared resources and the transactional requirements of each. As you apply this perspective, you may identify aspects of the Information view as obstacles to performance or scalability. In addition, considering scalability may suggest elements of the Information view that could be replicated or distributed in support of this goal.
Concurrency	Applying this perspective may result in changes to the concurrency design due to identifying problems such as excessive contention on key resources. Alternatively, considering performance and scalability may result in concurrency becoming a more important design element to meet these requirements. Elements of concurrency views (such as interprocess communication mechanisms) can also provide calibration metrics for performance models.
Development	One of the possible outputs of applying this perspective is a set of guidelines related to performance and scalability that should be followed during software development. These guidelines will probably take the form of dos and don'ts (e.g., patterns and antipatterns) that must be followed as the software is developed in order to avoid performance and scalability problems later when it is deployed. You will capture this information in the Development view.
Deployment	The Deployment view is a crucial input to the process of considering performance and scalability. Many parts of the system's performance models are derived from the contents of this view, which also provides a number of critical calibration metrics. In turn, applying this perspective will often suggest changes and refinements to the deployment environment, to allow it to support the performance and scalability needs of the system.
Operational	The application of this perspective highlights the need for performance monitoring and management capabilities.

time between the user initiating the request and the response being available for her use (e.g., the time from clicking a user interface button to seeing the response screen populated with data). For an infrastructure-oriented system such as a database, this could be the time between invoking a service and the service returning a response (e.g., the time from calling a query application programming interface to obtaining the query results).

We define two broad classes of response times you may want to consider separately.

1. *Responsiveness* considers how quickly the system responds to routine workloads such as interactive user requests. The response time for such operations is typically in the order of a few seconds. The key consideration for such workloads is user productivity, ensuring that the system does not slow down its users.

2. *Turnaround time* is the time taken to complete (turn around) larger tasks. This is typically measured in minutes or hours, and the key considerations are whether the task can be completed in the time available to it and the impact the task has on the system responsiveness while it is running.

These two classes of response times can affect different types of stakeholders and often require quite different technical solutions to make sure that requirements of each type are met.

EXAMPLE The following examples show how requirements could be specified for the two classes of response times.

Responsiveness

1. Under a load of 350 update transactions per minute, 95% of transactions should return control to the user within 5 seconds of pressing the submit button.

2. Under the reference load (defined in a separate document), 90% of service requests should return a reply to the calling program within the following times:
   - Open account: 30 seconds
   - Update account details: 10 seconds
   - Retrieve account status: 5 seconds
   - Retrieve balances: 5 seconds, plus 1 second per account accessed

Turnaround Time

1. Assuming a total daily throughput of 850,000 transactions, the process of establishing a consolidated position against each of the firm's external counterparties should take no longer than 4 hours, including writing the results back to a database. It can be assumed that no other system activity will take place during this period.

2. It must be possible to resynchronize the system with all of the production line monitoring stations and reset the database to reflect the current production line state within 5 minutes. It can be assumed that no status updates will be processed during the resynchronization period.

Throughput

Throughput is defined as the amount of workload the system is capable of handling in a unit time period. Throughput and response time have a complex interrelationship in most systems. In general, the shorter your transaction processing time, the higher the throughput your system can achieve. However, as the load on the system increases (and throughput rises), the response time for individual transactions tends to increase. Therefore, it is quite possible to end up with a situation where throughput goals can be met only at the expense of response time goals, or vice versa. We can illustrate this with a simple example.

EXAMPLE A database server can support up to 500 concurrent users performing sales transactions; however, as the number of concurrent users increases, the response time the users see increases as well.

- With 10 concurrent users, a typical transaction is processed in 2 seconds.
- With 100 concurrent users, a typical transaction is processed in 4 seconds.
- With 500 concurrent users, a typical transaction is processed in 14 seconds.

It takes 1 second of "thinking time" for a user to enter a transaction. If we have only 10 users, each user can theoretically perform 20 transactions per minute, and our total possible throughput is a modest 200 transactions per minute.

If the load on the system rises to 100 users, each user can process up to 12 transactions per minute. Our total possible throughput rises to 1,200 transactions per minute, but at the cost of doubling the response time.

> If we operate at our peak load of 500 concurrent users, each user can process up to 4 transactions per minute. Our total possible system throughput is 2,000 transactions per minute, but the response time cost has risen significantly for the users.

As the architect, you need to make sure that you and your stakeholders understand these interrelationships and that you have balanced your stakeholders' different performance goals.

Scalability

Most systems are subject to workload growth in some form. Scalability is the ability of a system to handle this increased workload, which may be due to an increase in the number of requests, transactions, messages, or jobs the system is required to process per unit of time or an increase in the complexity of these tasks.

Long-term scalability always has an associated time element that considers how soon the increase in workload is anticipated to arrive. You may also need to consider transient scalability—that is, the ability to handle short bursts of increased workload (such as increased traffic to an Internet news site during an international crisis).

Predictability

In addition to providing acceptable response time and throughput, another desirable property of a computer system is its ability to perform predictably. By this we mean that similar transactions complete in very similar amounts of time regardless of when they are executed. Similarly, the maximum transaction throughput the system can cope with should not vary significantly over time (in particular, it shouldn't decrease).

Predictability is often a more desirable quality than absolute performance.

> **EXAMPLE** Call center agents use a customer service system to answer customer queries over the telephone. Having identified the customer, the agent executes a transaction to retrieve the customer's details. Whether the response time for this transaction is 1 second or 6 seconds probably doesn't matter that much—5 seconds isn't a long pause during such a telephone conversation, and agents can incorporate this delay into their

conversations with the customers. Therefore, a predictable transaction time of 6 seconds is acceptable.

However, if the system is unpredictable and produces the result in any time from 1 second to 15 seconds, then even if the average transaction response time is significantly less than 6 seconds, this is still less acceptable to the agents because it will result in awkward conversation pauses for many of the longer retrievals.

Hardware Resource Requirements

A major part of the performance and scalability puzzle is working out how much (and what type of) hardware your system will need, and this is usually an early concern in any project, being captured as part of the Deployment view. Hardware must be considered early because it costs money, takes time to acquire, often needs people to operate it, and often needs to be housed in purpose-built environments. The amount of hardware needed for a system usually has a significant and very visible impact on its overall cost.

In general, more hardware means higher throughput and better response times, albeit at higher cost. Given this fundamental tension between cost and performance, your role is often to establish the minimum amount of hardware that will allow the system to meet its performance goals.

Peak Load Behavior

All computer systems eventually exhibit poor performance as the load on them increases. If you plot a graph of the average transaction response time against the load on the system, it will usually have the shape shown in Figure 25–1.

The system behaves well for a while: As workload increases, response time increases in a predictable, linear fashion. However, at a certain point things start to go very wrong, and the response times increase sharply. This point is known as the "knee" in the curve. Soon, the graph ends up as a nearly vertical line, indicating that response times have become so long that the system is effectively unusable. This behavior is usually caused by one or more critical resources in the system becoming so overloaded that it can no longer work effectively (e.g., a network card is so swamped by incoming connection requests that it cannot service any of them effectively).

This sort of behavior is exhibited by virtually every system we have come across. However, it obviously isn't acceptable to experience this effect during normal system operation. This means that your challenge is to identify where the "knee" in the performance graph for your system is and to make sure that the corresponding workload level will be irrelevant during normal system operation.

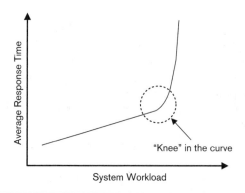

FIGURE 25-1 THE PERFORMANCE CURVE

ACTIVITIES: APPLYING THE PERFORMANCE AND SCALABILITY PERSPECTIVE

The activity diagram in Figure 25–2 illustrates a simple process for applying the Performance and Scalability perspective. In this section, we describe the activities in this process.

Capture the Performance Requirements

Ideally, you will already have a complete, consistent, and credible set of performance and scalability requirements as a result of the initial system requirements work performed. In reality, this usually isn't the case, and you need to collect these requirements, at a high level, as early as possible in the development lifecycle. Even if some requirements do exist, you need to verify their correctness and your understanding of them.

The performance requirements are often defined in business terms so that they are meaningful to the users of the system rather than the builders. Requirements such as "Be fast enough to support a 20,000-transaction-per-day back-office workload" are common and are useful because they describe the real stakeholder requirement rather than some abstract performance metric. However, at this stage, you need to translate such performance requirements into a set of key quantitative performance goals you are going to attempt to meet.

Setting such quantitative goals involves identifying the underlying performance metrics that are implicitly defined by the business-oriented requirements. From the previous example, you might end up with a definition of 5,000 information lookup requests, 10,000 specific transaction entry requests, and 5,000 report requests distributed over a 9-hour period, with a peak load of 20% of the transactions occurring in 45 minutes. This is a set of

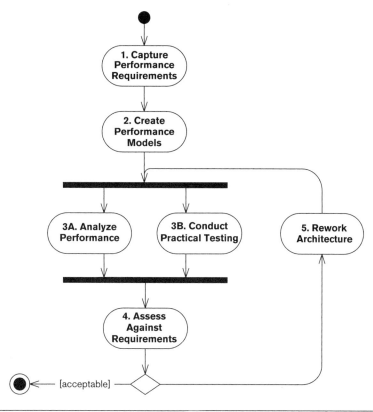

FIGURE 25-2 APPLYING THE PERFORMANCE AND SCALABILITY PERSPECTIVE

specific, quantitative goals, and you can establish whether or not you have met them by measurement and analysis.

A common problem with this process is understanding the business requirements enough to translate them into quantitative goals. Using experience, careful analysis, and the knowledge of domain experts who understand the workload are all possible solutions to this problem.

NOTATION Simplicity and clear communication are the goals when communicating performance requirements, and we have found that a simple approach based on text and tables is quite sufficient.

ACTIVITIES

Specify the Response Time Requirements. Response time targets are meaningful only in the context of a defined load. It may be easy for a computer system to process a single transaction in 3 seconds but much harder to achieve this target when it is receiving 500 transactions a second. This means that response time requirements need to specify the context as well as a clearly defined response time goal (which also defines when a transaction starts and ends). In most systems, response time under constant load will vary according to some sort of distribution curve. Most transactions will complete at or near the average response time, but some will take longer, and a few will complete more quickly. In most cases, it isn't reasonable to expect every transaction to complete within the target response time. It is more realistic to require a certain proportion (such as 90% or 95%) of transactions to meet the target.

Specify the Throughput Requirements. Throughput is typically defined in terms of transactions per unit time (second, minute, or hour), where a transaction is a clearly definable unit of work, recognizable to a user of the system. The transactions used for throughput planning should normally be derived from the system's most important usage scenarios (rather than a specific technology-oriented transaction item, such as a database insert statement).

Specify the Scalability Requirements. Scalability requirements are usually defined in terms of the increase in workload that the system must be able to absorb over particular time periods while continuing to meet its existing response and throughput goals. Scalability requirements should also make clear any changes to the system that will be needed to meet these increased workload levels.

Create the Performance Models

Being able to collect performance data isn't useful in itself. You need to use the data in an effective way to allow you to understand and improve your system's performance. A key part of this process is creating performance models that allow you to gain this insight. Such a model allows you to assess the maximum "theoretical" workload for your system, supplies useful estimates for capacity planning, and provides a set of measures against which the actual system can be compared to assess its performance.

The types of models you can use for performance analysis vary widely from a few simple calculations on a scrap of paper to sophisticated statistical models to complete online simulations of systems. All these models have their place, but given our degree of expertise and the space available, we will limit our discussion to relatively simple pencil-and-paper performance models involving basic representations of system structure with the simple statistics used to analyze them. The performance engineering books mentioned in the Further Reading section at the end of this chapter provide more information on performance modeling.

NOTATION We have found the following notation methods most helpful when creating performance models.

- *Performance modeling notations*: Specialists in this area have developed several graphical and mathematical performance modeling approaches, including execution graphs, augmented Petri Nets, approaches based on queuing theory, and statistical approaches (see the Further Reading section for more information). Most of the notations used in these approaches are extensions of previously existing notations, with the advantage of being tailored specifically for performance modeling. As with most specialist notations, they often have the disadvantages of complexity and unfamiliarity; many are not widely understood outside the specialist computer measurement community.

- *Ad hoc diagrams*: A simple block diagram notation is probably sufficient for many performance models because they are not terribly complex. In fact, you can use a UML deployment diagram with some ad hoc extensions as the basis for a performance model. Such an approach has the virtue of simplicity but may have limitations for more sophisticated modeling applications.

- *Text and tables*: Some of the performance model will probably need to be captured using text and tables to describe model elements, capture key metrics, and illustrate relationships between elements that the graphical notation does not make clear.

ACTIVITIES

Identify the Performance-Critical Structure. Use the Deployment view of the system as the basis of the model by simplifying it to its essential performance-critical elements—such as processes, nodes, network links, and the main data storage (such as your main databases). Create a new, simple block diagram of the system illustrating the main runtime system elements and how they are connected.

Identify the Key Performance Metrics. Review the block diagram and identify the parts that need to be annotated with performance data to allow the creation of performance estimates. This normally includes the processing time for the main functional elements of the system, the request latency between the main system processes, the length of time taken by a typical database operation, the number of concurrent requests that each major element can handle, and so on.

Estimate the Performance Metrics. At this stage, the values for most of the key performance metrics are probably unclear. For each such metric, you need to derive a reliable estimate of its value. Some may be fairly obvious from previous experiences that you or others on your team have had. For the rest of the metrics, try to create quick prototypes that allow you to derive estimates. If prototypes aren't practical, intelligent guesswork is probably your only remaining option. Whichever approach you use, make sure that the estimates are valid for a realistic workload and not just for a single transaction. When you've completed this process, the result will be a simple performance model you can use for prediction. To estimate the theoretical processing time for an element of system workload, you can trace its execution through the model and piece together the relevant performance estimates.

EXAMPLE Figure 25–3 shows an example of a simple performance model that might be built to investigate the performance of an order-entry process for an order-processing system.

The diagram shows that we have identified five performance-related parts of the system (plus the Browser Client), whose interactions we judge to be the crucial factors determining system performance. For each of these elements (or more accurately, those servicing others), we have estimated the response times that the element will provide to its clients under defined conditions. We have also estimated the communications latency between the elements, which varies widely (due to different technologies and deployment decisions).

This model provides two valuable insights. First, we can see how long we think a couple of crucial system transactions will take to execute. (We could extend this model or build other similar ones to investigate other aspects of the system's performance.) Second, the model helps us understand the set of performance-related assumptions we are making (such as the invocation latency being minimal between the Order Processor and the Price Calculator), which, if incorrect, may cause us problems later. The model also helps us focus on another step in the process, practical testing.

As we mentioned, the approach illustrated in Figure 25–3 is very simple. Although the model is helpful and provides useful insights, we made a number of important simplifications—for example, we're largely ignoring the modeling of queuing within the system. If you want to create more sophisticated performance models of your system, we recommend some books in the Further Reading section at the end of this chapter.

Analyze the Performance Models

In parallel with practical benchmark testing, you can calibrate the performance models with the previously estimated performance metrics and use the results to estimate likely system throughput under different scenarios. The advantage of using performance models is that analysis is cheaper, simpler,

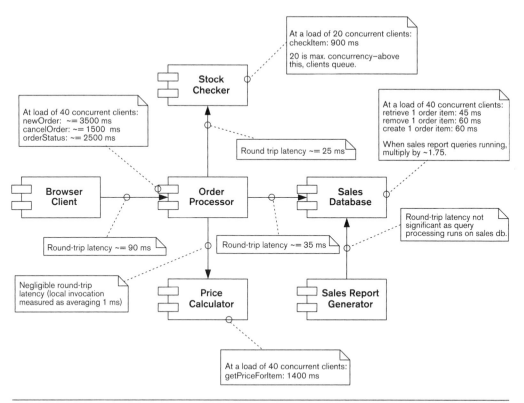

FIGURE 25-3 A SIMPLE PERFORMANCE MODEL

and quicker than benchmarking. The disadvantage is obviously that the results are only as good as the models, so they need to be carefully validated by some practical testing as well.

Consider using the performance models to explore a large number of scenarios quickly to find potential trouble spots, and then use this knowledge to drive more involved practical work.

NOTATION Analysis of performance models results in calculated performance data that you can usually represent in tabular form.

ACTIVITIES

Characterize the Workload. The first activity is to establish the "shape" of the workload your system needs to be able to process. This involves prioritizing and estimating the volume of each sort of request the system has been specified to handle, including an estimate of the routine processing needed.

Estimate the Performance. Having identified the kind of workload you expect, you can estimate the processing time of each piece of that workload. This involves using the performance models to identify the elements of the system involved in processing each piece of the workload and to determine how long the likely best- and worse-case durations will be. From this set of inputs, you can establish the estimated best- and worst-case processing times for each element of the expected workload. It is sensible to multiply these estimates by a factor that reflects the hidden inefficiencies likely to be present in the system. (A value of 20% is a good starting point for an information system.) At the same time, identify the least scalable element involved in processing each workload item, and use this information to estimate how many concurrent requests your system can handle.

Conduct Practical Testing

Although performance modeling is very valuable, it is of limited use in isolation; practical testing is also important. The testing you do can range from some simple isolated tests for assessing critical performance metrics to large-scale prototype benchmarking. The amount of practical testing you should perform depends on how confident you are that you can assess the likely performance of your system without it (and, of course, on how much time you have available to spend on this aspect of your architecture). For a system structure you have used before, with well-tested technology, in an application domain you have experience of, little practical testing may be needed. In a new domain, with new technology, or with a novel system architecture, you will probably want to perform a lot of tests.

NOTATION   You can write up test results in a short report if appropriate.

ACTIVITIES

Measure and Estimate the Performance Metrics. To support the process of creating a performance model, you need to measure or estimate values for a number of important performance metrics. A common performance testing activity is to perform a series of practical tests to estimate these metrics accurately. Such testing typically involves quickly prepared trial scenarios that allow a particular performance metric to be empirically tested (such as network response times from a Web server under load). The main pitfall to avoid with such testing is oversimplification of the test scenario, which results in much better performance than would be expected in a real deployment. Make sure that trial scenarios simulate a realistic context for the test metric (such as ensuring a realistic workload on the system element being tested).

Perform Benchmark Tests. Metric estimation is a highly specific activity that focuses on one microlevel metric. It can also be useful to perform more complex practical testing to find out what performance can be expected from a particular configuration of candidate system elements. Such testing is often referred to as *benchmarking* and usually involves creating a trial end-to-end system to allow system-level performance to be estimated. As such, its relationship to metric estimation is similar to the relationship between integration and unit testing. Benchmarking is more involved than simple microlevel performance testing, but the major pitfall is the same: namely, ensuring that the test is valid. Make sure that the limits of the benchmark are understood and that it captures enough of the key characteristics of the planned system to provide a useful insight into its likely performance. (For example, make sure that system elements perform enough processing to be representative of the elements in the system under development.)

Assess against the Requirements

Having completed performance analysis and practical testing, you can compare the results of this process against the performance requirements and draw some initial conclusions. These conclusions may indicate that all should be well or that modifications need to be made to the architecture to resolve potential performance problems. You may also believe that further testing and analysis are required because you made assumptions that you no longer feel comfortable with.

The result of this process should be a decision to either complete this cycle of performance work or circle back through the process. If the latter, you will need to make appropriate modifications to your proposed architecture and repeat the analysis and testing cycle as needed, to increase or deepen your knowledge of how the system will behave from a performance perspective.

NOTATION This activity is a process rather than a model-building activity. However, you do need to clearly document its outputs so that decisions, assumptions, and assessments are captured for everyone's use as the system development process moves forward. Document this activity's outputs as concisely as possible (probably by using plain text), and over time you will create a useful library of performance information that can be applied in other situations.

ACTIVITIES
Identify the Risks. Reconsider the performance risks you believe you are facing, based on your testing and analysis. Clearly record and justify those risks you think are still a problem and those that have been addressed. For those that are still troublesome, identify why they are still present, and use these conclusions to drive the next iteration of performance work, should you decide you need one.

Review the Requirements. Work through each of your performance requirements and demonstrate to your own satisfaction (and the satisfaction of any interested stakeholders) whether or not the proposed architecture will meet each requirement.

Rework the Architecture

The output of this performance work is likely to be a number of cross-view changes you need to make to your candidate architecture. The most likely impact will be to the functional and deployment designs, but other aspects of the architecture (particularly the information- and concurrency-related parts) are also candidates for performance-related changes. Many of the tactics described in the next section imply cross-view changes (e.g., in extreme cases, partitioning and parallelization can require changes to the functional, concurrency, information, and deployment structures in order to support effective partitioning and parallel execution of the workload and consolidation of the results).

After changing the architecture, move into the next iteration of the process by modifying your performance model and rerunning or adding practical testing, to establish whether or not the proposed changes have the required effects.

NOTATION   Use the same architectural notations used in your view models.

ACTIVITIES   Any sort of architecture definition activity required to improve performance is relevant here, particularly the tactics discussed in the next section.

ARCHITECTURAL TACTICS

Optimize Repeated Processing

An old software engineering heuristic states that most systems spend 80% of their time running 20% of the system's code. This certainly matches our experience that most systems have a small number of common operations that the system spends most of its time performing.

The resulting performance implication is that you should focus your performance efforts on that core 20% of your system. To state this in slightly more sophisticated terms:

operation total cost = operation invocation cost × operation invocation frequency

We can consider the total cost of a system operation to be the cost of a single invocation multiplied by the number of times we will invoke it during a unit time (e.g., per day). In turn, we can note that:

$$\text{system workload} = \sum\nolimits_{(1..n)} \text{operation total cost}$$

The total workload for our system, for a unit time, is the sum of all of the total operation costs over that unit time (where we have n possible operations in our system).

In order to focus your performance engineering effort, rank your system's operations by the total cost metric, and make sure that you optimize the operations at the top of the list first.

Having this information also helps you make intelligent tradeoffs between operation optimizations. In many cases, optimizing for one operation can have a negative impact for another. In general, when you have to make these tradeoffs, the needs of the frequent operations should take precedence.

EXAMPLE A message bus is a piece of software infrastructure that allows applications to exchange messages easily and efficiently. The message bus receives messages from senders, performs any data transformation required, calculates how to route the message to its intended recipients, and delivers the message to them.

In order to process messages efficiently, the message bus could maintain information on its nodes, the routes between them, and the connectivity characteristics of each (such as communication latency). The bus would use this information to derive the most optimal route between message senders and receivers. This speeds up the process of route selection (which is a frequent activity), but the tradeoff is that whenever a node or link is added or removed (which happens rarely), the entire set of route tables has to be recalculated, which is a potentially expensive operation.

The goal of the performance engineering process is to minimize the overall system workload; this is one of the few sure ways to improve system performance.

Reduce Contention via Replication

As we discussed in Chapter 18, whenever you have concurrent operations in your system, you have the potential for contention. This contention is often a major source of performance problems, causing reduction in throughput and wasted resources.

Eliminating contention can be a difficult process, particularly when you must deal with a single point of contention (such as a shared data structure inside an operating system process). This can occur when the contention involved is actually within the system's underlying infrastructure (e.g., an application server), rather than in the software over which you have direct control.

A possible solution for some contention problems is to replicate system elements—hardware, software, or data.

EXAMPLE Many large Web sites support many millions of page views per day, far beyond the capacity of even the largest computers. They provide this service by deploying vast server farms, made up of hundreds or even thousands of computers each running a separate instance of the Web server. Special hardware is used to allocate incoming requests evenly across the Web servers to ensure that response times are consistent and that usage is maximized.

Of course, in this scenario, the network connection into the server farm can still be a bottleneck. By replicating the server nodes, we may just be moving the bottleneck to a different part of the system. This is a very common feature of performance work—solving a problem simply uncovers the next bottleneck in the system!

EXAMPLE A lottery system supports remote point-of-sale terminals in retail locations throughout the country. When a terminal is switched on in the morning, it is necessary to enter a user name and password before the terminal can be used. This authentication is done through a single central database, which experiences very heavy load between 7 and 8:30 A.M., resulting in login times of up to a minute.

To alleviate this problem, several regional authorization databases are set up, with each one supporting about 10% of the overall terminal population. Programs are written to distribute login information to each database overnight. As a result, login times are significantly improved.

This approach works only in certain situations, and a limiting factor is that the system often needs to be designed to take advantage of replication from the outset. However, where possible, it is worth considering because it can be a lot easier to solve a contention problem by avoiding it completely in this way rather than having to solve it directly.

Prioritize Processing

The workload in your system will vary in terms of its importance, ranging from extremely critical processing that needs to be performed as quickly as possible to routine work such as housekeeping that can be completed over an extended period.

A problem in many otherwise well-built systems can emerge when the overall performance of the system is within target, but some important tasks still take too long to execute. In these systems, the underlying hardware is typically busy, and the expected overall throughput is being processed. But critical workload is being processed at the same rate as less important operations, and this leads to the perception of a performance problem.

To avoid this situation, partition the system's workload into priority groups (or classes), and add the ability to prioritize the workload to process. This allows you to ensure that your system's resources will be applied to the right element of workload at any point in time, so the perception of performance problems is much less likely. A low-level example of this approach is the priority class-based thread and process scheduling built into most modern operating systems.

When dealing with large information systems, this prioritizing usually involves identifying the business criticality of each class of workload. Those types of workloads that have to complete in a timely manner for business to continue (such as order processing) are naturally prioritized over workloads that, while important, will not immediately impact business operation (such as management reporting).

 EXAMPLE A Web-based system to support e-commerce may need to support order capture, customer account management, stock reporting, and sales reporting functions.

Probably all of the customer Web workload (such as order capture and customer account management) should be prioritized over other processing. The customers who use the Web site are extremely important stakeholders because a slow Web site will not only reduce immediate sales but may drive the customers to other vendors, thus damaging the business in the longer term.

In contrast, while the management team members are influential stakeholders, if the management reporting functions run slowly during times of peak load, it is unlikely to directly harm the business. Of course, making such a rational tradeoff can be challenging when dealing with live stakeholders.

The practical problem in most situations is finding the right balance between the different types of workloads. A number of factors need to be taken into account, including the relative importance of different stakeholders, the varying importance that different stakeholders place on different sorts of workloads, and the deadlines for processing various workloads. Finding the right balance for complex situations is often a case of applying your judgment to find an acceptable option, rather than discovering any absolute "right" answer.

Consolidate Related Workload

The processing of most operations in an information system requires a certain amount of context to be available in order for the processing to take place. The management of this context information can itself be a significant overhead when the operation to be performed is small or the context is expensive to locate (e.g., when loaded from a database).

To address this, consolidate related workloads into batches and process groups of related requests together. This pattern of processing normally allows a single initialization step, a number of operation processing steps, and then a single tear-down step—so saving the initialization and tear-down steps that would be required for each operation if processed separately.

EXAMPLE A generic rating engine uses actual and predicted foreign exchange rates to calculate values in different currencies. To use the engine, you supply an amount, a "from" currency, a "to" currency, and a date—either spot (now) or forward (in the future)—and the engine performs the required conversion. To do this, it has to calculate a table of forward exchange rates based on complex formulas. Although this calculation is fairly quick, because it is repeated for each value supplied it has a significant impact on performance.

The engine is enhanced to take a list of conversions as input, rather than just a single one. This improves performance significantly because, for a batch of a hundred values, the calculations have to be performed only once rather than a hundred times.

Such an optimization is inherently related to the structure of the system and the way operations are processed within the system, so it is something best considered as part of architecture definition. Doing so can lead to large efficiency gains for some systems.

Distribute Processing in Time

Some systems need to process a similar workload continually at all times of day or night. However, in our experience, such systems are pretty rare (although some Internet systems do fall into this category). Because most internal systems support people at work, and because people work during relatively fixed hours, systems often have different load requirements at different times of day. This means that the workload level for a system varies over time. The problem during the busy times is that (as we have already seen) concurrency tends to cause performance problems.

A useful system-level strategy for reducing system load, resource contention, and thus performance problems is to even out peaks and troughs of processing. Some peak workload is simply unavoidable—the result of the way people work. However, consider spending time during the architecture definition process to carefully analyze your system's workload during the peak times. In many cases you will find that some of the workload can be postponed to other times in your processing cycle. By moving these parts of the workload, you will improve performance during peak load times and use idle resources during quieter times.

Minimize Use of Shared Resources

At any particular time, each nonidle task running on a system is in one of two states:

1. Making use of a resource (e.g., a hardware resource such as processor, memory, disk, or network or a software resource such as a message service)

2. Waiting for a resource, either because it is busy (e.g., being used by another task) or not in a ready state (e.g., waiting for a head to move over a particular track on a disk or a software service to initialize)

As systems get busier and contention for shared resources increases, the waiting time takes proportionally more of the total elapsed time for tasks and contributes proportionally more to the overall response time.

Increasing the performance of resources that the task uses will help (because in general you have to wait less time for the tasks ahead of you in the queue to finish), although this may not be possible for a number of reasons, perhaps because you have reached the limits of the technology. The other way to alleviate this situation is to minimize the use of shared resources—that is, reduce the situations in which waiting has to occur. This is a complex topic, beyond the scope of this book, but you may want to consider the following strategies.

- Use techniques such as hardware multiplexing to eliminate hardware hot spots in your architecture.

- Favor short, simple transactions over long, complex ones where possible (because transactions tend to lock up resources for extended periods).

- Do not lock resources in human time (e.g., while waiting for a user to press a key).
- Try to access shared resources nonexclusively wherever possible.

Partition and Parallelize

If your system involves large, lengthy processes, a possible way to reduce their response time is to partition them into a number of smaller processes, execute these subprocesses in parallel, and, when the last subprocess is complete, consolidate all of the subprocess output into a single result. Whether this approach is likely to be effective in a particular situation depends on four primary factors:

1. Whether the overall process can be quickly and efficiently partitioned into subprocesses
2. Whether the resulting subprocesses can be executed independently to allow effective parallel processing
3. How much time it will take to consolidate the output of the subprocesses into a single result
4. Whether enough processing capacity is available to process the subprocesses in parallel faster than handling the same workload in a single process

If the overall process cannot be split easily into independent subprocesses, this technique isn't practical. Situations involving lengthy and expensive consolidation of subprocess output are suitable for this technique only if the consolidation cost is still small relative to that of the longer response time for the original process. Finally, if spare processing resources aren't available, parallelization is unlikely to be effective because the subprocesses will be executed one after the other and will be slower than the original design, due to the partitioning and consolidation overheads.

It is also important to remember that this approach is less efficient than using a single linear process (due to the partitioning and consolidation overheads) and achieves a reduction in response time at the price of requiring more processing resources.

EXAMPLE A feature offered by a sales management system is to generate a number of derived measures of sales performance (volume, profitability, average price, and so on) across the company, broken down by region. This feature is likely to involve a lengthy process of calculation over the sales information held in the system but is also likely to be a good candidate for partitioning and parallelization. If the request is partitioned into a process for each sales region (rather being run as a single process), each region's results can be calculated in parallel and the results consolidated to form the final report. If the underlying data can be efficiently accessed in n parallel streams, assuming similar data volumes per sales region, the parallel process is likely to complete in roughly $1/n^{th}$ of the time taken if run as a single process (plus some time for result consolidation, which is likely to be small compared to calculation time). This response time can be greatly reduced, at the cost of some processing efficiency.

Use Asynchronous Processing

One way to improve perceived response times for users is to carry out some processing asynchronously—that is, in the background, after the system has returned a response to the user.

EXAMPLE Several desktop computers share access to a single high-quality color printer by means of a shared printer server. Desktop applications send print requests to the print server, which manages them through a set of queues. Print requests for even the largest jobs complete as soon as the request has been received and acknowledged by the print server, rather than having to wait for the print to physically complete.

Once a document has been printed, the server notifies the originating PC, and a small message box is displayed to the user. Of course, this may happen some time later—possibly not until the next day in the case of very large print jobs. If printing fails for any reason, notification is also sent to the desktop, and it is the user's responsibility to resubmit the job.

You need to use this technique with some care, and only where it is really necessary, for several reasons. First, it is usually significantly more complex to implement, requiring some sort of background service to carry out the asynchronous parts of processing for you. More important, you have to develop strategies for dealing with situations where the background processing fails: It may be minutes or even hours after the transaction was initiated, and the user may not even be available to take corrective action. Finally, asynchronous processing doesn't actually reduce the amount of workload that needs to be performed or make the system more efficient (and thus actually solve the performance issue); it just moves the workload around.

Make Design Compromises

If other performance tactics you've tried have not resulted in acceptable performance or cannot be applied for some reason, you may need a more extreme approach. Many of the techniques of good architecture definition that we have described in this book can themselves cause performance problems in extreme situations. For example, a loosely coupled, highly modular, and coherent system tends to spend more time communicating between its modules than a tightly coupled, monolithic one does.

Although a loosely coupled and highly modular design should always be the goal, you should be aware that the benefits it provides might come at some performance cost. Where performance is a critical concern and other tactics have failed, you might need to compromise the ideal structure of your design, for example, by:

- Moving to a more tightly coupled, monolithic design to minimize internal communication delays and contention
- Denormalizing parts of your data model to optimize accesses to data
- Using very coarse-grained operations between distributed system elements
- Duplicating data or processing locally to minimize traffic over slow communication channels

Making such a change may improve performance but is likely to have costs in terms of maintainability and possibly even ease of use. You should carefully assess the desirability of these tradeoffs.

PROBLEMS AND PITFALLS

Imprecise Performance and Scalability Goals

It is far too common for even large projects to have vague, incomplete, or ambiguous performance goals or to have failed to consider the scalability of the system altogether. This is simply storing up trouble for the future—you won't have a suitable framework for designing, tuning, and building the system, and it won't be possible to determine unambiguously whether or not the system is performing acceptably.

RISK REDUCTION
- Define and obtain approval from your stakeholders for clear, measurable performance and scalability goals.
- Satisfy yourself that your performance and scalability goals are realistic and achievable.

- Communicate the goals to the architecture, design, and build teams so that they can be factored into their work.
- Make sure that acceptance criteria are based only on the agreed goals and do not include other (possibly implied) performance or scalability goals.

Unrealistic Models

The process of building a performance model can be an absorbing one, and the result is often a sophisticated model of the likely performance characteristics of the system. A problem that can result from an impressive model is an overreliance on its abilities. It is easy to be lulled into a false sense of security when a model suggests that no performance problems exist. A lack of problems revealed by a model does not necessarily mean that no problems exist in the real system; the model is an abstraction of reality and only as good as its match with that reality.

RISK REDUCTION

- Balance and augment the performance modeling activity with enough practical testing to make sure that the assumptions underpinning the models are valid and that the conclusions resulting from them are credible.
- Continue parallel practical testing right through the modeling process.
- Always check your modeling results against practical test results.

Use of Simple Measures for Complex Cases

Achieving acceptable performance in a computer system is a complex process, with many variables to worry about simultaneously. A common pitfall is to oversimplify the performance testing and modeling process to make it easier, but then to assume that its results will apply to much larger and more complex cases by simple analogy. Practical testing should reflect the real runtime environment you expect for your system, and if your performance models are very simple, the conclusions drawn from them must be used with care.

As a simple example, consider the practical testing you perform to calibrate your model. If these practical tests do not simulate a realistic runtime environment (e.g., by being single-threaded rather than heavily concurrent), the results of these tests are unlikely to reflect the way the real system will behave.

RISK REDUCTION

- Continually question the validity of your analysis and testing conclusions.
- Consider the differences between the test environment and the real system runtime environment to spot critical divergences that are likely to invalidate the performance engineering process.

Inappropriate Partitioning

In Chapter 16, we discussed poor partitioning as a possible pitfall for the Functional view, but it is often also problematic when considering performance. Partitioning becomes a problem when one or more elements appear to be involved in nearly all of the transactions in the system. This often means that these elements become bottlenecks and prevent acceptable performance being achieved anywhere in the system because of their dominant role.

A related problem, which is often a symptom of poor partitioning, is to ignore the performance differences of local and remote processing. We discuss this problem near the end of this chapter when we talk about network and in-process invocation.

RISK REDUCTION

- Watch for functional elements that are highly connected to a large percentage of the system's other functional elements (see the discussion of "God elements" in Chapter 16). These system elements may be your potential bottlenecks.

Invalid Environment and Platform Assumptions

Whenever an innovative system is developed, a level of risk exists because of assumptions that have to be made about its environment or the underlying technology. This risk can result from new technology that has not been widely used before (or perhaps not on this scale), or it can result from assumptions about the system's environment (e.g., peak request volume).

Some of these risks are unavoidable and are simply the result of being first. What is surprising is the number of projects that either run into performance problems in well-understood areas or simply don't control their risks, even when this is perfectly possible.

RISK REDUCTION

- Identify and validate your assumptions, and assess them for risks as part of performance analysis.

- Identify your possible mitigation strategies if your assumptions are proved incorrect.

Too Much Indirection

It has been said that any problem in software engineering can be solved by adding another level of indirection.[1] It is certainly true that indirection is a

---

1. Attributed to Andrew Koenig.

powerful tool—used wisely, it can make systems more flexible, easier to change, more powerful, and even more elegant. However, another famous adage also applies: There is no such thing as a free lunch!

A problem with indirection is that it introduces hidden work into the system. Some forms of indirection (e.g., object references in an object-oriented language) do not normally introduce enough overhead to cause a problem in anything apart from the most performance-critical situations. However, other forms of indirection (e.g., key mapping in a database) can add a significant percentage of overhead for certain sorts of processing (e.g., some updates may need two disk writes rather than one).

RISK REDUCTION

- Be careful how much indirection you introduce into the performance-critical parts of your system.
- If you have a lot of indirection in the implementation of critical path operations, carefully assess the tradeoff between the functional advantages and the performance disadvantages.

Concurrency-Related Contention

Any system with concurrent processing and shared resources has the potential for contention between threads of execution. In its most extreme form, this contention can slow a concurrent system to a crawl as threads spend most of their time "thrashing" in and out of wait states trying to obtain access to shared resources. Even in less extreme cases, such contention can become a significant bottleneck and cause performance problems throughout the system. Careful analysis and design of your system to avoid such bottlenecks is an important part of the performance work for concurrent systems.

RISK REDUCTION

- Inspect your Functional and Concurrency views to identify the elements of your system that must deal with a significant amount of concurrent processing.
- Investigate the proposed implementation of critical elements as part of your modeling, testing, and analysis process to convince yourself that they will not become bottlenecks that grind your system to a halt.
- During software construction, test the concurrent behavior of critical elements as early as possible.

Careless Allocation of Resources

Increases in computing power in recent years mean that, in general, we need to be much less conscious of using hardware resources frugally than used to be the case. However, an often-overlooked problem related to this new free-dom is the fact that the process of allocating and freeing runtime resources (such as memory or locks) requires resources itself. This is easy to forget be-cause the process is often implicit (such as the Java language's automatic gar-bage collection or a relational database's automatic lock allocation). However, this doesn't mean it is free!

A problem that can creep into many information systems is excessive al-location and freeing of runtime resources. This is often revealed by elements that appear to run much slower than expected without any obvious way for the time to be lost.

RISK REDUCTION

- Avoid large amounts of dynamic resource allocation and deallocation in critical path elements.

- Consider preallocating resources at less critical times (such as startup or during quiet periods).

- Consider whether allocated resources can be reused more cheaply than freeing and reallocating them.

- Work with software developers to understand the problem and document guidelines and patterns to explain good practice (in the Development view).

Disregard for Network and In-Process Invocation Differences

Modern computing technology provides the option of distributing a system across a number of machines and accessing resources located anywhere on the network. Such distribution is a major feature of many modern informa-tion systems. In fact, much of today's information systems technology aims to allow the location of deployed elements to be changed after they have been developed.

It is easy to accidentally ignore the performance differences between in-voking operations locally within an address space (process), between two processes on one machine, and between processes on machines located an immense distance apart. In reality, the response times of these different situa-tions can differ by an order of magnitude or more.

If you ignore this critical distinction, you run the risk of extremely un-pleasant performance surprises when you deploy the system and find that one or more of your critical interelement interactions is ten times slower than you had assumed due to the locations of key system elements.

RISK REDUCTION

- Consider interelement distribution and possible remote invocation as part of your fundamental architecture definition process.
- Make sure that the locations of elements and their interelement invocation costs are accurately reflected in your performance model to allow you to take possible invocation latencies into account.

CHECKLISTS

Checklist for Requirements Capture

- Have you identified approved performance targets, at a high level at least, with key stakeholders?
- Have you considered targets for both response time and throughput?
- Do your targets distinguish between observed performance (i.e., synchronous tasks) and actual performance (i.e., taking asynchronous activity into account)?
- Have you assessed your performance targets for reasonableness?
- Have you appropriately set expectations among your stakeholders of what is feasible in your architecture?
- Have you defined all performance targets within the context of a particular load on the system?

Checklist for Architecture Definition

- Have you identified the major potential performance problems in your architecture?
- Have you performed enough testing and analysis to understand the likely performance characteristics of your system?
- Do you know what workload your system can process? Have you prioritized the different classes of work?
- Do you know how far your proposed architecture can be scaled without major changes?
- Have you identified the performance-related assumptions you have made (and validated them if needed)?
- Have you reviewed your architecture for common performance pitfalls?

FURTHER READING

You can find a very practical yet thorough tutorial on the process of performance engineering for real systems in a book written by two well-known and widely regarded specialists in the field [SMIT02]. We have found this book very useful, and it has influenced much of our thinking in this area. A number of our performance pitfalls are similar to performance antipatterns in this book (particularly their God Class, Circuitous Treasure Hunt, One-Lane Bridge, and Excessive Dynamic Allocation), and this book provides valuable advice on recognizing and avoiding these problems.

Another comprehensive, if rather more daunting, explanation of performance engineering focuses on its quantitative aspects [JAIN91]. This book contains more information on statistical and simulation-based performance engineering than most of us will ever be able to apply, but it presents comprehensive explanations of a number of very usable techniques.

Two examples of practical, technology-focused performance books are Wise [WISE97] and Killelea [KILL98]. The first provides a lot of hands-on information on how to solve (and avoid) performance problems in distributed systems. The second focuses on Web-based systems and provides good examples of how to consider performance work for such systems.

Finally, if you'd like to check what Moore's Law really says, Intel makes it available via its Web site at www.intel.com/research/silicon/mooreslaw.htm.

26

THE AVAILABILITY AND RESILIENCE PERSPECTIVE

Desired Quality	The ability of the system to be fully or partly operational as and when required and to effectively handle failures that could affect system availability
Applicability	Any system that has complex or extended availability requirements, complex recovery processes, or a high profile (e.g., is visible to the public)
Concerns	Classes of service, planned downtime, unplanned downtime, time to repair, and disaster recovery
Activities	Capture the availability requirements, produce the availability schedule, estimate platform availability, estimate functional availability, assess against the requirements, and rework the architecture
Architectural Tactics	Select fault-tolerant hardware, use hardware clustering and load balancing, log transactions, apply software availability solutions, select or create fault-tolerant software, and identify backup and disaster recovery solutions
Problems and Pitfalls	Single point of failure, overambitious availability requirements, ineffective error detection, overlooked global availability requirements, and incompatible technologies

In the traditional data processing model of system availability, computers supported the mainstream business of the organization during the day (typically 9 A.M. to 5:30 P.M., Monday through Friday) by capturing orders, cash withdrawals, or other sorts of transactions. Then the computers reverted to batch mode during the night to perform tasks such as reconciliation, consolidation, and exchange of information with other systems.

Although we still see this model in some organizations, in recent years there has been a significant change in the way that most companies carry out their business, driven to a large extent by the Internet and the global operations of large organizations. The business day has in general become longer, often extending into the weekend (the traditional preserve of huge, long-running batch jobs), and near-continuous operation has become the norm in many places.

Today's requirement for many systems, therefore, is to be available for much, if not all, of the twenty-four hour cycle. With the improved reliability of hardware and, to a lesser extent, software, many expect that failures will be few and far between and that, where these do occur, recovery will be prompt, effective, and largely automated. As the large number of Web-site failures in the early years of Internet e-commerce showed, any system exposed directly to your customers must be up and running—if it isn't, your company's reputation will suffer.

This business environment means that getting your availability characteristics wrong can be very expensive. However, increased online availability comes at a cost, whether in terms of more hardware, increased software sophistication, or redundancy in your telecommunications network.

The Availability and Resilience perspective is important to any system that has complex availability and resilience requirements, is visible to the public in any way, or is complicated enough to warrant special analysis of recovery techniques.

APPLICABILITY TO VIEWS

Table 26–1 shows how the Availability and Resilience perspective affects each of the views we discussed in Part III.

CONCERNS

The fundamental concern of this perspective is system availability: the proportion of time that the system is up and running and available to provide a service to users. However, availability is a bit more complex than it first appears, as we'll discuss in the following subsections.

Classes of Service

When thinking about downtime, you don't need to restrict yourself to a binary available/unavailable model of service. It is often appropriate to consider different levels of service, ranging over a spectrum from full service to none.

TABLE 26-1 APPLICABILITY OF THE AVAILABILITY AND RESILIENCE PERSPECTIVE TO THE SIX VIEWS

View	Applicability
Functional	Availability is a key concern to user and acquirer stakeholders because it may impact the business's ability to operate effectively. Functional changes may sometimes be needed to support availability requirements, such as the ability to operate in an offline mode when a communications network is unavailable.
Information	A key availability consideration is the set of processes and systems for backup and recovery. Systems must be backed up in such a way that they can be recovered in a reasonable amount of time if a disaster occurs. Backups should not impact online availability, or if they do, they may need to be scheduled to occur outside the online day.
Concurrency	Features such as hardware replication and failover in your system may imply changes or enhancements to your concurrency model.
Development	Your approach to achieving availability may impose design constraints on the software modules. For example, all subsystems may have to support start, stop, pause, and restart commands to align with your failover strategy.
Deployment	Availability and resilience can have a big impact on the deployment environment. Availability requirements may mandate a fault-tolerant production environment (i.e., one in which each hardware component is duplicated and failover is automatic) or a separate disaster recovery site that can be quickly activated if the production site goes down. You may also need special software to support hardware redundancy or clustering.
Operational	Processes and mechanisms to allow the identification and recovery of problems in the production environment may be required. There may also be a need for geographically separate disaster recovery facilities. Processes for main site failover, network failover, and data recovery must be designed, tested, and implemented. If the standby site is physically remote from the production site—as it usually is—processes are also required to move production staff from one location to the other or to deploy suitably trained staff at the standby site.

EXAMPLE Consider a self-service banking system that allows users to manage their bank accounts at automated teller machines (ATMs). The ATM communicates in real time with a central computer that maintains information on the customers' accounts. *Full service* implies that customers can query balances and enter all supported types of transactions, and *no service* means that no inquiries or transactions can be done.

From time to time, the communications network between the ATM and the host computer may fail, may be switched off for maintenance, or may suffer from poor response due to heavy usage. When the network is unavailable or unresponsive, local processing could be carried out on the ATM without reference to the host, allowing the system to offer partial services, such as:

- Restricting users to balance inquiries only
- Restricting transactions to those below a certain limit
- Requiring increased time to carry out transactions
- Restricting users to deposits only

Although any system unavailability is usually undesirable, it may be easier (and probably considerably cheaper) to offer only restricted service during slack times of operation, rather than attempting a solution that offers full service for long periods.

Planned Downtime

In practice, all computer systems require occasional downtime in order to install new or repaired hardware, install operating system or software upgrades, or carry out offline tasks such as backup or data verification.

We call such unavailability *planned downtime* because it occurs according to a predetermined schedule that aligns with the broader requirements of the business. Planned downtime usually occurs overnight or at weekends because the need to access many systems is less at these times.

It's usually possible to make fairly accurate estimates of the length of time such tasks take and the frequency with which they need to be done, so you can usually make reasonable predictions about planned downtime.

Unplanned Downtime

Unplanned downtime, on the other hand, occurs because of a hardware or software fault that renders the system unusable. A CPU or disk may fail, network connectivity may be lost, the operating system may crash, or the application may suffer an error from which it cannot recover.

Compared with planned downtime, it's much harder to predict the time and frequency of unplanned downtime—especially downtime due to software failures. However, most systems suffer from unplanned downtime to a lesser or greater extent, and your analysis must account for this. In particular, if downtime is protracted, you may need to establish contingency procedures (manual or semiautomated) to allow business to continue.

Time to Repair

Failure, of course, is only half of the problem as far as availability is concerned; the other half is how long it takes to rectify the fault.

For hardware, this usually involves swapping out a faulty component with a working one and restarting the affected part of the system. For disks and other persistent storage, you need to add the time required to restore from backup the data that was on the disk. The time required to repair software is harder to quantify. An immediate "repair" may be as simple as restarting the affected part of the system; however, ensuring that the problem does not happen again may be much more complex. Fixing the software itself may involve conducting forensic analysis of the fault; designing, building, and testing the fix; deploying it; and dealing with any lost or damaged data.

Disaster Recovery

If a critical system fails entirely or the physical operational environment becomes unavailable (e.g., due to fire), an entire disaster recovery process may be required in order to restore service. Disaster recovery can involve the recreation of the entire system environment, including the hardware, communication network, and software platform as well as the system's own application software and data.

> **EXAMPLE** One of us did a study of system availability in the late 1980s for a major U.K. bank. The bank analyzed its reliance on systems and concluded that if it were to lose its main system (which managed all of the bank's retail accounts), it would go out of business within three days. For this reason, the bank invested in a separate (and very expensive) standby mainframe computer, solely for the purpose of switching over should the main production computer become unavailable.

In our example, the standby mainframe was kept idle in constant anticipation of catastrophe. In reality, it is more common to find standby machines being used for development, testing, training, or some other nonessential activity. However it is done, disaster recovery forms an essential part of any model of service availability. Disasters such as flood or fire are, fortunately, rare, but their impacts can be catastrophic.

Although the system's runtime environment can be replaced, data can't, so your model must also consider how you will recover data in the event of a disaster. You must determine how much data, if any, the business can afford to lose in the event of a disaster and how long it can survive while data is being recovered or repaired.

Many organizations have realized that service availability depends not just on the availability of an operational computing platform but also on the availability of staff, information, a working environment, and an internal and external communications infrastructure. This has developed into the idea of *business continuity*, which extends the system availability concept right into the organization to include people, places, and infrastructure. A discussion of this topic, important as it is, is outside the scope of this book, but we suggest some other books that cover this area in the Further Reading section at the end of this chapter.

ACTIVITIES: APPLYING THE AVAILABILITY AND RESILIENCE PERSPECTIVE

The activity diagram in Figure 26–1 illustrates a simple process for applying the Availability and Resilience perspective. In this section, we describe the activities in this process.

Capture the Availability Requirements

Ideally, your set of availability requirements was defined earlier as part of the system requirements process, but often this isn't the case. If you have the requirements already, you need to analyze, understand, and validate them; if not, you need to capture them as well. In either case, you must work with the stakeholders to understand and validate the system's availability requirements, categorizing them by class of service.

NOTATION A simple text-and-tables approach is usually the most effective and straightforward way to capture availability requirements.

ACTIVITIES
Identify the Types of Services Offered. Consider each of the services your system offers its users. Classify the services into groups based on their criticality to the system users' productivity.

Define the Levels of Services. For each type of service identified, define the availability required in terms of when the service is needed and whether or not all of its functions are necessary. If possible, identify one or more levels of degraded service that are still useful (e.g., if normal service involves placing an order and confirming a delivery date, a degraded level of service, where the order is placed but a delivery date is not available, might still be useful).

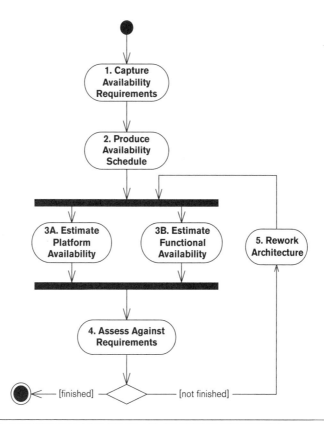

FIGURE 26-1 APPLYING THE AVAILABILITY AND RESILIENCE PERSPECTIVE

Define the Operational Service Levels. Based on the levels of service you aim to provide for each of your service types, define the set of operational service levels that the system as a whole will provide. This involves defining what services need to be available during normal operation and the possible levels of degraded operational availability. Work with the stakeholders to make sure that the levels of service specified are useful to them.

Produce the Availability Schedule

Based on the availability requirements you have validated with your stakeholders, create an availability schedule that defines when the different system services need to be available and any periods when services are not required (and so may not be available).

NOTATION You can present the availability schedule in a number of ways, the key being to use an approach that interested stakeholders can immediately comprehend. Here we list a few techniques we have found to be effective.

- *Text and tables*: The simplest way to represent an availability schedule is just as a set of tabular entries with textual annotations about when services are and are not required.
- *Graphical notations*: As an alternative to plain text and tables, you can represent availability schedules very effectively by using Gantt charts or similar diagrams (see Figure 26–2).

ACTIVITIES

Identify Normal Operational Availability. For each of the system's service types, work with the stakeholders to identify when this service is normally required. Make sure this includes seasonal availability, when the system may be needed at certain times of year but not at others (e.g., public holidays).

Identify Possible Unavailability. Attempt to identify regular times when services are definitely not required (e.g., weekends). These periods should be marked on the availability schedule as potential unavailability and are useful for scheduling workload that could otherwise reduce system availability if run during normal operational periods.

Estimate Platform Availability

In order to understand the potential availability of your system, you need a reasonably accurate estimate of the availability that your underlying hard-

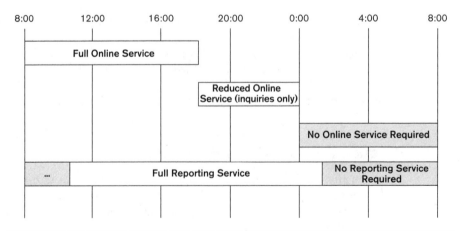

FIGURE 26–2 GANTT CHART OF A REQUIRED AVAILABILITY SCHEDULE

ware and software platform can provide. This measure is the maximum theoretical availability of your system (before operational constraints are applied, which will reduce availability further).

NOTATION Estimation of platform availability results in a set of statistical measures typically recorded as text and tables, although this information can also be useful for augmenting UML models in the Deployment view with availability information.

ACTIVITIES

Create the System Availability Model. You can predict (and therefore measure) availability by using some basic statistics. Availability models consider system availability on a component-by-component basis and usually consolidate these into an overall availability figure for the system as a whole.

Availability is defined as follows:

$$\text{availability} = \frac{\text{time the system is available}}{\text{elapsed time}}$$

Availability metrics are usually expressed as percentages, such as 99.99%, which represents a downtime of just under an hour a year, or 99.999%, a downtime of 5 minutes a year. (These two values are often shortened to the terms *four nines* and *five nines*, respectively.) A system that is available from 9 A.M. to 5 P.M., Monday to Friday, for example, has an availability of 40 hours/168 hours, or about 24%.

Unavailability is the converse of availability:

$$\text{unavailability} = \frac{\text{time the system is unavailable}}{\text{elapsed time}}$$

And, obviously:

$$\text{availability} + \text{unavailability} = 100\%$$

For hardware, it is possible to use published *mean time between failures* (MTBF, sometimes known as *mean time before fault*) measures to estimate how often failures are likely to occur. MTBF is defined as follows:

$$\text{MTBF} = \frac{\text{elapsed time}}{\text{number of failures}}$$

Mean time to repair (MTTR) is defined as the average time taken to repair a fault once notified and may be available from hardware manufacturers (or from supplier service-level agreements).

You can combine MTBF and MTTR to estimate hardware availability as follows:

$$\text{hardware availability} = \frac{\text{MTBF}}{\text{MTBF} + \text{MTTR}}$$

You may also be able to obtain reliability data to perform the same sort of calculation for your operating systems and middleware (where "repair" in this case is usually the same as "restart").

Using these formulas and the content of your Deployment view, it is reasonably straightforward to derive predicted measures of hardware (and perhaps system software) availability, although it is often difficult to predict the number of failures for an average site. When combining metrics for multiple components, you can use the rule that the system is only as available as its least-available component.

Unfortunately, there are rarely any reliable metrics that allow you to come up with meaningful estimates for application software availability, except for the most established and unchanging applications. This reason for this is that software doesn't fail according to established failure models, which are based on the degradation of physical materials and assume failure isolation. Software fails because it has to cope with unexpected conditions that it was not designed or tested to meet, and worse still, you cannot assume that software failures are isolated. These failures are much harder to predict and require quite different models to characterize them accurately.

However, if you want to try to produce a model of application software availability, you can attempt one by using the models in the Functional, Concurrency, and Deployment views as primary inputs. A number of books provide tutorials on software reliability modeling (see the Further Reading section for suggestions).

When estimating availability, try to present the results in terms of classes of service, for example, "Full service available 95%, at least restricted service available 99.9%." This involves looking at component usage by different types of functionality. (Such information is available primarily from your Functional view.)

Note that your availability model may have some subtleties, especially if the architecture is complex or the unavailability of some internal components of the architecture does not impact the perceived availability of the system as a whole.

EXAMPLE   A bank provides ISDN access for its larger branches and analog dial-up access for smaller or more remote branches. The bank's teller systems are built in such a way that they can work offline if the connection to the central server (which maintains the latest transaction and balance information) goes down for a short period of time.

> The perceived availability of this system, from the perspective of tellers and customers, is high, even though the underlying network may not be particularly robust.

Create the Incident Recovery Analysis. Consider the likely incidents that could affect your system's availability. For each, define the failure that could occur, its impact, the remedial actions to be taken, and the likely time needed to rectify the situation.

 EXAMPLE Table 26–2 shows an example of incident recovery analysis.

TABLE 26–2 INCIDENT RECOVERY SCENARIOS

Incident	Impact	Remedial Action	Time to Repair
Hardware (nondisk) failure	Reduced availability (throughput affected)	Replace the faulty component, and possibly reconfigure the hardware or the operating system	1 hour
Disk failure	Total unavailability (service offline)	Replace the faulty disk, and possibly recover data from backup and/or other means	6 hours including restore
Nontransient network failure	Temporary service outage, in-flight transactions aborted, some loss of throughput when using backup network	Switch over to standby network, possibly with reduced bandwidth	5 minutes
Operating system crash	Temporary service outage, normal availability within 5–10 minutes	Reboot; although crash may be symptomatic of some other problem (such as faulty memory or disk) that needs to be addressed	5 minutes for reboot
Data corruption	Affected accounts and transactions unavailable, failure of end-of-period reconciliation	Recover data from backup and possibly other means (such as replaying transaction logs)	6 hours
Application software failure	Variable, from temporary outage (10 minutes) to total outage due to corruption	Restart, depending on the application and the nature of the failure; may be necessary also to recover data in some way	Not quantified

Note that transient failures (e.g., the transient loss of a network connection) are not usually considered in this analysis, although it may be necessary to accommodate these in your architecture (e.g., by automatically reconnecting when the network becomes available again).

You may find it useful to walk through some scenarios to validate this analysis. Once the system is developed, you should thoroughly test the remedial actions specified to ensure that they actually work.

Estimate Functional Availability

Estimating the maximum likely availability of your underlying implementation platform provides you with an upper bound on the possible availability of your system. However, it is likely that the system design will impose further unavailability in the guise of planned downtime. Many information systems require some periods when the system cannot provide full operational service because of the need to perform internal processing (such as reconciliation, data maintenance, backups, summary and report processing, and so on).

In order to understand the level of functional availability your system can offer, draw up a functional availability schedule by working through the operational cycle of the system and identifying the periods of operation when the design of the system means that normal service cannot be provided.

You can create this new schedule by starting with the required availability schedule prepared previously and augmenting it with the system operations that may impact availability. Where possible, schedule these operations in the periods when the required availability schedule indicates that normal services are not needed.

NOTATION Representing functional availability involves capturing the periods during which different aspects of your system will be available. Here are a couple of techniques we have found effective for achieving this.

- *Text and tables*: The simplest way to represent the system's functional availability is as a set of tabular entries with textual annotations explaining the level of availability that can be provided in each period.

- *Graphical notations*: A graphical notation such as a Gantt chart (see Figure 26–3) is an effective alternative to a tabular presentation.

ACTIVITIES

Design the Functional Availability Schedule. If systems have planned downtime or periods of reduced availability (e.g., to support overnight batch runs), you should draw up schedules to model the offline activity. These will be driven partly by requirements determined by stakeholders (users, opera-

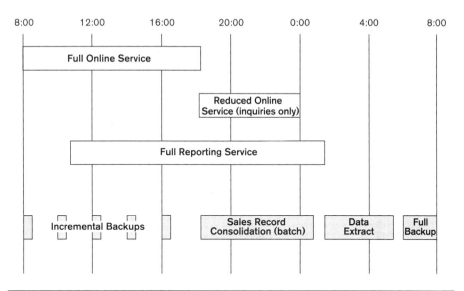

FIGURE 26–3 GANTT CHART OF A FUNCTIONAL AVAILABILITY SCHEDULE

tions staff, and so on), as captured in your Operational view, and partly by what is technically feasible for your architecture, as reflected in your Functional, Information, and Concurrency views.

For the online day periods, availability criteria are typically driven by the business's need to serve its customers. Online day schedules such as 9 A.M. to 5 P.M. or 8 A.M. to 6 P.M. are common. You also need to consider weekends and holiday periods, when availability may be curtailed (or possibly extended). For the overnight batch run, the most important consideration is whether all batch jobs can be completed during the overnight batch window.

For applications that aim for near 24-hour availability, it is rare to offer a full level of service throughout the period. Although you can never be certain that there won't be a customer who wants to buy one of your widgets at 3 A.M., the impact of a reduced level of service during these times is not usually severe. Your analysis needs to balance the costs of very high availability against the benefits it provides. The final decision will usually be made by your acquirer stakeholders.

Define the normal working day in consultation with your users, resisting the temptation to extend this longer than necessary—the longer the working day, the less time available for overnight batch processing (if applicable). When sizing the batch window, consider the worst-case elapsed times, which usually occur at period start or end (the start or end of the month, quarter, financial year, and so on).

Assess against the Requirements

There are two aspects to assessing your architecture against its availability requirements. First, ensure that the overall level of availability you can achieve is acceptable in the context of the system's requirements. Second, ensure that no particular availability risks are unacceptable even when the overall level of availability is sufficient.

If this assessment suggests that your architecture provides sufficient availability, you're done applying this perspective. Otherwise, if the overall level of availability is too low or there appear to be specific availability risks that are too high to be acceptable, the process continues with the next step, reworking the architecture to address the availability limitations in the current architecture.

NOTATION You can easily capture any outputs of this step by using text and tables, without resorting to special-purpose notations.

ACTIVITIES

Combine the Platform and Functional Availability Estimates. Combine the platform and functional availability estimates you created in the previous steps to arrive at an overall estimate for your system's availability. The functional availability figure provides you with an estimate of the routine availability of your system, while the platform availability estimate indicates how much unavailability you need to factor in due to unexpected technology failures.

If your functional availability estimate suggests 2 hours of downtime per day (meaning a functional availability of about 91.5%) and your platform availability suggests the loss of 6 days per year to technology failures (giving a platform availability of 98.3%), the overall system availability will be about 90% ($.915 \times .983 = .899$).

Identify Particular Availability Risks. Review the outputs of the platform and functional availability assessments, and review any particular situations you identified that could result in particularly acute availability risks. Things to watch for are situations where particularly long periods of unavailability can occur and situations where the impact of the unavailability is particularly significant (e.g., just after a new product launch or at the end of the financial year). Highlight these particularly significant availability risks, and ensure that they are acceptable to your stakeholders.

Rework the Architecture

If the architecture does not provide sufficient availability to meet the system's requirements, you will need to rework aspects of it to increase the availability it can offer. This is likely to center on the Deployment view (where you can add technological availability solutions) and the Functional and Information views (where you can modify the system's design to increase the amount of functional availability the system can offer).

NOTATION The notations used for this activity are the same ones used in the existing models for each view you're modifying.

ACTIVITIES

Reduce Functional Unavailability. Identify each of the features of the architecture that were found to cause a reduction in system availability during the assessment of functional availability. Consider addressing each one by reducing the amount of unavailability (e.g., by reducing or parallelizing tasks) or eliminating unavailability where possible (e.g., using replicated data as input to summary processing). For each, attempt to assess the cost of reducing the availability against the amount of extra availability achieved and, to keep costs under control, implement only those with the most favorable ratios.

Reduce Technology Unavailability. Work through the Deployment view to identify those parts of the deployment environment that are single points of failure and so could reduce the system's availability if they fail. For each failure point found, identify a possible solution (such as fault-tolerant hardware or high-availability clustering) that could eliminate that failure point. Again, balance the cost of the solution against the likelihood and impact of the failure, and select those solutions that give the greatest benefit at the lowest cost.

ARCHITECTURAL TACTICS

Select Fault-Tolerant Hardware

Fault-tolerant computing platforms can continue to operate without interruption even if a hardware component fails. These are typically implemented by means of redundant or duplicated hardware: each component—CPU, memory, disk, I/O port, and so on—is deployed in pairs, and if one of the pair fails, the other continues to operate while the fault is analyzed and the faulty part repaired or replaced. Such platforms, although expensive, deliver a very high level of system availability and often allow hardware upgrades to be performed while the system is online.

Redundant disk architectures (such as RAID[1] or mirrored disks) are a particularly common example. As shown in Figure 26–4, disk writes are applied to

---

1. RAID (Redundant Array of Inexpensive or Independent Disks) architectures are available in a variety of configurations, known as RAID levels, which variously provide resilience through mirroring, improved performance through striping, and/or error correction.

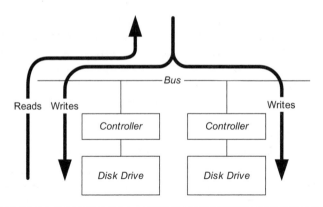

FIGURE 26–4 MIRRORED STORAGE HARDWARE

each side of the mirror, whereas reads come from only one side (or in some configurations, whichever side can return the information with the least amount of head movement). If either disk fails, the other can continue on its own until the faulty disk is replaced and resynchronized.

If you are deploying a fault-tolerant platform, remember that availability is only as good as your weakest component. Don't forget to include routers and networks, terminals, PCs, printers, tape drives, and so on in your availability analysis. Where fault-tolerant solutions do not exist for these components, you may have to develop strategies of your own (e.g., standby printing facilities).

Use Hardware Clustering and Load Balancing

High-availability clustering is a technique for protecting against failures by mirroring the whole computer rather than just a disk. In a clustered configuration, two or more identical computers (referred to as *nodes*) are deployed in parallel and share the total workload between them. If any one of the nodes fails, one of the remaining nodes takes over its workload and processing can continue (although the transactions in progress at the failed node may have to be resubmitted). This process is known as *failover*.

A variety of different clustering configurations are available, depending on how the nodes are connected to shared resources, such as memory, disk, and the communications network, and what failover scenarios are supported. Whatever approach you choose, incoming transactions must be allocated to one of the nodes. A technique called *load balancing* performs this allocation and helps ensure that the nodes are used to their fullest possible extent. Load balancing can be provided via hardware or (less commonly) software. Figure 26–5 illustrates an example configuration, where requests are load balanced between a

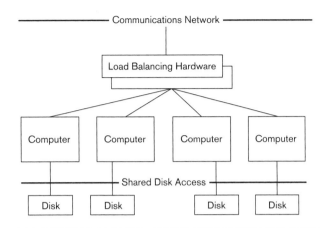

FIGURE 26–5 HIGH-AVAILABILITY CLUSTER

number of clustered nodes with shared disks to allow failover in case of node failure.

Clustering typically requires enhancements to the operating systems, middleware, and application programs that run on them. Special software is also required to manage the cluster. Some types of clusters (scalable clusters) can also be used to enhance performance due to their ability to reduce contention via replication (as we describe in Chapter 25).

Log Transactions

While it may be possible to recover some lost data from backups, that may not be the end of the story. For a number of reasons, backups may not bring data back to the state it was in at the point of failure.

- Backups may have been made only daily or periodically during the day, so the most recent transactions may not be included in the backup.

- It may be necessary to restore multiple databases to a consistent point in time, to maintain cross-database data integrity.

- An up-to-the-minute backup may be available but may have become corrupt due to a fault in the database storage mechanism in use.

In such scenarios, it is extremely useful to have a separate transaction log that can be replayed into the recovered database to bring it completely up-to-date, as shown in Figure 26–6. Such a capability may be provided by the storage mechanism, by front-end applications, or by underlying transaction management software; or you may have to develop it yourself.

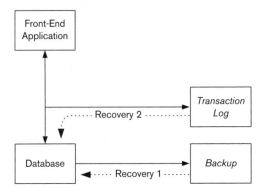

FIGURE 26-6 POINT-IN-TIME RECOVERY WITH A TRANSACTION LOG

An added benefit of such transaction logging is that you can use it to provide an audit trail.

Apply Software Availability Solutions

Fault-tolerant hardware platforms do not deliver *software* fault tolerance: They are just as vulnerable as ordinary platforms to operating system crashes or application failures. Safety-critical systems, such as aircraft guidance systems, achieve software fault tolerance by multiplexing software solutions (i.e., independently writing the application several times and employing a real-time "voting" system to compare the outputs of the different versions, allowing inconsistencies between them to be identified). However, the costs of delivering this level of sophistication mean that it is usually not appropriate or affordable for more mainstream architectures.

This said, you do still need to develop effective strategies to ensure the reliability and recoverability of your software. While this can be considered a design rather than an architectural issue, it has some architecturally significant aspects, such as:

- A robust strategy for data validation and dealing with rejected data
- A common strategy for detecting, logging, and responding to software errors
- A service to which error messages are logged and from which alerts and errors can be trapped
- The recording of full diagnostic information to help in subsequent analysis and repair

Select or Create Fault-Tolerant Software

Software can also be written to reconfigure itself in response to changing conditions, for example, by allocating itself more resources (such as shared memory) when under load or by automatically disabling certain features if they malfunction and offering only partial service until the problem is rectified. Such technology is still in its relative infancy in mainstream information system development but has been investigated widely by researchers and is appearing in some operating systems and infrastructure software. You can also use these approaches within your own application software to provide a degree of resilience where required.

EXAMPLE A desktop application reads from a preferences file when it starts up in order to restore the user's preferences for presentation (color, font, and so on). If this preferences file is not present, or if it has become damaged or corrupted, the application reverts to a standard, default configuration and creates a clean version of the preferences file.

Identify Backup and Disaster Recovery Solutions

Every system that manages persistent information (i.e., information that must be stored on stable storage and available across system restarts) must include mechanisms for backing up this information by writing it to a separate storage medium from which the information can be recovered in the case of system failure (particularly, disk failure).

Traditionally, some form of magnetic tape was used for backup, but this method suffers from several constraints: the speed at which data can be written to the backup media, the amount of information a single tape can store, and the reliability of the media. A backup that takes eighteen hours and requires two hundred tapes will be cumbersome and prone to failure.

High-volume backups are often done to disk, for example, over a very high speed local or wide area network. An alternative solution is to deploy mirrored data disks, unmirroring them temporarily while the backup is done, as shown in Figure 26–7.

While the first mirroring architectures placed the disks physically near one another, you can now mirror onto disks at another location, possibly many miles away, by means of high-bandwidth, highly reliable fiber-optic networks. Such a distributed mirroring solution, while expensive, can also form part of your disaster recovery architecture.

Most backup systems can perform online backups, that is, they can back up data while the system continues to run (with an acceptable degradation in

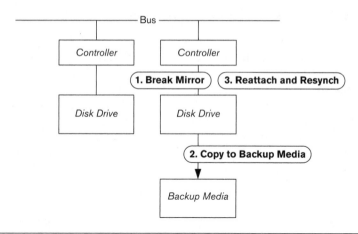

FIGURE 26–7 MIRRORING FOR AVAILABILITY

online performance). Others require that the system be taken down in order to perform the backup; if this applies to your situation, you will need to factor this into your recovery plans.

Any backup solution must maintain the transactional integrity of the data so that, when the data is restored, it is left in a transactionally consistent state. We discuss this issue further in Chapter 17.

PROBLEMS AND PITFALLS

Single Point of Failure

A system is only as reliable as its least-reliable component. A *single point of failure* is an individual element in an architecture that, if it fails, causes the whole architecture to fail.

EXAMPLE It is common to improve reliability by deploying mirrored disk configurations of the sort that we described earlier. This is a sensible precaution; disks contain mechanical parts, so they are more prone to failure than other hardware components.

However, in some mirrored configurations, the disk pairs share a common controller (the device that connects the disk to the main computer bus). If a controller fails, access to each disk in the pair is lost. The reliability of the controller thus becomes the key determinant of the reliability of the disk architecture.

The presence of a single point of failure can critically undermine the reliability of the system as a whole.

Risk Reduction

- Analyze your architectural models, particularly your Functional and Deployment views, for the presence of any single points of failure. If you find any, determine whether it is cost-effective to enhance these (perhaps by hardware duplication) to improve reliability.

Overambitious Availability Requirements

Availability schedules are, of course, driven by the needs of the business. However, like performance requirements, they usually require a tradeoff between necessity and cost. Increasing the length of the online day, for example, reduces the length of the overnight batch; this may necessitate more powerful hardware, or more sophisticated batch systems or scheduling, to complete the overnight batch run.

Many systems, particularly ones that provide services over the Internet, aim for 24/7 availability. This means that the system is never allowed to go down, ever—not even for maintenance or for software or operating system upgrades. This is extremely difficult to achieve and extremely expensive, even with today's very high availability computing platforms.

Risk Reduction

- Validate your high-availability requirements carefully (in particular, challenge requests for 24/7 operation if you hear them). Make sure these requirements are backed by a business need.
- Where high availability really is needed, make sure that your proposed technology platforms are suitable (and supported) for this degree of reliability.
- Make your stakeholders (particularly acquirers) aware of the costs of high availability to encourage them to set requirements at a realistic level.
- Tie any third parties into clear, quantitative service-level agreements to ensure that they do not affect your availability.

Ineffective Error Detection

In most systems, more code is devoted to trapping and dealing with errors than to implementing core functionality. It is tempting, especially if there are time pressures, to skimp on error handling, but this can be disastrous in the long run.

EXAMPLE A system collects information on ticket bookings from a number of airlines for the purpose of allocating to customers the bonus points that can be exchanged for free flights. Unfortunately, one of the routines that calculates the point values returns an error code that is not checked. This routine is failing because of a programming error, so customers are not being credited with points they are due.

Eventually, a customer complains that her point values have not been calculated correctly, and a large-scale corruption of data in the database is discovered. The system administrator attempts to restore the database from backup, but because the routine has been failing for a long time, all of the backups are corrupt as well.

The only solution to this situation is to fix the data in the database directly and to eventually write special programs to retrieve the booking information and recalculate the data in the whole database.

Your error-handling strategy (or lack of it) has a wide impact on your system, so you need to clearly define a strategy in the Development view.

RISK REDUCTION

- Define a clear, system-wide error-handling strategy that provides enough information for your availability needs.
- Define design standards for error handling such as the following.
  - All actions that can return an error are checked for success and failure.
  - When errors occur in a low-level routine, they are reported upward to the caller.
  - All errors are logged.
  - At the top level, any reported error is either fixed by the program (e.g., by retrying) or causes a user-visible halt.
- Capture error-handling strategy and standards as part of your Development view to ensure that error detection and handling is implemented consistently throughout the system.

Overlooked Global Availability Requirements

Any system that has global reach may need to be available around the clock.

EXAMPLE A foreign-exchange trading system is used by traders in Hong Kong, London, and New York. As the trading day is coming to an end in Hong Kong, it is starting in London, and a few hours later, it

> starts in New York. By the time New York trading has closed, the next day's trading is due to start in Hong Kong again.
>
> However, the system design mandates an end-of-day consolidation run, during which trading cannot take place. It is not possible to fit this run into the timetable at any point because the system is always being used by someone.

Although your system may not have global reach now, you should explore with your stakeholders whether the system might go global in the future. If so, you will save a lot of time by building in some high-availability features now.

RISK REDUCTION

- If required, take a global perspective when considering the availability of your system (also see the discussion of the Location perspective in Chapter 28).
- Where continuous uptime is a real requirement, reflect this in your architecture as early and visibly as possible.
- Confirm that your main architectural solutions are compatible with global needs (such as adding hardware to allow the transfer of processing between different servers to "follow the sun").

Incompatible Technologies

Many high-availability solutions have some specific requirements related to the software that will run on them. For example, a database or application server that caches information in shared memory may need to be redesigned to work in a clustered environment where each computer has its own cache.

Unless your software elements have been specifically written to run on such platforms, you may find that they perform badly or just won't work at all. It is particularly important that you make sure that all of the different pieces of third-party software work together perfectly. If they don't, it is very unlikely that they will work correctly during a failover situation.

RISK REDUCTION

- Use supplier data to confirm that your hardware and software elements are compatible with one another.
- If you have any doubt, consider a proof-of-concept, or ask your suppliers to put you in touch with their customers who are running similar configurations.

CHECKLISTS

Checklist for Requirements Capture

- Are availability requirements defined, documented, and approved?
- Are availability requirements driven by business needs?
- Do availability requirements consider different classes of service, if appropriate?
- Do availability requirements strike a realistic balance between cost and business needs?
- Do availability requirements consider online and batch availability?
- Do availability requirements take into account variations such as period end?
- Do availability requirements take into account future changes in business operations such as moving to a longer online day?
- Can availability requirements be met by the chosen hardware and software platform?
- Have you defined strategies for disaster recovery and business continuity?
- Do stakeholders have realistic expectations around unplanned downtime?

Checklist for Architecture Definition

- Does the proposed architectural solution meet the availability requirements? Can this be demonstrated, either theoretically or based on previous practical experience?
- Does the solution consider the time taken to recover from failure, e.g., to restore from backup if necessary?
- Does the backup solution provide for the transactional integrity of restored data?
- Does the backup solution support online backup, with acceptable degradation in performance? If not, is it feasible to take the system down in order to perform backups?
- Has consideration been given to restoring data from corrupt or incomplete backups?
- Will the system respond gracefully to software errors, logging and reporting them appropriately?

- Have you defined a standby site in the architecture, if appropriate? Is the standby site configured identically to the production site, or will it offer reduced performance? If the latter, is this reduced performance acceptable to the users?

- Have you defined and tested mechanisms for switching from production to standby environments? If not, when will you do this?

- Have you assessed the impact of the availability solution on functionality and performance? Is this impact acceptable?

- If high availability is particularly important, have you assessed the architecture for single points of failure and other weaknesses?

- If you developed a fault-tolerant model, does this extend to all vulnerable components (such as disk controllers)?

FURTHER READING

Two IT-oriented books on disaster recovery [HIAT99; TOIG00] explain how to plan for and cope with system disasters from an IT perspective. An alternative view from the business process perspective [BARN01] provides a lot of useful guidance in areas outside computer systems recovery that are still crucial to achieving effective overall disaster recovery.

A number of approaches exist for modeling and predicting software reliability using statistical models. You can find a readable introduction to these approaches in Neufelder [NEUF92], which explains how to create models to predict the reliability of a piece of software, including a comprehensive description of the various theoretical models available. For an alternative opinion, Butler and Finelli [BUTL93] and Whittaker and Voas [WHIT00] discuss problems with software reliability modeling, and the latter (which is the more accessible of the two) suggests factors that new software reliability models should take into account.

You can find a very thorough, practical, and readable discussion of how to create highly available systems using today's mainstream technology in Marcus and Stern [MARC00]. Written for the architect and system administrator, it goes into the practical details of actually getting highly available systems to work. Another book [PIED00] covers similar ground, but from a somewhat less technical perspective.

No list of availability references would be complete without Pfister [PFIS98], a classic, highly readable, and often entertaining tutorial on the technology of cluster computing, addressing both highly available clusters and scalable clusters. This book manages to make a complex and technical area both approachable and comprehensible, providing a thorough overview of the issues, techniques, and technologies involved in achieving clustered systems.

For those wanting more background on the theory and technology of system availability, a large number of references are available. Examples include the very technical review of the techniques used to create fault-tolerant hardware and software technology found in Jain [JAIN91] and the review and tutorial of the current state of the art for achieving fault-tolerant software found in Pullum [PULL01].

27

THE EVOLUTION PERSPECTIVE

Desired Quality	The ability of the system to be flexible in the face of the inevitable change that all systems experience after deployment, balanced against the costs of providing such flexibility
Applicability	Important for all systems to some extent; more important for longer lived and more widely used systems
Concerns	Magnitude of change, dimensions of change, likelihood of change, timescale for change, when to pay for change, development complexity, preservation of knowledge, and reliability of change
Activities	Characterize the evolution needs, assess the current ease of evolution, consider the evolution tradeoffs, and rework the architecture
Architectural Tactics	Contain change, create flexible interfaces, apply change-oriented architectural styles, build variation points into the software, use standard extension points, achieve reliable change, and preserve development environments
Problems and Pitfalls	Prioritization of the wrong dimensions, changes that never happen, impacts of evolution on critical quality properties, lost development environments, and ad hoc release management

A somewhat overused business maxim tells us that the only constant is change, and most software architects can identify strongly with this. The very ability of software to be "soft" means that stakeholders expect a software-based system to be able to evolve very quickly. Couple this expectation with other common factors such as misunderstood requirements, rapid business change, and the effect of actually delivering a system on end-user requirements, and it is easy to see why change is such a major factor in the lives of software architects.

The commonly adopted iterative approach to system delivery can make an ability to deal with change all the more important. When a system is delivered in iterations, its users can start using some parts of it much earlier and thus provide early feedback to the developers. This is an extremely valuable process because it allows requirements to be validated early. However, it also means that there is constant pressure during the delivery cycle to change the system's behavior.

Although, in principle, software is easy to change, experienced software developers agree that this is true only if change is explicitly considered during its development. Software developed without any concern for the changes that will likely be needed can be much harder to change than anyone expects.

We consider the process of dealing with change in the system development lifecycle under the term **evolution**, by which we mean all of the possible types of changes that a system may experience during its lifetime.

The Evolution perspective addresses the concerns related to dealing with evolution during the lifetime of a system and thus is relevant to most large-scale information systems because of the amount of change that most systems need to handle.

APPLICABILITY TO VIEWS

Table 27–1 shows how the Evolution perspective affects each of the views we discussed in Part III.

TABLE 27-1 APPLICABILITY OF THE EVOLUTION PERSPECTIVE TO THE SIX VIEWS

View	Applicability
Functional	If the evolution required is significant, the functional structure will need to reflect this.
Information	If environment or information evolution is needed, a flexible information model will be required.
Concurrency	Evolutionary needs may dictate particular element packaging or some constraints on the concurrency structure (e.g., that it must be very simple).
Development	Evolution requirements may have a significant impact on the development environment that needs to be defined (e.g., enforcing portability guidelines).
Deployment	This perspective rarely has a significant impact on the Deployment view because system evolution usually affects structures described in other views.
Operational	This perspective typically has less impact on the Operational view.

CONCERNS

Magnitude of Change

For some systems, potential changes are limited to defect rectification and minor cosmetic adjustments or tweaks to external interfaces. At the other extreme, some widely used, long-lived systems undergo a continual process of major evolution to meet the changing needs of their environments and are effectively rewritten every few years.

The most difficult problems occur when you expect only the former situation but the latter reality emerges during development or deployment. Such cases are likely to be expensive to remedy because the system will probably be hard to change, and complete redevelopment may be your only practical evolution option.

Dimensions of Change

Different types of evolution require different support in the system's architecture and have different costs and risks associated with them. If you can identify the dimensions of change required, you can narrow your system evolution to a more bounded, tractable problem.

We classify the important dimensions of change as follows.

- *Functional evolution*: This includes any change to the functions that the system provides, from simple defect corrections at one end of the scale to the addition or replacement of entire subsystems at the other.

- *Platform evolution*: Many successful systems need to evolve in terms of the software and hardware platforms on which they are deployed. This can include migrating platforms (e.g., from Windows-based servers to Linux-based servers) as well as extending the platforms the system can use (e.g., porting products to new platforms or extending existing PC-based client platforms to include Web-based access).

- *Environment evolution*: Most information systems need to be integrated with a number of other systems to be useful. This may involve retrieving information from systems on demand, processing the outputs of other systems, or providing information for other systems to process. As these other systems are created, evolve, and are removed, this may put evolution pressures on your system, so that although it does not have to change its functionality, it may need to change the way it integrates with other systems.

Likelihood of Change

It is often easy to identify many types of change that could be needed, but assessing the probability that the changes actually will be required may be much harder. Providing facilities for change in your system adds complexity and expense, so it is important to provide support only for changes that are likely to occur.

Timescale for Change

The likely timescale for the required change is also an important concern. The environment of most systems is changing constantly, which means that assumptions that are true today rarely survive intact over time. The further away the need for a change is, the less likely it is that the change will actually be needed in its currently identified form.

Requirements for changes that have no associated delivery date or a far-off delivery date may be of lower priority than changes with firm, short-term dates attached to them.

When to Pay for Change

There are two main strategies for dealing with changes to your system.

1. Design the most flexible system possible now to make it easy to change later. This is perhaps best characterized by the metasystem approach, where the system's information structure and functions are defined at runtime by configuration data.

2. Create the simplest system possible to meet immediate needs and to meet the challenge of making changes only when you absolutely have to. This is perhaps best characterized by the Extreme Programming (XP) mantras of "Do the simplest thing possible" and "You aren't going to need it," which capture the lesson that trying to guess the future and build the most flexible system possible is an expensive, risky, and complex business.

One of the major differences between these two strategies is when you pay for change. Developing highly flexible systems costs a lot more than developing simple, rigid ones, so the cost of change is loaded to the front of the systems lifecycle if you follow the first strategy. The tradeoff is that you hope these early costs will be paid back by cheap changes later. Developing the simplest system possible costs less up front because the system is simpler and quicker to deliver, but each later change is likely to cost more because you have no existing mechanism for implementing the change.

Getting the balance right between these two extreme positions avoids either wasted early effort or huge change costs later and helps you find a position that minimizes the overall costs of development.

Development Complexity

In nearly all cases, building in support for evolution increases the complexity of a system's design, sometimes by a huge amount. This added complexity costs more to develop (as discussed earlier) and may also bring problems related to system reliability and the time required to deliver early parts of the system. In some cases, complexity can even become an obstacle to system evolution.

Preservation of Knowledge

It is usually fairly obvious how to make changes to a system while it is being built—the people you need are available, knowledge about how the system works is fresh in their minds, and a development environment is available for making and testing the changes. Once the system moves from active development to a more stable deployed state, this may no longer be true.

An important concern for any system is how to preserve the knowledge required to make significant changes to the system as people move to other projects, memories fade, and the available technical environments change.

Reliability of Change

From the simplest bug fix to the most complex subsystem redevelopment, any system change can have a negative impact on the deployed system, so it is essential to have a set of processes and technologies to make this process as reliable as possible.

Automated testing, repeatable and well-understood processes, stable development environments, and effective configuration management are all key factors in addressing this concern as your system evolves.

ACTIVITIES: APPLYING THE EVOLUTION PERSPECTIVE

The activity diagram in Figure 27–1 illustrates a simple process for applying the Evolution perspective. In this section, we describe the activities in this process.

Characterize the Evolution Needs

This step is really one of further requirements analysis, this time to understand the requirements from the perspective of system evolution. The requirements for the system probably focus on what must be delivered, the system's

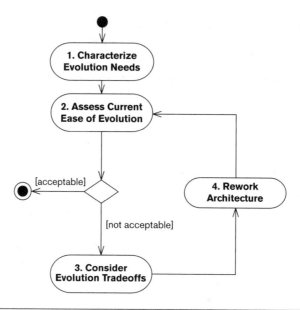

FIGURE 27-1 APPLYING THE EVOLUTION PERSPECTIVE

level of complexity, technical and project constraints, and so on. Now you must go back to the requirements and work out what will likely need to change over time.

You can characterize your evolution needs by using four dimensions.

1. *Type of change required*: Characterize each type of evolution into one of the dimensions described earlier (functional, platform, or environment).

2. *Magnitude of change required*: Establish how much effort each type of evolution will need. Is it just defect correction, or will large-scale, high-risk system changes be required? A useful way to present this is the effort required as a percentage of the initial system development effort.

3. *Likelihood of change*: Assess how likely it is that each of the types of change you have identified will actually be required. This allows you to focus on those that are most likely to occur.

4. *Timescale of required changes*: Are the changes required on an immediate, firm timetable (in effect, a phased delivery)? Or are they vague needs for changes some time in the future depending on external factors (such as system use)?

Evolution requirements often are not explicitly recorded, so you need to infer them from the existing documents and validate them through discussions with key stakeholders. When reading the requirements documents, look for elements such as:

- *Deferred functions*, any parts of the system requirements that explicitly define future extensions, or functions that need not be delivered initially
- *Gaps in requirements*, probably evolution requirements in disguise, which could not be defined initially due to incomplete requirements analysis
- *Vague or undefined requirements*, which indicate this area of the system is not well understood
- *Open-ended requirements*, for example, terms such as "like" or "including" in system requirements definitions, which suggest that extensions similar to the explicitly specified cases will be required

The result of this process should be a list of key evolution requirements for your system, with each characterized by its type, magnitude, and timescale. From this list you can quickly assess the overall importance and nature of the evolution that stakeholders will expect from your system.

To help you decide which requirements to prioritize, rank the requirements in terms of their relative magnitude divided by how many months from now you think they'll be needed. (So, for example, a change with an assigned magnitude of 60 needed in 12 months is allocated a score of 5, while a change with a magnitude of 30 needed in 3 months is allocated a value of 10.) Focus your attention on the top couple of requirements in this list: These are the large changes that are near enough to worry about.

NOTATION A simple text-and-tables approach is usually the most effective and straightforward way to present evolution needs.

ACTIVITIES

Analyze the Requirements. Perform a manual review and analysis of the requirements for your system in order to identify these evolution requirements.

Estimate Effort, Nearness, and Priority. Derive a magnitude for each change and divide it by when you think it will be needed.

Assess the Current Ease of Evolution

For each of the evolution requirements you have identified, work through a scenario of how you would change your system to meet the requirement when it becomes necessary. For each of these scenarios, note how much of the system must change and how difficult and risky the resulting set of changes is.

This assessment allows you to decide whether or not your architecture requires any changes to meet the evolution requirement.

The focus in this step is not to identify all the details of what needs to be done, but rather to assess whether the changes required could be accomplished at reasonable cost during the required timescales.

NOTATION A simple text-based approach is probably sufficient for capturing the results of your assessment.

ACTIVITIES

Assess the Architecture. This step is really a mini architectural evaluation of your system from the perspective of a single quality property (i.e., modifiability). Refer to Chapter 14 for a discussion of architectural assessment.

Perform a Risk Assessment. Given how well (or otherwise) your architecture supports the likely evolution requirements for the system, is this level of risk acceptable enough for your project to go forward?

Consider the Evolution Tradeoffs

If you feel that your architecture needs some changes to support the evolution requirements, consider the options for providing the flexibility you need. The key tradeoff to consider is whether to expend the effort of creating a flexible system during initial development or whether to defer this effort until system changes are actually required. This tradeoff depends very much on the type of system, the likelihood of changes actually being required, and the level of confidence you have about easily making major changes when needed, rather than during initial development.

The result of this step is a strategy for meeting your evolution requirements in terms of how the system will evolve and at what point the support for the evolution will be put into the system.

NOTATION A simple text-based approach is probably sufficient for capturing your strategy for meeting evolution requirements.

ACTIVITIES

Identify the Options. Consider all of the possible approaches to supporting evolution in your system, from doing nothing initially, through designing but not implementing various options, to the development of a fully flexible system from the outset. Assess the architectural impact of each possible option.

Assess the Options. Use a mini architectural assessment to consider which option is right for your system, considering the costs, risks, and priorities of your requirements.

Rework the Architecture

Use the best evolution strategy you identified to make the set of changes necessary for your architecture to support the evolution requirements.

NOTATION Reworking the architecture involves changing the views that describe it, so the notations used are dictated by the views you need to change.

ACTIVITIES
Revise the Architectural Design. Revise your architecture in line with the option(s) you selected in the previous step.

ARCHITECTURAL TACTICS

Contain Change

Typically, dealing with change in a small, well-defined part of your system isn't a problem. For example, changing a single software module to deal with a change to its interface to an external system is usually fairly straightforward. A change starts to be a problem when its effects ripple through a number of different parts of the system simultaneously. (For the interface dimension, for example, if the interface change requires a change to internal system interfaces, this is a much more serious problem than changing the single software module that provides the external interface.)

The architectural challenge is to design a system structure so that the required changes are as contained as possible. Normal sound design practice has a lot to offer in meeting this challenge. The following general design principles can help you localize the effects of change.

- *Encapsulation*: If your system elements are strongly encapsulated with well-defined, flexible interfaces, this will go a long way toward helping you isolate change. In particular, making sure that the internal data structures within your system elements are not visible to their callers helps keep those callers isolated from changes that need to be made within an element.

- *Separation of concerns*: Giving each of your system elements a clear and distinct set of responsibilities helps ensure that a change related to one aspect of your system affects only one element. Conversely, if the responsibilities of your system elements are not clear or a number of elements are involved in each part of the system's operation, most changes are likely to affect a large number of pieces of the system and thus will be expensive and risky to implement.

- *Single point of definition*: Make sure that all data types, values, configurations, and so on are defined only once. This prevents a change to, for example, a system data structure or interface value limit resulting in changes to a number of different parts of the system.

The real trick when containing change is being able to predict which types of changes will need to be contained in which locations. Of course, there is no magic way to do this; the best solution is early analysis.

Create Flexible Interfaces

When designing the main internal interfaces in your system (and between your system and its environment), think about how possible changes would affect those interfaces. Some interface designs are significantly more resilient to change than others. The next example shows a simple way to improve the flexibility of a functional interface.

EXAMPLE Consider the following interface fragment, which allows a caller to create an `Employee` object in the system and receive a newly allocated employee number as the return value:

```
interface EmployeeService
{

    integer createEmployee(String   forename,
                           String   surname,
                           SSNumber ss_number,
                           Date     date_of_birth) ;
    ...
}
```

Now consider how that interface would have to change if, for example, the need arose to add a set of initials to the definition of the `Employee` type. Obviously, you would need to add a new parameter to the interface and update all of the callers of the interface to supply a value for this new parameter.

The following alternative interface definition would be more flexible than the previous one if this type of change were required.

```
interface EmployeeService
{

    integer createEmployee(Employee emp) ;
    ...
}
```

The `Employee` type has been defined elsewhere (exactly once) and is used as part of the definition of this interface. In this case, assuming that the employees' middle initials are optional, it is quite possible to introduce this new feature and to affect only those system components that actually need to know about the initials, not all of the components that process `Employee` objects.

You can use a similar approach with information interfaces. For example, by using a self-describing message technology such as XML to define message formats and allowing new message elements to be optional, you can allow messages to be extended with little or no impact on system elements that do not need to use the extended form of the interface. Consider this approach particularly for your external interfaces if environment evolution is likely to be important for your system.

Having suggested this, we should note that such approaches are not without their costs, and you need to evaluate them in the context of your evolution requirements. To take interface flexibility to its logical extreme would involve dropping static typing of your interfaces altogether and establishing the types of all request parameters at runtime. Such a flexible approach can be more difficult to understand and test and may be less efficient at runtime. It can also introduce many subtle system problems because it is hard to check for information that is accidentally missing.

The specifics of how you can create flexible interfaces depend on the technology environment and problem domain of your system. However, considering the degree of flexibility required of your important interfaces and how to achieve it is an important aspect of addressing the evolution concerns of your system.

Apply Change-Oriented Architectural Styles

If you have significant requirements for system evolution, it may be worth considering the adoption of an overall architectural style that is particularly focused on supporting change. Metamodel-based systems provide a very high degree of flexibility in some problem domains (particularly database systems requiring significant schema evolution).

A detailed explanation of the relevant architectural styles isn't possible here due to space constraints. However, we give a brief example here.

EXAMPLE An investment bank could use a metamodel-based architectural style for one of its trading systems. Such a system needs to capture and process the details of deals involving many sorts of financial instruments such as bond purchases, foreign exchange transactions, money market transactions, equity trades, derivative transactions, and so on. However, new types of deals are invented regularly, meaning that there is a significant requirement to support functional evolution.

A traditional architecture for the system might identify a certain number of types of deals that the system can handle—perhaps foreign exchange, money market, and equity transactions. Each of these would be analyzed to work out its characteristics and processing, and the system would be built to support these functions. Perhaps the architect would spot some commonality between these different types of processing during design and would use some generic reusable processing for the common aspects. Later, bond transactions would need to be added, so a similar process would be repeated and the system changed in order to incorporate those functions.

In contrast, a metamodel-based architecture starts by considering fundamental concepts such as customers (counterparties), currencies, trading and settlement dates, trading limits, collections of trades for a particular trader (books), and so on. Then, instead of developing a system to process a particular set of transaction types, the architect designs a system to provide a set of facilities to implement the underlying concepts and provides a data-based configuration facility to allow the system's implementers to define the types of trades they want to perform in terms of these underlying concepts. Later, when new trade types are required, they are added by changing the configuration data, rather than the system code.

Such metamodel-based systems can provide the ability to support very rapid change because instead of modifying the system implementation to change its behavior, you can just reconfigure it—usually a much faster process.

Of course, there is no such thing as a free lunch—or, for that matter, a free system change. Metamodel-based systems are much more complex to develop and test than systems based on more static architectural styles. They are also inherently less efficient in terms of runtime performance, which can limit their applicability in environments where performance is a major concern.

Build Variation Points into the Software

A less extreme strategy than adopting a complete architectural style is to adopt specific, localized design solutions to support certain types of changes in specific places in the system. This approach involves identifying the locations where supporting a certain type of change is critically important and specifying a mechanism to achieve the change required. We term these places in the system **variation points** (borrowing the term from product-line architecture). Using variation points is an example of the architecture placing specific constraints on the software design process in order to achieve a particular quality property.

A large number of specific software design patterns have been published that attempt to introduce some form of variation point (Façade, Chain of Responsibility, and Bridge, to name only a few). Some of the general approaches we have found useful include the following.

- *Make elements replaceable*: Being able to replace certain elements in your system with an alternative implementation is a very useful mechanism for creating a variation point (and is widely used in commercial software). This typically involves developing the software so that the interface to an element and the element's implementation are kept separate and so that other elements depend only on the interface. This allows you to change the system's behavior by replacing an element at build time or, with some technologies, at runtime.

- *Parameterize operation with configuration parameters*: Specify that certain aspects of the processing carried out by your software can be parameterized. For example, parameterize the inputs, outputs, and accuracy required of a statistical processing element in the system to allow some aspects of the system's operation to be changed over time without modifying its implementation.

- *Use self-describing data and generic processing*: The simplest approach to processing data is almost always to hard-code the logic required, but this means that changes to the data require changes to the system. However, certain types of processing (e.g., format conversion) can often be performed in a more generic way if the structure of the input data is known. To deal with format changes in such situations, consider specifying the use of a self-describing data stream (such as XML) with the processing code being written in such a way that it uses the structure of the incoming data to guide its processing.

- *Separate physical and logical processing*: In many systems, data formats change frequently, but the actual processing required does not. This is an example of a case where separating the physical processing from the logical processing can create a useful variation point. If the software is partitioned to first process the physical format of the data and then perform the business (or logical) processing on the results, it is much easier to deal with a change in the physical format (e.g., from CSV files to XML files).

- *Break processes into steps*: Business processes are frequently made up of a number of steps that must be performed in sequence. However, the simplest approach to automating the process may be to implement it as a monolithic piece of software. You can introduce a possible variation point to support process change if instead you structure the software as a number of separate elements, one per step, that combine to form a process.

Like other software architecture decisions, you should introduce variation points carefully, balancing the cost involved in creating, maintaining, and using each variation point against the likelihood of it being used and its importance to stakeholder needs.

Use Standard Extension Points

A related approach to building in your own variation points is to consider how you can use extension points built into standard technologies to provide support for changes to your system. Many mainstream information systems technologies provide standard extension points (such as the J2EE platform's ability to easily add support for new types of databases, via the JDBC interface, and external systems, via the JCA interface). If you can use these standard technology solutions, you may find a number of flexible extension points, available for free, that you can adapt and use in a number of ways to meet your evolution requirements. For example, you could write custom adaptors that allow you to use standard application integration facilities to connect to your in-house systems as well as the packaged applications they are normally used for. This could allow you to avoid designing and building your own mechanism for future integration into in-house systems.

Achieve Reliable Change

A major challenge for the architects, developers, and administrators of many systems is dealing with change in a reliable way. You, like us, have probably seen a supposedly simple change turn out to have a number of serious side effects that caused major problems when deployed.

Change in any system can be risky, but it can be particularly difficult to deal with in software systems, where it often isn't possible to assess the impact visually and the system must be exhaustively tested to confirm your assumptions about postchange behavior.

If your system is one that needs to cope with change (and, of course, nearly all are, whether or not change is actually planned for), you need to make some architectural decisions that allow changes to be made reliably. A number of relevant strategies can help you with this.

- *Software configuration management*: A crucial part of dealing with software change is having a reliable configuration management system that allows you to control changes to the system's software modules and allows formal system versions to be clearly identified and retrieved.
- *Automated build process*: In addition to controlling the versions of the inputs to the software build process, it is important to make the build process itself reliable, consistent, and repeatable, to ensure that building

a particular version of the system always ends up with exactly the same result. Inevitably this means creating an automated system so that human error and inconsistency do not creep into the build process.

- *Automated release process*: For most systems, taking the outputs of the build process and packaging them for release and deployment isn't a simple process, and you need an automated system to do this reliably. Creating and maintaining the build and release systems takes valuable time and effort, but in our experience it's always cheaper than the alternative.

- *Environment configuration management*: In addition to controlling the versions of the software modules used in your system, you should control the development and production environments used for creating and running the system. These processes may be less well supported by existing tools, but it is important to carefully manage the exact versions of development tools and deployment platforms, as well as the precise configuration information for them, to avoid instability caused by mismatches between different environments.

- *Automated testing*: Testing is a crucial part of managing the process of system change. If you don't have a way to test the system, you won't know whether or not a change to it has been successful. One aspect of this involves making sure that you have a comprehensive set of tests so that you can assess the impact of a change on the system's behavior. The other aspect is automation. If you do have a comprehensive set of tests for a significant system, it will probably amount to hundreds or thousands of tests. It simply isn't possible to run this many tests in a reliable, timely, and efficient way without a high degree of automation.

- *Continuous integration*: When making changes, it is always best to receive bad news as early as possible. Given that large-scale system change often involves bad news, it is sensible to have a process to discover it as soon as you can. A good way to achieve this is to continually integrate the changing parts of your system rather than trying so-called big bang integration at the end of the process. Continuous integration involves bringing system changes together as often as possible and testing the result (at least once per day in most cases). Both the process of integration itself and the tests you run help uncover problems with the proposed changes as quickly as possible. This minimizes wasted effort and allows you to identify possible solutions.

Preserve Development Environments

Once a project has delivered a meaningful amount of functionality, the original development environment is often dismantled or evolved. Over time, you can easily reach the point where no one knows the exact set of compilers, operating systems, patches, libraries, build tools, and so on used to create the system. This can be a particular problem for product developers who support a wide range of platforms and product versions.

Part of your responsibility as an architect is to preserve the development environment in some way. Clearly record the details of the required development environment, and make sure that enough hardware and software is retained so that the environment can be precisely recreated if the need arises due to an evolution requirement (e.g., if a fault cannot be reproduced in the current development environment).

PROBLEMS AND PITFALLS

Prioritization of the Wrong Dimensions

When considering how to allow for change in your architecture, it is easy to focus on dimensions that you know about or that seem immediately important because key stakeholders stress their importance. However, the important change dimensions for a system may be found elsewhere. For example, if your background is primarily data-oriented, it is easy to focus on the environment dimension, whereas in reality the evolutionary challenge for your system may be to extend the number of client platforms from which users can access the system.

Focusing on the wrong things is a problem throughout architectural design. Focusing on the wrong evolutionary dimensions can result in an architecture that is more complex and expensive to build than simpler alternatives and yet still is not particularly easy to change when the actual changes needed emerge.

RISK REDUCTION
- If you decide to build in support for system change, do so only after working through enough solid analysis to be confident that you are focusing on the right change dimensions.

Changes That Never Happen

Myriad possible changes could credibly be made to any system. You can't realistically design an architecture that allows for them all, certainly not one that can also be delivered in a cost-effective and timely way with an acceptable level of risk. Any architecture that allows for *all* possible changes would be too complex and unwieldy to build. If you plan for evolution in your architectural design, you are explicitly or implicitly deciding to make some of the possible changes easier than others.

If you build in specific support for a certain type of change that is never actually needed, you end up with design "baggage" that has to be understood and accommodated by its developers until eventually someone is courageous enough to decide that the change is never going to happen and removes the support for it.

Providing support for any future change requires overhead in terms of design, implementation, and often runtime overhead, so supporting a number of changes that don't happen can be a major unnecessary cost for your system.

RISK REDUCTION

- Provide specific support for a type of change in your architecture only when you are confident it will be needed.

Impacts of Evolution on Critical Quality Properties

Building a system to support evolution is not without cost. In particular, highly flexible systems (such as the metamodel-based systems outlined earlier) can bring significant costs in terms of runtime efficiency and performance, as well as the more involved development process that their complexity implies. (Of course, this is not always the case, and a flexible system may actually be easier to tune for performance because it has a well-understood, flexible, modular structure that allows easy monitoring and analysis, varied deployment options, and so on.)

The danger with focusing too heavily on the goal of flexibility is that you could make a system that is very easy to change but fails to meet one or more fundamental quality properties such as performance or availability. Also, it is easy to create such a complex system that all of your energies end up focused on the flexibility problem, and you neglect other properties such as security or internationalization due to lack of time.

RISK REDUCTION

- Having decided on the support for evolution in your architecture, make sure that you maintain the balance between flexibility and the other important quality properties for your system.
- Use a process of continual architectural assessment (discussed in Chapter 14) to achieve this balance.

Lost Development Environments

We have already mentioned that the development (and test) environment is more likely to be lost than the deployment environment. In addition, development environments are often subject to independent change and evolution as development and support priorities and workload naturally change over time.

The problem with trying to recreate a development or test environment is that it often isn't clear exactly what is needed to do so.

- Do you require a specific version of a library, or will a later version be acceptable?
- Other than obvious tools like compilers, what other tools do you need to perform a complete build and release? For example, was a particular scripting language used and, if so, do you need to install any extensions to it?
- Do any of the major development tools require any software patches? (A common example is the compiler, which may change behavior with certain patches applied.)
- Do you need a particular underlying operating system version or chip model, or can you substitute them later, with supposedly compatible versions?

In our experience, it is quite rare to find that the answers to these questions are known, let alone recorded.

RISK REDUCTION
- Whenever an external element is introduced to the development environment, record its name, version, and origin along with the reason for its inclusion. This doesn't need to be terribly formal; a text file checked into your configuration management system is sufficient.
- Toward the end of the construction phase, try to recreate your development environment in a completely separate location that you haven't used before, and use the information recorded earlier to build the environment. Build your system and run your tests. This process rapidly reveals any missing elements from your list, which you can add to save others (or perhaps yourself) the same problem in the future.

Ad Hoc Release Management

When deploying to a test environment, it doesn't really matter if the process goes wrong because no one is seriously affected—some tests fail, people realize that deployment has failed and they have to redeploy, but system users are not affected. However, deployment beyond the test environment is much more serious, and any problems at best will be annoying for end users and administrators and at worst may threaten critical operations in the target organization. It is important to orchestrate and manage the release management process just as carefully as the process of building and testing the system.

Release management differs somewhat between turnkey and product development environments, with turnkey developers often being responsible for updating the actual production system, whereas product developers are responsible for creating an installable system for others to install. In reality, though, both of these types of release management can be complex and, if done badly, have a negative impact on important stakeholders (end users and system administrators, respectively).

RISK REDUCTION

- Invest in an automated release process to achieve reliability and repeatability. This will save effort for every release and will also help prevent problems caused by human error during the release process.

CHECKLISTS

Checklist for Requirements Capture

- Have you considered which evolutionary dimensions are most important for your system?
- Are you confident that you have done enough analysis to confirm that your prioritization of evolutionary dimensions is valid?
- Have you identified particular specific changes that will be required and the magnitude of each?
- Have you assessed the likelihood of each of your changes actually being needed?

Checklist for Architecture Definition

- Have you performed an architectural assessment to establish whether your architecture is sufficiently flexible to meet the evolutionary needs of your system?
- Where change is likely, does your architectural design contain the change as far as possible?
- Have you considered choosing an inherently change-oriented architectural style? If so, have you assessed the costs of doing so?
- Have you traded off the costs of your support for evolution against the needs of the system as a whole? Are any critical quality properties negatively impacted by the design you have adopted?
- Have you designed the architecture to accommodate only those changes you are confident will be needed?

- Can you recreate your development and test environments reliably?
- Can you reliably and repeatedly build, test, and release your system?
- Is your chosen evolutionary approach the cheapest and least risky option of delivering the initial system and the future evolution required?

FURTHER READING

A systematic approach to dealing with change at the implementation level by using a set of well-defined transformations known as refactorings is described in Fowler et al. [FOWL99]. A number of architectural styles are described in Buschmann et al. [BUSC96], including a metamodel-based system style called Reflection, which is particularly amenable to certain types of change.

There isn't much written material on evolution aimed at the architect specifically; however, Bass et al. [BASS03] does include a set of tactics to help achieve architectural modifiability. These tactics are fairly generic but suggest a lot of useful things to consider for your architecture. (The book also provides similar sets of tactics for availability, performance, security, testability, and usability.) In contrast, there are quite a number of books on software design patterns, many of which address change. Some useful ones to start with are Gamma et al. [GAMM95] and Coplien et al. [PLOP95–99].

Support for controlled variation and evolution is a major concern of software product-line architecture, and the concept of the variation point, which we mentioned earlier, is borrowed from the techniques used in this discipline. Two books [BASS03; BOSC00] provide introductions to creating software architectures for product lines as well as references to further reading in the area.

One SEI-sponsored book [CLEM02] is a practical guide to performing architectural evaluation including evaluating systems for modifiability, while another SEI book [SEAC03] presents an architecture-based evolution process for modernizing older systems.

Deferring the need to pay for change until it is actually needed is a core principle of the Extreme Programming approach. The original reference for Extreme Programming is Beck [BECK00].

28

OTHER PERSPECTIVES

So far, we have defined some important perspectives—Security, Performance and Scalability, Availability and Resilience, and Evolution—in reasonably full detail. We have found the concerns addressed by these perspectives to be relevant to most if not all information systems. If you do not apply these perspectives to your architectural views, you impose a serious risk of delivering systems that do not meet the explicit or implicit needs of your stakeholders: They may expose sensitive data to malicious attackers; they may perform poorly under heavy load; they may suffer from frequent and expensive interruptions in service; or they may be very difficult to change.

You may also need to consider a number of other perspectives when designing your architecture. We say "may" for several reasons.

- Not all of these other perspectives are relevant to all situations. For example, a system that operates only in one country is probably unaffected by the Internalization perspective.

- They may have a less significant impact on the architecture. For example, the concerns of the Usability perspective may not be that relevant to a server-based EAI or data movement system, which is only minimally exposed to users (although the usability needs of system administrators should not be ignored).

- They may relate to less highly visible system properties. A system operating in a lightly regulated business area, for example, is minimally affected by the concerns of the Regulation perspective.

Therefore, in this chapter we define the following *secondary* perspectives and for each one present a subset of the information we provided for the primary ones earlier in Part IV.

- *The Accessibility perspective* ensures that people with disabilities can use the system.

- *The Development Resource perspective* ensures that the system can be built, deployed, and operated within known constraints related to people, budget, time, and materials.

- *The Internationalization perspective* ensures the system's independence from any particular language, country, or cultural group.

- *The Location perspective* ensures that the system can overcome problems brought about by the absolute location of its elements and the distances between them.

- *The Regulation perspective* ensures that the system conforms to local and international laws, quasi-legal regulations, company policies, and other rules and standards.

- *The Usability perspective* ensures that the people who interact with the system can work effectively.

Given that you have only finite time—and probably not very much of that—to develop your AD, you will need to decide which of these perspectives are most relevant to you and how much time you want to spend applying them to your views.

THE ACCESSIBILITY PERSPECTIVE

Desired Quality	The ability of the system to be used by people with disabilities
Applicability	Any system that may be used or operated by people with disabilities or may be subject to legislation regarding disabilities
Concerns	Types of disability, functional availability, and disability regulation
Activities	Identification of system touch points, device independence, and content equivalence
Architectural Tactics	Assistive technologies, specialist input devices, and voice recognition
Problems and Pitfalls	Ignoring these needs until too late, lack of knowledge about regulation and legislation, and lack of knowledge about suitable solutions

In recent years, enlightened corporations have come to recognize the contributions that disabled people can make, and many have high-profile programs to encourage their active participation in business operations. Furthermore, many countries have passed legislation that prohibits discrimination against people with disabilities and obliges employers to provide facilities suitable to their needs.

For systems directly exposed to customers (e.g., Internet- or mobile communications–based systems, public kiosks, or automated teller machines), failing to address the needs of the disabled population can significantly reduce the systems' reach and effectiveness, in addition to reflecting unfavorably on the organization in the eyes of the public.

Accessibility should take into account not only the direct users of the system—i.e., those sitting at terminals—but the indirect users as well. For example, a financial system may need to provide bank statements in Braille for blind customers.

Consideration of disability aside, addressing accessibility concerns brings benefits in many cases by making systems more usable and efficient in their operation.

It is also important to assess architectures for compliance with legislative requirements and internal standards, as we discuss under the Regulation perspective.

Applicability to Views

Table 28–1 shows how the Accessibility perspective affects each of the views we discussed in Part III.

TABLE 28–1 APPLICABILITY OF THE ACCESSIBILITY PERSPECTIVE TO THE SIX VIEWS

View	Applicability
Functional	In theory, the functional structure should not really be affected by accessibility considerations—all functions should be available to disabled users in exactly the same way they are to able-bodied users. In practice, functional compromises may need to be made in some cases.
Information	The information structure is unlikely to be significantly affected, although it may be necessary, for example, to maintain information about disabilities of customers and/or users.
Concurrency	The concurrency structure of the system is unlikely to impact its accessibility, so the impact on this view is minimal.
Development	The Development view needs to raise awareness that accessibility issues are important. And, of course, you may need to accommodate disabled developers, too.
Deployment	The deployment environment is likely to be the most affected by this perspective. Special hardware (described in this section) may be needed to support disabled users.
Operational	The Operational view may have to take into account the needs of disabled users requiring support or the needs of disabled support staff themselves.

Concerns

Your system may need to be usable by people with a range of disabilities:

- People who are blind or partially sighted, who cannot read small print or differentiate items on low-contrast displays
- People who are color blind (this affects up to 10% of the male population)
- People who are totally deaf or hearing-impaired
- People who have difficulty processing information
- People with low levels of literacy or numeracy

Ideally, all functionality should be available to all users regardless of their level of ability. Where this is not the case, you should clearly identify the limitations and obtain stakeholder agreement.

Many countries have legal requirements with regard to disability, such as the Americans with Disabilities Act in the United States and the Disability Discrimination Act in the United Kingdom, and at a minimum you should always assess your systems against these. A number of standards, guidelines, and best-practice guides are also available, against which you can assess your architecture. (For more information, see the Further Reading section for this perspective.)

You should be aware of the implications of regulations before you begin architecture definition. It is much easier to design accessibility features into the architecture from the outset rather than to retrofit them at the end. Specialized knowledge may be required, and you should not be afraid to consult with experts where necessary.

Activities: Applying the Accessibility Perspective

A simple process follows.

- Identify the types of disabled users who may need to interact with your system (blind, deaf, movement-impaired, and so on).
- Identify all places where disabled users may interact with the system (*touch points*).
- Use your stakeholders to help identify all relevant regulations and specific concerns related to accessibility.
- At a high level, agree on requirements for the intersection of each type of user with each of the key touch points.

- Develop an architectural approach and, where appropriate, a more detailed solution that meets the requirements.
- Bench-test the solution against the requirements, using prototypes where appropriate.

Architectural Tactics

Hardware and software components that have been designed to meet the needs of disabled users are known as *assistive technologies*. Examples of these include the following.

- A *Braille display* is a mechanical device that dynamically raises and lowers dots in a Braille grid. Such devices typically display anything from one character to a whole line at a time.
- A *screen reader* is an adjunct to a visual display that reads the contents of the screen aloud to visually impaired users.
- A *screen magnifier* enlarges a portion of a screen so that users with partial vision can see it more easily.
- A *voice recognition system* provides an alternative to keyboard or mouse data entry by accepting commands spoken by the user.
- *Internet chat* technologies (e.g., Web-based help desks) allow people such as those who are deaf to communicate without using a telephone.
- Many types of specialist input devices are available for mobility-impaired users.

Designing presentation elements to be device-independent is generally a good practice and brings particular benefits where there is a need to support access by disabled users.

Presentation should not rely on one interface capability to convey meaning but should provide alternatives wherever possible. For example, screens and printouts should not rely solely on color or pictures to emphasize elements of text because they may not stand out to color-blind or partially sighted users or those using display devices that do not render color. Instead, use the technique of *content equivalence*—in other words, render content in different ways that convey the same meaning. For example, if a screen uses color to highlight incorrect input, it could also use an annotated arrow that points to the incorrect data.

Similarly, interaction should not rely on a single mechanism but should support alternatives where possible—for example, you could make a graphical user interface operable by both mouse and keyboard.

Where interactions involve a number of separate steps or are otherwise complex, aim for navigational simplicity. Screens should be clear in their use, consistent, and well designed. Avoid excessive use of special effects, such as blinking text or sounds, as these may not be perceived by some disabled users.

Problems and Pitfalls

Here are some common pitfalls to keep in mind for the Accessibility perspective.

- *Failure to think about how to address these issues until it's too late*: This can put you at risk of noncompliance with legislation or with the requirements of some key stakeholders.
- *Lack of knowledge about regulation and legislation*: You should consult experts if you are at all unsure.
- *Lack of knowledge about suitable solutions*: If you're unfamiliar with assistive technologies, get advice from specialist stakeholders.

Checklists

CHECKLIST FOR REQUIREMENTS CAPTURE

- Have you identified and obtained stakeholder approval of the extent to which the system must support the needs of disabled users?
- Have you provided for the needs of indirect disabled users, such as customers who need paperwork provided in Braille format?
- Have you identified the disability legislation that affects the system and assessed the system against it?
- Have you ensured that the system meets any internal accessibility standards?
- Have you considered all points at which the system has any human interaction? For example, have you considered operational management and monitoring of the system, or printed forms that are sent to customers to be filled in?

CHECKLIST FOR ARCHITECTURE DEFINITION

- How confident are you that your architectural assumptions are correct? Where you are not, are mitigating activities in place (such as a proof-of-concept)?
- Do the interactive elements of your architecture sufficiently separate presentation and content to meet the system's accessibility objectives?
- Are the interfaces between components (particularly those leading in and out of presentation devices) sufficiently generic to be able to take on board new devices without (much) rework?

- Does the architecture allow for presentation alternatives to convey meaning (e.g., text, pictures, and/or sound in a user interface)?
- Do standards for user interface design emphasize simplicity, consistency, and clarity in place? Does the architecture adhere to them?

Further Reading

Many of the references listed later under the Usability perspective also touch on Accessibility.

A number of Web sites are devoted to accessibility. Your best starting point is the Web Accessibility Initiative of the World Wide Web Consortium at www.w3.org/WAI. Also, most hardware and software vendors run disability portals, for example, Microsoft (www.microsoft.com/enable/), IBM (www.ibm.com/able/), and Sun Microsystems (www.sun.com/access/). Many governments also maintain online resources that provide best practice guidelines and explanations of accessibility legislation (such as the www.disabilityinfo.gov site in the United States and the www.disability.gov.uk site in the United Kingdom).

You can assess Web sites for their conformance to accessibility best practices by using online tools such as Bobby (http://bobby.watchfire.com/).

THE DEVELOPMENT RESOURCE PERSPECTIVE

Desired Quality	The ability of the system to be designed, built, deployed, and operated within known constraints related to people, budget, time, and materials
Applicability	Any system for which development time is limited, technical skills for development or operations are hard to find, or unusual or unfamiliar hardware or software is required
Concerns	Time constraints, cost constraints, required skill sets, available resources, budgets, and external dependencies
Activities	Cost estimation, development time estimation, development planning, dependency management, scoping, prototyping, and expectation management
Architectural Tactics	Incremental and iterative development, expectation management, descoping, prototyping and piloting, and fitness for purpose
Problems and Pitfalls	Overly ambitious timescales, failure to consider lead times, failure to consider physical constraints, underbudgeting, failure to provide staff training and consider familiarization needs, insufficient resource allocation for testing and rollout, insufficient time for likely rework, and overallocation of staff

In this context, a development resource may be a person, a piece of hardware or software, a building, a timescale, or money. (Note that runtime computing resources are a slightly different topic, which we discuss as part of the Performance and Scalability perspective in Chapter 25.)

All software projects are primarily constrained by time and cost. IT budgets are never unlimited, and although technology capabilities improve from year to year, so do the costs of building, deployment, and support. Today's rapidly changing business environments impose substantial pressures to deliver flexible systems ever more quickly. There may even be immovable timescale constraints, such as the arrival of new legislation, new regulations, or a new millennium. (At least that last one is unlikely to recur for another thousand years or so!)

You may think it odd or inappropriate that an architect should get involved in things like time and money. Certainly as an architect, none of these problems are directly yours to solve. However, they all impose constraints on your architectural choices. For example, if you have to wait a month before trained developers are available, you will have less time to build the system and less scope for incorporating complex features. If the budget will not stretch to a mainframe, there is little point in considering it as an architectural candidate. If the data center is full, a server farm is not an option unless space can be found elsewhere.

Applicability to Views

Table 28–2 shows how the Development Resource perspective affects each of the views we discussed in Part III.

Concerns

The constraints of people, budget, time, and materials lead to a number of more specific concerns.

- Appropriately skilled people are always a key resource constraint. If your architecture makes use of a technology unfamiliar to your developers, you will need to provide a large-scale retraining exercise.
- You should also consider the impact of your architecture on the existing support community. Retraining or recruitment may be necessary, and you may need to provide richer tools for operational management, analysis, and repair.
- Your users may need training in new technologies and new applications. This is particularly significant in large-scale rollouts of new or significantly modified applications. If users are unfamiliar with the software they will be using, you may want to put extra effort into usability.

TABLE 28-2 APPLICABILITY OF THE DEVELOPMENT RESOURCE PERSPECTIVE TO THE SIX VIEWS

View	Applicability
Functional	Resource constraints such as short timescales or limitations on available skills often impose restrictions on functionality and on functional qualities such as generality.
Information	Complex or particularly sophisticated information models may require a large staff of specialists to implement; lack of such staff may impose restrictions on your architectural options.
Concurrency	Concurrent architectures are often complex to implement, and you will need to consider the development and testing time and the skills of your developers when designing your architecture.
Development	Cost constraints may limit the number of separate development and test environments available to you, so you may need to formulate strategies for sharing these.
Deployment	Again, cost constraints may limit your options for deployment, particularly where redundancy and resilience are concerned.
Operational	You need to be aware of the cost implications of your proposed operational and support architecture.

- Deployment of new applications may necessitate large-scale infrastructure upgrades that are not immediately obvious to you. For example, a new application may require more memory than the standard PC desktop provides or more bandwidth than the corporate network can handle. In organizations with a large number of geographically distributed users, this sort of massive cost can kill a project.

- On large-scale programs, you should consider the impact on office space. It may be necessary to quickly commission space to house the development team, the support team, a test center, or the users. Extra data center space may be needed to store a new server farm or large amounts of shared disk storage.

- You should be aware of dependencies between development activities and of the overall critical path (the sequence of activities that, if a delay occurs to any of them, will delay the entire project). Here are some examples.

  - You may have mandated a hardware platform that has a long lead time for procurement and deployment, such as a mainframe computer or specialized hardware built to order.

  - You may be dependent on hardware, software, or services delivered by a third-party supplier.

- There may be lead times for recruiting and/or training specialized personnel.
- A large-scale rollout may have to align with other activities.

Consideration of these aspects provides an essential reality check that the system you are proposing will ever see the light of day. You may design the most flawless, performant, and extensible architecture possible, but if building it would take many years or hundreds of programmers, it will probably never get off the drawing board.

Activities: Applying the Development Resource Perspective

As you develop your architecture, regularly review the development resources likely to be required to realize it. Feed these findings back to the project managers as early as possible—particularly if new or unexpected resources are needed (e.g., specific design skills with a new technology or office space that isn't already available).

Your most important activity here is to not forget anything. If you follow the processes we describe in this book—identifying and engaging stakeholders, creating views, and applying perspectives to these views—you have a much better chance of success.

It may be appropriate to support any controversial architectural decisions with a risk analysis. Discussion of such a risk analysis is outside the scope of this book (see the Further Reading section for this perspective).

Architectural Tactics

Many traditional software engineering techniques, such as component-based development, software reuse, and the use of off-the-shelf software libraries, can contribute to development efficiencies.

A number of techniques are available to help you reduce timescale and/or cost where these are overriding concerns. It is fair to say, however, that at the time of writing, techniques such as Rapid Application Development (RAD) and Extreme Programming (XP) are not well proven in the context of large system development programs.

An iterative approach, such as that espoused by the Rational Unified Process (RUP) or Feature Driven Development (FDD), can help mitigate risk and uncertainty and can deliver key benefits early as part of a phased development. In practice, for complex developments, an iterative approach (as opposed to a big bang approach) seems to be the only one that has any chance of success.

Perhaps the most important technique is *expectation management*. Because of the relative immaturity of our profession, many software development projects go over time and/or budget, or they fail to deliver all of their promised improvement. It is essential that you communicate clearly with your stakeholders about what will be delivered to them and when and that you obtain their agreement to any compromises you have to make. You might want to present the quality triangle (see Chapter 2) to your stakeholders to help explain the slogan "Quality, speed, cost—pick two!"

Some specific techniques that may be relevant include the following.

- *Descoping*: Reduce the functional scope, or relax some of the required system characteristics such as flexibility or scalability, to reduce development times.

- *Prototyping or piloting*: These can help reduce risk (although they also may set an expectation that the system is more complete than it actually is).

- *Fitness for purpose*: Try not to be tempted to develop a system that is more sophisticated, complex, or flexible than the users actually need. If they want something quick and cheap, that is what you should deliver.

Problems and Pitfalls

In our experience, resource constraints are the single biggest cause of software project delays or failure. Many factors lead to projects being underresourced or optimistically planned. As an architect, you can draw on your own experience to identify plans unlikely to succeed and suggest alternative strategies for them.

In addition to straightforward underbudgeting, keep in mind some other common pitfalls.

- Overly ambitious timescales
- Failure to consider lead times
- Failure to consider physical constraints such as space, power, furniture, and so on
- Failure to provide staff training and consider familiarization needs
- Insufficient time and resources for testing, quality assurance, and rollout
- Insufficient time for rework required due to development mistakes, misunderstood requirements, and unexpected change
- Overallocation of staff, e.g., allocating staff to a project five days per week when, realistically, a maximum of about four days of productive work is possible each week

Checklists

CHECKLIST FOR REQUIREMENTS CAPTURE

- Have you understood the project's key constraints in terms of time and budget, as well as the room for maneuvering if your architecture mandates extra resources?

- Have you considered physical constraints such as existing capacity, office space, and availability of personnel?

- Have you balanced the benefits of new or unfamiliar technologies against the costs and risks of deploying them?

- Have you understood which compromises are more likely to be accepted where resource constraints necessitate this? To what extent would stakeholders consider limiting scope, functionality, or even quality? Are you sufficiently confident that savings would be realized by making such compromises?

- To what extent is there scope for deferring features until future releases of software?

- Do you understand which functional and operational principles absolutely cannot be compromised, no matter what the resource impact? (Examples might include quality, security, user/customer experience, regulatory compliance, and richness of features.)

CHECKLIST FOR ARCHITECTURE DEFINITION

- To what extent did you base your architecture on technologies already familiar to your developer community?

- To what extent did you base your architecture on proven, established technologies as opposed to innovative ones?

- Have you assessed your architecture against existing infrastructure capabilities (desktop platforms, network infrastructure, and so on) to see whether hardware or software upgrades are required?

- Have you included in plans the costs of additional infrastructures for disaster recovery, support, acceptance, and training?

- Where new or unfamiliar technologies are used, have you considered the impacts of staff training and support?

- Is your architecture simple enough to be built and supported by development/operations staff who have only recently been trained?

Further Reading

A wealth of material is available on managing projects and risk. Hall [HALL98] is a comprehensive guide to identifying and managing risk on complex projects in a structured way. McConnell [MCCO97] is a software project management handbook that focuses on delivering projects on time and within budget.

THE INTERNATIONALIZATION PERSPECTIVE

Desired Quality	The ability of the system to be independent from any particular language, country, or cultural group
Applicability	Any system that may need to be accessed by users or operational staff from different cultures or parts of the world, or in multiple languages, either now or in the future
Concerns	Character sets, text presentation and orientation, specific language needs, cultural norms, automatic translation, and cultural neutrality
Activities	Identification of system touch points, identification of regions of concern, internationalization of code, and localization of resources
Architectural Tactics	Separation of presentation and content, use of message catalogs, system-wide use of suitable character sets (e.g., Unicode), and specialized display and presentation hardware
Problems and Pitfalls	Platforms not available in required locales, initial consideration of similar languages only, internationalization performed late in the development process, incompatibilities between locales on servers

No longer can we assume that the *lingua franca* of generally available IT systems is English. Even if the users of the system speak English, the customers they are dealing with may not; their names may require support for non-English or non-Western alphabets; and if the system uses the Internet, it may be directly exposed to customers from any part of the world.

The Internationalization perspective is important, therefore, for any system that will have users who speak different languages or come from different countries. If systems are aimed at a specific locale with no plans to move it into a wider area, this perspective has limited relevance.

Because of its length, you may sometimes see the word *internalization* abbreviated as *I18N*. A related term is *localization* (sometimes abbreviated as *L10N*), which refers to the process of performing the specific work required to use an already internationalized system in a particular locale (e.g., the translation of system messages).

Applicability to Views

Table 28–3 shows how the Internationalization perspective affects each of the views we discussed in Part III.

TABLE 28-3 APPLICABILITY OF THE INTERNATIONALIZATION PERSPECTIVE TO THE SIX VIEWS

View	Applicability
Functional	The functional structure may need to reflect how presentation is separated from content. General functionality should be independent of location.
Information	The Information view defines which stored information needs to be internationalized and how this will be achieved. If data needs to be stored or presented in different units of measurement, you may need to define strategies to do this to an appropriate level of precision.
Concurrency	This perspective has minimal impact on the Concurrency view.
Development	The Development view will need to reflect the impact of these factors on the development environment. For example, internationalized test data may be required, or early access may be needed to specialized devices. User-visible messages must be populated into catalogs.
Deployment	The deployment environment may need to take into consideration such items as internationalized input and presentation devices. Don't forget that your underlying software and hardware platforms need to support the languages you're working with—there is little point in supporting Urdu if your operating system or relational database management system doesn't support it. Similarly, the underlying platform needs to be internationalized (e.g., to have the ability to store Unicode in data stores).
Operational	The Operational view may need to consider what functionality is provided to support the maintenance and administration of localized information and services, and how support will be provided to different locations.

Concerns

This perspective addresses the system's support for the following concerns.

- *Multiple character sets*: A character set is a mapping from a standard set of characters to a list of byte values. Western character sets such as ASCII or EBCDIC encode each letter in a single byte, while more complex character sets such as Kanji (Japanese) require more than one byte per character. Unicode is a two-byte character set that attempts to encapsulate all modern written languages.

- *Differently oriented text presentation* (horizontal, vertical, left to right, right to left): Some non-European languages such as Urdu are written right to left, for example.

- *Language-specific concerns such as*:
  - Pictographic languages (e.g., Chinese, Japanese), which represent words using pictures or symbols rather than a limited alphabet
  - Use of different languages to present static information (e.g., screen prompts, report headings and titles, error messages, online help and reference documentation, printed documentation such as user manuals and training materials)
  - Different spelling within the same broad language (e.g., British vs. American English)
  - Different usage, meaning, or significance of the same words or phrases in different cultures
- *Different cultural norms such as*:
  - Different units of measurement (metric, imperial, and so on) and automatic conversion of data between these, while maintaining suitable precision
  - Different date, time, and currency display and data entry formats
  - Different output sizes (paper, screens, and so on)
- The *automatic translation* of dynamic information for display or printing.
- *Cultural neutrality*: in other words, avoiding concepts that certain groups understand but others do not. This is most difficult to define or measure and is particularly important where systems rely heavily on metaphors or have highly graphical or abstract presentations.

You should consider all of the system's devices (screens, printers, keyboards, and so on) when addressing these concerns.

Activities: Applying the Internationalization Perspective

A simple process follows.

- Identify all places where a person interacts with the system (the touch points).
- Identify the scope of services and information that need to be internationalized at each of these touch points.
- Identify the system's regions of concern (the types of countries and locales from which the system can be touched and the specific set of locales if available).
- Develop an architectural approach and, where appropriate, a more detailed solution that meets these requirements.
- Bench-test the solution against the requirements.

Architectural Tactics

Successful internationalization depends on a clear separation of presentation and content. Screens can be created on the fly with titles, headings, and prompts pulled from library text in the appropriate language.

In many systems, information and error messages are held in dynamic message databases, with variable parameters inserted at runtime. Even if you are not concerned with internalization, this useful technique gives you much greater flexibility over message content.

To be compatible with the widest range of character sets, you should use a multibyte character set such as Unicode. Note, however, that many rendering devices do not support this fully, and it has sizing implications for the storage of large amounts of text data.

You may need to make use of specialized display and presentation hardware, such as Kanji keyboards for the entry of Japanese text.

Problems and Pitfalls

Here are some common pitfalls to keep in mind for the Internationalization perspective.

- Unavailability of the underlying platform in the correct locale.
- Consideration of only languages similar to your own when planning internationalization (e.g., forgetting about Asian languages and investigating just Western ones or vice versa).
- Attempts to internationalize the system late in the development cycle. This can be very expensive and disruptive. You don't need to do all the localization initially, but it's important to build in the internationalization mechanisms early.
- Incompatibilities between different locales on servers (e.g., some platforms may not support both Chinese and Japanese on the same server).

Checklists

Checklist for Requirements Capture
- Have you agreed with stakeholders on the extent to which systems must be operable in different languages or countries, either now or in the future?
- Have you considered all points at which the system has any human interaction? For example, have you considered operational management and monitoring of the system or printed forms sent to customers to be filled in?

- Have you identified whether there is a requirement for non-Western character sets such as Kanji, which have special requirements for entry and presentation of data?
- Does your analysis consider all types of interaction—screens, keyboards, printed reports, and so on?
- If the system needs to convert between different units of measurement, have you considered how this will be done while retaining suitable data precision?

CHECKLIST FOR ARCHITECTURE DEFINITION

- How confident are you that the architecture will meet all the requirements? Where you are not, are mitigating activities in place (such as a proof-of-concept)?
- Do the interactive elements of your architecture sufficiently separate presentation and content to meet the system's internationalization objectives?
- If non-Western character sets such as Kanji must be supported, do your input and output devices accommodate these?
- If standard text must be presented in multiple languages, have you designed facilities for maintaining such information?
- Does your system sizing take into consideration the extra capacity (disk storage, network bandwidth, and so on) required for multibyte character sets?

Further Reading

Luong et al. [LUON95] is a thorough explanation of the process required to create internationalized software by a team that worked together at Borland, internationalizing a number of products including C++ and dBase. Microsoft published a comprehensive guide to developing internationalized applications on Microsoft's operating systems [INTE02]. Lund [LUND98] is the definitive book on handling Chinese, Korean, Japanese, and Vietnamese data.

THE LOCATION PERSPECTIVE

Desired Quality	The ability of the system to overcome problems brought about by the absolute location of its elements and the distances between them
Applicability	Any system whose elements (or other systems with which it interacts) are or may be physically far from one another

Concerns	Time zones of operation, network link characteristics, resiliency to link failures, wide-area interoperability, high-volume operations, intercountry concerns (political, commercial, and legal), and physical variations between locations
Activities	Geographical mapping, estimation of link quality, estimation of latency, benchmarking, and modeling of geographical characteristics
Architectural Tactics	Avoidance of widely distributed transactions, architectural plans for wide-area link failure, and allowance for offline operation
Problems and Pitfalls	Invalid (wide-area) network assumptions; assumption of single point administration; assumption of one primary time zone; assumption of end-to-end security; assumption of an overnight batch period; failure to consider political, commercial, or legal differences; and assumption of a standard physical environment

The Location perspective addresses the problems that arise when systems or system elements are physically distant from one another. If all elements are located in the same place, you can usually disregard this perspective.

Be aware, however, that the physical separation of elements may not always be immediately obvious. For example, many systems have disaster recovery sites that are physically distant from the main operational site or may rely on links to external, distant systems. Such an architecture presents a number of challenges that you should address through this perspective.

Applicability to Views

Table 28–4 shows how the Location perspective affects each of the views we discussed in Part III.

Concerns

The Location perspective addresses a number of concerns.

- If system operation is time-dependent (as virtually all systems are), you must consider the impact on its operation of the different time zones and the overlapping of the operational day in different parts of the world. For example, when it is afternoon in London, it is late evening in Sydney and early morning in New York. The system may need to be able to operate simultaneously in online mode and in overnight mode.

- If elements are geographically very distant but need to communicate efficiently and seamlessly, wide-area network bandwidth, latency, reliability, and resilience become important.

TABLE 28-4 APPLICABILITY OF THE LOCATION PERSPECTIVE TO THE SIX VIEWS

View	Applicability
Functional	The Functional view is often presented independently of real-world location concerns; typically, these are modeled in the Deployment view.
Information	If data is highly distributed, the Information view should describe how information is kept synchronized, what update latencies are expected, how temporary discrepancies are handled, and how information is transformed between locations.
Concurrency	Concurrent processing across highly distributed parts of the system is likely to be problematic for reliability and latency reasons. The concurrency approach chosen may need to change in order to accommodate location realities.
Development	If system development is spread over multiple locations, the Development view needs to explain how software will be managed, integrated, and tested.
Deployment	The Deployment view must consider how systems are physically rolled out to disparate locations in a controlled, synchronized way and what is needed in order to test and accept this rollout. Significant issues such as latency, lead times, and costs are often associated with the selection and rollout of wide-area networks.
Operational	The Operational view needs to consider how widely distributed systems are monitored, managed, and repaired.

- If elements are distant, connectivity is typically less reliable than when they are nearby. The architecture may need to accommodate situations where wide-area connectivity has been lost for a time, but a (possibly degraded) service must continue to be provided.

- If communications are required over heterogeneous networks between elements in different countries, there may be issues related to compatibility and interoperability of protocols.

- If there is a need to perform high-volume operations remotely over the wide-area network, such as distributed backups or distributed software updates, you must consider the bandwidth and response implications of these.

- You may need to address the political, commercial, and legal implications of your location. For example, systems may be subject to different laws and regulations (which you can also address in the Regulation perspective), taxation regimes, working practices, and so on.

- The system may even need to accommodate differences in the physical characteristics of different locations, such as the type or reliability of electrical supply, the availability of telecommunication links, or even extremes of temperature or climate.

Activities: Applying the Location Perspective

A simple process follows.

- Map each physical component to a geographical location.
- Consider the physical distance and the communications infrastructure between each of these components.
- Capture and obtain agreement on operational requirements (response, latency, reliability, and so on) over each of these interfaces.
- Take into account any political, commercial, or legal implications. (We discuss legal implications in the section on the Regulation perspective later in this chapter).
- Develop an architectural approach and, where appropriate, a more detailed solution that meets these requirements.
- Bench-test the solution against requirements.

If a system's reach crosses national boundaries, you may want to create some models.

- You can model the 24-hour day across the time zones in the countries of operation and consider what the system will be doing while it is daytime in one zone and nighttime in another. If you need downtime for overnight batch processing, for example, how will this be accommodated if the system has to provide uninterrupted service?
- You can create a geographical model of system location to help understand the impact of long distances on information flows, multistep processes, and so on. Remember that, in general, the further dispersed the end points are, the worse your latency and reliability will be.

Architectural Tactics

You should generally avoid transactions that rely on the availability of widely distributed elements. However, this is not always possible, particularly in service-based architectures. In such cases, you can provide resilience in a number of ways. (Note that this area is very complicated and specialized, and we can only skim the surface in this book.)

The simplest approach is to minimize or remove the possibility of network failure by providing standby routes to use if the main route goes down. Modern protocols, particularly IP, provide this rerouting automatically, but your architecture still needs to include the standby network hardware and sufficient emergency bandwidth. Where this isn't automated, you also need to consider the processes whereby traffic reroutes from one pipe to another. Essentially, in this model, the network is as much part of the disaster recovery infrastructure as the computers are and must be designed to support this.

A more sophisticated solution is to provide the ability to work in offline mode. This may be an essential feature if resilient communications cannot be guaranteed.

EXAMPLE Banks and other types of retail financial institutions typically operate numerous widely distributed small branches. Although these branches may be semiautonomous, many processes require access to centrally located systems (in the data center or head office).

Financial transactions, for example, may need to be centrally authorized to reduce the risk of fraud; customer or account data may be managed on a central server to make it universally available; regulatory requirements may mandate that information be collated centrally and passed on to the relevant authorities.

The volume of traffic from any one local branch to the central site, however, is probably fairly small. It is not cost-effective, therefore, to use high-bandwidth resilient communications, and typically a solution such as ISDN or even dial-up will be deployed.

However, if communications are interrupted for any reason, the branches must be able to continue operations, possibly with a degraded level of service. If branches cannot accept financial transactions, the bank will soon go out of business.

In such a scenario, it is essential that local systems can operate offline, in other words, without connectivity to central servers. Typically this solution will "stack up" transactions to be applied when connectivity is restored.

Problems and Pitfalls

Here are some common pitfalls to keep in mind for the Location perspective.

- Assuming that networks are infinitely fast and have infinite capacity, zero latency, and 100% reliability
- Assuming that one administrator will provide management and support, rather than a team of administrators spread across multiple locations, time zones, and languages
- Assuming a single time zone for all significant operations
- Assuming that the entire end-to-end network is secure, when in reality much of it may run over uncontrolled third-party equipment

- Assuming the availability of an overnight batch period of operation for a system that has worldwide reach
- Failing to investigate (e.g., through expert local advice) the political, legal, and commercial environments of geographical areas unfamiliar to you
- Assuming that the physical environment (temperature, physical security, power supply, networking availability, and so on) will match that of the primary site

Checklists

CHECKLIST FOR REQUIREMENTS CAPTURE

- Have you understood and agreed on the physical location of each component of the architecture?
- Do you understand the requirements for throughput, response time, availability, and resilience for all connections between geographically distributed components?
- Are the performance and reliability expectations of the wide-area network realistic and achievable within the time and budget constraints and the capabilities of the available network infrastructures?
- If appropriate, have you understood and agreed on how the system will accommodate simultaneous operation in multiple time zones?
- If there is a requirement for separate online and batch modes of working, is this compatible with the need to operate in multiple time zones around the world?
- Have the bandwidth and response time requirements of high-volume operations such as distributed backups or distributed software updates been understood and approved?
- If there is a requirement to support offline operation when wide-area connectivity is not available, are the service-level requirements for these clear and achievable?
- Do the requirements take into account the legal and political implications of operating in different countries?
- Has the network infrastructure between sites been factored into disaster recovery requirements and plans?

CHECKLIST FOR ARCHITECTURE DEFINITION

- How confident are you that the architecture will meet all the requirements? Where you are not, are mitigating activities in place (such as a proof-of-concept)?

- Have you identified all points at which network protocol translations need to take place (e.g., TCP/IP to SPX/IPX), and does the architecture provide resilient, flexible components for these?
- If there is a requirement to support offline operation when wide-area connectivity is not available, does the architecture incorporate features to recover and resubmit information when connectivity is restored? Will these complete within an acceptable period of time?
- Do the disaster recovery capabilities of the architecture extend to the connectivity between distant locations?

Further Reading

This area doesn't get much attention in the written literature, and we aren't aware of any books that specifically address geographical location-related concerns for large systems.

THE REGULATION PERSPECTIVE

Desired Quality	The ability of the system to conform to local and international laws, quasi-legal regulations, company policies, and other rules and standards
Applicability	Any system that may be subject to laws or regulations
Concerns	Statutory industry regulation, privacy and data protection, cross-border legal restrictions, data retention and accountability, and organizational policy compliance
Activities	Compliance auditing
Architectural Tactics	Assessment of architecture against regulatory and legislative requirements
Problems and Pitfalls	Not understanding regulations or resulting obligations, and being unaware of statutory regulations

Unlike other system qualities, compliance with the law is an area where you cannot make compromises. Although you may be able to live with a system that is slow, occasionally unreliable, or potentially insecure, a system that does not comply with legal regulations may be prevented from going into production or may expose the organization to risk of prosecution.

Applicability to Views

Table 28–5 shows how the Regulation perspective affects each of the views we discussed in Part III.

TABLE 28-5 APPLICABILITY OF THE REGULATION PERSPECTIVE TO THE SIX VIEWS

View	Applicability
Functional	Regulations can have a significant impact on what the system does and how it works.
Information	Especially in Europe, there is a great deal of legislation related to the retention, use, and manipulation of personal information. The impact on the Information view may include privacy, access control, retention and archive, audit, availability, and distribution.
Concurrency	This perspective has little or no impact on the Concurrency view.
Development	This perspective has little or no impact on the Development view, although if production (live) test data is to be used, there may be restrictions on this.
Deployment	This perspective has little or no impact on the Deployment view, although health and safety legislation could have an impact on the hardware deployed.
Operational	This perspective has little or no impact on the Operational view.

Concerns

Software systems are potentially subject to a wide range of legislation. Most obvious are any laws that apply directly to the problem the system is intended to solve. For example, an accounting system needs to comply with financial regulations, or a human resources system with employment law.

However, many types of legislation may apply to systems regardless of what they actually do.

- *Finance*: This legislation can be frighteningly complex, with severe penalties for noncompliance. It covers a broad spectrum, including measures against fraud and money laundering, rules about corporate accounting and company law, regulations for local and national taxation, and requirements for fair and open treatment of customers.

- *Data protection*: More so in Europe than in North America (e.g., the Data Protection Act of the United Kingdom), this sort of legislation can impose stringent conditions under which personal data can be captured, stored, used, and retained, with severe penalties for noncompliance.

- *Data retention*: This is especially important where financial transactions or contractual agreements are involved. Financial regulations in most countries, for example, impose the requirement to archive financial transactions for a number of years before they can be destroyed. (Note that this does not necessarily mean electronic format, either: It may be necessary to keep paper copies or microfiche.)

- *Disability and antidiscrimination*: We discussed this earlier when we covered the Accessibility perspective.

- *Health and safety*: There is a small but significant category of IT-related industrial injuries such as eyestrain, repetitive stress injuries, and so forth. Incorrect or inappropriate use of computer equipment can cause harm to the users and impose liability on employers.

- *Environment*: These laws may necessitate disposing of waste in an eco-friendly way or reaching targets for the use of recycled materials.

- *Law enforcement*: In recent years, a number of laws (the USA PATRIOT Act in the United States, the Regulation of Investigatory Powers Act in the United Kingdom) have been passed that impose requirements on organizations to support the activities of law enforcement and antiterrorism agencies. Some of these laws have attracted controversy due to their wide-ranging scope.

- *Protection of corporate assets*: This includes areas such as protection of trademarks and copyright as well as Digital Rights Management, which restricts access to content such as prerecorded music held in digital form.

In addition to considering national and local laws, you also may need to take into account foreign or international laws if your system—particularly if it makes use of the Internet—has a presence in other countries. For example, some countries, particularly the United States, place severe restrictions on the export of some technologies such as encryption, although these constraints have been somewhat relaxed in recent years.

Even if your system is completely legal, you need to assess it against the organization's own internal policies for security, backup and restore, disaster recovery, and any business or technology standards that may be mandated or recommended.

Activities: Applying the Regulation Perspective

It is difficult to define a formal process here. You need to identify all relevant regulations (specialist stakeholder involvement will be required here) and then assess your architecture for compliance.

Conformance to directly applicable regulations (such as employment law for a human resources system) should be implicit to any specification of requirements. However, although stakeholders will typically understand the law as it applies to their area of interest, you may have to bring in outside experts to consider areas such as data protection, health and safety issues, or environmental protection. Do not complacently assume that these do not apply to software systems; this can be a very costly mistake to make.

Architectural Tactics

There are no solutions specific to this perspective. Rather, you should assess your architecture against regulatory and legislative requirements as we discussed earlier.

Problems and Pitfalls

Here are some common pitfalls to keep in mind for the Regulation perspective.

- Not understanding complex regulations fully
- Not fully understanding the obligations implied by regulations
- Being unaware of regulations entirely because you are new to a domain or because the law is changing so quickly

Checklists

CHECKLIST FOR REQUIREMENTS CAPTURE

- Have you identified all legislation that applies to the functionality the system supports (e.g., employment law for a human resources system, or company law for a financial system) and assessed the architecture for compliance with these?
- Have you identified the generic legislation that applies to software systems (e.g., health and safety, the environment, data protection) and assessed the architecture for compliance with these?
- Have you determined whether the system can be considered as touching on other countries in any way, and if so, what legislation it may be subject to as a result?
- Have you considered international law such as technology export restrictions?
- Have you identified the relevant internal business and technology regulations and standards? Have you assessed the architecture for compliance with these?
- If legislation requires registration with governmental agencies (e.g., the Data Protection Registrar in the United Kingdom), have you applied for this registration, or do you have plans to make this happen?
- Do your archive and retention plans conform to all applicable legislation?

CHECKLIST FOR ARCHITECTURE DEFINITION

- Does your architecture accommodate any required automated interfaces to regulatory bodies (e.g., automatic upload of accounting or taxation information)? Do these interfaces conform to prescribed business and technical standards?

- Does the architecture conform to any mandated technical standards?

Further Reading

Because regulations can change quickly and vary from country to country, we recommend that you obtain further information from the relevant authorities.

THE USABILITY PERSPECTIVE

Desired Quality	The ease with which people who interact with the system can work effectively
Applicability	Any system that has significant interaction with humans (users, operational staff, and so on) or that is exposed to members of the public
Concerns	User interface usability, business process flow, information quality, alignment of the human–computer interface (HCI) with working practices, alignment of the HCI with users' skills, maximization of the perceived usability, and ease of changing user interfaces
Activities	User interface design, participatory design, interface evaluation, and prototyping
Architectural Tactics	Separation of user interface from functional processing
Problems and Pitfalls	Failure to consider user capabilities, failure to use non-IT communication specialists, failure to consider how concerns from other perspectives affect usability, overly complex interfaces, assumption of a single type of user access, design based on technology rather than needs, inconsistent interfaces, disregard for organizational standards, and failure to separate interface and processing implementations

Applying the Usability perspective ensures that the system allows those who interact with it do so effectively. This perspective tends to focus on the end users of the system but should also address the concerns of any others who interact with it directly or indirectly, such as maintainers and support personnel.

Getting usability right can have a significant impact on the success of the system, so it is perhaps surprising that this perspective is all too often neglected. Usability is not just about making life easier for your stakeholders: It can significantly affect the success of your system. If you design a system that is awkward to use, meets users' needs poorly, or fails to help them do their jobs better, your users will do everything in their power not to use the system. You may find yourself deploying a white elephant—destined never to see the light of day.

It is easy to get bogged down in details here that are more appropriate to consider during design. With the Usability perspective, focus on architecturally significant issues, that is, ones that involve multiple stakeholders or have far-reaching impact.

Applicability to Views

Table 28–6 shows how the Usability perspective affects each of the views we discussed in Part III.

Concerns

This perspective addresses a wide range of rather loosely related concerns.

- The obvious concern is the usability of the user interface. (Remember that we are considering not only the end users of the system but also any person who interacts with it, such as operations staff, support personnel, maintainers, or trainers.)
- Process flow around the system should be simple, understandable, and consistent, especially where processes are complex, comprise multiple

TABLE 28-6 APPLICABILITY OF THE USABILITY PERSPECTIVE TO THE SIX VIEWS

View	Applicability
Functional	The functional structure indicates where the system's external interfaces are and thus where usability needs to be considered. It may be impacted by usability needs (e.g., the addition of interface services to support certain interaction styles) but is unlikely to be changed significantly.
Information	Information quality (the provision of accurate, relevant, consistent, and timely data) can have a large impact on usability.
Concurrency	This perspective typically has little or no impact on the Concurrency view.
Development	The results of applying the Usability perspective impact the Development view in terms of the guidelines, standards, and patterns that ensure the creation of a consistent and appropriate set of user interfaces for the system.
Deployment	This perspective has little or no impact on the Deployment view, although usability concerns could require changes to element deployment (e.g., due to response time requirements).
Operational	The Usability perspective should consider the usability needs of the system's administrators.

steps, or involve different types of users. Clear and straightforward process flow increases the likelihood of tasks being completed correctly and in a timely manner.

- Information quality has a large impact on usability. The provision of accurate, relevant, consistent, and timely data is essential to the efficient operation of any system. If information cannot be relied on, is not trusted, or is known (or believed) to be of poor quality, systems may not be used or may be used in a way other than their designers intended.

- The architecture should align with current or planned work practices. Where this does not happen, you should rework the architecture, or you may need to drive through some business changes. Business changes are particularly likely when implementing a general-purpose package for areas such as human resources, customer relationship management, or enterprise resource planning. Note that business change driven as a result of technology deployment is a very thorny activity for architects.

- The architecture should align with the current or planned skills of users. Where this is not the case, your plans should include provision for staff training.

- You should understand and be aware of *perceived* rather than *actual* system qualities such as reliability and performance. Here are some examples.

  - Making use of asynchronous transactions, where control returns to the user before the transaction has completed in the database, can provide significant improvements in observed response times.
  - Allowing local systems to continue operating in offline mode even though links to remote systems are down can deliver high perceived availability even when the underlying network is of relatively poor quality.

    These approaches add to the complexity of the architecture, however, so you must balance them against the difficulty of repairing data if asynchronous activities fail.

- The ease (or difficulty) of changing user interfaces can impact a system's usability. Difficult-to-change interfaces make it less likely that user feedback will be incorporated through routine modifications.

Activities: Applying the Usability Perspective

A simple process follows.

- Identify all places where people may interact with the system (touch points).
- Understand how users will interact with the system at each touch point. Are they performing quick, atomic transactions such as checking an

account balance or the status of an order, or something more measured such as browsing a catalog or doing some research?

- Understand the users' capabilities: How experienced are they at using computers and the interface technologies you have specified in your architecture? How experienced are they in the application or business function your system supports? How much training (if any) will they receive?

- Understand the context in which the system will be used. Is it an internal system that is tightly controlled and managed, or will it be exposed to the general public on a variety of platforms?

- Develop an architectural approach and, where appropriate, a more detailed solution that meets these requirements.

- Bench-test the solution against the requirements.

It is becoming increasingly common to bring in outside expertise (e.g., for graphic design and marketing) when designing interfaces exposed to the public. This helps ensure that the interface is not only functional and easy to use but also aesthetically pleasing, and that it conveys the right sales and marketing messages.

Architectural Tactics

The solutions relevant to the Usability perspective depend highly on the type of system being built, the capabilities and experience of the people who will use it, and the means by which they will access it. There are a number of specific approaches to designing particular types of interfaces (see the Further Reading section for this perspective).

One basic architectural principle to keep in mind is separating the implementation of the user interface from the functional processing. If the interface implementation is tangled with the functional processing, it becomes much harder to change or replace the interface than if the two are cleanly separated components. Having the interface as a separate component allows for much easier experimentation and change as a result of user feedback and could also enable simultaneous use of a number of alternative interfaces if desired.

Problems and Pitfalls

Here are some common pitfalls to keep in mind for the Usability perspective.

- Failing to take into account the capabilities, expertise, and experience of your users when designing interfaces

- Failing to bring non-IT professionals (e.g., marketing or graphic design specialists) into the architecture definition process

- Failing to consider how other perspectives—particularly Availability and Resilience, Performance and Scalability, and Internationalization—can impact usability
- Creating overly complex or inappropriately feature-stuffed interfaces
- Assuming a single type of user access (e.g., for Web and mobile platforms, assuming that all users have a high-bandwidth connection, fast processor, high-resolution color display, and so on)
- Crafting the interface around the technology rather than being driven by the business process and the needs of the users
- Using inconsistent or haphazard approaches to data entry validation, error management, user help, and so on
- Failing to comply with strict corporate guidelines for presentation (such as the use of fonts, logos, terminology, and punctuation) for externally visible interfaces such as Web pages
- Implementing the interface and the functional processing together without clear separation between them

Checklists

CHECKLIST FOR REQUIREMENTS CAPTURE
- Have you identified all of the system's key touch points?
- Have you identified all of the different types of users who will interact with the system?
- Do you understand the type of usage (occasional, regular, transactional, unstructured) for each of the touch points?
- Have you taken into account the needs of support and maintenance staff and other second-line users?
- Do you understand the capabilities, experience, and expertise of the system's users? Have you correctly mapped these into requirements for presentation and support?
- Have you taken into account any corporate standards for presentation and interaction, particularly for systems exposed to the public?

CHECKLIST FOR ARCHITECTURE DEFINITION
- For Web and mobile platforms, have you considered the variation in bandwidth, hardware capabilities (screen resolution), and rendering software?
- Do the interface designs align in a sensible way with the business processes they are automating?
- If your system is exposed to the general public, have you obtained any necessary approvals from your marketing department for the use of company logos and so on?

Further Reading

One of the earlier books on the topic, Nielsen [NIEL94], has an extensive bibliography and runs a Web site extolling its author's practice and principles. Shneiderman [SHNE97] is a readable book that takes the jargon and mystery out of the field of human–computer interactions. Bass and John [BASS01] describes a technique for making reasoned decisions about usability tradeoffs in an architectural context.

The Usability Professionals' Association (http://www.upassoc.org/), which supports the work of professionals in this field, publishes a magazine, a process for usability design, and much other material.

PART V

PUTTING IT ALL TOGETHER

29

Working as a Software Architect

In Parts I through IV, we explained the principles that underpin the role of the architect, the importance of your role in project delivery, the process of software architecture, and some of the pitfalls you are likely to encounter. We also introduced three key concepts—stakeholders, viewpoints, and perspectives—and explained how to create an effective architecture and capture it in a sound AD.

We have presented a lot of information along the way, and when you consider how to apply it, you may wonder where on earth to start! In this final chapter, we describe how to put into practice the guidance in this book, explaining when it is relevant during the project lifecycle and how to apply it to different types of projects.

THE ARCHITECT IN THE PROJECT LIFECYCLE

As we explained in Part II, you'll be closely involved in the development of your system throughout the project lifecycle, with your effort probably concentrating on the first third and last third of the project phases. In the following subsections, we outline your key tasks during each lifecycle phase and refer you to the appropriate parts of the book for further information.

Project Initiation

You should be heavily involved in the initiation stage of any large system development project. In addition to thinking about the technical solution, you will have to contribute to the planning process. You may be expected to draw up plans yourself or at least to contribute informed estimates. You should be clear about the architectural process you are going to follow and about how long it will take to complete. In practice, you will be most constrained by the time and resources available.

On a personal level, you should put together a list of responsibilities to define your role if such a definition does not exist. If it does, read through the responsibilities so you understand them, and make sure they are reasonable and realistic. If they aren't, work with your management to make adjustments. Table 29-1 summarizes your key tasks during this phase.

Stakeholder Identification

One of your first tasks is to identify your key stakeholders and start to engage with them. Draw up an initial list of business and technology stakeholders of all of the main types, making sure that the ones you select are informed, committed, authorized, and representative.

Once you have drawn up and reviewed your list, meet with the stakeholders at the earliest opportunity, either individually or in groups. You can explain to them the benefits of a stakeholder-based approach, your role and theirs, and what will be required of them. You can also start to discuss—at a high level—scope, requirements, and potential solutions. Table 29-2 summarizes your key tasks during this phase.

TABLE 29-1 KEY TASKS DURING PROJECT INITIATION

Description	Further Information
Understand the architecture definition process you are going to follow.	Chapter 7
Develop resource and time estimates and feed them into the overall project plan.	Bibliography
Review and approve of your personal job responsibilities.	Chapter 5

TABLE 29-2 KEY TASKS DURING STAKEHOLDER IDENTIFICATION

Description	Further Information
Draw up and review the list of key business and technology stakeholders.	Chapters 2 and 9
Brief the stakeholders individually or in groups to explain your role and ensure they understand what is required of them.	Chapter 9

Scope and Requirements Definition

If the system scope has not already been clearly defined with and approved by the sponsors, you need to tend to this as a matter of urgency. Work with your key business and technology stakeholders to define, review, and document the scope (producing a context diagram is useful here) and get it approved by the sponsor.

You will also need to familiarize yourself, at a high level at least, with the functional and nonfunctional requirements of the system. Of course, at this early stage, the requirements may not be approved or even captured, in which case you will need to keep yourself up-to-date with them as they take shape.

You need to carefully manage changes to the scope and requirements as you go forward. The project should have a standard change control process—if it doesn't, work with the project manager to define one and make sure everyone follows it. Table 29–3 summarizes your key tasks during this phase.

Architecture Definition

Your first step is to select a small number of viewpoints and focus on these. What "a small number" actually means, of course, depends on the nature of your system. Most architects start by considering a Functional view, possibly augmented with a Deployment view. You may also want to consider an Information or Concurrency view, if relevant. Don't be too ambitious at this point—it's better to focus on one or two viewpoints while your ideas about the solution start to crystallize. You can consider the other viewpoints later.

You then start to consider which perspectives you will want to apply to your views to ensure that the system's nonfunctional goals are achieved. You may choose to apply the same or different perspectives to all of your views (e.g., you might apply the Performance and Scalability perspective to your

TABLE 29–3 KEY TASKS DURING SCOPE AND REQUIREMENTS DEFINITION

Description	Further Information
Review the system scope with stakeholders and revise it as necessary.	Chapter 8
Document the scope in a context diagram.	Chapter 8
Familiarize yourself with the functional and nonfunctional requirements.	Chapter 8
Ensure that a change management process for scope and requirements is in place and is followed.	Bibliography
Identify scenarios to illustrate key requirements.	Chapter 10

Functional view and the Availability and Resilience perspective to your Deployment view).

At this point, you should work with your stakeholders to agree on which are the two or three most important perspectives. These probably include Performance and Scalability, Availability and Resilience, and possibly one or two others. Again, don't be too ambitious at this early stage.

Having selected your viewpoints and the perspectives to apply to them, draw up some early views by putting together some first-cut models. You don't need to worry too much about completeness or depth at this point; the objective is to give yourself a starting position to review with your stakeholders. As you develop the models, use the perspectives you have selected to understand the key quality properties for the system.

As we explained in Part II, architecture definition is iterative, involving multiple refinement steps as you evaluate, rework, and improve your models. This process is complete when you have addressed all major stakeholder concerns and believe that you can start system construction with an acceptable level of risk. Table 29–4 summarizes your key tasks during this phase.

TABLE 29–4 KEY TASKS DURING ARCHITECTURE DEFINITION

Description	Further Information
Select one or more viewpoints appropriate to the problem you are trying to solve.	Chapters 2 and 3, Part III
Review and understand the key concerns, models, and pitfalls for these viewpoints.	Part III
Select one or more perspectives appropriate to each of your viewpoints.	Chapters 2 and 4, Part IV
Review and understand the key concerns, strategies, and pitfalls for these perspectives.	Part IV
Decide on the initial set of model(s) for the viewpoints you have selected.	Part III
Review the key elements of each model and select an appropriate notation.	Part III
Draw up some first-cut models.	Chapter 12, Part III
Apply perspectives to the first-cut models.	Part IV
Identify scenarios for architectural evaluation.	Chapter 10
Validate the resulting candidate architectures.	Chapter 14
Iterate until you identify an acceptable architecture.	Chapter 7
Ensure that you have an effective AD.	Chapter 13

System Construction

During system construction, you may take on another role, such as design authority, as well as acting as the architect. During this phase, it is important that you spend enough of your time in an architectural role to allow you to oversee, mentor, and review during the software development process. This helps instill good practices and ensures that the system conforms to the architectural principles you have defined. Table 29–5 summarizes your key tasks during this phase.

System and User Acceptance Testing

As the system starts to take shape, early versions of it will probably be handed over to independent testers for system testing. Later, it will be installed in test environments to allow user stakeholders to test it to ensure it is fit for their use. The system and user acceptance testing phases of the project are crucial in order to ensure that effective testing is performed within the development organization, to obtain early feedback about the suitability of the implementation for production use, and to build confidence in the system within the user community. Table 29–6 summarizes your key tasks during this phase.

Operation

Once a system has moved into production, you will probably be preoccupied with new releases or projects on other systems. Even so, it is advantageous if you can retain a role when the system is operational. You are the main person

TABLE 29–5 KEY TASKS DURING SYSTEM CONSTRUCTION

Description	Further Information
Oversee the software development process, particularly in its early phases, to ensure that the right foundations are in place to implement the architecture faithfully.	Bibliography
Review representative samples of the implementation.	Chapter 19
Lead and mentor developers to ensure that they understand and follow good general practices and your specific architectural principles.	Bibliography

TABLE 29-6 KEY TASKS DURING SYSTEM AND USER ACCEPTANCE TESTING

Description	Further Information
Ensure that comprehensive system testing is planned.	Bibliography
Ensure that comprehensive user acceptance testing is planned.	Bibliography
Work with program and project managers to obtain the time and resources required to perform the planned testing.	Bibliography
Monitor the testing process to obtain early indications about the quality and suitability of the system.	Bibliography

with a system-wide view who also really understands the needs of the system's stakeholders and the history of the decisions that led to the system's architectural form. This means that you can usefully be involved during the operational life of the system, ensuring that it still meets stakeholder needs, analyzing problems or failures in production, making suggestions about possible future work, and keeping generally current with the health of the system. Table 29–7 summarizes your key tasks during this phase.

Decommissioning

All good things come to an end, and eventually your system will be decommissioned, or you may work on the decommissioning of other systems. Your skills as an architect can be just as usefully applied to decommissioning a system as to creating one, and you should make sure that you are fully consulted and involved in any decommissioning projects. Table 29–8 summarizes your key tasks during this phase.

TABLE 29-7 KEY TASKS DURING OPERATION

Description	Further Information
Regularly review operational problems or concerns.	Chapter 21
Occasionally engage with stakeholder groups to gauge their satisfaction with the system.	Chapter 9

TABLE 29–8 KEY TASKS DURING DECOMMISSIONING

Description	Further Information
Ensure that any decommissioned services are now obsolete or are replaced.	Chapters 8 and 9
Work with stakeholders to ensure that effective migration planning and processes are in place.	Chapter 21
Ensure that suitable data migration and archiving takes place when the system is decommissioned.	Chapters 17 and 24
Ensure that all regulatory constraints are met, where appropriate.	The Regulation Perspective section in Chapter 28

THE ARCHITECT IN DIFFERENT TYPES OF PROJECTS

Information systems architects are involved in many types of system development project, each with its own unique challenges. Sometimes it is a "green field" project, and you must understand the requirements from scratch; in other cases, an existing system needs to be modified, and you must define how the system can be changed at minimum cost and risk; and sometimes, rather than developing a distinct system, your project is to integrate existing systems.

Each of these project types has a different set of priorities, and this is reflected in the viewpoints and perspectives you need to consider. In the following subsections, we outline the architectural priorities for a number of common types of projects and refer back to material elsewhere in the book that is likely to be useful.

In-House System Development

By "in-house" development, we mean a classical information systems project, where a business need leads to the initiation of a system development project to create a new system within an organization. Such development projects require broad architectural involvement, from scoping the new system right through to ensuring that it enters production safely. Table 29–9 summarizes the architectural priorities for this type of project.

New Product Development

Developing a new product involves developing a system in something of a vacuum. Although you may have some ideas about the expected customers for

TABLE 29-9 ARCHITECTURAL PRIORITIES FOR IN-HOUSE SYSTEM DEVELOPMENT

Description	Further Information
Scope and requirements	Chapters 7 and 8
Stakeholder identification and engagement	Chapter 9
Design and validation of a new architecture	Parts II, III, and IV
Leading and overseeing construction	Chapter 19
Specification and acquisition of a deployment environment	Chapter 20
Supervision of migration to production	Chapter 21

the system, you probably don't have any direct contact with them because the system hasn't actually been developed yet. This means working extensively with proxy stakeholders (such as user groups and product managers) to understand likely customer needs. The ease of modification of a new product is likely to be paramount because most successful products have long lives spanning many releases. You will also need to lay the groundwork for a solid development environment that can support a sophisticated, multirelease lifecycle in the future. Table 29–10 summarizes the architectural priorities for this type of project.

Enterprise Application Integration System

An enterprise application integration (EAI) system is an interesting variant on an enterprise information system because it doesn't usually perform any

TABLE 29-10 ARCHITECTURAL PRIORITIES FOR NEW PRODUCT DEVELOPMENT

Description	Further Information
Scope and requirements	Chapters 7 and 8
Identification of and engagement with proxy stakeholders	Chapter 9
Design and validation of a new architecture	Parts II, III, and IV
Creation of an architecture that has the ability to evolve over time at low cost	Chapter 27
Assessment of requirements for customer deployment environments	Chapter 20
Creation of a solid development environment for long-term technical integrity	Chapter 19
Leading and overseeing construction	Chapter 19

TABLE 29-11 ARCHITECTURAL PRIORITIES FOR EAI SYSTEMS

Description	Further Information
Tight scoping of the integration to be provided	Chapter 8
Identification of and engagement with stakeholders outside the normal stakeholder community	Chapter 9
Identification of data sources and destinations	Chapter 17
Definition of common data formats, models, and transformations	Chapter 17
Creation of an architecture capable of high throughput and resilience	Chapters 25 and 26
Creation of an architecture that is easy to monitor and exhibits reliable error handling and failure recovery	Chapter 21

business processing itself. Rather, an EAI system links other operational systems to provide an integrated information systems environment. EAI systems are also interesting because they are often invisible to business users, who are one of the primary stakeholder groups of a classical information system. Although end users or acquirers may benefit from the new facilities that an EAI system enables, they are unlikely to have any direct contact with it. Table 29-11 summarizes the architectural priorities for this type of project.

Extension of an Existing System

Extending an existing system can be quite different from creating a new one. The existing system has set stakeholders' expectations, so it is important that any change to the system does not come as an unpleasant surprise. Having said this, we should note that extending a system is often an opportunity to revisit and improve weak areas of the existing architecture. Requirements management and scoping are often simpler than with a new system because the stakeholders have probably been identified already, and the requirements can often be specified in terms of enhancements to the existing facilities. Of course, one of the major challenges inherent in extending or changing something that already exists is understanding and dealing with the existing implementation and the decisions that have already been made, particularly if you have not been involved with the system before. Table 29-12 summarizes the architectural priorities for this type of project.

TABLE 29-12 ARCHITECTURAL PRIORITIES FOR EXTENSION OF AN EXISTING SYSTEM

Description	Further Information
Understanding and evaluation of the existing architecture	Chapter 14
Creation of models for the existing system if none exist	Chapter 12
Creation of an architecture that does not cause existing quality properties to be degraded	Part IV
Creation of an architecture that can be implemented without interrupting existing operations	Chapter 21
Management of the change to the system with the lowest risk possible	Chapter 27

Package Implementation

Implementing a software package is another interesting variation of the classical information systems implementation project, and these two types of projects share many common activities. However, when implementing a package, the core activity of the classical project—software development—is largely replaced by tailoring and configuration of a software package. A package implementation project also usually shares some of the characteristics of an EAI project because a large portion of the work to be performed involves integrating the package with existing data sources and destinations. Managing requirements and dealing with stakeholder expectations can also be a challenging part of these projects because a large proportion of the benefit of implementing a package will be lost if extensive tailoring and modification of the package is required. Table 29–13 summarizes the architectural priorities for this type of project.

TABLE 29-13 ARCHITECTURAL PRIORITIES FOR PACKAGE IMPLEMENTATION

Description	Further Information
Scoping and management of stakeholder expectations	Chapters 8 and 9
Understanding and evaluation of the package architecture	Chapter 14
Assurance that the package exhibits suitable quality properties	Part IV
Identification of data sources, destinations, and mappings	Chapter 17
Assurance of the package's manageability	Chapter 21
Design of a deployment environment for the package	Chapter 20

APPENDIX

OTHER VIEWPOINT SETS

The set of viewpoints we present in this book is by no means the only one that could be or has been proposed. While we believe it does a good job of partitioning the AD into a manageable number of sections and ensuring a widespread coverage of concerns, we know of a number of other viewpoint sets that approach the problem somewhat differently. In order to allow you to compare and contrast our viewpoints with some of the other viewpoint sets that exist, we summarize five other approaches in this appendix. You can find more details of our experiences with these viewpoint sets in Woods [WOOD04].

KRUCHTEN "4+1"

When we first started using architectural views, we began with Philippe Kruchten's "4+1" set. The viewpoint set we presented in this book is a direct evolution and development of the "4+1" set, so they have a lot in common. Table A–1 outlines the "4+1" viewpoints.

This approach also suggests the use of a set of functional usage scenarios (or use cases—the "+1" part of the name) to illustrate how the views work together. We also strongly endorse the use of scenarios for illustration and evaluation (although we suggest spending at least as much time on quality property scenarios as on functional usage scenarios).

In addition to extending and defining the viewpoints outlined in Table A–1, our approach adds two viewpoints to this set, Information and Operational.

- We added the Information viewpoint because the underlying information structure in a large-scale information system may be quite different from the desired functional structure and may be much longer lived than the processing elements that use it. The Information viewpoint also needs to deal with data-specific concerns such as latency, ownership, distribution, replication, and so on.

TABLE A-1 KRUCHTEN "4+1" VIEWPOINT CATALOG

Viewpoint	Definition
Logical	The logical representation of the system's functional structure, normally presumed to be a class model (in an object-oriented systems development context). Our Functional viewpoint is a development of this "4+1" viewpoint, renamed to make its content clear (because you could have a number of logical aspects to an architecture).
Process	The concurrency and synchronization aspects of the architecture. Our Concurrency viewpoint is a development of this "4+1" viewpoint, renamed to avoid confusion with business process modeling.
Development	The design-time software structure, identifying modules, subsystems, and layers and the concerns directly related to software development. Our Development viewpoint is based on this "4+1" viewpoint.
Physical	The identification of the nodes that the system's software will be executed on and the mapping of other architectural elements to these nodes. Our Deployment viewpoint is a development of this 4+1 viewpoint.

- We added the Operational viewpoint because of our experiences with information systems that were developed with little or no thought given to how they would be installed, migrated to, monitored, controlled, and managed in their production environments. There are often important constraints, stakeholders, and concerns in this area that we believe architects need to take seriously from an early point in the system lifecycle. The Operational viewpoint provides structure and guidance for this process.

You can learn more about these viewpoints in Kruchten [KRUC95].

RM-ODP

The Reference Model for Open Distributed Processing (RM-ODP) is an ISO standard framework for describing and discussing distributed systems technology. The framework is defined using a set of five viewpoints, as shown in Table A–2.

While the RM-ODP approach provides an interesting partitioning of the AD, it was actually created to support efforts to standardize distributed systems technology and (as its name suggests) imposes a reference model on the systems being described.

You can find a good tutorial on the use of the RM-ODP approach in Putman [PUTM00].

TABLE A-2 RM-ODP VIEWPOINT CATALOG

Viewpoint	Definition
Enterprise	Defines the context for the system and allows capture and organization of requirements.
Information	Describes the information required by the system using static, invariant, and dynamic schemas.
Computational	Contains an object-oriented model of the functional structure of the system, with a particular focus on interfaces and interactions.
Engineering	Describes the systems infrastructure required to implement the desired distribution of the system's elements. This description is performed using a specific reference model.
Technology	Defines the specific technology that will be used to build the system.

SIEMENS (HOFMEISTER, NORD, AND SONI)

While working at Siemens Research, Christine Hofmeister, Robert Nord, and Dilip Soni developed a set of four architectural viewpoints based on the way the Siemens software development teams approached software architecture. Table A–3 shows the Siemens viewpoint set.

TABLE A-3 SIEMENS VIEWPOINT CATALOG

Viewpoint	Definition
Conceptual	The conceptual functional structure of the system that defines a set of conceptual components linked by a set of connectors.
Module	The concrete structure of the subsystems and modules that will be realized in the system, the interfaces exposed by the modules, the intermodule dependencies, and any layering constraints in the structure.
Execution	The runtime structure of the system in terms of processes, threads, interprocess communication elements, and so on along with a mapping of modules to runtime elements.
Code	The design-time layout of the system as source code and the intermediate and delivered binary elements created from it.

A strength of this taxonomy is that the viewpoints are presented in fully worked form (rather than just being summaries of the kinds of information they should contain). Unfortunately, we found that this particular viewpoint set didn't work that well for information systems because it is specialized for the needs of embedded and real-time software development.

The Siemens viewpoint set is defined further in Hofmeister et al. [HOFM00].

SEI VIEWTYPES

A somewhat different set of viewpoints is the set of "viewtypes" developed by the Software Engineering Institute as part of its research on effective architectural description techniques. The set comprises three viewtypes, which are then specialized by a set of associated architectural styles for each viewtype, as shown in Table A–4. The styles define how a particular type of architectural structure should be captured within the overall approach defined by the viewtype.

The SEI viewtypes are somewhat different from the other viewpoint sets summarized here, primarily containing advice related to documenting, rather than creating, an architecture. They also introduce the notion of specializing a viewtype by using a particular architectural style. Although these viewtypes contain less information about the process of software architecture than some of the others, they contain a great deal of useful advice about documenting your architecture, which is likely to be relevant even if you are basing your approach on a different viewpoint set.

The SEI viewtype set is defined in Clements et al. [CLEM03].

GARLAND AND ANTHONY

Jeff Garland and Richard Anthony are practicing software architects who have written another practitioner-oriented guide to software architecture for information systems. They also define a viewpoint set, although it's rather different from ours, as shown in Table A–5.

This viewpoint set is much larger than the others; each viewpoint has a narrower scope. The advantage of this is that each view is clearly focused, has a manageable size, and plays an obvious role. The disadvantage is that it is harder to manage the problems of fragmentation in the AD and cross-view consistency.

These viewpoints are defined in Garland and Anthony [GARL03].

TABLE A-4 SEI VIEWTYPE CATALOG

Viewtype	Definition
Component and Connector	The Component and Connector viewtype is concerned with the system's runtime functional elements, their behaviors, and their interactions. The following styles defined for this viewtype all relate to commonly occurring runtime system organizations: • *Pipe-and-Filter* • *Shared-Data* • *Publish-Subscribe* • *Client-Server* • *Peer-to-Peer* • *Communicating-Processes*
Module	The Module viewtype is concerned with how the software comprising the system is structured as a set of implementation (code) units. The following styles are defined for the Module viewtype: • *Uses*: for capturing intermodule usage dependencies • *Generalization*: for capturing commonality and variation (inheritance) relationships between modules • *Decomposition*: for specifying how modules are composed from simpler elements • *Layered*: for specifying how modules are arranged in layers according to their level of abstraction
Allocation	The Allocation viewtype is concerned with how relationships between the different parts of the system and different aspects of their environment are captured. The following styles are defined for this viewtype: • *Deployment*: for specifying how software elements are mapped to elements of the deployment environment • *Implementation*: for specifying how software modules are mapped to the development environment (such as their location in a codeline) • *Work Assignment*: for mapping software modules to those responsible for creating, testing, and deploying them

TABLE A-5 GARLAND AND ANTHONY VIEWPOINT CATALOG

Viewpoint	Definition
Analysis Focused	Illustrates how the elements of the system work together in response to a functional usage scenario
Analysis Interaction	Presents the interaction diagram used during problem analysis
Analysis Overall	Consolidates the contents of the Analysis Focused view into a single model
Component	Defines the system's architecturally significant components and their connections
Component Interaction	Illustrates how the components interact in order to make the system work
Component State	Presents the state model(s) for a component or set of closely related components
Context	Defines the context within which the system exists, in terms of external actors and their interactions with the system
Deployment	Shows how software components are mapped to hardware entities in order to be executed
Layered Subsystem	Illustrates the subsystems to be implemented and the layers in the software design structure
Logical Data	Presents the logical view of the architecturally significant data structure
Physical Data	Presents the physical view of the architecturally significant data structure
Process	Defines the runtime concurrency structure (operating system processes that the system's components will be packaged into and interprocess communication mechanisms that will allow communication between them)
Process State	Presents the state transition model for the system's processes
Subsystem Interface Dependency	Defines the dependencies that exist between subsystems and the interfaces of other subsystems

BIBLIOGRAPHY

[AMBL02]   Ambler, Scott. *Agile Modeling: Effective Practices for eXtreme Programming and the Unified Process*. New York: Wiley, 2002.

[ANDE01]   Anderson, Ross. *Security Engineering*. New York: Wiley, 2001.

[BARB98]   Barbacci, M. "Are Software Architects like Building Architects?" *The Architect*, 1(2), September 1998. Available at www.sei.cmu .edu/news-at-sei/columns/the_architect/1998/September/ architect-sep98.htm.

[BARN01]   Barnes, James. *A Guide to Business Continuity Planning*. New York: Wiley, 2001.

[BASS01]   Bass, Len, and Bonnie John. "Supporting Usability through Software Architecture." *Computer*, 34(10):113–115, October 2001.

[BASS03]   Bass, Len, Paul Clements, and Rick Kazman. *Software Architecture in Practice*, 2nd ed. Boston, MA: Addison-Wesley, 2003.

[BAYS99]   Bays, Michael. *Software Release Methodology*. Upper Saddle River, NJ: Prentice Hall, 1999.

[BECK00]   Beck, Kent. *Extreme Programming Explained*. Boston, MA: Addison-Wesley, 2000.

[BEED02]   Beedle, Mike, and Ken Schwaber. *Agile Software Development with Scrum*. Upper Saddle River, NJ: Prentice Hall, 2002.

[BLOC01]   Bloch, Josh. *Effective Java*. Boston, MA: Addison-Wesley, 2001.

[BOSC00]   Bosch, J. *Design and Use of Software Architectures*. Boston, MA: Addison-Wesley, 2000.

[BUSC96]   Buschmann, Frank, et al. *Pattern-Oriented Software Architecture: A System of Patterns*. New York: Wiley, 1996.

[BUTL93]   Butler, Ricky, and George Finelli. "The Infeasibility of Quantifying the Reliability of Life-Critical Real-Time Software." *IEEE Transactions on Software Engineering*, 19(1):3–12, January 1993.

[CHEC99]   Checkland, Peter. *Systems Thinking, Systems Practice*. New York: Wiley, 1999.

[CHEE01]   Cheesman, John, and John Daniels. *UML Components*. Boston, MA: Addison-Wesley, 2001.

[CLEM02]   Clements, Paul, Rick Kazman, and Mark Klein. *Evaluating Software Architectures*. Boston, MA: Addison-Wesley, 2002.

[CLEM03]   Clements, Paul, et al. *Documenting Software Architectures*. Boston, MA: Addison-Wesley, 2003.

[COOK94]   Cook, Steve, and John Daniels. *Designing Object Systems*. Upper Saddle River, NJ: Prentice Hall, 1994.

[COPL91]   Coplien, James O. *Advanced C++ Programming Styles and Idioms*. Reading, MA: Addison-Wesley, 1991.

[DATE03]   Date, C. J. *An Introduction to Database Systems*. Boston, MA: Addison-Wesley, 2003.

[DOBR02]   Dobrica, Liliana, and Elia Niemela. "A Survey on Software Architecture Analysis Methods." *IEEE Transactions on Software Engineering*, 28(7):638–653, July 2002.

[DSOU99]   D'Sousa, Desmond, and Alan Wills. *Objects, Components and Frameworks with UML, the Catalysis Approach*. Reading, MA: Addison-Wesley, 1999.

[DYSO04]   Dyson, Paul, and Andrew Longshaw. *Architecting Enterprise Solutions: Patterns for High-Capability Internet-Based Systems*. New York: Wiley, 2004.

[ELMA99]   Elmasri, Ramez E., and Shamkant B. Navathe. *Fundamentals of Database Systems*. Reading, MA: Addison-Wesley, 1999.

[FOWL97]   Fowler, Martin. *Analysis Patterns*. Reading, MA: Addison-Wesley, 1997.

[FOWL99]   Fowler, Martin. *Refactoring*. Reading, MA: Addison-Wesley, 1999.

[FOWL00]   Fowler, Martin, and Kendall Scott. *UML Distilled*, 2nd ed. Boston, MA: Addison-Wesley, 2000.

[FOWL03]   Fowler, Martin. *Patterns of Enterprise Application Architecture*. Boston, MA: Addison-Wesley, 2003.

[FREE99]   Freeman, Eric, Suzanne Hupfer, and Ken Arnold. *JavaSpaces: Principles, Patterns and Practices*. Reading, MA: Addison-Wesley, 1999.

[GAMM95]   Gamma, Erich, Richard Helm, Ralph Johnson, and John Vlis-
           sides. *Design Patterns*. Reading: MA: Addison-Wesley, 1995.

[GARL03]   Garland, Jeff, and Richard Anthony. *Large Scale Software Ar-
           chitecture*. New York: Wiley, 2003.

[GILB93]   Gilb, Tom, and Dorothy Graham. *Software Inspection*. Reading,
           MA: Addison-Wesley, 1993.

[GIRA02]   Girauld, Claude, and Rudiger Valk. *Petri Nets for Systems Engi-
           neering*. Berlin: Springer-Verlag, 2002.

[GOOD99]   Goodyear, Mark. *Enterprise Systems Architecture*. Boca Raton,
           FL: CRC Press, 1999.

[HALL98]   Hall, Elaine. *Managing Risk*. Reading, MA: Addison-Wesley,
           1998.

[HARD01]   Hardman, Brett, Donald Flynn, and Konstatin Beznosov. *En-
           terprise Security with EJB and CORBA*. New York: Wiley, 2001.

[HARE87]   Harel, David. "Statecharts: A Visual Formalism for Complex
           Systems." *Science of Computer Programming*, 8(3):231–274,
           June 1987.

[HIAT99]   Hiatt, Charlotte. *A Primer for Disaster Recovery Planning in an
           IT Environment*. Hershey, PA: Idea Group Publishing, 1999.

[HOFM00]   Hofmeister, Christine, Robert Nord, and Dilip Soni. *Applied
           Software Architecture*. Boston, MA: Addison-Wesley, 2000.

[HOWA02]   Howard, Michael, and David LeBlanc. *Writing Secure Code*.
           Redmond, WA: Microsoft Press, 2002.

[IEEE00]   IEEE Computer Society. *Recommended Practice for Architec-
           tural Description*. IEEE Std-1471-2000. October 9, 2000.
           Available at http://standards.ieee.org/reading/ieee/std_public/
           description/se/1471-2000_desc.html.

[INTE02]   Dr. International. *Developing International Software*, 2nd ed.
           Redmond, WA: Microsoft Press, 2002.

[ISO96]   International Organization for Standardization. ISO Standard
           11197-3. "Information Technology—Metadata Registries
           (MDR)—Part 3: Registry Metamodel and Basic Attributes."
           Available at www. metadata-standards.org/11179/.

[JAIN91]   Jain, Raj. *The Art of Computer Systems Performance Analysis*.
           New York: Wiley, 1991.

[JALO94]   Jalote, Pankaj. *Fault Tolerance in Distributed Systems*. Upper
           Saddle River, NJ: Prentice Hall, 1994.

[JAZA00]   Jazayeri, Mehdi, Alexander Ran, and Frank van der Linden.
           *Software Architecture for Product Families: Principles and
           Practice*. Boston, MA: Addison-Wesley, 2000.

[KILL98]   Killelea, Patrick. *Web Performance Tuning*. Sebastopol, CA: O'Reilly, 1998.

[KIMW99]   Kim, Won (ed.). *Modern Database Management: Object-Oriented and Extended Relational Database Systems*. New York: ACM Press, 1999.

[KROE02]   Kroenke, David. *Database Processing: Fundamentals of Design*. Upper Saddle River, NJ: Prentice Hall, 2002.

[KRUC95]   Kruchten, Philippe. "Architectural Blueprints—The 4+1 View Model of Software Architecture." *IEEE Software*, 12(6):42–50, November 1995.

[KRUC00]   Kruchten, Philippe. *The Rational Unified Process: An Introduction*, 2nd ed. Boston, MA: Addison-Wesley, 2000.

[LAMP04]   Lampson, Butler. "Computer Security in the Real World." *Computer*, 37(6):37–46, June 2004.

[LEON00]   Leon, Alexis. *A Guide to Software Configuration Management*. Norwood, MA: Artech House, 2000.

[LEVE95]   Leveson, Nancy. *Safeware: System Safety and Computers*. Reading, MA: Addision-Wesley, 1995.

[LINT03]   Linthicum, David S. *Next Generation Application Integration: From Simple Information to Web Services*. Boston, MA: Addison-Wesley, 2003.

[LUND98]   Lund, Ken. *CKJV Information Processing*. Sebastopol, CA: O'Reilly, 1998.

[LUON95]   Luong, Tuoc, James Lok, and Kevin Driscoll. *Internationalization: Developing Software for Global Markets*. New York: Wiley, 1995.

[MAGE99]   Magee, Jeff, and Jeff Kramer. *Concurrency: State Models and Java Programs*. New York: Wiley, 1999.

[MAIE00]   Maier, Mark, and Eberhardt Rechtin. *The Art of Systems Architecting*, 2nd ed. Boca Raton, FL: CRC Press, 2000.

[MARC00]   Marcus, Evan, and Hal Stern. *Blueprints for High Availability*. New York: Wiley, 2000.

[MCCO97]   McConnell, Steve. *Software Project Survival Guide*. Redmond, WA: Microsoft Press, 1997.

[MCGO04]   McGovern, James, et al. *The Practical Guide to Enterprise Architecture*. Upper Saddle River, NJ: Prentice Hall, 2004.

[MEYE00]   Meyer, Bertrand. *Object-Oriented Software Construction*, 2nd ed. Upper Saddle River, NJ: Prentice Hall, 2000.

[MILN89]   Milner, Robin. *Communication and Concurrency*. Upper Saddle River, NJ: Prentice Hall, 1989.

[MITC02]   Mitchell, Richard, and Jim McKim. *Design by Contract by Example*. Boston, MA: Addison-Wesley, 2002.

[NEUF92]   Neufelder, Ann Marie. *Ensuring Software Reliability*. New York: Marcel Dekker, 1992.

[NIEL94]   Nielsen, Jakob. *Usability Engineering*. San Diego, CA: Academic Press, 1994.

[NUSE01]   Nuseibeh, Bashar. "Weaving Together Requirements and Architectures." *IEEE Computer*, 34(3):115–117, March 2001.

[PALM02]   Palmer, Steven, and Mac Felsing. *A Practical Guide to Feature Driven Development*. Upper Saddle River, NJ: Prentice Hall, 2002.

[PAUL02]   Paulish, Daniel J. *Architecture-Centric Software Project Management: A Practical Guide*. Boston, MA: Addison-Wesley, 2002.

[PERR92]   Perry, Dewayne, and Alexander Wolf. "Foundations for the Study of Software Architecture." *ACM SIGSOFT Software Engineering Notes*, 17(4):40–52, October 1992.

[PFIS98]   Pfister, Greg. *In Search of Clusters*, 2nd ed. Upper Saddle River, NJ: Prentice Hall, 1998.

[PIED00]   Piedad, Floyd, and Michael Hawkins. *High Availability: Design, Techniques and Processes*. New York: Wiley, 2000.

[PLOP95–99] Coplien, James, et al. *Pattern Languages of Program Design 1–4*. Reading, MA: Addison-Wesley, 1995–1999.

[PREE94]   Preece, Jenny, et al. *Human Computer Interaction*. Reading, MA: Addison-Wesley, 1994.

[PULL01]   Pullum, Laura. *Software Fault Tolerance Techniques and Implementation*. Norwood, MA: Artech House, 2001.

[PUTM00]   Putman, J. *Architecting with RM-ODP*. Upper Saddle River, NJ: Prentice Hall, 2000.

[REDM97]   Redman, Thomas C. *Data Quality for the Information Age*. Norwood, MA: Artech House, 1997.

[ROSC97]   Roscoe, A.W. *The Theory and Practice of Concurrency*. Upper Saddle River, NJ: Prentice Hall, 1997.

[RUHW00]   Ruh, William A., Francis X. Maginnis, and William J. Brown. *Enterprise Application Integration: A Wiley Tech Brief*. New York: Wiley, 2000.

[RUMB99]   Rumbaugh, James, Ivar Jacobson, and Grady Booch. *The Unified Modeling Language Reference Manual*. Reading, MA: Addison-Wesley, 1999.

[SCHM00]   Schmidt, Douglas, Michael Stal, Hans Rohnert, and Frank Buschmann. *Pattern Oriented Software Architecture, Volume 2, Patterns for Concurrent and Networked Objects*. New York: Wiley, 2000.

[SCHN95]   Schneier, Bruce. *Applied Cryptography*. New York: Wiley, 1995.

[SCHN01]   Schneier, Bruce. *Secrets and Lies*. New York: Wiley, 2001.

[SDL02]   The SDL Forum Society Web Site, www.sdl-forum.org.

[SEAC03]   Seacord, Robert, Daniel Plakosh, and Grace A. Lewis. *Modernizing Legacy Systems*. Boston, MA: Addison-Wesley, 2003.

[SHAW94]   Shaw, Mary. "Procedure Calls Are the Assembly Language of Software Interconnection: Connectors Deserve First-Class Status." Technical Report CMU-CS-94-107, CMU/SEI, 1994.

[SHAW96]   Shaw, Mary, and David Garlan. *Software Architecture—Perspectives on an Emerging Discipline*. Upper Saddle River, NJ: Prentice Hall, 1996.

[SHNE97]   Shneiderman, Ben. *Designing the User Interface*, 3rd ed. Reading, MA: Addison-Wesley, 1997.

[SMIT02]   Smith, Connie, and Lloyd Williams. *Performance Solutions: A Practical Guide to Creating Responsive, Scalable Software*. Boston, MA: Addison-Wesley, 2002.

[SOMM97]   Sommerville, Ian, and Pete Sawyer. *Requirements Engineering: A Good Practice Guide*. New York: Wiley, 1997.

[TOIG00]   Toigo, Jon William, Margaret Toigo, and Jon Toigo. *Disaster Recovery Planning: Strategies for Protecting Critical Information Assets*. Upper Saddle River, NJ: Prentice Hall, 2000.

[VIEG02]   Viega, Gary, and John McGraw. *Building Secure Software*. Boston, MA: Addison-Wesley, 2002.

[VOSS89]   Vossen, Ruediger, and Thomas Curtin. *Computer Operations Management*. New York: Wiley, 1989.

[WHIT00]   Whittaker, James, and Jeffrey Voas. "Toward a More Reliable Theory of Software Reliability." *IEEE Computer*, 33(12):36–42, December 2000.

[WIRF90]   Wirfs-Brock, Rebecca, Brian Wilkerson, and Lauren Weiner. *Designing Object-Oriented Software*. Upper Saddle River, NJ: Prentice Hall, 1990.

[WISE97]   Wise, Sid. *Client/Server Performance Tuning: Designing for Speed*. New York: McGraw-Hill, 1997.

[WOOD04]   Woods, Eoin. "Experiences Using Viewpoints for Information Systems Architecture: An Industrial Experience Report." In F. Oquendo et al. (eds.), *Software Architecture: First European Workshop, EWSA 2004, St Andrews, UK, May 21–22, 2004, Proceedings.* Springer Lecture Notes in Computer Science 3047, pp. 182–193. Berlin: Springer-Verlag, 2004.

[WYZA99]   Wyzalek, John, and Layne Bradley. *Handbook of Enterprise Operations Management*. Boca Raton, FL: Auerbach, 1999.

INDEX

A

Abstraction, in models, 167–168
Access, authorizing, 382–383
Access control policy, 374
Access control sets, 373
Accountability, security, 369, 384–385
Acquirers, 111, 112
Administration models. *See also* Operational viewpoint.
  activities, 340–341
  custom utilities, 341
  error conditions, 339–341
  example, 342–343
  monitoring facilities, 339, 341
  notation, 340
  overview, 339–340
  performance metrics, 341
  performance monitoring, 340
  performance scenarios, 341
  routine maintenance requirements, 340–341
  routine procedure requirements, 339
Age concerns, 245–246
Aggregation, 254
Agile development methods, 88–89
Agile modeling (AM), models, 171
Architects
  versus
    business analysts, 64
    design authorities, 64–66
    developers, 66
    project managers, 64
    technology specialists, 65–66
  core concepts, 62

  in different projects
    enterprise application integration (EAI), 514–515
    extending existing systems, 515–516
    in-house development, 513
    new product development, 513–514
    package implementation, 516
  domain, 63
  enterprise, 63
  organizational context, 64–66
  product, 63
  in project lifecycle
    architecture definition, 509–510
    decommissioning, 512–513
    operation, 511–512
    project initiation, 507–508
    requirements definition, 509
    scope definition, 509
    stakeholder identification, 508
    system construction, 510
    system testing, 510
    user acceptance testing, 510
  responsibilities, 67
  role of, 60–61
  skill set, 66–67
  solution, 63
  specializations, 63
Architectural acceptance criteria, 75
Architectural description (AD)
  contents
    appendices, 187–188
    concerns overview, 185
    document control, 184
    general principles, 185–186

Architecture description languages
  (ADLs), 164–165
Architecture design. *See* architecture
  definition.
Architecture models. *See* models.
Architecture Tradeoff Analysis Method
  (ATAM), 195, 199-204.
Archive concerns, 250–251
Assessors, 111, 113
Asset protection, 497
Associations, 252–253
Asynchronous processing, 419
ATAM. *See* Architecture Tradeoff Analy-
  sis Method
Attack trees, 375–376
Attributes, 252
Auditing sensitive events, 381–382
Authenticating principals, 382
Authorizing access, 382–383
Availability
  functional, 438–439, 441
  platform, 434–438
  requirements for, 432–433
  schedule, 433–434
  security aspects, 369, 385–386
  software, 444
  technology, 441

B
Backout strategy, 334, 336, 349
Backup. *See also* disaster recovery.
  concerns, 330–332
  models, 351
  solutions, 445–446
Books and publications
  Analysis Patterns, 159
  *Architectural Blueprints: The 4+1 View
    Model of Software Architecture*, 30
  IEEE Standard 1471, 182
  Pattern-Oriented Software Design, 138
  *Recommended Practice for Architec-
    tural Description*, 182
Boxes-and-lines diagrams, 222–223,
  224

Build process, 302
Build process, automating, 466–467
Business analysts *versus* architects, 64
Business goals and drivers, architectural
  limits and constraints, 92–93

C
Candidate architecture, 17, 80–85
Cardinality, 252
Change. *See* Evolution perspective.
Class of service, concerns, 428–430
Classes
  definition, 252–253
  of incidents, 344
  of stakeholders, 111–115
Client nodes, 311
Client/server approach, definition, 15
Code. *See* software.
Codeline model
  activities, 302
  build approach, 302
  configuration management, 302
  notation, 302
  overview, 301–302
  release process, 302
  source code structure, 302
Codeline organization concerns, 295
Cohesion, Functional viewpoint, 217
Committing updates, 248
Common design model
  activities, 301
  common processing, 298, 301
  common software, 299
  design constraints, 299–300, 301
  design patterns, 301
  notation, 299
  overview, 298–299
  standard design approaches, 299
  standard software elements, 301
Common processing concerns, 294
Communicating with stakeholders, scenarios, 123
Communication, via architecture definition, 74